THE NEW
FREELANCER'S
HANDBOOK

SUCCESSFUL SELF-EMPLOYMENT

FORMERLY TITLED *FREELANCE FOREVER*

32159

MARIETTA WHITTLESEY

A FIRESIDE BOOK · PUBLISHED BY SIMON & SCHUSTER INC.
NEW YORK · LONDON · TORONTO · SYDNEY · TOKYO

Fireside
Simon & Schuster Building
Rockefeller Center
1230 Avenue of the Americas
New York, New York 10020

Designed by Kathy Kikkert
Manufactured in the United States of America

10   9   8   7   6   5   4   3   2   1

ISBN 0-671-64582-X

Acknowledgments

I would like to thank the following freelancers for their enormous contribution to this book. Without their experience, their information and their words, it could never have come into being.

Writers: Michael Austin, Ann Derry, Stephen Fischer, Brendan Gill, Herbert Mitgang, John Payne, Robert Phelps, Martha Rhodes, Gerald Sykes, Edward Tivnan, David Weller.

Visual Artists: Miguel Bejarano, Christine Berthoin, Jean Brunel, Jim Caldwell, Ron Carboni, Muriel Castanyis, Simone di Bagno Guidi, Eileen Fisher, Mimi Glover Forer, Terry Gruber, Decatur Higgins, Christopher Makos, Russ Miller, Jim Morrison, Libby Moyer, Cynthia Navaretta, Mike Nikai, Nic Osborn, Robert Osborn, Margery Peters, Cisco Pichardo, Penelope Potter, Deborah Remington, Judith Rothchild, Bob Sabin, Kevin Sacco, Jan Sawka, Jonathan Scoville, Sally Spillane, Dominique Strandquest, Rei Yoshimura, Tom Zetterstrom.

Actors, Dancers, Mimes: Peter Boyden, Helen Haroldsen, Chip Keyes, Monica Meehan-McNamara, Roger the Jester Reed, Ellen Sandler, Cameron Thompson, Helen Townsend, Fiddle Viracola, Shelly Wyant.

Musicians: Dave Achelis, Katherine Carboni, Robelyn Schrade James, Compton Maddox, John Moses, Eliot Osborn, Dave Robinson and Stephen Tarshis.

My thanks to the following organizations for information that they supplied: The Authors Guild, The Center for Arts Information, Credit Union National Association, The Foundation Center, The Insurance Information Institute, The Internal Revenue Service, Volunteer Lawyers for the Arts.

I would also like to thank the following individuals for their contributions: Tony Outhwaite and Jane Wilson of JCA Literary Agency, Johnette Isham and David Niles of the Rhode Island School of Design, Elodie Osborn, Eugene Brissey, Laura Bachko, David Forer, Doug Booth, John Booth of the Twentieth Century Fund, Lori Antonacci and The Foundation for the Community of Artists, Ann Copeland, Alexina Shufeldt and Richard DeKoster, Peregrine Whittlesey and Gerald Freund, Thorn Welden, Chuck Radcliff and Sarah Jeffords, William F. Willis of Wagner McNeill, Gilbert Watkins and Irving Schwartz, CPAs of Schwartz and Hofflich, Josh Miller, Robert Baldwin, Susan

Moldow, Chad Hatfield of Classic Printers, Linda Young of Du-Art Film Labs, Jim McGarry, Robinson Leech, Jr., Linda Tuncy and Rose Genito of Salisbury Bank and Trust, Victoria Oscarsson of the Oscarsson-Hood Gallery, David Guc, Leslie Sarah Thompson, Jean Moore and Sharon Tingley, Carolyn Grancher, Tad Crawford, Edward Hallam Tuck, Scott Warner, Rubin Gorewitz, Ken Pepper, Lyn Austin of the Music Theatre Group, Paul Malagoli, Nellie Sabin, Martin Weidenbaum CPA, Barclay Prindle, Betty Lux, Dr. Robert Schell of Personnel Sciences Center, Dr. Eric Braverman of the Princeton Brain Bio Center, the late Frank Shames, Barbara Gilder Quint, Gina Ogden, and the late Jeffrey J. Steinberg.

On the editorial side, I want to thank my editor, Tim McGinnis, and Laura Yorke, his assistant, for their guidance and good ideas, and Susan Moldow for her original role as midwife.

Contents

Preface

I wrote *The New Freelancer's Handbook* because I realized that most freelancers do not know how to manage the business aspects of their lives. This is not because the typical freelancer is less bright than the typical employee—quite the contrary—but rather because freelancers are not given business-related information that is tailored to their needs. Pick up any publication which discusses the problems of working, and you will see that little of it is relevant to the freelancer's case.

As I thought about it, I realized that the average freelancer's life is about as different from an employee's as it could be. It wasn't just business information that was needed but information on how to deal with every aspect of freelance life. As a freelancer, you are your own employer and employee and your talent is your product. Nothing that you do in your life is ever completely separate from your work. Your work even extends into your emotional and romantic life. Freelancing thus requires a very different outlook from working at anything else. There is no five o'clock in your life. Your life involves both securing work and then doing it. Even your off-hours tend to be occupied with thoughts about your work—subliminally if not fully consciously.

Moreover, you make all the decisions about your own work. You receive little or no professional direction from superiors—the responsibility is all yours. Usually you don't even have the benefit of co-workers with whom to discuss problems. In fact, nothing is made easy for you. You don't have such perks as group health plans, unemployment and disability income, or employee credit unions. Nor do you have the security of a regular paycheck. What you do have is a far greater latitude in how you lead your life, freedom to create, and the satisfaction of using your time to work for yourself doing something that you care about doing.

I was not surprised to find in researching this book that most of the freelancers I talked with were not adequately informed about how to manage their businesses—if they even thought of what they were doing as a business. I believe that many freelance artists are poor businesspeople because they buy (or are sold) the popular misconception that art and business do not mix—that artists should not sully their spirits with crass commercial know-how. The traditional stereotype of the artist has been a sort of footloose and chaotic creature, one who constantly lived dangerously. This picture is more likely to depict hobbyists or failures than successful, established artists.

In order to cope effectively as a freelancer in today's world, you must become aware of two important survival lessons. They are the two most important lessons I ever learned, and they were taught me in college by the writer Gerald Sykes. They are simple axioms, but so true that they can pull you through much of what you have to confront as a freelancer. One is to remember that Nature doesn't give a damn about you, an individual, no matter how important you seem to yourself. And the second rule for survival is to become bilingual: to learn not only the language of your art but also the languages of business and commerce.

Nowadays, whether he likes it or not, the individual artist has to deal with many specialized languages in addition to that of his art form. If you can't be bothered to learn the new vocabularies in the world around you, these languages will be used against you by those who have mastered them, and you may not survive as an artist.

So you need to learn the vocabulary and thought processes of accountants, landlords and computers, to name but a few of those other languages. If you can become conversant with these idioms you will be able to survive in today's world without compromising your work. Those who remain "innocent" will probably fail to freelance forever.

When you realize that you have to make your own way as an artist and when you master the necessary idioms, you will have the basic tools for survival. You will realize that you are the only one who determines whether you will sink or sail. *The more waters you can sail in, the better your chances of a successful voyage.*

This book was conceived with the hope of making it possible for more freelancers to acquire the skills they need in order to thrive in all the situations in which they may find themselves.

Preface to the New Edition

When I wrote the first edition of *Freelance Forever* in 1979, a friend jokingly referred to it as "the Abbie Hoffman of self-help books." I was thrilled with the analogy at the time. We've all grown up a bit since then—even Abbie Hoffman—and our methods, goals and concerns may have changed accordingly. Nevertheless, freelancers now as then need to know how to work both inside and outside the system, how to be both risk-taking and painstaking. This edition of *The New Freelancer's Handbook* updates the first edition and more. I have learned more about freelancing, and I wanted the book to reflect the years of new experience that I have accumulated as a freelancer.

In this period, I have increased my freelance medical writing business to the point where it not only provides a decent income but also permits me significant time to work on my own writing and to ride horses. This is my idea of an almost perfect situation. Instead of never having enough clients, now I often have more than I can handle, and I have had to learn how to turn jobs down. Such concerns never occurred to me when I originally wrote the book, and because of this, I didn't ask the working freelancers I interviewed about that side of things. In pumping them just for information about how to struggle successfully, I only got part of the story. This book contains the rest of the story.

How to Use This Book

This book is not a how-to book for artists. It is a survival manual for freelancers. Freelancers live lives that are completely different from employees with a very different set of problems. Much more is left up to you. Part I, Living the Life, is designed to give you an idea of how to cope with those problems as successfully as possible. Time management is one of the most important aspects of being a successful freelancer, and so the first chapter tells you everything that I and the freelancers I interviewed have learned about coping with such problems as scheduling and disciplining yourself to get your work done on time. Getting work is half the job of freelancing, and the next chapter gives you advice on finding work in your field. The next two chapters should help you find and finance an affordable workspace and set it up so that you have the privacy and space you need. The next chapter, Getting the Job Done, gives you valuable clues about the actual mechanics of doing freelance work—dealing with clients, booking jobs and turning work down without jeopardizing your future chances with that client. I have also included interviews with users of freelancers' work detailing some of the problems they traditionally have with freelancers so that you can avoid those pitfalls when dealing with your clients. The next chapter, Stay in Touch, tells how to use the telephone, mails and special delivery services as economically and advantageously as possible. The last chapter in this section tells about some of the special advantages computers have for freelancers and how to decide which one is right for you. Part II, Your Mind and Body, addresses psychological problems peculiar to freelancers and their special psycho-physiological needs and offers some traditional but often ignored solutions as well as some new ones that freelancers have worked out for themselves. Part III, Money Matters, explains as straightforwardly as possible how to cope with major business responsibilities such as taxes, grants, credit, collecting what's owed you, insurance, legal matters and budgeting. New to this edition is a section on how to charge for your work. All sections contain sources of further information. In addition, at the end of the book, you will find an appendix of useful organizations and of further reading, organized by profession. Because many good books disappear from store shelves in a matter of weeks never to be seen again, some of the books I will refer to throughout this book may be very difficult to buy. They are nevertheless worth the read. If your local library doesn't have the books you are looking for, don't forget the excellent interlibrary loan systems that allow your home library to borrow books from other libraries. Sometimes you have to wait weeks or more to get what you want, but eventually some obscure little town's library will produce it for you.

I suggest that you read through the whole appendix—not just for those organizations and references that you think apply to your own art form. Some organizations and other resources offer assistance to several types of artists.

This book is aimed at freelancers in the arts even though much of the information is applicable to any self-employed person. Thus, the terms *artist* and *freelancer* are used interchangeably.

In many ways, this book has been a collaborative project. I could never have come up with all the information and advice in this book by myself. I am a writer by profession, and although I have had a lot of exposure to the theater and to the art worlds, I do not know all the ins and outs as well as freelancers who make their living in these worlds. Therefore, much of the valuable information in this book is contained in excerpts from my interviews with the successful freelancers whose advice on various subjects appears as extracts throughout the text. While some readers may feel that the interviews can be passed over in favor of the harder facts in the main body of the text, I would advise you to listen to the firsthand advice given by other freelancers. I have always found the experience of others to be every bit as helpful as hard information.

In fact, when I was first starting out I would collar successful writers at parties and pump them to find out how they lived and worked. I still read all interviews of artists with a voracious curiosity. I am far more interested in learning an artist's thoughts on the problems we all share and in hearing how she solves them than I am in reading criticism of her work.

Freelancing is a highly individual business which you must learn by trial and error and from the mistakes and successes of others. There is a great deal of individual variation in how people get by, and I think this is an essential point for freelancers to learn. School tends to instill in all of us at a very early age that there is only one "right way." Such an attitude is nothing but a burden to the prospective freelancer. I hope that my inclusion of quotes on many subjects by many artists will help my readers understand that the "right way" is whatever works for you.

My own instincts have always been toward self-employment. I never had summer jobs, because from an early age I realized that I could make more money and have more free time if I ran my own business. Except for a couple of temporary stints as an employee, I have freelanced all my adult life. This has given me the time and the leisure to work steadily at my writing. Naturally my fortunes wax and wane, and I eat better at some times than at others, but to me it's all part of the bargain.

Philologists among my readers may quarrel with my spelling of the word *freelancer*. Webster's gives a choice of *free lancer* or *free-lancer*. The former seems more apt for the original definition of the word. A free lancer was a mercenary knight who owed no loyalty to any one king or country (hence, perhaps, some of the modern-day distrust of freelancers who likewise have no loyalties to any employers but themselves). I find *free-lancer* too cumbersome. Therefore, I have chosen *freelancer*, a spelling which has become so acceptable as to be used by the *New York Times*.

Finally, I would like to explain my use of genders. I am aware of, and sensitive to, the sexism couched in the English language. Yet I am also a great admirer of our language and hate to see such atrocities as "(s)he" inflicted upon it in the name of feminism. I also refuse to turn every sentence into an awkward and overly long string of words by switching it around in order to avoid using *his* or *her*. The integrity of some sentences dictates that a choice be made, so I have randomly used one or the other without regard for conventions of gender and role. I hope thereby to have done my small bit against sexism while doing my utmost not to violate the language in the name of politics.

Salisbury, Connecticut
September 1987

Epigrams

"Life is a juggling act on a high wire for me right now," says a recent graduate of UCLA Film School. Siri is fairly certain that she wants to freelance as a cinematographer. She prefers the idea of freelancing for several reasons. She doesn't like to work for the same outfit day after day, and she wants to continue to live in her hometown which is thirty miles from Los Angeles. Most important, she figures that freelancing will give her more opportunity to work on her own experimental videos.

She did well at school and, on the strength of her reputation as a student cinematographer, got some freelance work as a production assistant for two producers who often hire UCLA students. While on the set, she was able to use her considerable carpentry skills to make herself indispensable. Both producers enjoyed working with her, and both have promised her more work when they have suitable projects. However, promises of future work don't put bread on the table, so she is working as a freelance carpenter for a contractor in her town and making $12 per hour.

"I'm not hurting for money the way a lot of my friends who went directly from film school to pavement pounding in search of stardom are, but my dilemma isn't so different from theirs. I want to establish myself in the film business—even as a production assistant to start—so that I don't have to be a carpenter forever. It means having plenty of energy, because when I get home from a hard day of work, I have to do one of two things: either I have to get to work on one of my own video projects or I try to cultivate clients by entering contests, sending out résumés and making phone calls. Weekends are totally devoted to my own work, and I take the occasional day off from work to go into the city in search of clients or to see movies. It gets tiring and sometimes I wonder if I'll ever get to the point where I can support myself doing my own work or something close to it. I guess I'm lucky that I have a viable means of support so that I don't have to get locked into a job that would limit my flexibility to advance my career."

"I never thought I'd have so much freelance work that I'd actually pray for no more clients to call each day." Edward, like many writers, hoped that he could support himself by writing fiction. Although he has been fortunate enough to have one novel published, it hasn't made him rich or even famous. Nevertheless, he does have his foot in the door, and several publishers are interested in his second book when it is finished. Now that he has a family to help support, he knows that even if he does sell his next novel, he can't count on it to go far toward paying his bills.

As the difficulty of being a fiction writer began to dawn more and more clearly, Edward saw the handwriting on the wall and looked for ways to support himself and his work. As it turned out, he needed to look no further than his computer. Edward had bought his computer early. While many people were still debating whether computers would become widespread members of society or whether they were just a fad, Edward began to learn about them from the inside out. While others were just overcoming their computer phobia, he was writing programs. At one point, he even considered giving up writing for a lucrative job in software design. However, as he was pondering this move, one of his hacker friends told him about all the opportunities for freelance technical writers who could explain in words how to run software. This sort of writer can make upwards of $300 per day, and their work is in high demand.

"I had never earned so much money in my life. It can be a real danger for an artist to make a lot of money, because it can seem like an end in itself and you drift away from what you care about. I was determined that this would not happen to me." But Edward skirted this danger while simultaneously avoiding the money problems of many artists. In order to make his life work, he has become even more disciplined. Now he gets up an hour earlier so as to have some uninterrupted time for writing fiction. After he has put in his two hours at his desk, he swims a half mile at a local pool and then comes home to work on his technical manuals. On days when he doesn't have any computer writing work, he has more time to give to his own work.

"It's all really working for me right now. I feel I've got it all pulled together into a full and satisfying life with none of the life-wasting deprivation of being a starving artist in a garret. No matter what people say, you don't have to starve to be an artist, and artists don't have to be broke to produce good work. If you're always broke, you spend too much time worrying about money and not enough on your work. That's no help. Also, being too broke deprives you of many new experiences that might broaden your mind or influence your work. Instead of traveling or being able to buy books or go to the theater, you just sit there in your room and eat peanut butter.

"Unfortunately it's just a reality of our society that the average artist isn't valued and can't necessarily support himself decently with his own noncommercial creations. If you don't have a private income or some other special situation then you have to figure out a way to pay the bills that gives you enough to live on and flexible enough hours so that you can devote time to your personal vision. With luck and persistence you can do it all. Or at least that's how I feel now. I'm very optimistic."

Jack has been a successful cartoonist and illustrator for the last five years. He has created a line of comics that is published by a large comic book publisher and does a prodigious amount of freelance illustrating as well. Until two months ago, Jack was earning about $30,000 a year from all these sources. "Then, thanks to a rather fluky set of circumstances that developed over a couple of months, I lost 80 percent of my clients over a very short period of time. It was nobody's fault really, just one of those things. For instance, one company (based in Germany) pulled out of the U.S. because the dollar was in such bad shape it was no longer cost effective to ship products to the United States. Another art director that I did work for on a monthly basis at least decided to go back to school and get a Ph.D. His replacement brought a stable of help to the position and did not hire freelancers. One comic company that I had regular work with folded overnight, and a rather avant-garde publication in Phoenix switched from illustrations to heavy reliance on photos. Bang! Just like that. Naturally any semblance of security went out the window. Fortunately, I have trained myself to be very versatile, and I managed to pick up a great deal of T-shirt art work and corporate image design work to help in the interim. It was a bit like the choir all taking a breath at the same time . . . suddenly everything gets very quiet."

Things are slowly picking up for Jack. He has moved a bit more into the corporate identity design field, and he is doing some work for record companies. His story is not unique. Freelancers who work hard to build up a good list of clients occasionally do have setbacks in which everything goes wrong at once even though they have worked very hard and incurred no one's ire.

There are as many different scenarios of freelancing as there are people in business for themselves, but their lives tend to have many themes in common. This book should help you with some of the predictable problems of freelancing.

PART ONE

LIVING
THE LIFE

CHAPTER ONE

MANAGING YOUR LIFE

Perhaps the single hardest aspect of being a freelancer is being your own ringmaster cracking the whip over your own back. Since your decision to freelance may be due in part to a dislike of outside ringmasters, one of the things you must be very good at is making yourself work along and get things done. While you may have more latitude as to hours, attire and locus, you are constantly battling Parkinson's Law: work expands to fill the time allotted to its completion. Many writers, for instance, are aware that it is better to ask for a shorter deadline by which to deliver a manuscript, since work speed and efficiency are so often determined by the length of the deadline. A constant battle with procrastination can be exhausting and overwhelming, and is one of the reasons many freelancers have to give up. This need not happen to you if you learn how to control your time rather than letting it control you. Getting control of your time involves several factors: identifying your peak hours, learning how to plan and schedule the time you do have, learning how to get started and developing your own ways of coping with procrastination.

YOUR PEAK HOURS

I was always taught at school that you could not possibly do any decent work unless you were sitting in a straight-backed chair in a silent room and it was morning. Over the years, I realized that I work best sitting on the floor, listening to music, from about eight o'clock at night until one or two in the morning. Everyone has his own way of working. Certain habits can be adjusted slightly, but one characteristic which is highly variable among individuals is each one's best work time. You must discover your own peak hours for yourself. This is something which is peculiar to your body's built-in clock and should not be decided for you solely according to external pressures if you can help it.

How do you know which is your best time of day? Well, the condition of your mind when you wake up in the morning is a preliminary clue. Do you feel lazy and dull-witted when you wake up, or do you find that you get going right away? Some people do their best work soon after they awaken and fade as the day goes on. Others get a burst of energy or feel suddenly clear-headed and able to concentrate much later in the day or at night. Pay attention to how you work at different times of the day, and you will see that there are definite variations in your ability to focus on your work. The physiological correlate of these psychological peaks is a rise in your body temperature. If you live alone, you may already have discovered what your best hours are: your individuality in this regard tends to get overridden by family or friends' needs if you live with them. Therefore, it isn't a bad idea to discover your peak hours and make them yours before you try to work and live with others. The stress of constantly adapting your internal peak hours to other people's schedules is more exhausting than you realize.

An interesting theory of inner clock scheduling appeared in an article in *Psychology Today*. It holds that we are still living in primitive bodies adapted to withstand the heat of the African plains, where humankind originated, instead of the life in the temperate zones that we have inhabited for the last million years. Our primitive ancestors had to slow down and stay in the shade during the early afternoon. The authors of the article suggested that we would all do better if we worked a little bit later into the afternoon, lunching at one thirty or two when our bodies slow down anyway. As it is, they argue, we go to lunch while we are still in peak running form, we then eat and fall into an afternoon slump from which we don't revive until about time to go home. They advise a later lunch with a little slow time afterwards and staying a little later in order to take advantage of another high energy period in the late afternoon from around five to six.

This is a consideration that you can make when you work for yourself. I work best at night, so I arrange my days when possible to work from after breakfast until eleven and then pursue other interests until about four. I work again from four to about six, and then for a few hours after dinner. On days when deadlines threaten I work all day long if necessary.

Here's another theory that I like: light is extremely important to all mammals for the regulation of various physiological cycles, a fact usually ignored by modern medicine. Many physiologists say that humans, unlike other animals and plants, do not rely on light to synchronize all their body's cycles, but rather regulate their body's clocks only with external environmental clues such as mealtimes and hours of going to work and coming home. However, research done by Dr. Rutger Wever of the Max Planck Institute in West Germany disputes this. His research indicates that sufficient lighting will affect humans just as it does animals. He and other doctors feel that most people working indoors do not get enough of this light intensity—the equivalent of fifteen 100-watt bulbs burning for several hours in your living room. They contend that living pattern disturbances, insomnia and depression may come from being chronically underexposed to light. They suggest that you work near an unshaded window. The time of day also influences the effect that the light has on living patterns. These researchers suggest that if you have trouble getting up in the morning and going to bed at night, spend more time in early morning light. It will set your biological clock forward a few hours. You might try running before breakfast or walking to work if you work away from home. Conversely, if you fall asleep and get up too early, you may need to spend more time outdoors just before sunset to set your clock backward. By paying attention to the type and amount of light you absorb you can influence your peak hours to your advantage and establish firmer time use habits.

There are things to be said for both night and day hours. Naturally, if there is business involved in your work to any significant degree, you will have to be available during external business hours (though perhaps not every day). If you work best during the day you're more likely to be in sync with the rest of the world, which enables you to work and play when most of your friends probably do also. For freelancers with children of school age this can work out very well, since you can work while they're at school. Some freelancers who have young children find that they can get up an hour or two earlier in the morning and get a lot of work done in the peaceful predawn hours while everyone else is still asleep. Working during the day also gives you the advantage of being able to consult with the outside world as you need rather than having to wait until morning the way night owls sometimes do.

On the other hand, there may be a physiological reason why some people may work better at night, and it is a characteristic they share with radio and television sets. As the sun goes down there is less radio and microwave interference in the atmosphere, which appears to calm people who are sensitive to these atmospheric changes. In some as yet unelucidated way, humans are affected by these waves. If you work at night you will find that it is extremely peaceful, but you may also find it inconvenient, at least during any stages of your work that involve the outside world. One successful way of getting around that is to do all your phone and library work, or your support work, during the day and your creative work—or whatever you need your whole mind for— at night. The advent of various on-line computer databases gives more latitude to those who work at night, since you can access information by telephone twenty-four hours a day (see chapter 7).

A painter had this to say: "First of all you have to figure out whether you are a day person or a night person. Save your high-energy period for yourself and for your work. You sell your secondary time. I was a high-efficiency waitress, I really burned, but in terms of my head I turned that time off. During the day is when I really cook. I'd go home at one or two in the morning and then I'd get up early and paint all day until four or five o'clock."

Whatever time of day you find best is the one you should choose insofar as the other people in your life permit you to do so. But even though today we recognize the physiological idiosyncrasies which determine one's peak hours, this acceptance is fairly recent. The artists who are old enough to be interviewed for this book grew up at a time when it was still thought very sloppy, or bohemian at best, to do one's work at night and sleep late into the morning. Many people who find they work better later expressed guilt at this and somehow equated daytime work with better discipline and increased efficiency:

I have the feeling I'd get more done if I were up by nine every morning. Instead I just feel myself floating into it, but there I am still going strong at three or four in the morning. —Actress-Director

I like the nighttime for really cracking a scene, or starting something new, because you're a little tired, a little looser, and you make interesting mistakes. To me, when you're doing the muscle part, where you know what

you're doing, the day is better because you're clearer and you can see obstacles more. Different times for different things. —Writer-Lyricist

I work during the day, but that's because I'm a puritan prig. I always believed in working at night, as though the real me would emerge at night, but I've never been able to stay awake long enough to get much work done. Most people only get up in the morning because they have to work in the business world. —Writer

I find that I am at my most energetic and efficient after midnight, unless I have tried to do a lot during the day. I try to work earlier mainly because of societal pressures; one wants to be able to play with one's peers occasionally. But I am undeniably clearest around 1 A.M. If I were a novelist this wouldn't be so inconvenient, but as a journalist it is difficult because I have no access to information at that hour, and by the time 9 A.M. comes I have lost my enthusiasm and concentration and am usually sound asleep. Somehow, I don't seem to start reviving again until 4:30 or so when, again, everyone else is going home. —Writer

My husband and I have always worked at our outside jobs during the day and then come home and painted until one or two in the morning, at which time we eat a small dinner. It's the only way we can afford to paint at all. —Painter

According to Dr. Robert Chell of Personnel Sciences in New York City anyone's limit of undivided attention on any one task is about forty minutes. This doesn't mean that you should quit after forty minutes, but just that you should get up and stretch. He also suggests doing a different task for forty minutes and then going back to your original one as a way to improve your concentration.

It is also up to you to decide whether you prefer to interweave your tasks or do one thing all of one day or all one week. Most experts suggest that you try to plan for as much variety as possible in order to keep yourself awake. What you must figure out for yourself is how much variety keeps you on your toes and how much is distracting. James Dickey wrote in his journal *Sorties:* "The whole point is to do some writing, some guitar playing, and something physical every day, no matter what. That is the only way to live and get your work done."

PLANS AND SCHEDULES

Plans and schedules are at least as important to freelancers as they are to executives and students. One of the stupidest remarks I ever heard from a fellow freelancer was when another writer collaborating on an assignment with me shouted as I chided him for being three hours late for a scheduled work session,

"Oh, don't hassle me. This isn't an office. I said I was sorry. Why are you freelancing if you're so uptight about schedules and plans?"

"Why are *you* freelancing?" I thought. "You'll never survive if you can't learn to be on time."

It seems to be par for the course that freelancers are either drowning in excess time with no work to do or else don't have enough time even to take a deep breath for fear of missing a deadline. In order to cope with these extremes, freelancers must learn how to wait constructively when nothing seems to be happening and how to plan and schedule effectively so that they can get everything done with a minimum of stress when things are cooking.

In order to plan your time you first have to have some idea of what needs to be done and in what order. Priority items are all those which you are being paid to do and those with deadlines. Aside from those immediate priorities you must decide which additional steps, such as soliciting new clients, will help to move you along to where you want your work to be, and put them down just below the immediate priorities. It really helps to put all this down on paper before your eyes so that it is less labyrinthine. There are a variety of ways to do this. Perhaps the simplest way is to make three headings: Outside Work, Work for Self, and Nonbusiness. Under each heading you can put a list of all the assignments, tasks and other steps related to these three parts of your time.

I use these three divisions to include: (1) work commissioned or assigned by outside sources, paid assignments; (2) creative work of my own (which is as important as paid work, probably more so unless you are strictly a commercial freelancer); (3) nonbusiness is everything from sports activities to painting your kitchen. While these obviously have nothing to do with your work, personal goals are important to your life in that your work should not be the only area in which you have dreams and goals. Some of your time must go to these other matters, and success breeds success. The attainment of a personal goal, such as losing that ten pounds, will promote a feeling of self-control that will carry over into your freelance work.

GOALS

Life is too short to allow you to do everything without concern for relative importance. With planning for the long term, and day-to-day scheduling, you can achieve much more than by just doing whatever presents itself in random order.

It helps to think a little ahead and set up long- and short-term goals for yourself. This doesn't mean setting yourself on any irrevocable course. All it means is sorting out just which of the many options open to you are the ones that mean the most. You have to make your goals realistic too, or they won't mean anything. In order to set realistic goals they must be (1) specific and (2) broken down into steps.

Specificity of your goals will ensure that you know what you are striving for. It is not much help to say to yourself that you want to become a great photographer before you die. Such a resolution leaves a great deal of room. You need to zero in more. This doesn't mean that your goals won't change, that you are locking yourself in. It just means that you have a closer idea of what you really want. Sometimes when deciding what your goals are it is helpful to imagine that you are writing an idealized obituary of yourself. Forget all the reasons that you think you can't do what you want to do. The very first step is to identify what you *really* want to do, suspending for the moment any judgments as to possibility or suitability.

Another caution is to *make sure you know whose goals they are*. Are they your goals, or are they goals set for you by your parents, your school or your spouse? All too often we have difficulties in reaching goals because they are not even our goals. Rather, they are admonitions and shoulds that we've internalized from these ghostly authority figures. So, another important test for each of the goals you write down is—whose idea was that anyway?

You should also set deadlines for the completion of your goals, otherwise they are just vague strivings which you can always rationalize away. In order to make these deadlines attainable you need to break each goal down into a number of tasks, each with its own deadline. These tasks can then be performed one at a time, reinforcing your commitment and your energies as you complete them successfully. Success is infectious. It is well known to psychologists that a person with a past history of successes will be able to carry over a generalized feeling of success in his approach to later goals, which will be easier to accomplish in such an aura of confidence.

A GOOD SCHEDULE IS FLEXIBLE

On top of the time that you must block off for work that you are committed to and tasks related to your own goals, you need time for just thinking and marinating in your own juices, as well as time to eat, sleep and entertain yourself.

One of the most common mistakes people make when planning their time is to try to schedule themselves too rigidly. This is detrimental because it's impossible for anyone in the modern world of bureaucracies, crowded highways and slow mails to run totally on schedule at all times. On top of this, there is always the element of chance and uncertainty that you would be a fool to think you can eliminate. You never know when death, marriage, or a myriad of other, less epochal occurrences will interrupt your schedule. And, as with any physical event, the less flexible your plan, the more disruptive any chance occurrences will be. If every fifteen-minute hole is filled, you will find yourself feeling guilty for always cutting into time you had allotted for other projects, because you have no flexibility. An inflexible schedule is difficult enough for an IBM executive; for an artist it is out of the question. The very nature of creative work dictates that you must have plenty of time to let your mind wander and free associate—time when you aren't pressed to do anything.

"The fact is that disorder is the condition of the mind's fertility," writes Paul Valéry in A *Course in Poetics*. The sort of disorder Valéry means is not the sort that comes when you miss deadlines or overdraw at the bank. It is the freedom to let chaos reign over your intellectual processes, which can only come when the administrative and income-producing aspects of your life are in order and don't require constant attention.

Nor does this mean that creative people should not have some inflexibly scheduled time for getting work done—almost all freelancers agree that you must. Creative work is the result of disciplined, concentrated effort. Most freelancers also feel that your work time should be the same every day—or at least planned and not haphazardly at any time you can bear to get into it.

SCHEDULING YOUR TIME

With all this in mind, take a monthly or yearly calendar and follow these suggestions for planning your time:

* For each *professional* and each *personal creative deadline* outline all the steps that you will need to take to complete each project on time. With a list of those steps in front of you, decide how much time you need to complete each step and in what order they flow most logically. Michael Le Boeuf, time expert and author of *Working Smart* (Warner Books), recommends that you allow 1.5 times as much time as you think you will need in order to compensate for unavoidable delays, mood changes and unexpected snags. Thus, if you figure a job will take you six hours, allow nine. This gives you a more realistic outer time limit against which to measure your progress. Assign the steps for each project to days within the deadline period for that project. It is mainly an individual matter whether you give your prime time to professional projects or work for yourself during your prime time. This may depend partly on how close you are to a professional deadline, how hard the work is and how draining you find it. Of two illustrators with identical newspaper deadlines as well as individual projects, one may use his peak hours to do outside work, because doing the job well and getting more assignments is important. The second may do outside work in off-hours, because he finds it easy to knock off outside assignments. The point is that no matter how much or how little effort contracted-for work costs you in comparison to your own work, the end result must satisfy your client.
* On your calendar, write in red all *professional deadlines* (i.e., deadlines you must meet for magazines or production schedules of various sorts— all outside deadlines). Then go back and assign each step leading to it to a particular time slot and pencil it in.
* Now write in red *personal creative deadlines* (deadlines you have set for the accomplishment of various tasks pertaining to your own creative work). Pencil in which part of the work you want to accomplish on each day.
* Next, write in *personal nonprofessional deadlines* (weight-loss deadlines, mailing deadlines, etc.). Allow yourself a certain amount of time each day and each week, and then rope off this time for yourself.
* Next come miscellaneous appointments and dates. This may seem self-indulgent, but I assure you it's not. This gives you the time to keep your personal life running smoothly. You need an hour a day, at least a day a week, and a weekend a month in which you should consciously avoid thinking about your work. This is harder than you think, particularly if you love your work and particularly if you work at home.

You should now have penciled-in tasks to be completed each day, along with the steps and appointments necessary to accomplish this. The completed chart should be very helpful in helping you to organize your time and then using this time most efficiently. Make sure to keep it up-to-date, keeping a month or two ahead insofar as you can in such a capricious business.

• *Make a daily schedule too.* In order to get the maximum day-to-day benefit from planning, you should also make a schedule for each day. This is something that you should make a habit of doing first thing each morning or last thing as you are winding up, and you should keep it with you during the day.

You probably haven't had a daily schedule since the fourth grade, but you need one all the same. A schedule helps you organize the tasks you must accomplish by the end of the day. It is really the day's program. It needn't be any big deal. I organize mine like this:

WORK
  Work on Chapter 9
  Proofread short story
  Dr. Novick's paper in Science
  Retype Times *piece*
  4 P.M. *meeting at* News

ERRANDS
  Stamps
  Cat food
  Ballet tickets

PHONE CALLS
  Dr. Forer
  Joyce at 8 A.M.

CORRESPONDENCE
  Query to Elektra
  Thank Dr. Bailey
  Lunch with AP guy

If there are any especially urgent matters, I usually write these across the top.

A schedule can help you coordinate the two facets of your job as a freelancer: finding the work and then doing it. Though you may not think of the time you spend entertaining prospective clients or talking on the telephone as work, it is an essential part of freelancing. Time must be allotted for it on a regular basis. You must decide whether you need to spend an hour a day or an hour a week lining up new work. It will vary according to your workload.

AIDS TO KEEPING TRACK OF YOUR TIME

One graphic designer I interviewed had a novel concept that she had developed to help her stop wasting her time. Here it is in her own words:

Sometimes I forget where I have to go or where I have been, and then I start feeling very guilty at all the lost time. I began to realize that in this business it's really not nine to five, and what matters is what happened that day, what you accomplished, how much time you spent. So I developed a little trick whereby I keep a second book which I work on every time I am in a taxi or on the subway. Usually I can count on that happening every few days, so I always have time to fill it in. I just write down in it what I did, where I went, how many hours it took, any important ideas that came out of it. Also, if I have something important coming up in the future, I'll write in it as if it were a calendar in addition to my appointment book. This book is mainly after the fact, while the other is my upcoming appointments. I leave that one on my desk and cross out the things in it as they are done. This second book I carry with me. It is very important because I go back and look at it in order to decide if something was worth it, or whether I wasted my time in a way that I can prevent the next time.

Another helpful thing you can buy is the large-size weekly calendars. Several types are made, laid out differently for different needs. A very useful layout for the freelancer with several projects going at once is the Eaton's Week-At-A-Glance for "Group Practice," since it has several parallel columns so that you can have the day's work for each project side by side.

HOW TO WAIT CONSTRUCTIVELY

Some freelancers may find that they are occupied all of the time, even when they're not on a job. To others—particularly performers—life may seem to be made up of a few weeks of work surrounded by long arid periods of unemployment. These hiatuses can be devastating and are often at the heart of many artists' decisions to get into something else. For some people such a decision is the most realistic move, considering the enormous odds and the level of talent of the competition. At the same time, some extremely talented people become discouraged and give up too early because they are unable to wait constructively. Simply waiting is anti-life, since there's always the nagging question, "Waiting for what?" A significant number of the people I talked to had the same observation: breaks always seem to come when you can't stop what you're doing to accept them. Conversely, these people also noticed that the years they spend sitting by the telephone are the ones when nothing advances in their careers.

Long periods of unemployment are the freelancer's lot, but they can be turned around and made constructive if you just make a point of doing so. The combination of waiting and being impoverished isn't a great deal of fun.

If this is your predicament, you may need to take a temporary job which will help to fill your time as well as your wallet. If you have enough to live on in the immediate future, you might do better trying to drum up some work in your field. This has the advantage of occupying your time and helping you move forward in your work. If you are lucky and canny you will be able to use this off-time to line up some assignments.

One of the keys is not to think of the time you spend between jobs as dead time. Employees seem to be happy enough to have some free time. So should you be. If you know how to wait you will be able to rebound from this time as though from a vacation. It is only ruined when you begin to think of it as an ending.

It is most important not to sit passively by. In fact, waiting is the wrong word, because it connotes a time apart from the rest of your life, which this time should not be. Every day in your life should count. Consider that each day you live has its unique impact, and if you are glued to the telephone and television you are receiving less impact than you might have if you looked at it in a different way. It's a matter of taking life as a whole, and not identifying so deeply with your work that you don't consider yourself alive if you aren't out there doing it.

Waiting seems to pose the heaviest and the most frequent problems to performers. This is because performers, more than others, need accessories. A writer can work for her own pleasure, as can any sort of visual artist, but a performer needs at least an audience, and maybe also a stage and a script and supporting performers.

LINING UP FUTURE WORK

When you are busy working on a project you often do not have the time to line up your next projects and keep the ball rolling. Nevertheless, it is a good idea to line up projects in advance, so that when you have finished one there will be no waiting at loose ends.

If you have allowed your work life to come to a halt and are now sitting around feeling depressed, you are not using your time well. It would be far better to use the time to get more work. In the delight that you feel at getting one job out of the way, you should not allow yourself to slack off. Doing the work and turning it in is only one part of your job. The other part is procuring new work. The times when you are not actively working are ideal in which to do this.

Lining up work should be approached on many fronts. Try to get as many things happening as possible, since some almost always end up being delayed or falling through:

- Talk to your agent, rep or manager if you have one.
- Use this time to catch up with friends in your field and other relevant ones. It is in informal meetings like this that ideas come. Part of the trick is to keep your net widely spread so that you are on people's minds when a suitable job comes up. The occasional lunch or drink with these people when you have the time will keep you and them current.
- This is a good time to expand your own horizons. Read, go to films, plays, concerts, exhibitions. These will serve to jog your unconscious into coming up with totally new ideas that you can sell.
- Writing query letters, showing your portfolio and otherwise selling yourself is hard work. Ideally, you should put aside some time every week for this sort of chore—naturally, not when you're working on deadline and can't afford the time (though even when on deadline you may find that spare moments can be put to good use drafting letters or making appointments to show your work). You have time to do this on a larger scale when you are not in the middle of a project.
- As one freelancer says, when you're working on a project you should be looking for more work, and when you're out looking for more work you

really should be working at home. This is a difficulty of freelancing that you really must master. It's all too easy to forget that after you turn in the piece you're working on that you're going to need some new work immediately to pay the next month's bills.

• Catch up on your rest and exercise. This is not meant to be facetious. You have probably observed how some of your most brilliant ideas come when you are dozing off or participating in a sport you like. When you are working very single-mindedly on a project, you tend to neglect your mind and body by not exercising, not sleeping enough and not eating well. These practices do not facilitate the creative process. You'll be amazed at how many new ideas you'll come up with if you loosen your reins for a few days. Then, do not fail to act on those ideas. You've had a rest, now sit down and write that letter.

The following comments illustrate the ways in which several freelancers deal with waiting:

I haven't worked in six months, and my last work was a day's work in a film, so I haven't been on stage in a year. That's really hard. My bottom line is that when nothing is giving you that boost, you create situations in your life that do that. Classes, friends, fixing up your apartment can all help you get through these times. You have to create some kind of meaningful routine and schedule for yourself just so that days of empty spaces don't go by in your appointment book. —Actress

The most difficult things about being a freelancer are those long periods of unemployment. You should learn to live with them early on, because that's the other side of not working fifty weeks a year and having two weeks' paid vacation. There are those times when you don't work at all—your life is a vacation—totally empty. You try to create a life separate from your profession which gives your life quality and joy. —Illustrator

I do lots of things which keep my interest level high and broaden my base of operations, so that I become more and more in control instead of being controlled by what work is available. That's what being a freelancer is about. Your objective is to control your life. So if I'm not performing, I'm writing or practicing or just hanging out meeting people—something you should never undervalue. —Composer-Musician

PROCRASTINATION

Procrastination is slow death to even the best-laid plans. It is a terrible affliction composed of equal parts of fear, poor organization and conflict. It can expand the simplest task into an awesome three-week project. The worst thing about procrastination is that it is totally maladaptive, and it solves nothing. Freelancers who cannot avoid procrastinating generally either find themselves back in better-supervised work environments or find themselves very hungry.

Here are some hints for avoiding procrastination and getting started:

- Procrastination often arises when there is a hidden conflict or fear related to the attainment of a goal. It is often useful to ask yourself what you expect to happen when your task is finished and what you fear.
- Force yourself to take a quick look at what you have to do. Often you will find that this will get you caught up in it.
- Similarly, take five minutes to break down the task into a sequence of steps and write them down. Outline it if it is a written piece. Some people estimate how long each step will take and write down their estimate next to the task.
- If your procrastination procedure is to read the papers, wait until you've scheduled a break to go and buy them. The exercise will get the blood flowing to your brain again, and you'll probably come back clearer-thinking, unless of course you also stop off to buy groceries, have a beer, go window shopping or anything else you shouldn't be doing.
- If your style is to clean your nest before you can settle down to work, try to keep the house passably clean. This is really a way of trying to calm inner anxiety by making your outer environment reflect your mind. Someone who has to tidy her desk obsessively is trying to do the psychic equivalent at the same time. With practice, you can learn to compartmentalize your anxieties better, so that the dirty kitchen floor can be forgotten for the duration of your work by simply closing the door.
- The telephone is the devil's own invention as far as the chronic procrastinator is concerned. Unplug it if you can or turn off the bell. If you can't silence the ring in any way, deaden it by putting the phone in another room or under pillows. A handy combination is an answering machine hooked up to a phone which has been unplugged. You have no excuse to answer the phone, since you'll get all your messages later anyway.
- Bring the television set out of the closet only after you work. Better yet, don't have one in the house.
- Use spare minutes, when you know your available time is limited, to get started on something you've been avoiding. Some people just dread the thought of the loneliness and long hours of silence that are necessary to complete a job. By forcing yourself to confront it for a limited amount of time, you may be able to see that it is the fear you have projected on it that is making it so threatening.
- Self-hypnosis is extremely helpful in finding out why you procrastinate, why you have a conflict about reaching your goal. Self-hypnosis, which can be taught to you, is a valuable tool for attacking the problem on a daily basis.
- Sometimes you have a choice of steps to take. It helps to choose the one most suited to the mood you're in rather than always forcing yourself to finish the worst thing first according to some misguided puritan notion.

- Give yourself a reward for starting a task you've been avoiding.
- Punish yourself for procrastinating by making yourself do some lower-priority housework or something apart from your work which you also hate. How about cleaning the cat's pan and bowls and then picking the hair filters out of all the bathroom drains? I'm sure you have your own private horrors.
- Try making yourself sit totally unoccupied for five minutes. DO NOTH-ING. You'll be begging to get to work after four minutes.

DISCIPLINE

The need for disciplined work habits was perhaps the only topic I discussed with freelancers about which there was total unanimity. If you are not disciplined you will not survive as a freelancer. It is just this slight edge in self-motivation and discipline which distinguishes the good freelancer from the good employee. You might think (and many would-be freelancers do mistakenly believe) that because freelancers have no diurnal work rhythms imposed from above, they have less need of organizing their time. Yet have you ever noticed how with twenty-four hours free in a day you accomplish far less than when you're juggling job, social life, plus one or two unexpected last-minute considerations? "Work expands to fill the time available for its completion." It's one thing if you allow this to happen on someone else's time. If they permit it, or don't notice it, you've gotten away with something. It becomes a different thing, however, if you waste your own time, and it takes both discipline and motivation to keep from doing so.

The difficulty many of us have with discipline is its negative connotation left over from childhood or school days. "To discipline" can mean "to punish," and most of us don't want to punish ourselves—at least not consciously. The times the word "discipline" came up when we were children usually were times we were forced to do things against our will and thus lost our autonomy. Therefore we tend to think that when discipline enters, our freedom goes out the door. But if you examine this position logically, you can't help but realize that it is false, except perhaps for those who don't have to work. A lack of discipline merely restricts your freedom by doubling or tripling the time it takes you to do things, as well as by complicating your free time with guilt. Furthermore, a lack of discipline is very bad for your self-esteem, and it manifests itself continually when your work is not going well. Having a reasonable amount of discipline does not make you a Pollyanna or the class grind; it simply enables you to freelance.

Most of the freelancers, even the most highly successful, felt that they could stand some improvement in this area. Yet even the very fact that they were able to succeed as freelancers pointed to a level of self-discipline beyond that of the average person. As you will see, the nearly unanimous answer to the question "What motivates you?" was "The deadline," or "Starvation." Yet most people, when facing starvation, would turn to the employment agencies. To carry on with some of the least appreciated and most demanding work there is, with no one else to crack the whip, requires a fundamental dedication to one's work and better-than-average self-discipline.

None of us is disciplined in every action all the time. Being disciplined does *not* mean being infallible. When you are dieting, one slip doesn't mean that you should abandon the whole diet. The same thing is true of professional discipline. A disciplined artist is one who has a high level of dedication and is serious toward her work. As with everything that we have discussed in this chapter, discipline breeds more discipline. Here are some tips to help you develop it:

Start slowly. Don't try to change ten years of undisciplined work habits overnight. A good way to start getting control of your life is to gain discipline over some nonworking aspects of it. Lose that five pounds, clean that attic. Bit by bit you begin to perceive yourself as being in control, a disciplined person.

• Start now. It won't be any easier tomorrow.
• Remember that discipline exists for *all* of us. If you wish to continue free-lancing, you are in charge of disciplining yourself. If this doesn't appeal, maybe freelancing isn't for you.
• Try self-hypnosis. It can work wonders with discipline problems.

Most of the freelancers quoted here are successful, and their attitudes about discipline may suggest why. It's rarely easy for anyone, but those who care about their work find a way to discipline themselves:

Sometimes you have to scare yourself before you can really get anything done. It's like term-paper time over and over constantly, only it's your life.
—Photographer

I'm not that well motivated. I'm very well disciplined. If I have work I can do it. The only time I'm motivated as far as creating work for myself is when I'm broke. I need to be broke or I need not to have done any work for a while, but that means I can't have any distraction like a social life. Earning money and avoiding starvation are always the best incentives.
—Graphic Artist

I do my best work on weekends. I start as if I'm getting up to go to the office, but rather than walking out the door I walk to the other side of the room and I sit there. If I procrastinate, if I let it slide till one or two o'clock, then I have problems. Then I have to read for a while, look at someone else's books, get pissed off that I'm not doing anything. Or I buy the New York Times Book Review of Children's Books—*that always makes me feel guilty if I'm not in it. Reading about other people's stuff gets me going a lot of times.*
—Illustrator

I'm fairly disciplined. I spent a lot of time in the academic world as a classical scholar. I have a monkish personality. Someone who can sit down with Thucydides and Herodotus and enjoy them has got to be disciplined. I have great powers of concentration—not all of the time, but if I have a certain

amount of time, and work to be done, I can sit down and do it. Writing is a job; it's work. If you're going to be professional about it as a freelancer, you have to treat it as work. You have to sit down every day and do it. You can't think that it's just going to somehow magically appear in the typewriter, because it's not. You have to do it, or else you're going to starve to death.
                 —Writer

My big problem is getting started when I don't have a specific project. Once I'm on it I can usually stay with it, but I find it takes hours to get into it. My intelligence tells me I'd be much better up at eight and at my desk by nine; a regular day schedule would have an enforced discipline to it. I know that's the way to accomplish more, the healthiest way; but instead I find myself sort of floating into it.   *—Theater Director*

I think if you love your work and believe in it you have no trouble with discipline. Everybody is lazy. It's natural. You must press yourself to reach a routine, so that whether the weather is brilliant or the winter is cold, you still get up, drink your coffee and get to work. Even if you have no extremely good ideas, you must work. The only chance of giving birth to a good idea is to work daily. Good ideas come from ten bad ideas. Everybody must work as much as possible. When you have a routine it's like being a long-distance runner. Everybody knows that in the middle of the race nobody is concentrating—they continue to drive from routine. Only the start and finish are important.   *—Painter*

PRODUCTIVITY

Productivity is only partly a function of discipline and proper planning and scheduling. Creative productivity may be extremely variable over months and years, and this is often a source of guilt and misunderstanding among creative people. According to Dr. Silvano Arieti, a psychiatrist who has written a great deal about creativity, "productivity does not follow a constant pattern in creative men. Periods of great creativity alternate with periods devoted to scholarship, observation, or even mere meditation. At times a cycle seems to repeat itself."[*]

Variations in the cycle of productivity are something to be aware of, although not as a rationalization for a lack of discipline. You may be able to discover the length of your cycle and to what other cycles (e.g., menstrual, lunar, seasonal) it relates. Once you have some idea of what to expect, you can use your high-productivity periods to get a great deal accomplished less painfully, and you can berate yourself a little less during the less efficient part of your cycle.

Also, the nature of creative work is such that what seems like inactivity may actually be an essential part of creation. As I've quoted so often, "You need a lot of time to sit around and stew in your own juices."

It is internalized guilt from your childhood which makes you feel that you

[*]Silvano Arieti, *Creativity, The Magic Synthesis* (New York: Basic Books, 1976), p. 382.

aren't getting much accomplished unless you appear to be busy at every moment. This association between busyness and productivity is undoubtedly one of the most stifling aspects of being an employee. For several freelancers, it was this continual emphasis on at least *looking* busy which made them decide to go freelance at any cost.

Remember: you're not a machine. You may not always be able to turn out forty hours of work per week. You may never be able to—or on some jobs you may, but don't expect to. Producing original work—even commercial work that doesn't come from the depths of your soul—requires an enormous expenditure of effort. My mother, who was a well-known fiction writer in her time, somewhere dug up the "fact" that eight hours of writing requires as much energy as eight hours of digging ditches. I don't know how strictly true this is, but when I'm in the middle of a long day of work and my energy is flagging, I often remember it.

STAYING AWAKE TO WORK

Because you are doing a job which has to get done no matter what the hour, you may find yourself staying awake through entire nights as you work fearfully to meet a deadline. This part always used to frighten me more than any other. I am not very good at keeping myself going when all I really want to do is go to bed. When the thoughts of a warm, yielding bed and a support under my aching back become too insistent, it is almost impossible for me to stay awake productively. Usually what I do then is to allow myself a short nap, depending upon how much time I can spare from the project at hand. This I do with the reasoning that I can do a far better job if I am alert and rested rather than craving only my bed. Try taking a half-hour nap. It works wonders. If you have a little more time, you might try giving yourself one full sleep cycle, which is about ninety minutes on the average. The advantage of doing this is that your body is not forced awake right in the middle of a dream, when awakening is the most traumatic and when you are unlikely to feel refreshed. If, however, you take a whole sleep cycle, your body takes you on a trip through several levels of sleep and several changes in brain waves, and delivers you neatly at the threshold of consciousness at the end. You may also find that even such brief submersion will refresh your creativity as well.

There will be times, however, when you just can't take even half an hour out to sleep, and here are some suggestions as to how to keep going.

NUTRITION

Nutrition for the specific purpose of staying awake used to be sort of a hit-or-miss affair. Either you figured out by experimenting what foods worked for you or you took popular wisdom which stated at one point that a chocolate bar would keep you awake and then swung to the opinion that you should eat complex carbohydrates such as grains for energy. Recently, research at MIT has yielded much more finely tuned advice on eating for energy and relaxation.

Much of this has been done by Dr. Judith Wurtman whose work goes one level deeper into the composition of food and looks at amino acids.

Amino acids, which are the basic constituents of proteins, are very important in determining your mood and level of energy or relaxation. This is because amino acids are also constituents of the protein neurotransmitters that act as fuel for different types of nerve cells. The neurotransmitters, norepinephrine and dopamine, are activating and mood-elevating, while serotonin helps you to calm down, to focus and even to sleep. The research is subtle and complicated. (If you're interested be sure to get Dr. Wurtman's fascinating book, *Managing Your Mind and Mood Through Food.*) The basic information that you need for your life is as follows:

- Eat a high-protein, low-carbohydrate meal when you want to stay awake. Proteins contain tyrosine, a precursor to energizing norepinephrine and dopamine. With minimal carbohydrates (starches and sugars) in a meal, these substances are speeded to your brain where they can help give you a boost. A couple of ounces of lean meat will be the best energizer. Also good are boiled eggs, low-fat yogurt and cottage or skim milk cheese. You want to avoid fat not only because it isn't very good for you, but also because fat slows down digestion and consequently the breakdown of protein into various amino acids and their conveyance to the brain. Also, eating large amounts of protein will only make you fat and will not increase production of norepinephrine and dopamine. Your brain is extremely sensitive to very small changes effected by the foods you eat.

  Although you can buy tyrosine and tryptophan over the counter now, don't take these directly unless you are under careful medical supervision. They are drugs and have side effects. Tyrosine can raise your blood pressure, and tryptophan can make you too sleepy.

- Avoid eating carbohydrates when you want to stay awake. A candy bar will jazz you up for a few minutes, because of the sugar, but then it will slow you right down, because the carbohydrates provide the brain with more of the raw materials it needs to make serotonin, the calming neurotransmitter.

- Caffeine is a good stimulant. Save your second cup of coffee for that moment in your workday when you need a lift. On those days where your nerves are worn to a frazzle but you're still beginning to feel tired, Dr. Wurtman advises that you add a couple of cookies or crackers to your caffeine break. The caffeine will give you a lift, and the small amount of carbohydrate will help your brain get a supply of the amino acid tryptophan to make serotonin which will help calm and focus you.

EXERCISE

The feelings that we associate with fatigue can often be relieved by increasing our body's supply of oxygen. Without question, the best way to accomplish this is through exercise. While a short period of calisthenics or a brisk run around the block can help somewhat when you feel spasms of fatigue in your eyelids, it won't solve your energy problems over the long term. The way to keep your energy level high all the time is by exercising hard on a regular basis. This increases your body's efficiency at using oxygen, so that when a big effort is required you aren't immediately exhausted.

But suppose you aren't used to exercising on a regular basis, but still need to stay up to make a deadline? If you are anywhere near the water, a swim is probably the best wake-up there is. (A cold shower, while not exercise, is also bracing.) A walk or a short run may help, as can five minutes of jumping rope. One of my favorite methods is to put on a record and dance for five or ten minutes. Anything that loosens you up and gets your blood circulation up will be helpful in keeping you awake. The effect will be enhanced if you put your work out of your mind for the duration of your break.

If you know that you will be up for a while, you can prevent fatigue to some extent by exercising for about three minutes of every half hour. Just put down the tools of your trade and do some stretches or some sit-ups. Anything that gets the blood flowing back into your brain is bound to be useful in this regard. Likewise, standing on your head for a few minutes can be extremely refreshing for the person who has been hunched over a desk or drawing board for hours. Some people find that Yoga will give them back some energy. Even if you don't do Yoga, deep breathing exercises may help.

If breathing and exercise don't get you going again, there is a good reason. Your body is trying to make a point: you need sleep. It becomes increasingly costly to force yourself to stay up much past this point. To do so usually requires drugs.

DRUGS IF YOU MUST

Everybody's body is different. You really have to experiment for yourself to see just what works for yours. Naturally, any drugs you take to stay awake, even caffeine, will eventually take their toll. They shouldn't be used in place of a professional attitude toward your work which helps you get it done on time. If you find yourself working under terrible pressure for weeks on end, you should consider giving yourself a rest as soon as it is practical, because such a schedule is punishing, and if allowed to take its toll will defeat the whole purpose of getting out of the rat race to freelance in the first place.

Drugs should be considered a last resort for staying awake, although my interviews with freelancers of all ages did not reveal that this attitude is widespread. It is not for puritanical reasons that I say drugs should be a last resort, but because drugs can take so much out of you that you cannot keep taking them in order to work without ultimately paying a price with regard to your health and your sensibilities. The immediate resorting to drugs makes it temporarily possible to work beyond your limits. If this is rarely required in your freelance work then do as you wish, but if you always have to work long and hard, you need a solution that will always work.

In the legal nonprescription class are such drugs as No-Doze or generic caffeine tablets, which are equal to about ten cups of coffee. These do the job quicker than coffee, and without all the acid. Several of the freelancers I interviewed used these because they are less debilitating and expensive than coke or speed, and in a pinch they do the trick. Most popular were time-release caffeine capsules, such as Wakespan. Again, even these over-the-counter "coffee pills" should be used only occasionally. Research is showing more and more compellingly that caffeine is not so great for our hearts and our stomachs. Many doctors are now suggesting that you limit yourself to two cups of coffee per day.

Still, on balance, caffeine is an excellent, quite safe stimulant which has been shown to improve concentration and performance. In fact, of the artists I surveyed, only one did not drink coffee. Not only did they almost all drink coffee, most also had sophisticated brewing devices that allowed the coffee to emerge at its most flavorful—Melitta, or some other drip method. Hot coffee in the winter and iced coffee kept in a jug in the refrigerator in the summer are my own preferred solutions for ordinary workdays.

Tea can be just as stimulating as coffee. In fact, it actually contains more caffeine, particularly if you let it steep. An alternative is Celestial Seasoning's Morning Thunder Tea, which a hardworking recording engineer friend swears by for staying awake during the frequent twenty-four-hour days that he puts in at his studio.

The following advice comes from the co-owner of a small printing and design firm in New York. During the years they were setting up their business there seemed to be days on end when neither owner would sleep. I was always very impressed by their stamina and their ability to maintain such a punishing schedule without cracking.

Sometimes a business overpowers your life, and you have to do whatever you have to do to make it successful. You can decide just how committed you want to be. We decided we were never going to turn down work at that stage. That meant that there were going to be periods of being up for three days straight.

You can do these long stints without drugs. In fact, I don't recommend using drugs to stay awake. Try to relax and pace yourself when you have to work through the night or longer. (The longest stint I did was seventy-two hours straight.) Frequent showers are very helpful if at all possible. Be sure to drink plenty of water and eat some light high-protein foods. Little perks like taking five minutes out to wash your face or wash your hair in the sink can help immensely. Otherwise, play little mind games such as mentally calculating how much you are going to make. Above all, don't panic. Panic is a common reaction to the prospect of sleep deprivation, but see it as a project that will end and keep calm. You'll get by a lot better.

TIME: YOUR MOST VALUABLE RESOURCE

Controlling your time—finding your peak hours, scheduling, avoiding procrastination and increasing your self-discipline—is a *sine qua non* of freelancing. Freelancing, like all work, requires you to parcel out some of your time in exchange for money; but instead of selling your time to an employer, your time is your own resource. Learning to marshal this resource and put it to work for you is, quite simply, the cog around which everything in your freelance life turns.

The sooner you learn how to control your time, the more time you will have both for your work and for playing.

Discipline yourself, but realize that there will be fluctuations in your level of discipline. Don't expect such perfect adherence to your own rules that a lost day causes you to feel you've failed completely. Creative minds work in special ways. Occasionally you need a "lost" day. Accept this, and then get back to work the next day.

CHAPTER TWO

GETTING WORK

A very important difference between freelancers and employees is that freelancers must solicit their own work. As one freelancer said, "You wake up every morning and you're unemployed"—unless you become practiced at getting work.

The amount of work around will vary. (August seems to be the doldrums—a time of high despair among freelancers.) There is never enough to go around in any case, but you can greatly improve your odds by having good contacts and a good agent or rep. Here is some advice on both subjects.

CONNECTIONS

You don't have to be Paloma Picasso or Michael Douglas in order to have connections. Connections are friends and assorted people you meet who maybe couldn't quite be called friends. Nobody can do everything by herself, but perhaps more than anyone else, the freelancer is called upon to try. Connections are people who can help you, and whom you can also help.

Connections range from a friend who works in the post office and can hand-cancel letters for you (this beats the postage meter rollback trick described in chapter 17) to people who work in your field to people at the bank. These people can help you do things expediently, thus relieving some of the burden of trying to be your own everything.

There is nothing opportunistic about being friendly to a wide variety of people and exchanging business cards. They need you just as much as you need them. Freelancing in any field requires friends, inside tips, and luck just as much as talent. "The amount of talent can be stretched with the right timing and the right people," explains one artist.

One often hears the role of connections in getting work down-played. This is particularly true in articles written for the purpose of encouraging people to try their luck at writing or painting or performing. However, anyone who freelances knows that it is a grapevine business. There is a predictable wait of a few years before you really start to succeed as a freelancer, and it is during this period that you are creating and extending your vine. Of course a few people shoot right to the top, but for most there are those long years of making contacts and learning how to use them. One television writer said:

When you have to work to get work, everything becomes doubly tiring. It's a very social business. You have cocktail parties to go to. You always go out to lunch to discuss something. It's great. That's one of the things I like about this business, but when you're freelancing you have to do that even more because that's one of the ways you get jobs. You never go to personnel offices and say, "I want to write." No one gets jobs that way, particularly not writing jobs. You have to go to parties on the chance of meeting a producer. You meet people and you get along with them and you follow it up or they follow you up. It takes a lot of time and money. I've started wearing a jacket and not always blue jeans. I should have done that a long time ago. It's important. It's so fucking stupid, but it matters to those people.

There is most definitely an attitude and rhythm that you must pick up in order to freelance successfully, and most people take a while to catch on to it. The only way to defeat the inertia of freelancing is to start lots of projects cooking, so that when one is not going well or is finished you can put it aside, take a short breather, and then attend to whatever you have on the back burner and in the oven. The only way to have these numerous projects mean anything is to know the people who can help you implement them.

HOW TO MAKE CONNECTIONS

The best way to make connections is just to try to be as pleasant as possible to people you meet and talk to them. You never know when someone will be able to be helpful in some way or when you will get a phone call from someone requesting your help. You'll certainly never know if you don't talk to them and find out what they do. It's not just powerful people in your own field that you need to meet and talk to, either. As a freelancer you need all sorts of help. You can make contacts anywhere from the corner newsstand to a cocktail party. This is a large world, and the only way to ensure that you will meet the people who could help you and whom you could help is actively to go and meet them.

• One way to do this is through mutual friends. Your friends will be more apt to introduce you to people who can help you if you introduce them to people who may be able to help them. It never hurts to invest tax-deductible money in dinner parties or other gatherings for just this purpose. Remember, in a business where initiative is all, you must get used to the idea of going after what you want and also helping others when you have the opportunity so that they might do the same for you if you're lucky. (Don't *expect* anything back and that way you won't come to hate everyone you know. In the creative world people pull real jaw-droppers on one another every other day.)
• Another important strategy for making connections is to join a few professional societies. Usually, at least once a year, they hold some sort of social gathering for their members. Go to these and don't be afraid to circulate and talk to people you don't know.
• Go to lectures or classes that pertain to what you do, and then be sure to go talk to some of the people afterwards. Most people who lecture or

teach are very generous about helping up-and-coming people. This holds true even of many famous people whose very names may be enough to humble you. Try not to let them, though. Key figures in your field who like your work can be very valuable to you as mentors, as job connections and as references on grant applications.

- You'd be surprised at how many artists are willing to talk to people who write them intelligent letters and show interest in their work. (Remember, this works best as a two-way street.) There's no harm at trying this approach. If they snap back or don't reply, you have lost nothing.
- Within any field there is a group of "in" people. Although work is often gotten in other ways, these people often do hire other "in" people. This group can be hard to crack, but once you get invited to one party, book-warming, opening or vernissage, you can often snag invitations to the next ones. Or at least you can find out when the next event is and crash it. (If you do crash, polish your act: dress and act appropriately. Once you become a fixture no one will question your right to be there. It's a time-honored method.)
- Don't just limit yourself to gatherings that pertain to your field, particularly if you do any commercial work. While you may meet valuable connections who can help you with your work, it is from people who aren't writers or artists that you often get commercial work. Go to meetings for causes that interest you. It's here that you may find people looking for freelancers with your skills. A group may well need your help designing logos, illustrating pamphlets, making a film, writing publicity—if not now, perhaps later. Try to meet the people who have organized the meeting and offer your services.
- A good way to meet a specific person is to get some publication (it can be a small one, published by your professional group or a small newspaper) to let you interview that person.
- Once you have an agent or rep, these people can often arrange for you to meet anyone you need to.

These methods are all perfectly acceptable ways of meeting connections—ways which don't require any particular chutzpah and won't be looked at askance. Sometimes, though, you won't get to meet a particular important person unless you *are* willing to use every bit of gall at your disposal. If you take the "what have I got to lose?" attitude and combine it with a real faith in what you have to offer, you may get further than you expect. Your approach will have to be tailored to the particular situation. Here are a few of the more outrageous methods of meeting people that I've heard of:

- One actress, learning that a particular film director (who was casting his next movie) was to lunch in the restaurant where she worked, immediately put the situation to her advantage. First, she made sure she would be serving his table. Then, throughout the meal she displayed her (very genuine) talents. She sang and tap-danced on her way to and from the kitchen, annoying everyone else but charming the director. Eventually, she became one of the stars of his next movie.

• Several freelancers seduced people they needed to know.
• One screenwriter simply found out where a certain very famous playwright lived and arrived at his house late one afternoon bearing an excellent bottle of red wine. Instead of being annoyed at the intrusion, the playwright was impressed by the young man's courage, and they have since worked together on several projects. Other freelancers have found that favors are often tendered those who show up with good drugs at the right time.

Diversity of contacts is important. Ten other freelancers, no matter how well known, may be less important than ten people in other fields. I asked a number of freelancers who their key contacts had been over recent months. Here are their answers:

A magazine editor, a policeman who sells cheap pot and someone who works in a film distributor's office and can give me things to read and also provide me with names and telephone numbers.
                                                              —Writer

A girl who worked in a deco boutique who started coming on to me and was only too happy to lend me costumes and bibelots for a play; a drama critic whose name I should not mention and another producer whose name I will also leave out.   *—Theater Producer*

It turned out that the cousin of the guy in my hardware store gets really good photographic equipment for very cheap through some racket I'd rather not know about. A woman living alone in a friendly neighborhood will find a lot of protective, kind people who always seem to have cousins and in-laws who range from cops to, well, camera equipment salesmen. Also, after a while, you're known on the block and you're less likely to be hassled.
                                                —Photographer-Writer

The best connection I made recently was a guy hanging out on the street who turned me on to a loft which was about one-fifth as expensive as any of the others around and in which I am now happily ensconced.
                                                              —Painter

I've been compiling a Rolodex and making and keeping contacts. Most of it starts out being social and snowballs from there. It might be a model who introduces you to an art director. You need a good business card too.
                                                        —Photographer

Directly related to fashion is making contacts with clothes stores. I used to go shopping with my girl friend and she'd buy a lot of clothes and I'd talk to them and ask if they'd ever lend clothes in return for pictures. Again, you're paying for everything and they are lending you something for twenty-four hours. In New York everyone wants something for what they give you.
                                                        —Photographer

I try to give a few parties a year to replenish my connection bank. This
makes me feel a little calculating, like Nancy Kissinger, but it's so impor-
tant. I'm always meeting people in other fields who I try to match up with
my friends. You never know when an important new circuit will be forged
in this way.   —*Writer-Producer*

An excellent sourcebook for women is *Networking: The Great New Way*
for Women to Get Ahead by Mary Scott Welch (Harcourt Brace Jovanov-
ich). This book lists network organizations for women in different fields in
every state. Try your library for this one.

AGENTS, REPS AND MANAGERS

If you are supposed to spend so much of your time making and grooming
connections, then what, you ask, is left for your agent, rep or manager to
do?

First of all, if you already have an agent, the answer is that he may be doing
much of the legwork for you with regard to getting you jobs, contracts or gigs.
But it never hurts for you to meet new people as well. As most freelancers
know, it usually takes good connections and real talent to attract a representative
these days. Freelancing is not a sellers' market. It's the users of your work and
the middlemen who have the numbers on their side. This is not to say that
these people aren't open to new talent, but rather that they feel they don't have
to go begging for it.

Agents, besides helping you to find new clients or jobs, also help you to get
the most favorable deals for your work. Agents are familiar with the intricacies
of the particular terms and contracts that might come your way. A good agent
may be able to get you more money or more favorable terms with respect to
rights or artistic control over the final product, things that the average freelancer
rarely has the clout to do for herself.

If you do not have an agent or rep, you may well find that you have to be
already on your way before one will want to take you on. This is true whether
you be an actor, photographer, musician or writer.

WRITERS. Authors may have more trouble finding a legitimate agent than
finding a publisher, since there are fewer reputable agencies than publishers.
If you have any possible ins to a good agent (a friend who works in the office,
a writing teacher or another writer who can introduce you), use them and try
to get the agent to read your work.

If you are unusually talented, or unusually lucky, or if the agent is hungry,
you may be able to pick up an agent this way. More likely you will have to
find your own way through the catch-22 situation of first getting a commitment
or a strong bite from a publisher and then calling an agent to help you with
the contract.

A good agent is a godsend to a writer. Your agent's knowledge of each editor's tendencies and preferences is more finely tuned than yours and can save you time. It is also undeniable that publishers and magazines see agent-submitted work as more professional. In fact, some magazines and a few publishers will not look at unsolicited works submitted by authors, and most take them less seriously, no matter what they say. You must realize, however, that many agents will not handle magazine submissions except as a favor or where they can earn good money. Most feel that the $25 they stand to earn on a $250 magazine article is not worth their while.

Writers who wish to sell to magazines should have the most recent edition of *Writer's Market*, published by Writer's Digest.

Don't get involved with a so-called literary agency that charges a reading fee. This is not kosher in the world of reputable agents who actually have clout with publishers. Your best bet is an established agent who has plenty of experience and good relationships with editors at top houses. You can get the names of reputable agents and their specialties through one of these organizations:

THE SOCIETY OF AUTHORS' REPRE-
SENTATIVES (SAR)
39½ Washington Square
New York, NY 10012
(212) 228-9740

INDEPENDENT LITERARY AGENTS
ASSOCIATION, INC.
c/o Sanford J. Greenberger Associates
55 Fifth Avenue
New York, NY 10003
(212) 206-5600

Also, you can check on a potential agent with the Authors League. And check out the agent by meeting with him in person and, if possible, by talking to some of his other clients.

Don't underestimate how useful an agent can be for the 10 percent (or occasionally 15 percent) that he will cost you. I made the mistake of handling my first book contract myself. I incorrectly assumed that the hard part had been getting the offer and saw no need for an agent. Consequently, I did not get a very good deal, particularly with regard to an advance, and collecting royalties has been a constant trial.

VISUAL ARTISTS. As with writers, visual artists do not usually attract representatives until they have managed to obtain some level of recognition and a recognizable style which can be used to sell them. The procedure for trying to get a rep to notice you, the visual artist, is much the same as what a writer must go through. Start by making appointments to leave your portfolio with any reps you can get introduced to and hope that you will be picked up.

Many reps and artists feel that the beginning freelancer is better off trying to sell her work on her own. Many art directors and galleries will see artists' portfolios by appointment without the phone call having to come from an agent. When you have more prestige as an artist, a rep can help get you bigger and better deals and can help you with your more complicated contracts and rights transactions. Many reps are members of the Society of Photographer and Artist Representatives (SPAR). SPAR publishes a newsletter that contains a listing of artists seeking representation. You can add yourself to this list. SPAR also publishes a directory of reps, which is available from SPAR, 1123 Broadway, New York, NY 10010; (212) 924-6023.

You can also hook up with a good rep by talking to working artists in your field and finding out who they have used successfully. You should expect to pay a rep in the neighborhood of 15 percent to 30 percent of a deal, the higher end usually being for artists who live out of town.

MUSICIANS. As with the other professions mentioned so far, the average beginning freelance musician is not likely to attract an agent. Most musicians I talked to felt that it was next to impossible to get an agent unless you had already somehow gotten a record deal.

You are more likely to acquire a manager at an early stage of your career. A manager has some of the same functions as an agent, but your manager is your mentor too, and takes part in directing your career in the sense of helping you create an image, advising you in all aspects of your life, telling you what songs to play at a gig and making connections for you. Unlike an agent, a manager is not legally bound to solicit work for you. When your manager has made you bankable and you are doing good business, an agent can get you even bigger deals.

Generally, in the music business, agents and managers find you. You can facilitate this by appearing in showcases and gigging as frequently as you can. It never hurts to send announcements of your dates to any managers you know of, and even to check back on the day of the gig to see if they want a table.

There are no regulatory bodies that function as quality controls for music agents and managers. Previous track record and the references of other clients are your best bet as far as checking on someone who has shown interest in managing you. You want a manager who has a strong belief in you, coupled with a good business sense and an unassailable knowledge of the music industry. Remember that the record companies and others who employ you are, in effect, hiring you and your manager as a package, so find a manager who is truly worthy of representing you.

How much your manager receives in commission should be negotiated, using a lawyer who is familiar with the very complicated music business. The Songwriters Guild or Volunteer Lawyers for the Arts can supply you with names. Expect to pay in the neighborhood of 10 to 25 percent over a stated term for a manager, although the amount could be higher—depending upon your situation.

ACTORS. Actors' agents work differently in New York and in Hollywood. Hollywood is closed to you if you don't have an agent, whereas in New York you can still get in to plenty of auditions without one. If a Hollywood agent takes you on you are asked to sign an exclusive contract. A New York agent who is interested in you may not even sign you immediately, but may instead send you out for some jobs and see how you do. You can even have several agents sending you out on this basis.

You can get a preliminary list of franchised agents from Equity, SAG, AGVA or AFTRA. Agents are given a franchise so that they may represent performers in the union in question. These agents are then bound to use union contracts and to charge no more than 10 percent to their clients.

It is hard to get a Hollywood agent until you have something on film to show them or extensive stage credits. The numbers being on their side, they let you figure out how to get to a level where you have some work to show. A New York agent is somewhat easier to come by. It is important to try to find an agent who is hungry enough to care about you, the small fish, but who is well enough connected to get you work. It is a good idea to try to check out what other sorts of clients a prospective agent handles—so that there aren't fourteen others of your type all competing for the same jobs. One way to do this is to see who handles actors of your type and who has none by looking in *The Player's Guide* (New York) or *The Academy Directory* (Hollywood). These giant books display the photos, and sometimes dimensions and past credits, of thousands of actors according to type: ingenue, character men, leading women, etc. Once you have a narrowed list of potential agents, drop into their offices with your photo and résumé. Get into the habit, right from the start, of dropping in to agents' offices rather than mailing correspondence. Even though you may be met with something of a persona-non-grata reception, it is best to keep reminding agents of your presence. Some agents have a big sign-in sheet, and actors are meant to drop in once a week and show how much they want to work by signing in. It is hard to say whether this is just a power trip by the agent and a waste of time or not. It is worth trying for six months, and you are not limited to that one agent if you haven't signed a contract.

Actors' agents are not only franchised by the union but are also licensed by the state as an employment agency would be. Agents' commissions are presently 10 percent across the board in the industry.

Some actors also hire personal managers, although this is more common in the music world. Many naive performers have lost a significant percentage (10 percent, 20 percent, even up to 50 percent) of their earnings to managers who don't do anything that they themselves couldn't have done. Tempting as it may be to have someone looking after your comfort, don't hire a manager who doesn't have good contacts and a knowledge of the theater. You can pick out your own wardrobe. You can get the names of managers from the Conference of Personal Managers, 1650 Broadway, New York, NY 10019; (212) 265-3366.

SOME GENERAL RULES
REGARDING AGENTS

No matter what your profession, there are some general words of advice germane to any field.

First of all, there is a debate as to whether you should try to get an agent from a big agency, such as I.C.M., or whether the small, hungry agent is better. Unless you are an established, bankable talent you are probably better off (and much more likely to be taken) at a medium-sized or small agency where you will get more attention, where the agents aren't overfed, and the numbers are more on your side. This doesn't mean that you should go to someone so new to the business that she has no contacts and no track record with publishers or producers. Often an excellent and viable choice is a young agent in an established office with a known letterhead.

Never forget that your agent should be your ally. You should both be working toward the same goal: your advancement as an artist. This means that you should both keep your ears to the ground for possible work. There is no way your agent can unearth every possibility for you, so don't neglect the connection-making part of your job.

Don't underestimate the importance of having an agent you personally respond to. If you don't feel comfortable with the one you have chosen, try to improve the relationship or else try to find someone else. The wrong agent can bring your career to an abrupt halt.

PRESENTING YOURSELF AND YOUR WORK

SHOWING YOUR WORK

When taking your work to show prospective agents or clients, there are some basic rules of presentation that you should be aware of.

Writers generally need only some tear sheets of published work or cleanly typed or printed-out copies of unpublished work. When sending them around to editors, you can just put them in a manila envelope with a stamped envelope addressed to you. When I take my work around to see prospective clients, I carry a large portfolio of the sort visual artists carry with plastic-covered sheets. In it, I have copies of most of my major magazine pieces with the magazine's cover on the front side and a copy of the article on the reverse. I also keep photocopies of my best work, copies of my books and several copies of my résumé on hand in the pockets in the back.

Commercial visual artists generally carry work around in these portfolios also. Although some present their work as slides, most art directors prefer to see the work itself. Painters and sculptors whose work isn't portable are generally limited to slides and studio visits. One fine arts photographer that I interviewed feels that neither slides nor even portfolios with plastic sleeves make an adequate presentation of his prints, so he lugs around matted prints. Along with your portfolio, you should always carry several copies of a well-typed and copy-edited résumé. Visual artists occasionally put so much effort into their portfolio's appearance and then neglect to do the same with their résumé. Misspellings and typos really do detract from the impression you make—even though you aren't trying to sell your editorial services. If you don't have an eye for these things, get someone who does to proofread your résumé before you copy it.

The art directors and artists I spoke to about the presentation of portfolios had the following suggestions:

- Be sure to replace the plastic sleeves of portfolios when they begin to look gummy and scratched so that your presentation looks really crisp.
- Your portfolio should be organized so as to give the best impression of what you can do in the shortest amount of time.
- Gear your portfolio to a specific interview. Put the work relevant to the

particular assignment that you are seeking up front. You can keep any
extra work that you like in the back. Figure out your niche and have
your portfolio speak to it. The competent generalist gets less work than
the person whom art directors remember because she is good at a specific type of thing. This doesn't mean that you can't change your focus
during your career, but just remember to carve out an area where you
really are the best and try to hone your presentation to demonstrate this.

• Enclosing the artwork itself in a plastic sleeve before you put it in the
portfolio is a good idea, because it allows you to switch your portfolio
around quickly when you need to change its focus to go after a particular job and because it protects the artwork from dirty fingers or spilled
coffee should the person looking at it decide to remove it from the portfolio.

• Don't leave your portfolio with original work in it at an agency or company if at all possible. Certainly never let it sit somewhere over the
weekend. It's not so much that the art director is going to steal work or
ideas (although this has probably happened), but rather that other people who see it might not respect its value and it might get lost or
wrecked. Instead, try to have a little promotion package of stats or even
color Xeroxes that you can leave behind, along with a résumé for people who can't review your portfolio while you are there. Even though
you would obviously rather show them the originals, people who know
what they are looking at should be able to tell by looking at copies
whether they want to look further.

One printer who sees a lot of artists' portfolios offered some additional tips
on portfolio presentation:

• Beginning designers often do not have clean, professional-looking, well-
displayed portfolios. Even if you are newly graduated from art school
and don't have printed work to show, you have to be able to display
tight comps and camera-ready art ability in order for a client or printer
to hire you. Creative design solutions are extremely effective in demon-
strating a designer's ability.

• It is important to show a range of ability in your portfolio. If the client
doesn't know all the types of work you can do, you may miss getting
jobs.

Musicians, vocalists and composers can choose between sending a cassette
or going to the trouble and expense of having an LP or a 45 pressed. Most of
the musicians I talked to felt that since A&R people at record companies are
inundated daily with cassettes, the band who sends in an attractive record in
a sleeve with an eye-catching cover design and a picture of the band will be
well ahead. They point out that cassettes not only look undistinguished, but
the sound quality is poor and the timing is usually off. "If you want to make
an impression," says one band manager and producer, "press your own record."

Numerous independent production companies will take your master, get it
pressed and even make up a jacket cover for you for about $1,000 for 1,000

singles. You can then distribute and sell these records yourself at gigs and at record stores to make back some of your cost.

Film and video makers need to have a ten- or fifteen-minute reel to show prospective funding sources, museums and clients. The industry standard is now ³/₄-inch video, and everyone you are likely to be showing your work to will be able to screen this format. Some people suggest that you also make a number of ½-inch dubs so that the person can take your reel home and look at it if so desired. Along with your show reel, you should have on hand copies of your résumé neatly typed and perhaps some reviews of your work if you have any.

DRESSING FOR SUCCESS

If you are working with clients, and particularly if you are pounding the pavements looking for new clients, your appearance can be quite important. Many creative types disdain the advice to dress for success much to their detriment. No matter what you think about how fair or relevant it is, some people just don't put as much faith in people who don't look the part or, worse, who present themselves sloppily or unfashionably. Since they have so few clues to go by when deciding whether or not they want to hire you, they have to use every clue available to help them make their decision. A person who can't be bothered to look decent for an interview may well be the sort who cannot be bothered to go the extra distance to make a project right. Like it or not, your appearance can become decisive.

• Observe the dress of the world you are working in. While some potential clients may be a tie-and-jacket operation, others may be more relaxed. A general rule is that on a job interview you should dress as you would if you were working there, but one notch higher. Thus, if you are trying to get illustration jobs from the art director of a rock and roll magazine, where jeans are the uniform, it might be in order to wear a jacket and tie with your jeans. If the person interviewing you is wearing a suit, so should you be.

• When venturing into the corporate world, there is nothing more impressive for a man than a really well-cut, well-fitting suit, and it's worth scrimping and saving a bit to get one. If you are really broke, you can sometimes come across some old gentleman's cast-off English-made suit for $25 to $50 at thrift shops in better parts of town.

• If wearing a well-cut suit makes you feel more like an investment banker than an artist, you might want to pair it with an unconventional shirt or tie. Whatever else you add to it, a good suit makes a good impression on most people.

• Women, particularly freelancers in the arts, shouldn't feel that they have to dress in scaled-down mens' suits in order to make the right impression in the corporate world. To me, nothing looks more pitiful. A really flattering, fashionable dress that is neither seductive nor prim makes a good impression.

• No matter what you wear, be neat and clean. You'd be surprised to see how grungy some people are when looking for freelance work.

CHAPTER THREE

WHERE TO WORK

Freelancers have different housing needs, depending on their professions, incomes, family sizes and a host of other factors. What is right for one freelancer may not fit another's needs at all. The only way to find out what sort of housing is right for you is to analyze all of the pertinent factors: cost, location, size, how you intend to use it, how many people will be living with you, and so on.

COST

Cost is obviously a major factor when you are deciding what type of housing you need. Housing costs are skyrocketing. The old rule of thumb that one's housing expenditure should be about one quarter of one's income is now the impossible dream—particularly for the average freelancer, one quarter of whose income wouldn't pay for a donkey shed these days. You may find that you will have to lay out 50 percent of your income, or even more, in order to house yourself and your work. When trying to cut costs, one possibility is to share a work space with others and rent a small living space separately. Or you may prefer to spend a larger part of your income on housing a private work space, while cutting total costs by sharing a living area with others. One thing to remember in this regard is that you may be able to get a tax deduction for the percentage of your housing costs spent on maintaining your work space (see page 323, Business Deductions Allowed Sole Proprietors).

In some situations you may be able to reduce your rent through bartering arrangements. Here are some possibilities:

- Building superintendents are given free housing, and also a salary if their duties are extensive. Some superintendents do repairs and are available to tenants most of the day. Others merely arrange for outside repairmen to come and occasionally swab the halls. For the work-at-home freelancer this can be an excellent solution to the problem of exorbitant rent. Check real estate ads and talk to building management firms about it. Firms which handle many buildings are listed in the Yellow Pages. Look also by mailboxes or in elevators for names of building managers.
- If the owner of your building likes your work, you may be able to trade off

art, writing or musical services for rent. Sadly, this sort of barter is less likely to occur in cities than in the country, where real estate dealings are often on a more personal level. If you engage in this type of trade, you should know that the IRS expects you and the other person involved to declare the fair market value of the real estate and the artwork on your tax returns.

• If you are handy, you may be able to get a rent reduction in return for doing work on your apartment that the owner would otherwise have to pay someone to do.

• House sitting or caretaking is still a viable option if you live in the country. Unfortunately, most city dwellers realize that their apartments are such valuable commodities that they can easily be sublet.

AMOUNT OF SPACE

While it's always nice to have plenty of space, you can make a little go a long way if you have to. In most cities now, decent housing space is at a premium. People who move from the country to the city are often appalled at the claustrophobia-inducing little studios in which they find themselves living. But clever apartment dwellers, forced to live and perhaps also to work in dehumanizing ten-by-fifteen-foot plasterboard studios, have created an entirely new interior architecture of lofts, balconies and dividers which can render these little cubbyholes into usable spaces. Because one cannot usually make major structural changes in a landlord's property (at least, not without his permission—and then the improvements are legally his), people are making these improvements portable. If you don't need a great deal of space, perhaps you can use some of these new ideas to transform marginally adequate areas into better working or living spaces. Or you may be able to make work areas from unused spaces such as closets, the kitchen or your car. (For more information on transforming minimum spaces into decent living-working areas, see the section, How to Deal with a Lack of Space, in chapter 4.)

Obviously some freelancers, such as dancers, film makers, photographers and sculptors, cannot get by with tiny studios no matter how ingeniously transformed. Members of these professions should consider renting or sharing a living-working loft, or sharing a work area with others while living alone. These options are discussed in the following sections of this chapter.

LOCATION: CITY OR COUNTRY?

Freelancers must also decide what sort of surroundings they want to live in. Should they locate off in a peaceful part of the country, or should they be right in the center of things in a city? There are points in favor of both alternatives, and a lot depends upon your personality, where you grew up and the sort of work you do. A balance sheet approach may clarify your thoughts on this question.

LIVING IN THE COUNTRY—ADVANTAGES

- The biggest advantage of living in the country is the peace and quiet of typical rural American life. Some people find this lack of noise and distraction a tremendous boon to their work.
- Living in the country is distinctly healthier. A healthier body and mind can often make for higher productivity.
- Living in the country is sometimes cheaper than living in the city; but you will usually need a car, and you will have to pay for your own heating in most places.
- Living in the country usually requires more direct involvement with your environment. Some people benefit from chopping wood and feeling self-sufficient. Others find this kind of life too time-consuming.

LIVING IN THE CITY—ADVANTAGES

- You are closer to the art-business world. Publishers, museums, agents, galleries, schools, magazines, reference libraries and so on—all are in the cities.
- You don't need a car in most cities.
- Some people need the stimulation of a city and find that the country only makes them sleepy.

Perhaps the question to answer first is whether or not you need to be around people in order to do what you do. Do you need frequent contact with your agent, editor, rep, teacher, etc.? Many transactions with these people can be handled by phone, but some really can't. Suppose you are an actress and your New York agent calls and tells you about an audition in three hours. Will you be able to make it? Not if you are living in Vermont. Obviously, performers who depend on auditions or sudden production crises to get work must be within commuting distance.

And do you need to be around humanity in order to create your art? Some people who think they crave the stillness of the country find that they can't work there because their solitude is too concentrated. Some people need to have ongoing human stimulation. Others prefer to have none, or to store memories of it and then go off to the country and spew it all out on paper or canvas or a dance floor. From the freelancers I interviewed, I found that performers are less drawn to a country life. This is undoubtedly due to their work, which requires a steady availability to other people. Those whose major availability must be to their canvas or their pen have a greater latitude in deciding where they want to live.

There are, of course, bucolic outer suburbs surrounding even the most sprawling cities. These can be a very happy compromise, since you can commute to the city reasonably conveniently but can also find some of the pleasures of living in the country. The best way to find these places is to drive around until you stumble on some little town that the state highway commission neglected to plunder and then to proceed to the town real estate agents. In places like these it also makes sense to talk to the owner of the liquor store or the druggist, or to some other person about town who is likely to be able to put you onto real estate you might otherwise not hear about. If you are by yourself you may find a lot of people with spare rooms or attics to rent. I have done this successfully in both Scotland and Greece, and others I know have done it in New England.

It is usually best to rent in an area for a year or two at the least before you buy. That will give you enough time to decide if you're in the right town and which sections of the town appeal most to you.

HOME OR OUTSIDE WORK SPACE?

Employees generally don't have to worry about where to work. And, in the beginning, freelancers may have equally little choice if they can't afford to work away from home. The chance to work at home can be one of the most appealing features of freelancing; but some find that it can be a next-to-impossible situation, or one which is doubly draining due to the extra amount of concentration it seems to take to get anything accomplished. Naturally, the success of your attempts to work at home will be partially determined by how understanding your mate is, if you have one, how many children you have and how well you can focus on your work (disregarding the dirty dishes or the television).

WORKING AT HOME—ADVANTAGES

• If you have a family, there is a potential benefit in being closer to home: you are there when needed, and all your work is centralized.
• If you live alone, there is an advantage in having the run of your house while you work. If you have the discipline and concentration to enjoy the comforts without going all to pieces, home can be the most pleasant work environment as well as the most convenient and the cheapest.
• Many people have idiosyncratic postures or environments that they work best in, and these people suffer in offices. At home you have the freedom to work naked, or lying on the floor, in plangent silence or with the stereo on at maximum loudness. If catering to your idiosyncrasies frees your mind and doesn't just cause you to indulge yourself into a stupor, the home workplace can make a big difference.
• You save on carfare.
• You can eat better. You are close enough to the markets to buy fresh produce at off-peak hours. In the words of one freelancer, "no more awful coffee and donuts from the coffee wagon."
• If you are a parent, you have the advantage of being able to be around for your children's growing up. If this means a lot to you, you must be able to work it out so that you don't end up wishing to God you could work away from home. (See chapter 12, The Freelancer Parent, for a fuller discussion of how to make this work out.)

• You are free to work at your most productive hours, and to set your own hours.

WORKING AT HOME—DISADVANTAGES

• Self-discipline can be a big problem when your desk is ten feet away from your bed or the booze closet.
• There is no psychological separation between work and home.
• If you live with someone else this means that you are working, living and trying to have a relationship within the confines of a small world. It can make you begin to feel very claustrophobic. Here is how one commercial artist who lives and works with a partner feels: "You really have to give up a lot. Otherwise it's just a struggle all the time. As far as the creative end, it's pretty good, because we have the same hours, same projects, same interests. But after work is done for the day you still have to see the same face, with no break." His partner adds, "The best thing we've done recently is to put plants between our desks—now he doesn't feel he has to stare at my face all day. It's amazing how a simple thing like that has given us our space."
• According to a screenplay writer, "You are always in sight of your work, and there are no institutionalized breaks, such as lunch hours, coffee breaks and five P.M., that make such a breeze of employed life."
• For the intents and purposes of family members, you are "at home" unless you make specific rules to the contrary.

There are a number of ways to solve these problems. If you decide to work at home and have difficulties convincing your family of the importance of what you are doing, see chapter 12, The Freelancer Parent, which tells how to cope with families.

Sometimes the only way to solve your difficulties due to working at home is by not working at home or at least by creating the option to go somewhere else. But where? Do you want a permanent work space, or is only a temporary solution needed?

SHARING WORK SPACE

If you desire a permanent place in which to work away from home, you will need either an office or studio that you can afford on your own or one which is large enough to share. Writers can often make do with little rabbit hutches. Visual artists and dancers obviously need more room; and for them, going in with some people on a large space can be a great deal. It can also be a drag and a waste of money. Here is some helpful advice gleaned from several freelancers:

• Sharing doesn't always work out unless they are as professional about their work as you are about yours.
• Always get everything on paper. If it's a new lease, try hard to get both names on it, but realize that when you do that it means that each of you is liable for your own and your partner's expenses. If you decide to

share with someone who has been leasing the studio for a while, make sure your agreements as to the term of your sublet, hours of access, the rent, notice of termination and any equipment that you own or use in common is covered by a *written* contract. Be suspicious of any starving artist who wants to share a studio. You don't need the burden of someone else's financial woes or even their hard-luck stories. You may end up fighting for equal usage unless you make a deal about hours and access and have it on paper.

• If you and your partners decide to pool your money to buy expensive equipment, you must first come to some sort of *written* understanding about who owns what and about what will happen if one of you wants to sell it.

FINDING A SPACE TO SHARE

There are several ways to go about finding a space to share. If you are looking for a place to live, you will find agencies in most cities that cater expressly to people looking for roommates. These agencies screen applicants and then list them in a file. Most agencies cross-index applicants according to their personal habits (e.g., smokers, nonsmokers), how much space they want, how much they can pay and where they want to live. Then, rather like a dating service, they introduce you to potential roommates with whom you might mesh. For this service you will pay, in most places, a nonrefundable fee of $50 to $75. People who are looking for roommates to move into their house or apartment are not charged a fee. Most agencies will let you have a month to determine whether you and your new roommate are compatible. If you are not, the agency should help you to find a new person.

Even if you are only looking for a place to work, you may find one of these services useful. Many times you can be matched up with someone who has rented an apartment for a long time and is paying a reasonably low rent compared with the prevailing prices. If you are lucky, you may find that one of these is within your budget for working space even on top of your home rent. You might also try placing an ad to find a stranger who would be willing to rent you the extra bedroom or corner of the living room for work space during the day when they're at work. This could work well for everyone concerned: you would get a break on the rent, since you'd use the space only during the day, and they wouldn't have to see you.

If you don't want to pay an agency fee and you trust your own judgment of people, you should check the real-estate section of the local newspapers under "Shares" or "Roommates Wanted"; or, if you already have the space but need someone to share it, put in an ad. If you are screening people, be sure to ask for recent references and do check them. First, find out if the person under consideration is reliable about money and has a regular source of income (you have enough to worry about in getting your half up). Is he or she pleasant to be around? If possible, try to spend an evening with serious candidates. That ought to give you sufficient time to discover anything you don't feel comfortable with.

Another way around the expensive agency route is to advertise through any unions or professional groups which serve members of your craft. This way, you will at least be able to find someone of a similar ilk. Either place an ad in the membership publication, put a notice on the bulletin board or make your needs known to an appropriate member of the association's staff.

I think that the best sharing situations occur with people you link up with through word of mouth, or mutual friends, or people already known to you. People who are sent to you by friends are usually more conscientious than those who know that if the arrangement sours they will never have to see you or anyone known to you again.

FINDING OTHER
ECONOMICAL WORK SPACES

If you are just looking for a small office in which to write or think, you might try looking in the real estate ads among furnished rooms and unfurnished rooms. Depending upon how much you can afford, you might be able to find something. In many cities you can find furnished studios for $50 to $100 per week. Some of these even have housekeeping services and fresh linen (I fully endorse the keeping of at least a cot in an outside office. This gives you the option of staying with your work all day and night and taking little naps as you go. Writers especially seem to take short lie-downs in the middle of workdays. Writers' offices at many television studios have beds as well as desks).

In my small town in northern Connecticut, the local lawyer's office is in a small house. Two unused rooms in it are rented out to self-employed people, one a writer and the other a jewelry maker. You can often come across the same situation in cities, where there are extra rooms in office suites rented to outsiders.

You may find rooms to let within the apartments or houses of older people. A newspaper ad is a good way of finding one of these (such an ad, incidentally, is tax-deductible as a business expense). You never know when your ad will catch the eye of some old lady who has been thinking about renting out one of the children's rooms but hasn't been able to face the thought of a stranger living under her roof. To many people in that boat, a struggling artist or writer working there part-time will be a happy solution. Along the same lines, try asking your friends if any of their parents have a spare room.

In New York, and probably in other old cities as well, some of the older large apartment buildings have servants' quarters. These were usually built in a little colony up near the roof. Today, almost none of them is occupied by servants, but one is usually available to each apartment owner for a small ($25 to $150) monthly rental. Some buildings will permit apartment owners to let them out to friends or family members. These rooms are not advertised: you must find them through friends. One poet I know lived in one. It was a six-by-twelve rabbit hutch, but she was the sole inhabitant of the roof and had a marvelous view. Unfortunately, the stuffy building management did not allow her to have male visitors, but otherwise she was quite happy with her $60-a-month pad.

For more temporary relief from working at home, you might go to the library.

Some larger libraries have private reading and study rooms. At some you can even rent a little carrel with a typewriter. In New York, certain privileged writers have been able to make use of a small workroom, known as the Writers' Room, operated by a group of writers and supported by book publishers and the New York State Council on the Arts. It is in the Frederick Lewis Allen Memorial Room in the Main Public Library. For further information you can write to The Writers' Room, 8 West 40th Street, New York, NY 10017.

Some cities have subscription libraries which you join for a small annual fee. Reading rooms in these libraries tend to be quieter and more comfortable than those in public libraries. At the Society Library of New York City, one can usually find several writers in various stages of manuscript preparation ranged about the reading room. Those who come early enough take care to grab one of the three comfortable armchairs next to the windows.

In Washington, DC, there exists an organization called The WorkPlace. There writers, academics and business people can rent office space on a full- or part-time basis. An answering service, secretarial services and conference space are available. For further information you can contact: The WorkPlace, 1302 18th Street, NW, Suite 203, Washington, DC 20036; (202) 944-3640.

THE REAL ESTATE SCENE

After you have decided what sort of space is right for you, you must then decide whether you wish to rent, to buy or to get a loft, which is a rather hazy category of occupancy. There are things to be said for and against each possibility, so the choice between ownership and tenancy must be decided in the light of your particular situation.

RENTING—ADVANTAGES

- When you rent, your only tie to your space is your commitment to pay the rent for the term of the lease.
- You have a relatively small cash outlay.
- You have no maintenance costs save those incurred in keeping your abode clean.
- You pay no property or school taxes.

RENTING—DISADVANTAGES

- In the long run, renting costs more because it is money paid to a landlord that you will never see again in any form. It is buying you nothing but time in the rented space.
- You get none of the tax credits that homeowners with mortgages are allowed.
- A rental is not an appreciating investment the way your property is.

BUYING—ADVANTAGES

- Property you have bought brings important tax advantages: you can write off the interest on your mortgage, as well as property and school taxes.
- Houses and land are usually sound investments, particularly during times of inflation.
- Each monthly payment is bringing you closer to full ownership, while rental money is kissed good-bye each month.

BUYING—DISADVANTAGES

- You will be responsible for property taxes and possibly a school tax and utility taxes.
- Owning and maintaining a property may tie up a large proportion of your capital. Even though real estate is basically a sound investment, you have no guarantee of being able to get your money out when you need it.
- A lot more of your time and money must go into the maintenance of a property that you own.

HOW TO RENT A SPACE

If you do decide that renting is for you, then all you have to do is find the space, sign the lease and pony up the money. Because rental space is now at a premium in almost every city, and even in many rural areas, you will very likely need an agent. Agents charge from 10 percent to 12 percent of a year's rent in most places. The agency has various listings with which they try to match you, according to your requirements. If the landlord accepts you, the agent draws up a lease and collects his commission for finding the apartment, and that is the last you see of him.

The hard part, for freelancers of moderate means, can be in getting a landlord to accept them. Landlords want to know that you have an amount roughly equal to four times your rent coming in each month, and they want to know the name of your employer so that they can verify this to their satisfaction. Obviously this puts the self-employed person with a sporadic income in a very untenable position. This attitude may be shortsighted: as one painter pointed out, most serious artists will do their damndest to scrape up their rent money, since if they are evicted they have nowhere to do their work. Nevertheless, the difficulty remains.

In some cities you may be able to find some sort of privately funded artists' housing. Your best source of information on this score would be some of the professional associations in your field listed at the back of this book or your local arts council.

HOW TO BE ACCEPTED BY THE LANDLORD

The most common way of getting around the problem of getting accepted by slumlords who act as though they are renting space in Buckingham Palace is to lie on your application.

It is not advisable to lie casually. Lie only to the degree you absolutely must, but never past the point of plausibility. If you seem believable, most agents won't check you out too thoroughly, and they may even advise the landlord that you seem to be perfectly acceptable.

Even if you do get an apartment by lying blatantly, your lies can come back to haunt you later. All may go well until the landlord is looking for a reason to retaliate against you for reporting code violations, seeking rent abatement or simply for occupying an apartment which could be rented to someone else for more money. He may then dig up your application, and the misrepresentations that you made can reappear most inopportunely.

All but the most celebrated of freelancers are never going to be considered "quality" people by the average philistine landlord, insurance company or credit institution, although of all these it is generally easiest to pass muster with a landlord. The first rule is to go in dressed up as though you can pay the rent and have money left over. Some people find it difficult to dress for effect, but suppress the desire to flaunt your alternativeness to those who don't respect your originality. Play it straight and play it polite—at least until you have the signed lease in your file.

Aside from being well dressed and well spoken, it will be impressive if you can put down some prominent name as a reference. Even if you don't really know such people, there is scope here for a great deal of creative mendacity. Rare is the slumlord who will actually check with a dazzling biggie, and if you are caught it's a little less grave than misrepresenting your income (and harder to pin on you).

Unless you have a friend with a business who will cover for you, don't lie outright about having a job. While personal references aren't always checked, employers almost always are. If the landlord checks back and nobody has heard of you, you will lose the apartment and possibly any deposits you left to "hold" it. Still, it often won't do to put down actor, writer, artist, etc. Landlords read such words as *gypsy*, unless you have a parent or a patron who is willing to co-sign.

If a person co-signs, he or she is accepting a great responsibility. The co-signer is responsible for the rent if you skip out, and even if you die.

Another possibility is to say that you are a student. Landlords often assume that parents will help out a student, though in larger cities you may find that landlords are meticulous about securing such assurance in advance. Still, even in large cities, cheap housing with understanding landlords is found more frequently around universities. College bulletin boards are a fertile source of rentals and sublets in your bracket. An informal takeover sublet can often be the answer, since you may only have to satisfy the inquiries of the former tenant who can't wait to graduate and, in many cases, leave the state altogether. Late spring, late summer and around Christmas are all good times to find sublets left by graduating students.

You may find that you have to take a job just to acquire the respectability to obtain a lease. If you do, try to get one that can help your career in some way. For instance, artists might consider working at an art store where they will also be able to buy supplies at a discount. Quiet bookstores can be havens for writers. A couple of writers I know even find that such an atmosphere, customers' inquiries and all, is far more compatible with their work than their own hearths.

If you have some degree of financial success as a freelancer, and have the IRS forms for a year or two to prove it, you will not be forced to such measures—unless you are trying to buy into a snazzy co-op.

APARTMENT REFERRAL SERVICES

One word of caution is necessary regarding the so-called apartment referral services that are springing up in many cities. It is amazing that they continue to flourish in spite of the fact that so many people know that they are fraudulent. They operate differently from agencies in that they charge you a set fee to register. You are then provided with a list of apartments supposedly meeting your requirements. You can call in daily to get new listings for a specified period—usually ninety days. The services' involvement ends here, the moment you pay your fee. It is then up to you to make the calls, get the keys and see the apartments. But you will find in many cases that the apartments have been rented long ago, or were never up for rent, or simply don't exist. So you call in for "new listings," and if there are any, it's the same story with them as well. In short, stay away from referral services. I never knew anyone to find a space through them.

BUYING REAL ESTATE

Buying real estate is a bigger commitment than simply renting it, because you have more costs and because your obligation to assume these costs does not run out at the end of a specified term.

FINDING A PROPERTY

Finding a property to buy is not so different from finding one to rent. Your choices are to go to an agency (in this case the fee is usually paid by the seller, not you, the buyer), to look in the classifieds or to find something through word of mouth. Obviously, when contemplating buying a place you will want to investigate it more thoroughly than you would a rental. If you are really serious about it, you should have the property inspected for soundness of structure, termites, adequacy of water supply and energy consumption. If any repairs are recommended, get estimates in advance.

Once you have found a prospective property, you must take a *careful* look at your finances and decide whether you can really afford to buy it. It is very easy to get carried away with the romance of finally owning some property and then rationalizing this notion with talk about the tax advantages of ownership. While there are real financial advantages to buying as opposed to renting, such advantages won't work for you if you can't really afford the property to begin with. There are some handy rules of thumb that can help you decide whether you can afford the property you are contemplating.

1. You will have to come up with the cash for a down payment—anywhere from 10 percent to 30 percent of the selling price, and possibly more. Do you have it?
2. As in the case of the 25 percent rule of thumb for renters, your monthly costs (i.e., mortgage payment, property and school taxes, insurance, upkeep and utilities) should not surpass 30–40 percent of your monthly income. While this rule must sometimes be stretched for renters caught in the housing shortage, you should go slowly, since as a homeowner you cannot walk away from these costs and rent somewhere else cheaper.

Contact an accountant before you get too serious about buying property. Even if you have trouble asking yourself the tough financial questions, it's his job. While it may spoil your fun if the accountant concludes that you just don't have the wherewithal, believe him. Owning property is a dream most of us have, but it is no help to the development of your work if you are enslaved to a house and mortgage and can no longer afford to take creative risks. Buying a house prematurely is as bad for your art as having a baby prematurely.

Besides the accountant, you will also need a lawyer to supervise the closing, although you really should involve one much earlier than that. She may be able to help guide your choice of a property from the point of view of tax savings and investment possibilities, as well as to conduct a title search which will assure you that the seller does indeed have the clear right to sell to you.

FINANCING YOUR PROPERTY

If you have a realtor whom you trust, don't underestimate his or her knowledge of local mortgage policies. If you can, find an agent who has worked with artists and understands some of your special fiscal considerations. He may know of mortgage possibilities you have never considered. It is naturally to a realtor's advantage to help you get the financing you need.

While it is difficult to buy property if you don't have a steady five-figure income, it isn't totally impossible. There are a few federally funded programs which purport, with a number of restrictions and exclusions, to help low-income citizens to obtain housing. There are also many different sorts of mortgages available everywhere. The amount of mortgage money available is really determined by local banks and can vary greatly from area to area.

Shop around when you are doing business with banks. The bank just down the street may have a far more advantageous deal for you. When you look for mortgage money, visit the following institutions:

Savings and loan associations
Savings banks
Commercial banks
Mortgage companies

Wherever you go for a mortgage, prospective lenders will take two things into account: (1) the value of the property (so that if the deal goes sour and you can't make the payments, they can be certain of getting their money back), and (2) your ability to repay (see the section Strategies for Getting Credit in chapter 17 for an explanation of how lenders make this determination).

Savings and loan associations are the biggest lenders in the mortgage market. You are often able to get by with a down payment as low as 10 percent at one of these institutions.

Savings banks now exist nationwide. These institutions, like savings and loan associations, are often more willing to take a risk on a freelancer than are commercial banks.

Commercial banks tend to be the most conservative and abstemious lenders. Unless you really look all right on paper a commercial bank will probably shy away from you when they find you are a freelancer. Exceptions to this general rule sometimes occur in small towns where you are well known to the banker.

Mortgage companies are private firms that are in the business of lending mortgage money. Although their interest rates are higher, they may be more flexible than the banks. If you do end up doing business with a mortgage company, do so only with your lawyer's knowledge.

SOME SPECIAL MORTGAGE POSSIBILITIES FOR FREELANCERS

Purchase money mortgages
FHA, FmHA and VA loans
Variable rate mortgages
Graduated mortgages
Special unconventional mortgages

Purchase money mortgages are direct loans from the seller to the buyer on mutually agreeable terms. This can be a good bet for freelancers if the seller will accept you, since interest rates for these loans are often a few percentage points below the going rate. On the other hand, since the seller is lending his own money, he may be more cautious about accepting you as a risk than a financial institution might be.

The FHA (Federal Housing Administration) insures mortgages for qualified buyers. This deal works well, because FHA is a little more liberal in picking home buyers it will underwrite than banks are in deciding to whom to give a mortgage. Armed with FHA insurance, you can often attract a lender who might have turned you down without the guarantee of government-backed mortgage insurance. Because the lender is insured against your defaulting, you are able to get a longer mortgage term, which means smaller monthly payments. The other plus of this program is that you can make a much smaller down payment—currently 3 percent of the first $25,000 of the mortgage and 5 percent of the amount between $25,000 and the ceiling in your area. The maximum amount of mortgage you may have insured under this program varies from state to state and even among counties. (If you install solar energy equipment, you will be given mortgage insurance on a higher amount, which certainly seems an enlightened policy.) Unlike Farmers Home Administration loans, the FHA program has no income ceiling and no ceiling on the amount that you spend on the house. The ceiling is merely the maximum amount you can have FHA-insured.

To get an FHA loan guarantee you apply to an FHA-approved local bank.

(Banks like this program, because their loan to you is insured by the government and they can charge you the market interest rate, thus losing nothing financially and gaining maximal security.) Your realtor can also help you get FHA mortgage insurance. FHA requires an appraisal and has standards as to construction, location and habitability.

Of interest also to freelancers is the *Graduated Mortgage Plan* offered by the FHA under Section 245 of the Federal Housing Act. Under this scheme your mortgage payments increase in small increments over the first five or ten years depending upon the plan that you choose. This program is likely to attract people with low incomes (but who still can afford a down payment and the monthly mortgage charges), who have some realistic expectation that their income will be steadily increasing so as to cover the increasing payments. One disadvantage of this program is that you will pay more interest than you would with a level term loan. The interest rate is set by the bank, and it is to the bank that you apply for a loan under the FHA Graduated Payment Mortgage program.

For further information, contact your closest Federal Housing Administration Office or the main branch at (202) 453-4623.

The FmHA (Farmers Home Administration) may extend loans to people living in rural areas who are unable to get loans from other sources. At present, the maximum you may borrow is $95,000. Maximum income limits are fairly stringent (which is good news to low-income freelancers) and vary from state to state. Although having assets such as stocks or savings will not disqualify you from getting an FmHA loan if other lenders won't take you because of a low or sporadic income, you may be asked to put any such assets into your house either as part of the purchase money or for repairs. You can contact the FmHA either through your county office or by calling them in Washington: (202) 233-4000.

The VA (Veterans Administration) will loan up to 100 percent of the appraised value of a property to veterans. So with such a loan you can often get a property with no down payment. This service is free of charge for veterans. For further information, contact the Veterans Administration, Washington, DC 20420; (202) 233-4000.

Variable Rate Mortgages of various sorts are commonly available. The interest rate is tied to the bank's general financial picture as well as to the prime rate. Your variable interest rate can go up or down and can be adjusted every one, two or three years, depending upon the term that you agree to. Although these loans can be somewhat risky, because you may get stuck paying a much higher monthly payment if the interest rate goes up, there is some protection in that there is usually a cap on how high the interest rate can rise.

Unconventional mortgages of various sorts are becoming less unconventional. With rising mortgage rates, many potential buyers have been priced out of the market. In an effort to help people in this bind (and to drum up some business for themselves), the banks have begun to devise a variety of unconventional mortgages. Variable-rate mortgages are now so common as to no longer fit this category—though a few years ago they would have been almost impossible to find. *Balloon mortgages* work in different ways. Some deals require that you pay off only interest until the loan matures, or interest plus a small amount of the principal, leaving a "balloon amount" left over and due at the end. *Interest-only loans* are worth considering, particularly if you believe that your property is going to appreciate (as it almost always does). You pay off only the interest. When you sell the property, or obtain another mortgage, you pay back the principal. Also, some banks will give a lower interest rate in return for a share of the profit when the property is sold.

Not all such unconventional mortgages will be available everywhere. And sometimes somewhat different sorts will be available. This is another reason why you should shop extensively: some banks (usually savings banks and savings and loan associations) are more creative than others. Some will have no truck with any of the new flexible or deferred-payment mortgages.

ADDITIONAL COSTS

Once you have gotten your mortgage straightened out, do not forget about the miscellaneous closing costs and your lawyer's fees. Such costs, including title search, possible surveys and the preparation of various documents, normally amount to about ½ to 1 percent of the selling price. Have at least this much in your checking account at the time of the closing so that you aren't embarrassingly short.

CO-OPS AND CONDOMINIUMS

Buying into a co-op building or a condo is an alternative that is slightly different from the outright purchase of a property. When you buy into a co-op, you are buying a share in an apartment building. This share entitles you to live in your apartment, pay a monthly portion of the upkeep expenses and vote at shareholders' meetings. You do *not* own your co-op in the usual sense. If you decide to sell it, you must first get the approval of the other shareholders. A condominium is similar to a co-op in that members own certain areas in common and split the cost of maintaining them. The difference is that you actually *do* own your condo unit and can sell it to whomever you please.

The information given above on financing and buying real estate applies to co-ops and condominiums, as well as to houses of which you are the sole owner. When you buy into such properties, you should check carefully on any loans attached to them since such loans become, in part, your obligation to pay.

LOFTS

Lofts are one of the most popular types of housing for artists even though they are not the safest of investments. They can be rented, bought, or rented with improvements that were put in by former tenants and are bought separately for what is called a fixture fee.

For once, California was not the fountainhead of a major new trend. New York spawned the loft movement, and most of the laws and zoning regulations pertaining to lofts follow New York's example.

THE DANGERS OF RENTING LOFTS

You should always involve a lawyer in any decisions you make regarding buying or renting a loft. Loft dwellers do not yet have much protection, either in the case of tenure or in disputes over ownership of fixtures. A common scenario has been as follows:

In 1970, a working artist, a photographer, say, moves into a raw loft in a ruined-looking downtown area. Over the years, as his business prospers, he begins to make improvements in the loft, putting in an estimated $15,000 of his scarce money over the time period. Outside his window, he begins to see more and more activity. By 1973 the area has begun to remind him of St. Germain or the King's Road, but for the few remaining light manufacturers and small businesses. One day, toward the end of 1978, our friend is notified that his building is being co-opped. He is given an opportunity to buy in for $25,000 (substantially less than the offering to outsiders, scores of whom are nevertheless beating down the owner's door with fistfuls of dollars).

Our photographer is now in a bind. He can't afford to buy in, nor can he afford to lose the $15,000 worth of improvements that he put into his home. While his landlord is sorry about this, he would like the photographer to hurry up and either buy in or get out—minus the $15,000 and minus all the fixtures except those that are not "affixed" to the building. The photographer has little choice but to move. Four weeks later, a well-paid young lawyer moves in, feeling very bohemian in his artist's loft.

This situation has been caused by the greed of developers and owners whose only real concern is the appreciation of their investment. While the law still states that only certified artists may live and work in the zoned areas, in many cities this law is being widely evaded by those who have the money to pay the high rents or buy-in costs. What once were artists' communities have been overrun in a shameful way. Even if nonartists could actually be prohibited from taking spaces that should rightfully be occupied by artists, there wouldn't be enough lofts to meet the needs of serious, qualified and certified artists. At present, many people have no choice but to pay high fixture fees to move into illegal spaces on commercial leases.

Such people, living in illegal conversions, are often unable to take forthright action against code violations and other breaches in the warranty of habitability. It has been alleged that landlords have been invoking the illegality of the situation as a reason for throwing out the low-paying artist tenants so that the building can be brought up to code compliance and the lofts rented out to high-paying refugees from the straight world.

Another development has been the problems suffered by tenants who sublet from a middleman who has an agreement with the building owner. Typically, these middlemen renovate lofts and then sublet them to others. If, however, this net lessee runs into financial difficulties, as often happens, the tenants may find themselves faced with the choice of either bailing out the middleman in order to protect their investment or losing whatever they invested in their spaces altogether.

SECURING YOUR INVESTMENT

Unfortunately, too many people go through the steps of acquiring a loft backwards. They begin thinking about the cosmetics of renovation before they fully secure their investment. Many other loft dwellers move knowingly into illegal conversions in hopes that the zoning laws will change before long. Many artists in New York are in just this position because of the acute shortage of lofts.

Generally you will be faced with some sort of fixture fee to cover improvements put in by the previous tenants. You must ascertain, with a lawyer's help, your right to charge a similar fee to your successors. This is important, because a landlord does not *have* to do this for you. Technically anything that is physically affixed to the premises belongs to the landlord. Any agreements you make in this regard (or in any other regard) must be *on paper* to do you any good in case of a later dispute.

When considering a loft to rent you must take into account how much of a fixture fee you will be paying. For example, you find a marvelous deal which you can rent for $150 per month after paying a $12,000 fixture fee to cover the new kitchen, sunken bath tub, and refinished floors put in by the previous tenant. What this price translates to is that over a two-year term your "real rent" is $650 per month—unless you can recover the fixture fee at the end of your tenancy. If you can't be sure of doing that, you should strive either to get a long-term lease or the option to renew at the end of a shorter period. Tad Crawford points out, in *The Visual Artist and the Law*, that if your building is slated for demolition a renewal lease to extend your tenure up to the time of actual demolition can buy you some time if, as so often happens, destruction is delayed. You will also want a clause giving you the right either to terminate your lease after a certain period of time or to sublet.

Another point on which you should make sure your agreement is clear is specification of exactly what you are getting for your rent payments: who pays for heat and utilities? for garbage collection? Sometimes, unlike the case of renting apartments in the city, the tenant is responsible for these expenses.

Anyone contemplating signing a lease for a loft simply must use the services of a competent lawyer experienced in such situations or he will probably pay a penalty later.

RENOVATING A LOFT

How much renovation you should undertake in a loft depends on several factors:

1. How secure your lease is.
2. The recoverability of what you put in.
3. Your present and foreseeable future income.
4. The demand for lofts in your area.
5. The availability and cost of credit, and your credit rating.
6. How handy you are.

Before deciding to go ahead with any major restorative work, you should read *Pioneering in the Urban Wilderness* by Jim Stratton (Urizen Books, 1977). This book is invaluable for loft owners and prospective buyers not only for its advice about contracts and leases, but also because its numerous photographs show some of the more frequent steps in the renovation of a loft.

I also recommend a book called *Artists' Housing and Loft Living.* This work, a thorough treatment of the subject (including material on certification, zoning, leases and more) is available from: Volunteer Lawyers for the Arts, 1285 Avenue of the Americas, New York, NY 10019.

ARTIST'S CERTIFICATION

In New York City you must be certified as a working artist in order to qualify for a living-working loft in the Soho area or in a legally designated AIR (Artist in Residence) space in another area. Your application for certification is reviewed by a committee at the Department of Cultural Affairs, 2 Columbus Circle, New York, NY 10019; (212) 974-1150. The committee consists of twenty people—half artists and half administrative people in the arts. Your application will include a résumé and slides of photos of your work as well as an explanation of your need for a large work space. It will be judged only "to evaluate your degree of commitment to your work and your need for large space, not to make aesthetic judgments."

REHABILITATING YOUR HOUSING

An interesting alternative to buying prime housing is the present movement toward rehabilitating decaying city neighborhoods with funds provided by the government, the city or sometimes local corporations.

If you are handy and think you have the skills to do major rehabilitative work (which is a lot more complicated than even a fairly extensive loft renovation), and if you have the time to spare from your work, you may be able to acquire a beautiful old building for a song, or even for nothing.

For further information, contact one of these organizations:

NEIGHBORHOOD REINVESTMENT CORP.
1325 G Street, NW
Washington, DC 20005
(202) 376-2400

PARTNERS FOR LIVABLE PLACES
2120 P Street, NW
Washington, DC 20037
(202) 887-5990

BACK TO THE CITY
12 East 41st Street
New York, NY 10017
(212) 532-3100

A book that you might find useful on this subject is Richard Reed's *Return to the City: How to Restore Old Buildings and Ourselves in America's Historic Urban Neighborhoods* (Doubleday, 1979).

FURTHER LEGAL ASPECTS OF HOUSING

YOUR RIGHTS AS A RENTER

After you have passed muster with your landlord and secured a lease, your troubles may not be over. Many tenants find themselves in difficulty with their landlords after they have moved in. In order to protect yourself against typical landlord tactics, you really need to know something about the law.

Since the early 1960's, tenants' rights have progressed steadily. Until that time, landlord-tenant dealings were based on English Common Law premises, whereby the only solid right the tenant had was to "quiet enjoyment" of the property; the landlord's only clear duties were to provide the property and to collect the rent. In 1969 the courts finally recognized that the modern-day tenant is not renting a mere plot of arable land (for which the English law might be appropriate), but rather a package consisting of heat, plumbing, doors that work, janitorial services and other goods and services. Therefore, it was determined that tenant-landlord relationships should be governed by contract law. Where before the tenant was required to pay the rent whether or not adequate services were provided by the landlord, the new approach requires that the fulfillment of contractual obligations by both the tenant and the landlord be interdependent. In other words, you no longer have to pay for what you don't receive. Tenants' rights are now guaranteed by the warranty of habitability which states that tenants' rental agreements, written or oral, entitle them to decent housing—i.e., safe, sanitary and warm housing. This warranty of habitability is recognized in all but ten states as of the writing of this book. In states where it is recognized, you have a basis for withholding or reducing rent when services are not provided or housing is substandard.

Of course you may still be evicted (and on very short notice) for nonpayment of rent. However, in almost all states, a landlord has to take you to court to have you evicted, and if you show up in court with the cash or a certified check in hand, you can restore yourself. You can also present your case for withholding or reducing the rent. If you are being charged with some other breach of your rental agreement, such as having pets illegally, you might be able to satisfy the landlord without going to court simply by "curing" the breach—i.e., in this case, giving the pets away. An eviction notice *can* be withdrawn.

In any case, you should *always* respond to a notice to appear in court in this and any other instance in which you are served. If you don't, the other side automatically wins by default, and in the case of housing disputes, you can be put out. Generally, once a default judgment is entered against you, you won't have much luck reopening the case.

When a final judgment is entered against you, a sheriff will be sent to evict you. If you refuse to go, it is perfectly legal for the sheriff to put you and your belongings on the street (literally). Many states will grant a "stay of execution" based on the extreme inconvenience to the tenant of immediate eviction. This stay might give you an extra week or two to get out—the period varies from state to state (in New York it is six months; in Louisiana and Delaware it is twenty-four hours).

REMEDIES AGAINST LANDLORD NEGLECT

Unfortunately, tenants don't usually learn about the contractual obligations of both sides involved in a rental agreement until there is a problem. The usual consequence of this ignorance is, quite simply, the screwing of the tenant in any of a number of ways. If you do not know how to assert your rights to decent housing effectively, or how to proceed if you don't get them, you will not be able to handle such matters as retaliations by vindictive landlords whom you have reported, difficulties in recovering your security deposits, and other common problems.

Actually, most landlord problems can be avoided altogether if you know your rights and act that way. A good policy is to have on hand the names of tenant groups in your area. These organizations can be very helpful in helping you to fight a landlord, as can small local newspapers, if the ones in your area are sympathetic to tenant problems.

Tenants' groups, often very difficult to locate, can be found through local consumer or legal aid organizations, or by calling a local radio station or newspaper. Metropolitan Council on Housing (198 Broadway, New York, NY 10010 [212] 693-0550) also publishes useful information.

Through the Minnesota Tenants Union (P.O. Box 8641, Lake Street Station, Minneapolis, MN 55408; [612] 871-7485) you can get a book entitled *If You Pay Rent You've Got Rights Too.*

The New Jersey Tenants Organization is a group with a membership of about one million, and they can provide you with useful ammunition. Their telephone number is (201) 342-3775.

In addition, the following are books worth reading:

Blumberg, Richard E., and Grow, James R. *The Rights of Tenants.* Avon. This ACLU handbook is part of a series of *"Rights of . . ."* books. Other subjects in this series include veterans, young people, students, gay people, the poor, suspects, teachers and women. The books are particularly handy for those with enough legal background to make use of the citations and fairly technical explanations. Others may find the texts a bit dry and difficult to deal with.

Striker, John M., and Shapiro, Andrew O. *Supertenant: New York City Tenant Handbook.* Holt, Rinehart & Winston, 1978. This book is a perennially popular volume crammed with useful strategies. It is geared to New York City residents and New York law, but many of the tactics suggested can help you out anywhere.

CHAPTER FOUR
ORGANIZING YOUR WORKSPACE

A definite workplace is crucial to your job as a freelancer no matter what your profession. An artist or a journalist might need a whole room, or even a space completely separate from the house, while an actor might get by with only a shelf on which to store his photographs and résumés. Depending upon what you do, you may not always work *in* your space. Some freelancers work in clients' offices, in the field, or in front of audiences. Nevertheless, every freelancer, no matter how occupied, needs a "work territory," even if it is no more than a desk where she can store her work-related items and work *from*.

This chapter is devoted to giving suggestions on how to create a workplace for yourself and how to get the fullest use from a small space (see also chapter 3 for a discussion of where to work).

CREATING YOUR OWN WORK AREA

Your work area should suit you. As I have mentioned before, some artists choose to work in eccentric places. If you can allow yourself this indulgence without becoming too relaxed to work, it will probably aid your concentration. In many cases, fighting your desire to work on the fire escape or in bed is more distracting than just giving in and getting on with it. No matter what you were told to the contrary at school, not everyone works best at a desk. Proust, Descartes and John Lennon wrote in bed. Thomas Wolfe wrote on top of an icebox, and Churchill wrote standing up.

When planning your work space, you must take into consideration what your needs are and how much space is available to you. You should decide how much privacy and quiet you require, how much space you will need for work and storage, whether or not you must think about others who live with you, whether you will be receiving clients there, and how many people will be working there.

The amount of extra space in the typical small urban apartment offers about as much usable area as the cabin of a small boat and not much more privacy. With the help of various modular components, nomadic furniture and specially designed organizers, you can double the use of every inch of floor, wall and even ceiling space, thereby creating a usable work area even in a small modern studio.

HOW TO DEAL WITH A LACK OF PRIVACY

Privacy problems take two forms: visual and auditory. It is difficult to work while you are constantly in someone else's sight, and it can be distracting to have to see somebody else when you're working. Many artists also find that they don't like leaving their works-in-progress lying around for everyone in the family to scrutinize. The writer Dorothy Parker was reputedly so bothered by this that she would throw a towel over her typewriter anytime she left work in it. These are the major drawbacks to putting your work area in a corner of the bedroom or living room. While spare corners are often all that are available, you usually can do something to make them more workable. Here are some suggestions for improving your visual privacy:

• A portable screen is one of the cheapest answers. You can build one to your taste cheaply with scraps of wood, hinges and either plywood, canvas, fabric or paper panels. If there are any good junk shops in your area, see if you can't pick up a screen there.
• More expensive, but more decorative, are Japanese *byobu,* or sliding panels, made of thin strips of wood and translucent paper. Living space in Japan is limited, and often several generations live together under one roof. They have therefore refined the use of space and the creation of the illusion of privacy into an art. These panels fit into slots in the floor. They can be rolled back or removed completely when the whole room is needed, or they can be shut completely when a separate room is needed. If you are handy, you can make byobu yourself.
• Curtains are also a good solution. You can install a track on the ceiling so that you can divide a room or close off a corner. The curtains are fitted with small balls which enable them to stay in the track. For less money, you can just put up a pole, and the curtains can slide along it on rings.
• If you are handy or can get assistance it is not hard at all to put up a dry wall and thereby create your own little room in a corner. If you rent your living quarters you should obviously get your landlord's *written* permission to make such a change. If the room you start with is of sufficient size that it doesn't look cramped when you have finished, the landlord may be quite willing to go along with you and then advertise the apartment as having one extra room the next time it is rented.

Visual privacy, however, often is not sufficient. Children and spouses do play stereos and TVs, use the vacuum cleaner, and have friends over; and you may find these noises unbearable. I know I do, and noise pollution in several households where I have lived has driven me and my work out into the streets. Even in cases where you have managed to get visual privacy, noise can intrude horribly. It is less easy to deal with unwanted sound, but here are some suggestions:

• If there is room in your work area, rugs, curtains and furniture as well as paintings and other objects on the wall can be used to absorb sound.
• If you have some money and own your place, you can install acoustical tile on the walls and ceiling. It's not pretty, but it does the trick.

- You can make your own acoustical tile by putting up egg crates, bottoms against the wall. The crenellations absorb some of the sound that intrudes. I was once in a studio where this had been done. The egg crates had been painted white, and the overall effect was not at all displeasing.
- Rugs put up on the wall are a more expensive, more attractive solution.
- Ask family members to use headphones for the stereo.
- Wear earplugs yourself.

HOW TO DEAL WITH A LACK OF SPACE

As I have said, the best way to deal with a lack of space is to double the use of everything. Aside from the lack of privacy, the main reason limited space is a problem is that you reduce your living area too much; and too much going on in a small area gives rise to a cluttered appearance and claustrophobia. Here are some space saving suggestions:

- If you live alone (or with a sympathetic partner) you can choose whether to make your space mainly a studio or mainly a living space. If you decide on the former you might buy an old-fashioned Murphy bed, which folds back up against the wall during the day, thus freeing the whole area under the bed, normally just a breeding field for dust puppies. Less radical and more easily portable is a convertible sofa-bed that can also serve as a seat for clients. Slightly less elegant would be a trundle bed or "hi-riser" which, if covered, can serve as a sofa by day and then convert to a double bed at night.
- If you must go the other way from living quarters to studio space, you may want to build a worktable that rests on a bar screwed into the wall at one end and is supported by one leg that folds down and preferably rests in a slot in the floor like a chart table in a sailboat.
- I have seen worktables with folding legs that are stored up by the ceiling and descend on pulleys when they are needed. One of these did not have legs, but rather was suspended over the floor and anchored by means of clothesline attached to the corners of the table and then to rings in the floor. The table was waist-height and very steady for working on. When it wasn't needed, it was simply freed at the bottom and hoisted to the ceiling.
- If you have high ceilings and own your space or have a very relaxed landlord, you can build a small balcony to work on. This, however, is a project that you should not embark on unless you are a good builder and have a working knowledge of loads and structural design. Less dangerous, and also portable, is a freestanding loft structure that is not attached to the walls and cannot be claimed by your landlord as a fixture. The simplest of these is just a strong, three-sided box. You can work on the upper floor and use the inside as a bedroom or living room, or you can sleep on top and use the little room beneath as a work area.
- If you are fortunate enough to live in a structure that was put up prior to the '50's, you may have an extra closet that you can convert to a work-

space with a few simple renovations, such as the installation of a built-in desk or of the wall and floor supports for a portable folding table. With the addition of a vent, a large closet can be turned into an adequate home darkroom.

- If you are the person likeliest to do food preparation and your work is not the sort that would be ruined by a deposit of airborne grease, you may not mind working in the kitchen. My only advice is that you should only consider this a permanent arrangement if the room is large enough to allow you to have your own desk or worktable that is not also the chopping board.
- A highly adaptable and portable work surface for visual artists and writers is the Cardan Drafting Board, which features a drafting table anchored to two standards which can be mounted on the wall. Both the height and the angle of the surface are adjustable, and the whole board can be stored flat. It is available from Sam Flax, 111 Eighth Avenue, New York, NY 10011, or from the manufacturer: Rangine Corporation, 14 Felton Street, Waltham, MA 02154.
- If you work in bed, an old-fashioned breakfast tray with side pockets and a decent-sized work surface can bought for about $60. This is the sort of item that you might be able to find in a junk store or a tag sale for a lot less, or you can build one yourself with three pieces of wood and minimal carpentry skills. Another good surface for working in bed is an ironing board across the bed.

For further ideas, some useful books are:

Davidson, Margaret. *Successful Studios and Work Centers.* Available from Structures Publishing Co., Box 1002, 24277 Indoplex Circle, Farmington, MI 48024.

Hennessey, James, and Papanek, Victor. *Nomadic Furniture.* Pantheon, 1974. This book tells how to build simple and highly portable furniture.

Liman, Ellen. *The Space Maker Book.* Wallaby Books, 1978.

Naar, Jon, and Siple, Molly. *Living in One Room.* Vintage Books, 1976. This book assumes no knowledge of carpentry and thus is an excellent manual for beginners who want to build their own modular furniture.

STORAGE

No matter what you do, work seems to expand geometrically, and more and more space must be taken away from other uses to accommodate its by-products. Here are some ideas and sources for the storage needs of different kinds of artists:

WRITERS AND PERFORMERS can usually get by with a filing cabinet. If you can afford them, metal ones hold the most papers and also are flame resistant. You can find a decent two-drawer file for around $50 if you look for sales or discount stores that sell office equipment. These and other useful office items such as steel desks, desk-top files and swivel chairs can be bought secondhand either at stores which specialize in such items or at tag sales or government-surplus sales. Less expensive than metal files are the cardboard-box files that can be bought at office supply stores. Smaller items can be stored in alphabetized accordion files also found at office supply stores. Most writers will also begin to have a book storage problem rather early on in their careers. Bookshelves are easy to build onto your wall, but it is best not to do this when you rent unless it is worth it to you to fill any holes you make before you leave. The simplest kind to put up are those with standards and brackets. Once you have mounted the standards so that both are parallel and equidistant from the floor, all you have to do is screw in the brackets and place the shelves on top. More shelves can be added easily, and shelf heights are adjustable. Go to the cheapest hardware store you know to buy these components, for they add up to quite a lot. The cheapest shelves to get in most places are plastic laminates, some of which look very much like wood and some of which are made in solid colors. A less expensive bookcase can be made of wood or laminate propped up at each end by bricks or cinderblocks. And you may find a standing bookcase at a tag sale or thrift shop for even less.

PHOTOGRAPHERS must store prints, negatives and darkroom supplies. Foremost is an orderly, dustproof filing system for negatives and slides that enables you to locate them quickly. Most photographers favor some sort of written cross-index with each roll of film identified by a number. While it may seem time-consuming to record information about the subject matter of each roll of film, you will find that if you work professionally you will amass sets of negatives or slides at an alarming rate.

A small collection of slides might be stored in an accordian file with alphabetized pockets and a master list of what is in each pocket. Slides may also be stored in a looseleaf binder inside vinyl slide covers. If you don't expect to amass a large number of negatives, they too can be put in a protective folder which you staple to the back of a contact sheet. The contact sheets can be stapled across the top onto heavy paper and stored in a ringed binder. Long-term storage of both negatives and slides is done at about 21°C with a low humidity.

Unused film keeps best in your refrigerator, and darkroom solutions should be stored in labeled dark glass bottles which should be kept close to full to retard oxidation.

PAINTERS AND GRAPHIC ARTISTS need to store both materials and work. Taborets and stack trays for storing materials are available in a variety of sizes and types at some of the suppliers listed below, as are flat and vertical files and racks for paintings and prints. These storage units can be expensive when bought from art supply houses, but it is worth browsing through these catalogues to get an idea of some storage solutions that you can make yourself. Storage containers for pastels, tubes of paint or magic markers can often be found more cheaply at large hardware stores, which carry them for tool storage. Unless you are a good carpenter, flat print files are fairly hard to build well, but racks for paintings are within the reach of everyone. Many excellent items can be found at one of the following:

DICK BLICK
Dept. AA, P.O. Box 1267
Galesburg, IL 61401
(Easels, files, storage components, also books and paints.)

EBERHARD FABER
Crestwood
Wilkes-Barre, PA 18773
(Studio furniture.)

SAM FLAX
111 Eighth Avenue
New York, NY 10011
(212)260-6000
or
1515 Spring Street
Atlanta, GA 30305
(Studio furniture, drawing, mounting, storage supplies, paints, brushes and tools. The catalogue is a must to have on hand.)

KOLE ENTERPRISES, INC.
35553 Northwest 50th Street
Miami, FL 33102
(305) 633-2556

STUDIO CONCEPTS
Dept. AA, Box 17124
West Hartford, CT 06117

STURDI-CRAFT MARKETING EAST
200 Boylston Street
Chestnut Hill, MA 02167
(617) 969-4700
(Excellent low-cost modular wall storage systems, which are sold through Sears and J.C. Penney, among others.)

Another book which may also be of some help in solving your storage problems is:

Goodchild, Jon, and Henkin, William. *By Design: A Graphic Sourcebook of Materials.* Quick Fox, 1980.

FREELANCERS TELL THEIR FAVORITE ORGANIZER

A freelancer must be organized to survive. The average freelancer does not have the services of secretaries and file clerks to keep track of things. You need to know where you're going and what must be done each day as well as where all related pieces of paper lie on your desk. Here are some of the favorite organizing tools of my interviewees:

FILING

I use baskets. I have a separate basket for each project, and I use them as adjuncts to filing cabinets, which I use more for dead items or financial dealings. —Writer

Plastic desk trays can double or even triple your desk space, and they're so handy for filing all the in-process stuff which you use too often to put in

your file cabinet. With the trays you can keep the size of the piles down to a workable size, so that you don't go through them three weeks later and find that you've forgotten what you had there. —Graphic Designer

My life changed when I got my file cabinet. It really did transform things. I could find things immediately. It gives you a sense of organization and propriety. If your files are in order you can't be disheveled. One night I worked all night setting up my file system, but from then on I've been shocked at how well I've kept it up. —Director-Actress

SCHEDULING

I use what is called an architect's diary, which they sell at Bloomingdale's. It is very large and has a week at a time. What is special about it is that it has time slots from 8:30 A.M. until 11:30 P.M. Anything else is obviously not realistic for freelancers. I mean, who ever heard of a freelancer working from nine to five? —Graphic Designer

I have an appointment book. That's a must—a freelancer without an appointment book is an impossibility. I have an Eaton's Week-at-a-Glance, because I like to know what kind of week I've got, and I've got paper clips in it with pertinent business cards and telephone numbers.
—Actress

I recently got into those enormous Year-at-a-Glance calendars. These help you plan your time over the long run, so that you don't have to schedule all your jobs too densely. It aids you in deciding when it's time for a vacation. It's also good when you're sitting around waiting for work and berating yourself for being a useless schmuck to look back and see how much you've accomplished in past months. It's almost like having an activity graph of your time. —Illustrator

TELEPHONING

I guess you'd call this sort of a negative organizer: a telephone that unplugs. A ringing telephone is one of the real enemies of organization and concentration. It used to drive me to a frenzy. Now I know that whenever I need to work I can do so without being intruded upon.
—Writer

I'd be much unhappier without my telephone neck cradle. In this business you get put on hold a lot, and if you had to just sit there all that time, you'd waste at least an hour a day. With the cradle you can hold on and do something else at the same time without getting torticollis.
—Photographer

MISCELLANEOUS ORGANIZERS

My prime organizer is my watch. It's like having someone keeping an eye on you all the time. I waste so much time. I need to keep track of how long I spend in each activity. A watch with a timer would probably be even handier—mainly to time nonworking phone calls and breaks.
—*Artist*

A businesslike pencil sharpener—the kind they used to have in school, which is affixed to the wall with holes for different sized pencils. Don't get the electric kind—the kind you crank will give you far more satisfaction of your obsessive-compulsive urges for sharpness. Psychology and mind games are germane here. Sharp pencils and clean lines translate into sharp thinking and clean logic, if you see what I mean. —*Writer*

A blackboard is essential. I managed to get a music teacher's blackboard from a school furniture dealer. It has a smooth slate surface on one side for errands, thoughts, inspirational quotes and the like; the other side has several staffs, which are incredibly handy for composing. It also saves paper and thus our vanishing forests, which I think is important.
—*Composer*

I have to be able to visualize my whole plot on paper. After using progressively larger sheets, I found the solution. They make enormous sketch pads for artists. Buy the biggest newsprint pad you can find at an art supply house. I use separate pages for each character, and I also outline my plot on one of these and stick it up on the wall. Somehow this helps me design my stories better. —*Novelist*

I found that having an assistant helps organize me. Even if I've been puttering around all weekend avoiding my work, I find that the knowledge that she will be coming in on Monday forces me to organize a bit, so that she will have things to do and not have a wasted day. Then of course, if you get started, you often find that you have the momentum to keep on going.
—*Painter*

CHAPTER FIVE

GETTING THE JOB DONE

Merely finding work is usually the big problem for freelancers who are just starting out. Those whose business has taken off may have more of a problem finding the time to do all the jobs they have and making all their deadlines. Moreover, busy freelancers have the additional challenge of handling clients and keeping them happy. With some clients this requires no more effort than merely doing the work competently and on time. With others, this may be the hardest part of the job.

BOOKING JOBS

A busy freelancer may be booked steadily for months ahead, thus creating a steady work flow, or she may experience crazy periods where several new jobs are offered on the same day. While to the beginning freelancer who is just scraping by this may sound like bliss, it can actually be every bit as stressful as starving. If you work in a low-key freelance area where some clients are willing to wait their turn, then life is easy for you. You either tell them you will call them when you can get to their job, or you estimate how long it will take to finish the other jobs on your agenda and schedule them for a specific date. But if you work in a more hectic business—advertising, say—things can get unpleasantly frantic.

Sometimes an art director or editor will call you up to see whether you are available in a month to do a job with an adequate amount of time for its completion. Such jobs and clients are sunbeams in the life of a freelancer, because they permit you to plan your own time and allow a normal amount of leisure. All too often, however, freelancers are not brought in until after the staff person in charge of a project for a company has failed to deliver or suddenly realizes that he is overburdened. Suddenly the deadline looms, and they pull out their file of tried and true freelancers or of untried people who have sent résumés, and they call you up. Can you do this job that someone on staff had five months to finish—in three days? Of course if you've been sitting idly hoping for work you won't mind at all. (Nevertheless, don't commit yourself to doing the job on an extremely short deadline until you have seen the job itself. This is particularly true for beginning freelancers who may not know their capabilities under pressure and for whom the client may be unfamiliar.) But what if you are already working on a job or even two? This situation often arises for popular freelancers, and it can be quite agonizing. You'd like the extra money, but you don't know how much time you really have to devote to another job or whether you can really deliver. You feel nervous about turning down any proffered job—especially if this is a new client—in case they never call you again. On the other hand, they won't call you again if you botch this job, either. So what do you do?

First, think about your current project. Is it something you feel comfortable and confident doing, or are you already straining your limits? Are you working round the clock, or are there hours into which you could squeeze another job? Can the current job be put on hold for a day or two while you can get up to speed on the new project? Do you have other jobs waiting in the wings that may need some attention before you get this second job off your plate?

Some people really can't work on three things at once. I can. In fact, sometimes I wonder how I'd ever make any real money if I couldn't, but there are some things to consider:

- I try to accommodate emergency jobs whenever possible. There are two reasons: you can charge a supplement for rush jobs. (See chapter 15— most of the freelancers I know tack on from 25 to 50 percent extra.) Secondly, new clients often arrive on your doorstep with the wolf at their heels, and they are desperate. If you save their necks now and acquit yourself well, you've got your foot in the door, and you may find that suddenly they have lots of work for you, not all of it rush, rush.
- I do, however, turn down jobs I know would seriously compromise the jobs I am already doing. Why do three things at once if you can give each project only 65 percent instead of your customary 100 percent? You'll just disappoint several clients.
- Find out all you can about the work being offered. Sometimes you can manage to fit in extra work if it is different from the job you are already engaged in, and you can pretend it's relief from the first job and put in a longer day. While I cannot necessarily write three articles simultaneously on a short deadline, I can write an article, a short video script, and edit a technical medical monograph, particularly if they are all on different subjects. This may require a seventeen-hour day, but the long day is much less exhausting if you are using different skills. Obviously there is a point of diminishing returns past which your work on a project may become far less fruitful. Ordinarily a walk or a leisurely meal might be in order after you quit for the day, but in emergency situations a switch to another project will generally give you a second wind.

  This sort of schedule is grueling. I cannot recommend it as a steady diet, but sometimes that's what it takes to pay the bills or keep a good client. One freelance graphic designer says she and her partner handle their frequent thirty-six hour workdays by occasionally going over to their blackboard and inscribing an enormous dollar sign to remind themselves that they are raking in major bucks for their efforts.
- Sometimes you can negotiate more time if you tell the client that you'll

take the job if you could spend two days in squaring away a current project. After slaving day and night to get jobs in on time and then watching clients not even get around to looking at them for a week, I have learned that their deadlines are not always quite what they say. Unfortunately, many employers have learned from bad past experiences that they must tell the freelancer that he has only a week before the job has to go to the printer when, in fact, he may have two weeks or more. Often, if clients realize that the panic of finding someone to do the job is over and that the buck is passed they feel safe in giving a little more time.

On the other hand, some deadlines really are firm, and when you agree to a twenty-four-hour turnaround, you'd better be prepared to deliver. Assume this to be the case with all new clients. Nothing impresses them more than a freelancer who actually makes the short deadline as promised. Freelancers who handle deadlines responsibly are considered rare birds and are generally given lots of work and passed along to friends looking for good freelancers as well.

As you get to know a client better, you'll be able to judge when they are panicking unnecessarily and when the deadline is real. When they get to know you and realize that you really do deliver, the two of you may be able to negotiate deadlines to make them as equitable as possible for all concerned.

TURNING WORK DOWN

Sometimes you just have to turn down a job. This can be painful when it's more lucrative than the work you're already doing or if the offer represents the first advance from a client you've been wooing. As with everything, there are ways and there are ways. While no prospective client, especially a harried one whose neck is in a noose at her company, is going to jump for joy when you turn her down in her hour of need, you can try to ensure that she will try you again.

• Explain your situation vis à vis other projects on your plate. Occasionally the client will decide that she wants you no matter what and that she will shave time elsewhere so as to give you the job. At the least, you can make her understand that you're not turning her down frivolously. Also, you come across as a responsible professional who doesn't jeopardize his clients and who is much in demand.
• If it's a new client, do send him a follow-up letter, again apologizing for the poor timing and expressing the hope that he will try you again. If he doesn't yet have your résumé and work samples, send them along now and request a meeting to take place after the smoke clears.
• If you know another good freelancer, give his or her name to the client. Of course you run the risk that the client will be so delighted with your friend that he never calls you back. You can reduce the risk of this by following the steps outlined above. Also, unless your friend is a dud, in

which case he won't threaten your future assignments, he too may have an overflow to pass on to you. For example, I have a friend in the same technical writing field as I. We exchange jobs all the time to help each other out, and we charge each other 10 percent for them.

CLIENT RELATIONS

As an independent businessperson, you will have to give some thought to client relations. Some freelancers actually enjoy this part of their business while others do their best to avoid any contact. Basically, client contact can be divided into three phases: initial contact, daily working relationship and, sometimes, termination.

Your initial contact usually occurs after you or your agent have done your legwork (see chapter 2, Getting Work) and have hooked an individual or a company which needs your services. Generally, you will be asked to come in to your prospective client's place of business to talk about the job at hand. If your facilities and equipment have a bearing on how well you will do the job (e.g. printers, photographers), or if you have large pieces of work to show (e.g., sculptors, painters), then the client will need to come to you.

Presumably, at this point, the prospective client either is definite about hiring you or has greatly narrowed the field, so this meeting is not strictly a selling job but rather a discussion of what the client wants done and when, and how you can make it happen and for what price (see also chapter 15, What's It Worth?). Still, it is indirectly a selling job in that you should do your best to look and act on your toes (see also page 49, Dressing for Success). If the client comes to your studio, be sure that it is at least workmanlike and that you have a reasonable place to sit and talk. If all goes well, this initial contact will end with your getting the job.

DAILY WORKING RELATIONS

In some cases, your first meeting will be your last real contact with a client except for telephone consultations about the work. This is likely to be the case if your client is part of a larger company such as an art director, editor or project director. These people have plenty to do in their own offices, have hired you to get the job done and may well not feel the need to talk to you unless you have questions or problems or unless they have additional input for you.

"When I first started working," says one illustrator, "I probably drove art directors and book designers nuts, because I felt they expected me to give them progress reports. So I'd dutifully check in daily and tell them how things were going along. Then I began to realize that most of them didn't care. All they wanted was to get the work in on time without having to expend any more energy on it themselves. That was why they had hired me. When I realized this it really took the pressure off. I stopped talking like a guilty child who felt compelled to tell teacher that I really was putting in the time, and I just spent the time making sure the job was done on time and properly."

I know that tendency that you have to keep assuring people that you're really doing their job and not just slacking off. It's a mild paranoia that makes you feel that people in the nine-to-five world are suspicious of you, the freelancer, and that you have to keep checking in. But you really don't have to. In fact, your own anxiety may be infectious, and you may end up by making your employer nervous about your level of professionalism.

On the other hand, do be available to them. Some clients get nervous about their deadline, and they like to be able to call you and check up that everything is on schedule. Nothing robs them of confidence more than a freelancer who is supposed to be at work on their project yet who can never be reached. Always leave your answering machine on when you go out or make sure someone is home to receive messages. Call back promptly. Your client may just want to be told that the job is proceeding apace, or she may want to give you additional instructions or discuss changes.

Remember too that not all your clients are going to know anything about what they have hired you to do. They assume that you know your job. A project director whose expertise is really marketing may not have any idea of how the writer she hired to write a brochure actually produces the finished project. This means that your client may have a very unrealistic idea of how much effort and time your job will require, the process by which you work and even, in some cases, how good a job you have done for her. For instance, from your viewpoint, the real work may be the ideation which may require far more time than the actual execution. A client who doesn't understand this may become very alarmed to find that you haven't started to execute the final product. Her alarm can make you nervous. Don't let it. You know how you work. Explain calmly and politely to your client that the work will be done on time and to her specs but that she should leave the rest up to you.

Don't hesitate to call up a client if you have a legitimate question or problem. No one appreciates having a job come in slightly or more seriously wrong because you didn't want to bother her. In fact, if it's an important rush job that will require you to work nights and/or weekends, you should ask your client for a home number so that you don't have to hold up a job until morning. Most people are willing to have you call them at home if necessary. If they aren't, then the job couldn't be a real emergency.

Some clients assume that since many freelancers work where they live, they can be called at home any time of the day or night. While this may be true during a real deadline crisis, you don't want to be taken advantage of at other times. The occasional obnoxious user of your services may fall into the habit of calling you late at night or on weekends. I think this happens because they figure they don't have to catch you during business hours. If they don't get all their calls made during business hours, they figure they can call you whenever. If this becomes habitual, you must politely and firmly state your limits. Tell them that although you work any hours you need to when there's a big push on, you otherwise like to have nights and weekends for yourself and your family just like everyone else.

One freelance graphic designer had such problems with clients calling at all hours (and when they didn't reach him at his studio some even hunted him down at home without apologizing for the disturbance) that he finally put a night and weekend tape on his answering machine that said, "Wildebeest Graphics is closed right now. You can reach us tomorrow/Monday morning. If you have an emergency, please leave your name and number, and I will call you back."

The point is not to make it impossible to reach you. One of the features of freelancing is that you are available for emergencies. But you don't want clients to get into the habit of letting you take up the slack caused by their poor planning.

In short, in your daily working relationship with clients you should be affable but professional. Stand your own ground—this is foremost a working relationship between equals. Don't be afraid to state your needs and expectations. Hiding them in a misguided effort to be easy to get along with will cost you in the long run. Either you will get pushed to the point where suppression no longer works and you will throw a tantrum, or you will make too little money on your jobs.

Another client relations problem involves house style and tailoring your work to other people's needs. Frankly, for me that's one of the most depressing aspects of doing commercial work. I have my own style, and I think it's quite good. Certainly, when writing to order, I try to adapt to their needs by carefully studying the magazine or by finding out my target audience. Sometimes, despite your best efforts to produce what they want, you don't succeed, and they want you to rework it in a way that makes you want to throw up. I usually hang up after talking with them and feel very angry and want to pay them back the money and chuck the whole job. Then I calm down and realize that I am not acting like a pro and that I need the money. It often turns out that you have written something too personal, or too sophisticated for the market, so you are asked to do what I call "dumbing it down." This is very condescending of me, but it reflects the problem of trying to be a commercial and a fine artist at the same time. I'm always afraid that my own work is going to suffer if I have to do too much writing for people with an eighth-grade education and no imagination or desire to learn. That's a common fear. So I spend even more time on my own work where things can be done my way. I have found that I am far less bothered by having to redo work to make my client happy if I am also writing something of my own that no one can make me change.

My husband once told me a story about his father, an illustrator and well-known cartoonist, who started out, like many of us, working in advertising. After having been up for days on end toiling over an ad that he couldn't seem to get right for the client, he was just relaxing in the calm after he had sent the drawing off when the telephone rang. It was the client with a simple request. Couldn't he please put a smile on the bumblebee's face? He looked so ominous he'd scare people, and no one would buy the product. Well, my father-in-law, who later became famous for his satanic drawings about war and man's follies, roared, "No, I will NOT put a smile on the bumblebee's face!" and he hung up. He was lucky. The client used the drawing anyway, and it appeared with a smile drawn in by someone else. I usually don't get my way like that, but whenever a client calls up with some absurd "dumbing down" task, I always make myself think of it as putting the smile on the bumblebee and try to laugh my way through it.

You have to remember that the client's always right if you want to get paid. Swallow your pride about your artistic originality and do your best to do as you have been asked. It's part of being a reliable, professional freelancer rather than one who has the reputation of being a talented prima donna who can only be used in special situations.

LONG-TERM CLIENT RELATIONS

Over the long term, whether or not you are actually engaged in doing a job for them, you should continue to curry favor with your clients on a year-round basis. The goodwill of your clients is one of your principal assets, ranking just behind your talent and your persistence. So don't ever let your clients forget about you and replace you. Even if you are not currently working for them, you want to be the person whose name comes to mind when they think *freelancer*. Here are some good ways to stay current:

- Have an attractive postcard designed with your name and address for them to post on their bulletin board. If you're a visual artist, it should bear one of your works as well as your name and address. If a performer, a photograph of you. Writers and various types of consultants will also want to present themselves in an eye-catching way. For instance, the artist who designed my postcard made one side look like a legal pad with a bulleted list of the services I provide plus my name, address and phone number. If you have a logo, your postcard could just be your logo and contact information.

    I send these cards out to clients once or twice a year (if you have a big promotion budget, you might want to have several different cards printed and send them out quarterly or even monthly) and am always gratified to see these cards in evidence in people's offices. These cards also go out in my package to prospective new clients along with my résumé, business card (for their Rolodex), and a cover letter in which I usually mention that I have also enclosed a postcard for their bulletin board. Again, it's all psychological. The fact that you spent the time and money to produce a nice promotion piece and made the effort to send it out impresses people with your professionalism.
- Besides sending your cards, you may want to check in by telephone occasionally. This can supplement your cards well as so many people are so busy that although they mean to respond to your card, it gets buried and they never do. They may actually have a job for you coming up in a couple of months which you'd like to know about now. You may not hear about it until a week before they need you if you rely solely on your cards to get you work.
- Commercial visual artists may be able to reduce their promotional costs by asking for several hundred run-on copies of jobs that they do for clients. These reprints, obtained at your client's print run-on cost, should cost you little or nothing and may make excellent promotional pieces.

- Send Christmas or Hanukkah cards to your clients and other friends of
  your business. They are a tax-deductible business expense. The holidays
  are a time when you can remember other people in your clients' offices.
  Secretaries, receptionists and assistants are all happy to be remembered
  at this time of year. It never hurts these people to think well of you;
  some of it may rub off onto their boss. Also, today's assistants are tomorrow's clients.

TERMINATION OF CLIENTS

Sometimes you have to divorce clients. If hostilities such as nonpayment,
habitual late payment or unreasonable behavior are the cause of the break,
then it's easy. You simply write a letter stating that your and their best interests
would be better served by terminating the relationship (see page 304, Breaking
a Contract).

Generally, if there are bad feelings, both parties will be happy to end the
relationship. Sometimes, however, you have to end things with a faithful client
because either you have more lucrative or interesting work or you are changing
your focus. Do this with great sensitivity, because a cardinal rule of freelancing
is never to lose a friend. Write a nice letter explaining your circumstances and
give your client plenty of notice. If you work with him on a very steady basis,
you should make a cut-off date thirty to sixty days in the future. If it's a client
who really has been pleasant and loyal, it wouldn't be excessive even to ask
him out to lunch. If you can possibly recommend someone else to take on his
work, do mention him or her, and if your client is interested, you should offer
to set up an appointment for him. In any case, you should never shut the
door. Tell your client how much you have enjoyed working with him and that
you really do regret ending the association. This way if your client's budget or
needs change, he may come back to you. You can abet this by keeping old
clients on your Christmas card list.

ADVICE FROM THE OTHER SIDE OF THE DESK

Here is some advice from users of freelancers' services that may be useful to
you in your relationships with your clients:

- Don't be difficult. As obvious as this would seem, you'd be surprised how
  many freelancers have the reputation of being difficult prima donnas.
  They may be whiny or arrogant. They may renege on contractual obligations or simply just be grudging about going that extra mile to do the
  job right. Since we generally hire freelancers in emergencies, we consider those extra miles part of the job.
- Be available. I'm not interested in your weekend plans. Freelancers are on
  call seven days a week as long as they are on a project. Generally a
  freelancer is paid a little more than a staffer at a time when there is a
  serious deadline, and they are expected to be available.
- I don't mind dealing with anyone so long as I know where I can reach

him. If he wants to work at a friend's beach house, fine. I just need to know how to reach him by telephone and how to get next-day express to him.

• The worst freelancers are those who delay delivery. If I say I really need it on a given day, I mean it. Some people don't, so it is worth asking if there is some fudge time included in the deadline. I really dislike having my plans loused up, because I am expecting a piece of finished work on a given day and instead get a call that it won't be ready for three more days. Freelancers often don't seem to consider that I may have set aside time to do my part of the work. If the work isn't there for me to start on, it may cause me real problems. I really hate having to wreck my weekends because some freelancer hasn't made an agreed-upon deadline.

• Show some interest in the work. Call to check in after you have sent in your job. Give your client three or four days and then call. If the work is acceptable, now is the time to ask politely when you might expect your payment.

• Give yourself time to complete a job. It's worse than useless for a freelancer to say that she can do a job in two days just so that I'll hire her if she then turns around and doesn't deliver for a week.

• If you're a writer turn in a neat job. Don't assume that our people are going to put it on our word processing system before it goes to our client. If you can't type or don't have a word processor, have it done by a pro. If your client plans to send it on directly to their client and therefore expects it to look perfect, advise them that you are a writer and not a typist and ask whether you can charge them for the services of a typist.

Chad Hatfield, vice president of Classic Printers in Prescott, Arizona, has a detailed list of some of the common problems he, as a printer, encounters when working with graphic designers:

1. The designer didn't understand what the client wanted to get across.
2. Missed deadlines.
3. Excessive errors and omissions on the finished artwork. "If you have questions, ask . . . don't guess with someone else's money!"
4. The finished artwork was not approved before it was sent to the printer.
5. The designer seemed flaky and disorganized.
6. The designer was a prima donna who was inflexible about altering design concepts.
7. The designer did not take notes or record the instructions given him by the client.
8. The designer was hard to reach.
9. The designer did not provide written instructions and a mock-up of the finished art. This is important. No one is a mind reader.

CHAPTER SIX
STAY IN TOUCH

Making and keeping yourself visible is something every freelancer must become practiced at. It is this making oneself visible frequently enough to be noticed that distinguishes the successful freelancer from a person who only works once in a while. If you are a commercial artist, art directors have to see your work and be brought up to date on your progress at regular intervals. If you are a performer, people have to hear your tapes, see you perform or at least get a postcard with your picture on it every few months. The point of all this is that no one can give you work if (a) they don't know who you are, (b) they haven't heard from you in so long they've forgotten you or (c) no one can find you. You must try to stay in touch.

ON THE TELEPHONE

As far as the telephone is concerned, you must be set up to receive messages when you are not at home, and you must learn how to get through to busy people who are doing their best to avoid unsolicited calls.

Some people feel uncomfortable on the phone, but this is something that you, as a freelancer, must master, because the telephone is the major line between you and those who can give you work. You can use the telephone to your advantage—to save time and to foster new connections.

It is also important to know the ways in which you can save money when you use your phone. If you know about the different rates, plus some of the tricks, the telephone doesn't have to eat up quite as much of your budget.

USEFUL PHONE COMPANY OFFERINGS

Within the last few years the phone company has come out with a number of handy new services for busy people who don't have the benefits of secretaries or receptionists:

Call waiting is a service which alerts you when another person is trying to get through to you while you're already talking on the line. It permits you to hold the first call, answer the incoming one, and even switch back and forth between the two. This service is worthwhile, since you aren't forced to hold off all your phone calling while waiting for a particular call to come through.

Call forwarding enables you to receive calls at any number you go to during the day. This is particularly useful for freelancers who go out on jobs.

Threeway calling can be useful if you do some sort of collaborative work, since you can get a third party in on a conversation.

Conference calling is available in some parts of the country.

NEW TELEPHONE EQUIPMENT

An alternative to paying a monthly charge to the telephone company for some of the services mentioned above is to buy one of the new telephones that will do the same job. For instance, you can now buy telephones for about $100 which offer conference calling and one-touch dialing of up to about thirty frequently called numbers. For about the same price, you can buy your own call-forwarding system.

ANSWERING MACHINES

Not all of the above-mentioned telephone company services are available countrywide, although they undoubtedly will be in the near future. You can, however, hook up an answering machine to any telephone. Some require the installation of a separate jack, but if you have one of the new modular phones you can buy what is called a "T" jack and hook the machine into your line. Alternatively, if you know someone who is handy with telephones, he will be able to splice the machine into your line. If you do this, remember to have the friend show you how to disconnect it when the telephone repairman is coming (you are not supposed to outwit the phone company) and thus avoid paying $25 or more for the installation of a separate jack.

For the freelancer, an answering machine is a gift of God. Not only does it record messages, but it enables you to screen your calls so that you can receive important ones but fend off creditors and other tiresome individuals (at least until you feel like coming to the phone). With modular telephones, which unplug, or those with an adjustable bell, you can have the machine answer and record your calls without even being disturbed by the ringing. Most of these machines cost between $100 and $300, depending on who makes them and how many extras they have.

If you move around a lot in the course of a day, you might want to buy a more expensive model with a remote key. This enables you to replay your messages without going home. All you do is dial your number, hold the remote beeper up to the receiver, and the signal will cause your tape to rewind and play back your messages. These machines cost more, and many freelancers complain that the remote control never works right. If you do decide to buy a machine with this remote control feature, don't skimp on the machine that you choose and double-check the service warranty.

One thing to remember when recording your outgoing message is that anyone can dial your number, intentionally or not, and people have been robbed because they left messages indicating precisely whether or not they were at home or how long they would be gone. Women should be especially careful or consider asking a male friend to record the message. Something along the line of "I'm not available right now, but if you'll leave a message after the tone

I will call you back as soon as possible," or "I'm working right now and can't come to the phone . . ." is sufficiently noncommittal. Or simply say, "You have reached Aching Back Productions. Please leave a message, and we will return your call."

You will probably receive lots of advice about your machine from non-freelance friends and family who seem to resent this mechanical anti-intrusion device and often feel silly talking to it. What can you do? They simply don't understand the exigencies of your profession, and for a freelancer some sort of answering device or service is a must. Concerning an answering service, if you plan to be in business for more than a few months, you can buy your own machine for what you would pay a service.

If you have more than one telephone number, you can either buy separate telephones and answering machines for each line or buy devices that allow you to turn one-line equipment into two-line equipment. They are called line controllers or switches and cost about $50.

ANSWERING SERVICES

There are two kinds of answering services: those which answer your telephone from an outside office, and those which provide an alternative number that people can call to leave you a message. With both types you call in for messages, which is an advantage in that you don't have to go home to get your calls from a machine. The first kind of service, in which your phone is answered, is more expensive and requires a one-time installation fee. So many of the people I talked to had quarrels with this sort of service that I do not feel it is a great value for the amount of money it costs. This includes the installation charge (average cost is $50) and then the monthly fee, which ranges from $40 to $75. In addition, some of these services function only during "business hours," which isn't very useful for the average freelancer, whose business hours more closely approximate the hours in a day. Make certain you are getting twenty-four-hour service, if you think you need it.

The second sort of service, where you have a separate number, is frequently used by actors and models. Often on their résumés you will see their home number and also that of their service. There is an abundance of these services in New York and in Los Angeles, and they at least have the advantage of being familiar to agents and casting people. They are also economical and fairly reliable. This contrasts with the other kind, which often comes under attack because if seems as though whoever is supposed to be picking up the phone has gone permanently to the bathroom. A good way to find a reliable service is to look in one of the trades, such as *Variety* and *Backstage*. An average monthly charge for this sort of service twenty-four hours a day is $60. Again, some companies may charge extra if you exceed a certain number of calls per month.

LONG-DISTANCE TELEPHONE WORK

If you live away from the major cities, you will be using long-distance telephone a lot. It is one of the most successful ways to eradicate the impression of some city people that you are out in the sticks and should not be used when the timing is tight. However, you may find that you are paying as much to the telephone company as to the landlord each month. There are ways to reduce your bill. Much is to be learned from the pages at the front or rear of your phone book that tell you the rates and give dialing instructions.

Peak and off-peak hours. You pay the highest rates for calls made during business hours (8 A.M. to 5 P.M.). These are billed at the full weekday rate. Between 5 P.M. and 11 P.M. on weeknights, calls are discounted 35 percent (this discount also applies all day on major holidays). The biggest discount is from 11 P.M. to 8 A.M. weeknights, all day Saturday, and Sunday until 5 P.M., when you save 60 percent.

Understanding these hours, you can plan when you make your long-distance calls. You can't call most business acquaintances at 8 A.M., but if you live in a different time zone, 8 A.M. your time could be 9, 10 or 11 A.M. for someone east of you. Many people work until at least 5 P.M. so that you can call at 5:01 and find people within your zone and to the west of you still at work. If you are calling the West Coast from New York, you can't call them cheaply the first thing in their day, because they are just getting to work when it is noon in New York. You can call beginning at 5:01 P.M., when they are in the middle of their workday. If you know a business has an answering machine, you can call at night and leave a message for them to call you.

Station-to-station calls are cheaper if you can be sure the person is in and ready to talk. If the person is not likely to be in, you can call person-to-person and leave a message without being charged—but should your party be there, the rate is higher. Of course, calling collect is cheapest, and I occasionally do it if I am doing a job for a big company or calling a familiar editor who doesn't mind.

Dial direct. Always attempt to dial direct. This is much cheaper than an operator-assisted call. In many cases you can now direct dial around the world. The overseas operator (dial 01) can give you the necessary country and city codes.

Bill necessary phone calls. Sometimes a client will let you bill necessary calls that you make from your number to his. I always like to do this, if possible, since it is one less bit of money that I am in danger of losing should my client hang me up later.

Toll-free numbers. Don't forget that many large companies and government agencies have toll-free numbers which you can find by dialing (800) 555-1212. A directory of toll-free numbers is available from AT&T.

Avoid Directory Assistance charges. A useful reference volume that will save you money on directory assistance charges is the *National Directory of Addresses and Telephone Numbers* (ed. Stanley R. Greenfield, Bantam Books). This book contains most government numbers, and many associations, unions, communications industry numbers, as well as banks, hospitals, universities and hotels.

Calling cards. If you make any significant number of calls from outside telephones, you should get a calling card from your local phone company. Charging calls to your home telephone via your card is cheaper than having the operator bill to your home phone or to a third party (which can be done only if someone at that number accepts the charges). Also, it's comforting to know that in an emergency you can make a call even if you don't have a penny in your pocket.

COMPETING LONG-DISTANCE SYSTEMS

If your monthly long-distance bills are routinely over $50, you should look into some of the competing long-distance transmitters which may save you as much as 30 to 60 percent. Some of these work via satellite, others via microwave equipment. As long as you have a push-button phone, you don't need to change your equipment in order to link up with these. If you determine that one of these services would be cost-effective for you, the charge to convert your telephone to push-button service is nominal. You do, however, have to live within one of the company's service areas.

Two nonprofit groups can assist you in deciding whether you would save money using one of the long-distance services. For $35 an outfit called Telecommunications Research and Action Center (TRAC)—P.O. Box 12038, Washington, DC 20005; (202) 462-2520—will analyze one of your phone bills to demonstrate how much the same bill would be if you were hooked up to each of seven alternate long-distance carriers. The Center for the Study of Services (CSS) will also analyze your long-distance bill for a fee ranging between $10 and $75. Write CSS Long Distance Cost Comparison Department, 806 15th Street, NW. Suite 925, Washington, DC 20005; or call (800) 441-8933.

Two other books that might be of interest are:

Newton, Harry. *101 Money-Saving Secrets Your Phone Company Won't Tell You.* It's available from Telecom Library, 12 West 21st Street, New York, NY 10010.

The Complete Guide to Lower Phone Costs. Available from Consumer's Checkbook, 806 15th Street, NW, Suite 925, Washington, DC 20005.

GETTING THROUGH ON THE TELEPHONE

Cerberus was the mythical three-headed dog who guarded the entrance to Hades, and it would seem that this is just who guards the portals of all the important agents, editors, recording executives and other assorted biggies. It almost seems that such people consider it a test of dedication whether or not you will be persistent enough to get through to them. After all, enough hungry people will figure out a way to reach them to keep them in business, and they don't need the rest of us. So how *does* one get past Cerberus the secretary? The rule seems to be: the more important the person, the more efficient his secretary is at screening calls. If you sometimes get the feeling that secretaries or receptionists are being downright spiteful about denying you access to their bosses, you are probably right. For all they know, you might be about to replace them. So, the strategy begins with your approach to the secretary: don't alienate, but rather make him or her your ally. By this I mean speak pleasantly and learn the secretary's name.

Generally, the best way to get through is first to write a letter telling who you are, what you have to offer and what you've done in the past. Naturally, if you can drop a name meaningfully, do so. That is to say, if you are trying to get to Richard Avedon and your photography teacher is a friend of his, mention that or say that he recommended that you speak to Avedon. The point is the mention of the name. It's not that name-dropping will get you anywhere, in and of itself, if you're no good at what you do, but it can help to distinguish you from the hordes at the door in a busy person's eyes. Generally they won't refuse to see you if you use a name.

Another way to get names to use is by asking each person you talk to for a couple of other names. Then, in your initial letter or phone call to one of those others, use the first person's name, saying, "Mrs. Steinway at Rasta Man Communications suggested I call/write you."

Another good trick: after you have first dropped a note identifying yourself, when the secretary asks who you are, give your name and say "she is expecting my call." You generally get through this way, but be prepared to identify yourself again, as the busy person in question will probably not remember your name from the letter. Also, remember that it's all right to refuse to tell the secretary or receptionist what the call is in reference to by just saying, "It's a personal matter."

When you do get your quarry on the line, don't waste time. Even if she isn't looking for anyone at the moment, ask for exactly five minutes to show your work or discuss your ideas. Also, in this situation, do show some familiarity with the publication or program you are trying to work for. It's far more impressive to hear a person say, "I have several ideas for your 'Freebies' column which I'd very much like to discuss with you in person," than to hear some vague and passive chatter. Do your homework first! (See also the section Connections in chapter 2.)

Here are some suggestions from freelancers on how to get through the barriers between you and whomever you wish to meet:

I've found that the best way to initiate a working relationship is a meeting in person, so do whatever you can to initiate such. First you have to arouse enough interest for them to tell you to send in some ideas or some drawings, which isn't hard to do at all. Many editors and art directors will tell you to send in some ideas on paper, almost as a way to get rid of you. So, a favorite trick of mine is to go to a magazine at the end of the day, around 5:30 or 6:00, after the receptionist has left but when most of the important people are still in their offices. You are able to wander through the corridors, delivery in hand, until you reach your target's office. You then stick your head in and say something to the effect that there's no receptionist in sight and you don't like leaving your work just lying around. Don't be a jerk and hang around if your victim looks obviously displeased to see you, but I have often found this a very fruitful sort of initial encounter.
—Writer-Illustrator

It's important to note when people say to call back in two weeks, because if you bug them enough they will see you. They're putting you through a little test: "How many times can this person stick it out?" You don't want to be obnoxious, but you do have to be persistent. You have to develop a talent for getting through to the art director. I will sometimes get the name of one art director from another one, and then I will say, "So and so told me to call you." If I see a new magazine, I call up and get the general information about when they see portfolios, who the art director is and whether they talk to people directly. The first time I just talk to the receptionist, then I wait for an hour for subtlety's sake and call back in a different voice and ask to speak to the art director by name. Sometimes you get through. The best art director will have the best secretary at screening calls. After a while you just have to seduce the secretary in some way. Sometimes you should just drop in and say, "It's too bad he's busy, but I really think you should see this stuff." A lot of times these ancillary people are artists themselves, and the art director will listen to what they say on these matters.

—Photographer

I've found it helpful to sound very familiar, so I might ask for Bill if the person is named William, or Patsy for Patricia, etc. Also, don't use a questioning tone of voice. Better a crisp "Bill Hitchens, please" than "May I speak to Mr. Hitchens, please?" which gives them more room to say "No, you may not." Also, speak quickly so that the receptionist gets the feeling that you'd be annoyed at being detained further. It's all psychological, but that's the name of the game. It's any edge you can get in this type of business where there are a hundred people for every open spot.

—Actor

HELPING THEM CONTACT YOU

Sometimes, believe it or not, some of these busy, important people will want to get back to you. If you have an answering machine, tell that to their secretaries and also indicate when you will be there to answer in person. Many people are less enthusiastic if they think they'll have to make five calls to reach you in person. If you have the call-forwarding device mentioned at the beginning of this section, you will have no problem on this score.

Try to find out when the person is likely to call back, and be there then. If it's someone important enough, it's perfectly warranted to stay in all day and wait for the call.

If the person is calling back with a message that can be given to you secondhand, you can always give the number of a friend at work and have him get the message to you.

If you have a rep or an agent, it often sounds impressive if you give that number and identify it as such.

HOW TO BE INACCESSIBLE YOURSELF

While we're on the subject of accessibility by telephone, there are a multitude of reasons why you might want to have an unlisted number—usually having to do with unwanted calls from creditors, or suitors of the obscene variety. However, having an unlisted number isn't the foxiest way to do this even though it sounds glamorous. There are two reasons. First of all, the information operator tells them that you do exist, may even verify the address and then says that at your request the number is not given out. Many young actresses hoping to appear seasoned, or in demand, do this as though anticipating a tiresome rush of fans calling at all hours. Second, you have to pay extra to have an unlisted number. You are entitled to one listing for free as part of your basic service, and there is no qualification as to what *name* you use. You do have to use a name, rather than the name of your business, or you will be forced to pay the higher business rates, but it's quite all right to put in a long Slavic name with a vowel-to-consonant ratio of one to four. This is far better than the alternative of having an unlisted number, since no one will be able to locate you.

THE MAILS

The United States Postal Service is a mysterious bureaucracy whose secrets are closely guarded—even, it often seems, from its own employees at the local level. To wit, try asking the same question at a couple of different post offices, and your inquiries are likely to be met with as many different answers and opinions. I went for years dismissing a friend as senilely inaccurate for advising me to mail manuscripts "Special Handling," just on the strength of one inquiry at the post office. "Special *Handling?*" the man at the window repeated incredulously, *"Special Handling?* I've never heard of it. There's no such thing. Special Delivery, maybe, but no Special Handling."

To know the regulations for size and closure of mail and follow them is your best protection against having packages and letters returned or lost en route. In addition, knowing the rates and rules in advance may prevent a trip to the post office altogether. (In my small town this would deprive me of a morning's gossip and camaraderie, but to my counterparts in large cities, the thought of avoiding a trip to the P.O. is thoroughly delicious.) In fact, if you have an accurate scale, a chart of postage rates and other information available from your post office, a zip code directory and a supply of stamps, you can mail out most of your correspondence yourself.

Imperfect as it is, the U.S. Postal Service does offer a variety of services that are extremely helpful to freelancers. Not all of them are well publicized, so I will describe them in detail in this chapter.

CLASSES OF MAIL

Here is a compendium of different classes of mail available to you:

First-Class Mail is given the fastest handling possible. It also may not be opened for postal inspection. First-Class Mail weighing in excess of twelve ounces is called *priority mail*. Be sure to mark items larger than letter-size "First-Class."

Use First-Class for postcards and personal correspondence as well as for transportation of checks, money orders and short manuscripts.

Priority mail is used when you want larger packages to move with the same speed as First-Class letters. Priority mail is used for packages which weigh more than twelve ounces but no more than seventy pounds, with a maximum size of 108 inches in length and girth combined. If you use priority mail frequently, it would be wise to ask the post office for a chart telling the prices per weight to each postal zone.

Use stickers or clearly mark the packages "Priority" on all sides to ensure they receive the handling you are paying for.

Second-Class is used generally by magazines and newspapers which meet postal service requirements. You may also use Second-Class to mail individual copies of these.

Third-Class is most often used for large mailings and includes two rate structures: the bulk rate and the single rate. It is used for printed matter and parcels of merchandise which weigh less than sixteen ounces. Manuscripts and galleys may be sent Third-Class, though by the time they arrive someone else will be likely to have published the same thing. If you do mail something Third-Class, remember it is to consist of printed matter only. Personal communications go First-Class.

Fouth-Class. Beware of Special Fourth-Class: Manuscripts; it is for typed or handwritten originals only, and it moves like molasses. You cannot send photocopies this way. Fourth-Class Books is only for items larger than twenty-four pages and stapled.

Other parcels, weighing one pound or more, go Fourth-Class. If you are mailing the package from a large post office to another large one, the size limits are: under forty pounds and less than eighty-five inches in length and girth combined.

There is also a special Fourth-Class With Letter Enclosed rate. But in general fourth-class moves too slowly to be worth a freelancer's time.

HOW TO GET MAIL THERE QUICKLY: EXPRESS MAIL, SPECIAL HANDLING

While all these normal classes of mail are useful for ordinary purposes, suppose you have to mail an assignment to somebody in Atlanta who needs it the next day. An extremely useful service is *Express Mail*, which offers next-day service between most metropolitan, and many rural areas in the U.S. as well as to some European Cities.

Using this service, you can send anything mailable and weighing up to seventy pounds. The cost is determined by the weight of the package or letter and the distance it must travel, and whether the addressee picks it up at the post office or it is delivered directly to her door. You must have your shipment at the post office by 5 P.M., and it is guaranteed to be in its recipient's hands no later than 3 P.M. the next day—or the recipient can pick it up as early as 10 A.M. of the next business day. You will receive a receipt at the post office, and your shipment can be insured for up to $500 at no extra charge.

Even faster than simple Express Mail is *Express Mail Same Day Airport Service*. This is available between most large airports. You must take your parcel out to the airport mail processing area, which is usually in the cargo area. From there it will be dispatched as quickly as airline schedules permit, and your addressee can claim it at its destination within hours. Express Mail service is also available between many cities in the United States and the United Kingdom, The Netherlands, Brazil, Hong Kong, Australia, Japan, Belgium and France.

The difference between Express Mail and *Special Delivery* is that Express actually gets there faster, while Special Delivery is like giving a letter to somebody to deliver on horseback. It is supposed to mean that the letter will be delivered outside normal mail delivery hours and on Sundays and holidays as long as the addressee lives within a one-mile radius of the post office. However, Special Delivery is traditionally a way of asking for trouble and fouling up the delivery so badly that you'll end up wishing you had just sent it First-Class.

Third- and Fourth-Class mail may also go *Special Handling*, which costs the required regular postage plus a modest dollar or so for the first ten pounds and a little more thereafter. It moves a little faster than First-Class, but (according to the post office) not as fast as Special Delivery. Be that as it may, one still gets the impression that for Special Delivery, final arrival is sacrificed to speed. Special Handling is very useful for mailing manuscripts that you don't want to pay to send Express Mail.

HOW TO GET MAIL THERE SAFELY

For some mail it is not only important that it get there quickly, but also that it get there *safely* and that you have a record of its existence to wave at the postmaster in case there is a problem. You have several options in this case:

1. Items worth up to $500 can be insured against loss or damage for a nominal charge in addition to the postage.
2. *Registered Mail*. Irreplaceable articles and all items worth more than $500 should be registered. You must declare the full value of what you are mailing, and you can get coverage up to many million for domestic mailings. You are given a receipt of mailing, and your item receives special handling. You may also pay extra and get a return receipt which will show to whom, where and when the item was delivered. For a slightly larger fee, you can request a return receipt even after you have already mailed the item.
3. Items worth more than $400 can be sent First-Class, priority or parcel post. For items insured for more than $20, the postman gets a receipt of delivery from the recipient for post office records. You can also get insurance for international parcel post.
4. *Express Mail*. When you send something Express, you get a receipt and your item can be insured for up to $500 at no extra charge. (Note: If you are mailing manuscripts, your only real insurance is a photocopy in your file, though you can get proof of delivery. See below.)
5. *Certified Mail*. Certified mail is for items of no intrinsic value. It provides you with a mailing receipt, and for a small amount extra, you can get a return receipt which

identifies the item by number and shows the date it was delivered and who signed for it.

6. You can request *Restricted Delivery Service* with insured, certified or registered mail so that delivery is made only to the addressee or someone who is authorized in writing to receive the addressee's mail.

7. *Certificate of mailing*. A certificate of mailing does not provide insurance coverage for loss or damage, but it does give proof of mailing. This can be a useful tool in the practice of creative debtorship, as described in chapter 17. With a certificate of mailing to prove that you mailed an item to your landlord or any other creditor, you can stall for a couple of weeks anyway by simply mailing something—but not a check—to the creditor in question. You have proof that you mailed check number X (always be precise when pulling this sort of con) on such and such a day. You can even have a photocopy of the allegedly mailed check on hand. People are often slow to notice the irrelevancies of such things as photocopies in this sort of situation. If they stopped to think, they'd realize that anybody can make such a copy as "proof." When your creditor calls up threatening you, you can offer to show him the certificate of mailing and the copy, and ask him to wait for a few days; or if he insists, send him a new check. In either case, all you do is drop the original into an envelope which was stamped by a postage meter the day you said you mailed it. Even if you don't have access to a postage meter, someone you know probably does.

According to a postal employee friend, individuals using this sort of con are not likely to have a problem. However, sometimes these predated letters are returned. It is a trick that large companies are not above themselves. The selfsame postal employee told me about the time a certain large, well-known brokerage house tried this trick with five hundred dividend checks. The post office returned the entire mailing because the meter had been set two weeks behind the actual delivery date. If this doesn't vindicate you—the smallest of businessmen—in the legal sense, it certainly does in the moral sense.

8. *COD*. Collect-on-delivery may be used if the recipient is going to pay for merchandise when it is delivered. The postman collects the amount due, the postage and the COD fee. COD can be used for First- and Third-Class, and for parcel post and registered mail.

9. *Money Orders*. M.O.'s are a safe way to mail up to $700 in cash. You have a numbered stub in case of loss, and you can get a copy of paid money orders for up to two years after they are paid.

Do not lose your evidence of mailing insured, registered or COD mail. You may want to file a claim later. You get the claim forms from your post office and file them there. Only you, the mailer, may file a claim for a complete loss. You or the intended recipient can file a claim for partial loss or damage.

INTERNATIONAL MAILING

Mailing letters and packages to other countries can be done using the same classes of mail as domestic mailing, but do be aware that the slower classes move even more slowly to other countries. Not only is the journey physically longer, but it is not just jingoism to say that mail-handling by foreign postal employees may be less conscientious than that of our own U.S.P.S. personnel. I would recommend that you use First-Class or priority mail for any mail that is to leave our borders. Another good choice for letters to be mailed out of this country is an *aerogram*, which saves you money on postage, paper and an envelope.

International reply coupons are extremely good to know about when you are sending abroad mail to which you want a reply mailed back. You can't send a stamped, self-addressed envelope, as protocal would dictate, since foreign postage rates differ and U.S. stamps are useless abroad. You therefore buy enough international reply coupons to cover return postage (bearing in mind that the postage rates in other countries are often much higher) and enclose them in the letter. The recipient can then exchange them at her post office for postage. These coupons can also be bought in other countries and exchanged by you in America.

But two cautions regarding these coupons: many smaller post offices are not familiar with them, and not all countries are party to the agreement which permits their use.

Night letters are another inexpensive way to make quick contact with someone abroad. They are the cheapest sort of cable and guaranteed to arrive the next morning. To send a night letter, call the nearest Western Union, RCA or ITT.

MCI Mail (see page 112).

SIZE STANDARDS FOR MAIL

A surcharge will be added on to the postage for nonstandard-size mail. The following dimensions are considered nonstandard for First-Class, weight one ounce or less, and single-piece third-class, weight two ounces or less:

1. Exceeding 6½" in height, 11½" in length, ¼" in thickness.
2. A length of less than 1.3 times the height or more than 2.5 times the height.
3. A thickness of less than 0.007" (about the thickness of a postcard).
4. Size under 3½" in height, 5" in length and not rectangular in shape.

SOME ADDITIONAL MAILING TIPS

1. Letters arrive much more quickly if you use the dreary two-letter abbreviations for states, with no punctuation: e.g., TX or NY.
2. Letters which contain payments should always bear a return address.
3. Always have a good supply of paper, envelopes and manila envelopes on hand. It makes sense to buy these in bulk from office supply stores.
4. Cardboard tubes are good for mailing prints and other artwork on paper.
5. The post office itself is now an excellent source of handy mailers. They sell three sizes of square boxes and for books and manuscripts they sell three sizes of jiffy bags. I often use their prestamped envelopes, which come in letter or legal size. Handy also are prestamped postcards and reply postcards.
6. Invest in an accurate mail scale—the balance kind—and use it.
7. Get a chart of postal rates from your post office.
8. Buy $10 worth of stamps at a time, so that you are not constantly in and out of the post office. The best times to go are first thing in the morning until about eleven and then from late afternoon until closing. It will also be easier to keep track of postal expenses for tax purposes if you buy in large quantities rather than a few stamps at a time.

9. Don't use Scotch tape on anything but First-Class Mail, or the post office won't accept it. Pressure-sensitive filament tape should be used instead. The post office will accept twine-tied packages but prefers not to, because they sometimes get fouled in the handling equipment.

10. The post office advises you not to use paper wrapping for boxes, if possible, for sometimes the wrapping is lost. It is safer to mark the address directly on the box.

MAILGRAMS

Mailgrams are a wonderful invention under the jurisdiction of Western Union. If sent before 7 P.M., Mailgrams are guaranteed to arrive in the following day's mail. Messages sent up until midnight may also arrive, but they're not guaranteed to do so. Mailgrams are very handy when you want to make sure someone notices your letter, for they look enough like telegrams to call attention to themselves. Yet they are less expensive. One freelance writer I met even uses mailgrams for sending important queries to editors and producers.

FAX MACHINES

More and more people are using telefacsimile, or fax, machines to transmit and receive via telephone lines anything that can be committed to paper except photographs. Fax machines work much like a personal computer hooked to a modem. However, fax machines allow you to transmit to recipient faxes layouts, existing documents or pages from books without an optical scanner which would be needed to transmit via modem anything not in the computer's memory. Fax machines also double as copiers, and most are about the size of a typewriter. New portable ones, made in the Far East, fit into a briefcase and cost about $1,000. Fax generally requires its own telephone line which you can also use for outgoing calls. If your fax is hooked up, it will answer your telephone with a cacophony of electronic noises.

Of course it's not worth your spending the $1,500 to $2,000 that fax hardware costs if your clients can't receive faxed messages from you. However, more and more businesses now have fax. It will soon be nearly ubiquitous. My feeling is that if the promised electronic cottage is really built, it will be fax technology rather than the present Babel of incompatible computers that will make telecommuting a reality. Faxes can be especially useful for artists who want to show rough layouts to clients for direction or writers who want to send manuscripts instantaneously. Fax can transmit at the rate of about a page a minute, costing you only for the call.

SPECIAL DELIVERY SERVICES

You may have been hearing recently about various alternatives to the mails, which are often achingly, puzzlingly slow. One of these is the package services run by Greyhound, Amtrak, Trailways and the airlines. To find these, look in the Yellow Pages under "Air Cargo," or in the White Pages under the bus companies or Amtrak. In the Yellow Pages you will also find companies such as Emery Air Freight and Endicott Overseas Express, which are private companies offering the same sort of fast, highly reliable service. These services can provide insurance up to a higher amount, and many people find them quicker and more reliable.

United Parcel Service. UPS will pick up pieces of work at your home or studio and deliver them within the continental United States. To have UPS pick up, call the nearest office one day in advance of the pickup and request the service. You will need to know the weight, dimensions and value of the parcel. UPS will carry nothing over seventy pounds with a combined length and girth of no more than 108 inches. Packages are automatically insured up to $100, and you can pay 25¢ per $100 of additional insurance.

Federal Express: FedEx serves the entire United States, Canada and many other international destinations as well. Even many quite rural areas have FedEx drop boxes where you can leave off packages and letters and pick up FedEx mailers and labels. (I keep a stack of each at home so that I can fill them out in my office and then just toss the shipment into the collection box.)

Several types of Federal Express service are offered.

1. Standard Air: this takes one to two days for delivery.
2. Priority One: overnight delivery of packages weighing up to 150 pounds using your packaging. Overnight delivery using FedEx packaging is also available. Packages of thirty or fewer letter-size pages may go as an overnight letter in a special FedEx mailer. If you slip in more than this maximum, higher rates will be charged.

For both these services, delivery can take an extra day or two if you live in an area not regularly serviced by FedEx.

FedEx is liable for loss or damage of your shipments up to $100. However, you can purchase higher coverage up to $25,000.

There is a variety of extra services that FedEx will provide for a price. These include Saturday pickup and delivery and constant surveillance of your shipment.

You can pay for FedEx with cash or a credit card, or you can bill it to your own or someone else's FedEx account. Most of the companies I write for provide me with their FedEx number and usually even some pretyped mailing labels so that I don't have to lay out any money to mail my assignments. Try to set up such an arrangement with any frequent clients, because it's one less up-front expense from your pocket.

For further information on FedEx, call (800) 238-5355.

Emery Air Freight. EAF has offices in most major cities of the world. They will ship anything from an envelope to objects weighing tons. There are no size limits and no ceiling on the amount of insurance that you may buy. A particularly useful service is their express small package service, which handles packages weighing less than seventy pounds between EAF's express points. Delivery can be either to a terminal or door-to-door.

Greyhound Package Express. Greyhound and most other bus lines have package express services that will carry packages from the bus terminals to cities and towns serviced by that line. These services are fast, and particularly useful to freelancers living in rural areas. They may not, however, provide door-to-door service and the recipient may be required to make a trip to the bus depot.

Electronic Mail. If you have a computer and a modem, you can avail yourself of electronic mail offered by CompuServe and MCI Mail (see chapter 6).

USE THE MAILS TO
MAKE YOURSELF NOTICED

Most freelancers felt that it was important in any profession to stay in touch with clients, managers, editors and others via the mail. Here are some of their comments about using the mails to stay visible.

I mail out cards to people and then follow them up with a call saying that I'd like to show them my portfolio, or to people I've worked with I say, "I have some new work. Let me bring you up to date."
—*Illustrator*

It's not that expensive to have cards made up in quantity from photographs. If I've been working recently, I get a photograph of me in a particular part made into cards which I send to agents and casting directors. And of course you should always send flyers of anything you're appearing in to these same people. —*Actress*

Often a gallery will make postcards for you to send out to friends, critics and buyers. Have a mailing list, add to it frequently, and compulsively, and use it whenever you have a show coming up. —*Painter*

I send out notices for all my gigs with some sort of wacky, eye-catching photo and the vital information as to time and location underneath. You can have these photo-offset fairly cheaply. I send them to recording business people and also to friends. If any remain, I put them in the windows of cooperating stores and bars and affix them to lampposts with gaffer's tape.
—*Musician*

APPEARANCES

The appearance of what you mail out assumes an importance way out of proportion to its actual relevance to your work. To those of us who never cared about the appearance of our homework in school, it's a bit annoying to find that appearances and first impressions are even more important in freelancing than they were then. Here are some basic rules:

- Strive for neatness. This is important not only when typing letters but even when affixing labels to mailing tubes. Particularly if you are a visual artist, your eye is expected to care about things like that. It is the Zen level of reverence for daily tasks that you must reach.
- Use a fresh typewriter ribbon. Never let the type get dim and muzzy. Keep a stiff brush by your machine so that you can keep the type clean: filled-in O's and P's look unprofessional.
- People who have to read a lot of typed pages *hate* corrasable bond. The

type often rubs off it in transit, and when the person reads it, it is often a blurred, filthy mess. Use correction fluid or film and heavy, white bond. Best of all, if you can swing it, buy one of the new correction cartridge typewriters which make for foolproof corrections.

• If you're a poor or slow typist, why waste your time and talent even attempting to type your own correspondence or manuscripts? You can easily locate typists: students, other freelance friends and moonlighting secretaries are excellent choices. Look on bulletin boards for them or place your own ad. If you have a substantial job, check writers' magazines and book-review journals. Many of these have directories of typists. You can also find typing services in the Yellow Pages, but do be aware that these will tend to be more expensive than moonlighters and freelancers who have no overhead.

STATIONERY

If you engage in any sort of commercial work, you will need a system: a letterhead, envelopes and business cards. Personalized invoice forms are nice too. (See page 104). If you mail things in manila envelopes, mailing tubes or film mailers, you should probably also include labels with your name and return address. Photographers and other graphic artists need stamps for the back of their photos. These stamps should also contain a copyright notice: the symbol © and your name and the year, as well as your address and phone number. Visual artists will need postcards with an example of their work on front. Performers will need cards that bear their photographs.

The design of your letterhead and business cards should depend on what business you are in and what image you are trying to project. Business cards and letterheads can often be made up quite cheaply at small printing stores. However, you are often limited as to layout and typeface at these places. I think the best deal, and by far the most elegant stationery (short of engraved, which does cost a lot), is that done by a process called thermography. This can be done very quickly and cheaply and is raised like engraving. You generally have a choice of black, brown, red, blue or green ink, and a bewilderment of typefaces. If you do not have a good eye for this sort of thing, you might ask a graphic artist friend to help you lay out your card and choose a compatible typeface. For a small additional cost, you can have your own logo printed. Thermographed stationery can often be bought wherever you would normally buy stationery in your area: business stationery stores, printers, office supply stores.

You'll find that your whole act as an individual freelancer will be taken more seriously once you have proper stationery, and of course decent business cards look far more respectable than the flaps of matchbooks and cocktail napkins.

COPYING

Try to scrounge up a little extra and have résumés, grant proposals and similar presentations photo-offset rather than photocopied. The copy really does look cleaner.

If you do photocopy something whose purpose is to impress somebody, remember that you will get a better copy from a better machine.

Some copy stores now offer color Xerox. Much depends on how good the Xerox operator is, and many have no particular talent with color and light. So, while it can't be used for accurate representation of a visual artist's work, it can be useful for making flyers or other items where visual quality is secondary. It also tends to be rather expensive.

If you have a computer you can make endless copies of any documents stored in its memory. Furthermore, you can keep them on permanent file on a disk. Do be sure to have a duplicate disk of any important documents.

Writers and others who end up doing a lot of copying may want to spring for their own copier. Although the prices are steep ($500–$1,300) nothing beats the convenience of being able to crank out good copies the minute you need them without having to make a big expedition to do so.

An old, inexpensive standby which we have forgotten in the age of the word processor is carbon paper. Loose carbon paper is very trying to use as it dyes your fingers, is hard to handle because it's slippery and seems always to get put in backwards and not work at all. Much of the trouble with carbon paper can be avoided by using copying film instead. This doesn't smear on your fingers, it's easier to handle than carbon paper, and it prints an image in ink rather than carbon and wax particles. It costs a little more than ordinary carbon paper, but a sheet of it makes about ten times as many copies as does a sheet of carbon paper—so your cost per copy is considerably less.

Another handy product which does fine for making copies of queries, letters and anything else you want for your files consists of a piece of carbon paper and a plain sheet. You insert this into your typewriter beneath the paper you are typing on. When you finish the page you just tear the carbon off and you have a copy. Two brand names are Snap Pak and Carbon Mate. I always keep them on hand since they make it so easy to make a copy and mail the original immediately rather than waiting till you pass a photocopier. This lessens the temptation to just dispense with making a copy at all, which you can really pay for through the nose, particularly in business affairs. It should be axiomatic with you to make a copy of everything you mail out. It's your only prayer if something goes wrong.

RETURN MAIL

Getting back replies or having your work returned is the necessary counterpart to sending them off in the first place. Here are some important reminders regarding return mail:

- When mailing manuscripts that you want returned—and you should always want them returned—you must enclose a stamped envelope with your return address (abbreviated S.A.S.E.). I generally paper clip the stamps to the envelope, so that if they buy the manuscript the stamps aren't wasted, are usually returned in fact. Some people also feel that you should enclose a stamped envelope when you are querying editors or art directors or other potential employers. I don't feel this is necessary or fair.

• You should always put a return address on anything that you mail out. It is preferable for you to have stationery with your address printed on it. If you send out large packages or mailing tubes, you must have labels with this information.

• When sending out artwork that is to be returned, you must send it in a packing that can be reused. If you can roll it, excellent reusable plastic shipping tubes can be bought at large art supply stores. If it is to be laid flat, make sure to enclose plenty of stiffeners and a manila envelope of the same size with equal postage. Films should be sent in cases. Although many users of your work will be meticulous, and even may return your work better wrapped than you sent it, you can't expect this.

• If your work is sent certified or registered and insured, enclose explicit instructions (and payment if it's a poor or unreliable company or gallery) regarding how it is to be returned to you. Photocopy these instructions in case they fail to comply and you wish to sue them.

• If you move around a lot because you are broke and have no permanent address or because you tour, you should have a post office box that remains the same as long as you are close enough to it to collect mail. These boxes can be rented in several sizes for a nominal sum by the year and the half year.

A useful book for people who are planning to ship artwork is:

Way to Go! Crating Artwork for Travel. It is available from The Gallery Association of New York State, Box 345, Hamilton, NY 13346.

CHAPTER SEVEN
COMPUTERS FOR FREELANCERS

When I wrote the first edition of this book eight years ago, my editor advised me to at least mention the advent of the personal computer. I didn't, because I, like many "creative types," suffered from a rather limiting and shortsighted fear of computers. At that point I just couldn't see what those complicated machines could do for artists. Now I find it necessary to devote an entire chapter to the subject.

As one advertising executive recently told me, "A freelancer without a computer is an impossibility." Having now worked on an Apple Macintosh for the last three years, I can only concur. A simple personal computer can vastly increase your manpower without your having to take on any employees.

Perhaps the most graphic illustration for me of the difference between working with or without a computer has been during the rewriting of this book. Previously, the manuscript had to be painfully typed by me (after being edited, because the smallest changes could mean retyping a whole page), retyped at my expense by a professional typist, onerously re-edited and fact-checked, retyped in full, photocopied and then pasted up as last-minute changes came in.

This time around, I need only type each page once. Once the material is entered, additions, deletions and corrections can be done and undone in seconds with no more effort on my part than pushing a few buttons. If I find I have misspelled a word throughout the manuscript, I need never again spend three hours poring over the text to make the corrections. The Mac changes every misspelling in a couple of minutes.

Freelancers can put computers to many uses. A computer can type, file, draw, compute, send messages, play music, hold a conversation, publish, analyze and entertain, to name just a few of its capabilities. All you do is supply the appropriate software that allows it to function in a specific role.

Here it should also be stated that not everyone needs a computer. It is, after all, an expensive tool with a steep and potentially frustrating learning curve. Technophobes beware: the computer evangelists can be very persuasive. But if you can't sit down and write out a list of the ways a computer would transform your own professional life, then it would be a good idea to delay that purchase until the benefits are clear.

Nor will a computer replace effort on your part. If you think that buying a computer will turn you from someone who doesn't have a good negative filing system into a model of organization, you will be disappointed. You still have to enter the information accurately and do a certain amount of work yourself before your computer can help you out. Some freelancers will find that despite the explosion in computer capabilities, no computer that they can afford will be able significantly to improve the quality of their work or even the speed with which they can do it.

So before you commit your money, spend some time investigating how useful a computer is going to be in your work. (Of course, if you are a real gadgeteer, this warning will not deter you. You'd be surprised at the number of people who own computers not because they are particularly useful to them but just because of all the gee-whiz things they can do. If you're the type who feels that cross-indexing your record collection is worth doing, then you probably already have a computer for carrying out these momentous tasks.)

Here are just a few of the "legitimate" ways in which computers can be useful to freelancers:

ALL FREELANCERS: personal financial management, keeping tax records, writing letters, billing, keeping track of names and addresses, sending mail electronically, creating business forms, playing games, interactive learning.

WRITERS: writing and editing (word processing), sending copy electronically to a client or publisher, self-publishing projects, on-line research.

GRAPHIC DESIGNERS AND ILLUSTRATORS: presentation slides and graphics, line art, charts and graphs, image manipulation and enhancement, setting type.

PHOTOGRAPHERS: filing negatives and slides, producing slide shows.

MUSICIANS: controlling MIDI-equipped synthesizers, arranging and orchestration, score printing.

The computer world is growing more complicated by the day, even as the machines become easier to operate. One of its most confusing aspects to outsiders is its specialized vocabulary and odd way of using the language. Nevertheless, most people have by now heard the terms *hardware* and *software*. The former means the actual machine itself, usually consisting of a processing unit with a screen, a keyboard and add-ons such as a disk drive, printer or modem. Software is the program that tells the machine what to do.

CHOOSING YOUR HARDWARE

Once you have decided that your life might really become easier with the purchase of a personal computer, you must complicate it further by deciding what kind to buy. Most computer experts would counsel you to make this decision based on factors such as price, flexibility and what you intend to do with the computer.

Hardware is currently dominated by Apple and the ubiquitous IBM, the latter group including the hordes of IBM-compatible computers known as "clones." The "architectures," or hardware designs, of these two main groups are very different from each other, so that programs written to run specifically on an IBM computer, for instance, will not run on an Apple. To complicate matters even more, there are incompatibilities within each manufacturer's product line, so that a program written for an Apple Macintosh will not run on an Apple II-GS, and an add-on memory board for an IBM-PS/2-series computer is useless with an older XT model.

Each manufacturer has its vehement partisans, so it can be difficult to get an answer as to which is the better one for you. The best advice I can give you, once again, is to consider very carefully what you plan to do with the computer. This will lead you to the kind of software you plan to use, and often you will find the choice of hardware then becomes obvious. In a battle between features and budget, be careful of false economies: if a computer doesn't do all you expect and need it to do, it could cost you a lot more money in the future.

That one caveat aside, I should add that there is so much excellent software available for each computer model that, unless your needs are very specific and out of the ordinary, it is difficult to go wrong no matter which one you buy. Writers who want to take the drudgery out of doing their work and just need a computer to type on, and maybe keep the books, don't necessarily need anything very fancy. Many are happy with a cheap IBM-compatible computer and low-end daisy-wheel printer. On the other hand, most people in the know agree that some form of Macintosh is the best choice for people whose work involves graphics, because the best graphics software is being written for the Mac. The Macintosh is also ideal for latent Luddites like me, since it is easy to use and can virtually be unpacked, plugged in and pressed into service without my having to know anything about how it works.

Eventually the choice of a computer depends on how comfortable you feel with it. Some people prefer the no-nonsense IBM approach, while others feel the easy-to-understand Mac is best for anybody involved in creative endeavors, because it is so easy to run you can push aside operating difficulties and focus on your work. The best way to decide for yourself is to try as many of your friends' machines as you can.

Here are a few additional items to consider in your hardware purchase:

HARDWARE COMPATIBILITY. Although the Macintosh has been making impressive inroads into the major corporations, IBM is still the overwhelming standard. If your clients are mainly large companies, that could be important. You can give a 5¼-inch IBM-compatible disk to nearly any corporate client in the land, and there will be a machine somewhere on the premises that can read it. Despite the constantly growing ranks of pin-striped Macintoshes, Apple is still a long way away from being a standard presence in corporate America.

Compatibility is also a pricing consideration. Many IBM "clones" are more powerful and offer better values than their official IBM counterparts, and their presence in the market has certainly had a beneficial effect on the pricing of "true-blue" IBM machines over the years. For its part, Apple has expressed its intention to protect its proprietary hardware and software technology with all the legal might a Fortune 500 corporation can muster. So if you want a Macintosh, you must get it from Apple or from an authorized value-added reseller. There won't be any clones.

SOFTWARE COMPATIBILITY. The hardware divisions between the IBM and Apple worlds are deep, but the software gap has been closing since Microsoft Corporation introduced its Windows "operating environment," or user interface, for the IBM and compatibles. Programs designed to run under Windows, like Aldus Corporation's PageMaker, can offer performance comparable to the Macintosh when coupled with a fast computer and high-resolution graphics display. The software industry's desire for "hardware independence"—the ability to write generic programs that can be made available in versions for any personal computer, to expand software markets across hardware lines—virtually insures that this trend will catch on. So if that Macintosh program won't run on an IBM now, it may well be that a new version of it will someday.

EXPANDABILITY. Here's where planning ahead can save you money in the long run. As your workload increases, you might find yourself needing more storage space. A high-capacity hard disk drive is a tremendous convenience and only one of the myriad add-ons available for personal computers, also including extra memory, accelerator boards to make the computer run faster, modems for telephone transmission of data, specialized graphics adapters—nearly anything you want to do with a computer, there's a device available to do it. But there has to be a way to connect these devices to the computer.

On IBM-compatible computers, which are sold as basic, no-frills boxes that you can configure any way you want, the normal way is through add-on boards that you plug into "slots" on the main circuit board. The original PC had five of these slots; later models have eight. You can never have too many, since you'd be surprised how fast they can go.

Expansion of the Macintosh is limited: the Plus has no slots and the SE has only one. To a great degree this is offset by the use of peripheral devices that have their own "brains" and don't require circuit boards in the computer, and by the number of features already built into the computer. With some ingenious hardware modifications, you can use a larger display than the standard nine-inch screen that comes with the computer. But for true hardware expandability, you must go to the very expensive Macintosh II, and truth to tell, most people in the Apple world can live perfectly happily without it.

COMFORT. People can be very finicky about their keyboards. If you're a writer, you'll be spending a lot of time with yours, so you'll want to make sure it's one you're comfortable with. Other "creature comfort" items to consider: the amount of room the computer takes up on your desk and the color of the screen.

PRINTERS. Most printers fall into one of three categories: laser, dot matrix and daisy wheel. Not too long ago the daisy-wheel printer, which takes its name from the shape of its print wheel, was the cream of the printer crop and priced accordingly. Prices have fallen dramatically in a few short years, and you can now buy a decent daisy-wheel printer for $250 or so. These printers are slow and noisy, and they cannot print graphics. But they will produce IBM Selectric–

quality text in many different typefaces, and if that's all you need, they will do it well.

With the advent of high-quality dot matrix printers, however, the daisy wheel may be on the verge of obsolescence. Dot matrix printers, which used to be known for producing ugly text that was difficult at best to read, form characters out of dots. Most will allow you to print in a fast "draft" mode or slower, higher quality mode. Many now have a "near-letter-quality" mode that produces perfectly presentable text, though not quite as good as the daisy wheel. They also will print graphics, although of limited quality. The best—and most expensive—dot matrix printers have print heads with twenty-four pins, and the Apple ImageWriter LQ printer, at 216 dots per inch, approaches the resolution of the LaserWriter printer at about one-fifth the price.

If you are a writer, using your computer mostly as a glorified typewriter, you can turn out perfectly presentable copy on an inexpensive daisy-wheel or dot matrix printer with a fresh ribbon. Similarly, if you just print out invoices or letters, there's no need to buy an expensive printer unless you have money to play with and are very fussy.

If, however, you are trying to produce camera-ready artwork or text, your capabilities are limited by your printer. No matter how sophisticated your graphics program, you won't be able to produce professional quality work with anything less than a laser printer. Despite the usual industry hype boasting "near-typeset" quality text—in fact, current laser printers resolve three hundred dots per inch, while a typesetter resolves a minimum of twelve hundred—the laser printer is the state of the art for personal computers in both text and graphics. A laser printer can use proportionally spaced typefaces to give text a typeset look, and the quality is excellent. (*Inside Macintosh*, published by Addison-Wesley, was produced on an Apple LaserWriter.) But be prepared to spend a lot of money for that look. The cheapest laser printers will set you back at least $1,500 and from there the sky is the limit. Those offering PostScript, a programming language for specifying the elements of a printed page, cost much more—the LaserWriter Plus, for instance, comes in at about $4,500.

WHERE TO BUY

There are essentially two places to go: to a full-service computer store or to a mail-order dealer. Forget about the K-Marts and toy stores. We're talking about business machines here.

Your local computer retailer will tell you that you're better off dealing with him, rather than a cheaper mail-order house, since he can give you advice and after-sale support. He might also tell you how aggravating and time-consuming it is to return defective products by mail, how difficult it is to service machines purchased by mail and how many crooked mail-order operations there are.

There is some truth there, but it's not quite the whole story. Yes, to buy safely by mail you have to know exactly what you want, whereas a good salesperson can be an invaluable help to you in building a system around your specific needs. Shopping locally does have the distinct advantage that if anything goes wrong, you can go in and scream at the manager until you get some relief. (That can be satisfying even if you don't actually get any relief.) If the store has a good repair department, it is sometimes faster and more convenient, and perhaps even cheaper, to have a computer serviced where you bought it. There are indeed some fly-by-night mail-order operations, but in general, the major firms that advertise in the computer magazines offer prompt and reliable service, at a lower cost than the local retailer, albeit with greater demands on the customer's knowledge.

Personally, I believe that it is best to buy from people you know and trust and with whom you can have an ongoing relationship. Thus I favor the local retailer. But I don't believe in blind faith, and when you shop for a computer store, you should do so with caution, knowing that you're going to be spending some real money there.

Unfortunately, the computer retail business has grown more rapidly than the supply of high-caliber sales personnel, and it is all too easy to get bad advice. Beware the incompetent, the teenage prodigy and the huckster who would just as soon sell you a car as a computer. Think twice when someone tells you that the product his store carries is "the same as" the one you want. He may be right—who knows, it may actually be better—but computers are sophisticated and complex machines, and you lose if he's wrong.

Even if you don't know anything about computers, you can still pay close attention to how the store personnel treat their customers. Are they patient with new customers? Do they appear to know what they're talking about, and can they say it in English, or do they assault you with technobabble? Do they want to sell you what they like or what you need? Will they lead you away from a product you don't need as quickly as they'll lead you toward one you do? Do they treat customers as a necessary annoyance between video games? You can tell a lot about the quality of the store's after-sale support by the length of time it takes the salesperson to put down his coffee and wait on a customer.

Above all, ask questions and don't be afraid of looking ignorant. The good computer salesperson will do his best to bring the mountain to Mohammed.

BUYING SOFTWARE

Buying software can be particularly tricky. A quick glance at one of the computer magazines will reveal a bewilderment of software. With programs often retailing at upwards of $500, "try before you buy" is the rule. This poses a problem if the program you're interested in is not among the top sellers, as the dealer may not have a demonstration copy if he carries the program at all. Before you even go down to the computer store, see if you can find a friend who has some programs and will let you play with them—not every program will be to your liking despite the manufacturer's or salesperson's claims.

All of the computer magazines (if you can bear to read them) carry software reviews, as does *Whole Earth News*, which also publishes *The Whole Earth*

Software Catalogue. Macintosh users will find a handy listing, with thumbnail descriptions, of all the best-selling software each month in *MacUser.*

One common way of acquiring software is to make copies of friends' programs. If the program is free public-domain software or "shareware" obtained through a users' group or an electronic bulletin board, copying it is perfectly acceptable and even encouraged. But if it is a commercial software package, unauthorized copying is a violation of the licensing agreement (you might be surprised to know that you don't actually "buy" commercial software; it's actually more like a permanent lease) and the copyright laws, and could expose you to civil and/or criminal penalties if you're caught.

Apropos of copying, many software products have protection mechanisms that prevent you from making unauthorized copies. These protections range from a program code that checks for the presence of defects deliberately made in the program disk to elaborate hardware "keys" you must attach to your computer before the program will run.

In the case of games, copy protection is not a problem. But I would advise you to avoid, whenever possible, any business program that prevents you from freely making backup copies or requires alteration of your hardware for the sole purpose of using a copy.

This is a complex and volatile issue within the software community. But the fact remains that if something were to happen to your program disk—and believe me, things do happen to disks!—you would be stuck for however long it takes the manufacturer to send you a backup copy, for which you would be expected to pay as much as $25.

Some software packages allow you to make one copy of the program on your hard disk. Usually the backup procedure creates errors on the hard disk in specific places, so that the program will know it's an authorized copy when it finds them. If you are willing to let a computer program mess with your hard disk and all the valuable data on it, you're much braver than I am.

As for the hardware "keys," they have been known to interfere with the operation of peripheral devices such as printers or modems, besides being a general nuisance. Fortunately, they are relatively new and so far not in wide use.

INFORMATION NETWORKS AND OTHER SPECIAL SERVICES

If your work involves research, an on-line information network such as Dialog or BSR After Dark can be a valuable tool, offering bibliographies and abstracts or published articles on nearly any conceivable subject—very handy when you don't want to go to the library or it's two in the morning. You can find out what's happening in the world through up-to-the-minute AP and UPI summaries on services such as CompuServe and the Source. These networks offer a variety of other services, such as travel booking and investment advice, and all you need is a major credit card for charging your on-line time. They offer member-to-member communication whereby you can leave messages for other members in their electronic mailboxes, and forums which permit you to have group discussions with people across the country on a variety of subjects. This latter service might be particularly interesting to people in the arts since there are writers' and musicians' groups, as well as many other special-interest groups, holding forums.

If you normally send work to your clients by mail or Federal Express, you may be interested in MCI Mail, a service that allows you to send text and images via modem to MCI, which will then deliver hard copy to your client within two hours. Because this is faster than FedEx, you can have longer to work on your assignment.

If you wish to make use of any of these services, you will need a modem. Your computer store will sell you a modem package which will include the modem itself and compatible software that you will need to use it. It is worth it to spend a little extra on a modem that can transmit data at twelve hundred bits per second, which is pretty much the standard nowadays (though it will probably be replaced eventually by the newer twenty-four hundred bps modems that are gaining in popularity). Although the slower three hundred bps modems are still available and are cheaper, the money you save will soon be eaten up by higher telephone bills.

SPECIAL SERVICES

COMPUSERVE, INC.
5000 Arlington Centre Boulevard
Columbus, OH 43220
(800) 848-8199
(614) 457-8600 (in Ohio)

DIALOG INFORMATION SERVICES INC.
3460 Hillview Avenue
Palo Alto, CA 94304
(800) 528-6050

GENERAL ELECTRIC INFORMATION SERVICES CO. (GEnie)
401 North Washington Street
Rockville, MD 20850
(800) 638-9636
(301) 340-4000

SOURCE TELECOMPUTING CORP.
1616 Anderson Road
McLean, VA 22102
(800) 336-3366
(703) 821-6666

MCI MAIL
1900 M Street, NW
Box 1001
Washington, DC 20036
(800) 624-2255

PART TWO

YOUR MIND AND BODY

CHAPTER EIGHT

OCCUPATIONAL HAZARDS TO THE PSYCHE

Freelancers have all the money problems of most economically disadvantaged minorities. They have problems in the creation of their art. They have problems which arise from being artists in a country where the pantheon has places only for Money, Power and Efficiency. And they have the ordinary day-to-day anxieties and stresses which don't even relate to their work. Many of the stresses and frustrations which are the building blocks of neurosis are built-in occupational hazards of freelance work. The successful freelancer can skirt these dangers, but many people become lost to them for long periods. Dealing with them effectively is almost a prerequisite skill for successful freelancers.

These occupational hazards are problems common to everyone. I mention them in this book because they *are* occupational hazards, and nowhere is the connection between the person and the occupation closer than among freelancers. Quite literally, your work is you and you are your work.

"Writing is an abnormal activity for the human body. If you think of women who are butterfly swimmers and those great muscles they get—or a fencer's legs—they all have these abnormalities. Writers have that, but their abnormalities come with what they exercise! It's not surprising that they're nuts. Just to keep doing it is hard," says a Hollywood screenwriter.

In a country where the sort of work you do as a freelancer is considered low-priority at best, you begin to perceive yourself as a low-priority person. And everywhere you go—the rental agency, the bank, the insurance company—your low status is confirmed. Nothing is made easy, and if you haven't developed a resilient ego and skillful coping behavior, you are a perfect target for debilitating depression, anxiety and addictive behavior.

"LIKE A TURTLE ON ITS BACK"

Like a Turtle on Its Back is the title of a French film whose protagonist is a blocked writer. The simile is well-chosen, for it perfectly expresses the frustrated, helpless feeling of being blocked.

All artists may experience some degree of blocking, but according to both popular and academic opinion, the blocks are most frequently an anguish of writers. In any case, both the causes and the cures are the same no matter the occupation of the blocked individual.

Blocks may come at any stage of the work. Some people may sweat the most blood over the first brush strokes or the first words. Others may be stopped at the center of a work, perhaps even knowing what will come at the end but yet being unable to create the connective tissue. Others may be unable to make necessary changes or revisions.

Much of the writing on creative blocks has been contributed by the psychoanalysts: Freud, Jung, Rank and others later. However, equally valid thinking on blocks comes from artists themselves. The earlier work concentrates on childhood experiences and primal fears, while later papers admit that blocks can be a necessary safety valve to protect the artist from the "violence of the creative experience," in Rank's words.

The fear hypothesis seems a particularly reasonable explanation of the sort of block that causes an artist to be unable to begin a work. According to a paper by Dr. Richard Robertiello,* victims of creative blocks place too high an importance on being creative, in many cases because their parents instilled in them this lack of proportion. To these people, creativity is "the one and only avenue of achieving recognition, the public equivalent of maternal love. . . . The victim of the block is afraid to create for fear of being rejected and thus destroying forever the illusion of being able to achieve love and recognition. He would rather maintain the illusion that some day he might achieve this than risk the rage, hurt and depression connected with a possible rejection." Tom Wolfe, quoting Anthony Burgess in a recent excellent review of this subject by R. D. Rosen† says, "Writer's block is almost always ordinary fear. The first fear is that you can't do what you've announced you would do, even if you've only announced it to yourself."

Perfectionism is also a common factor in artistic blocks. Nothing can be perfect, yet some people are unable even to get started, because they seem to think that everyone else's works arrive fully formed. This kind of rigid perfectionism is maladaptive, is usually a remnant of unrealistic parental or educational standards and leaves little room for true creativity. Comparisons can also cause problems. Don't compare yourself to Shakespeare and Michelangelo—even great artists like Updike and Klee don't measure up to standards like that.

COPING WITH BLOCKS

There are a few strategies to prevent blocks in the first place, and all of them focus on bringing buried material closer to the surface, so that you can see what is really going on and why you might be afraid of it.

• The first method was reported in a writer's magazine about ten years ago. I remain indebted to its inventor, though I have been unable to track down who he was. It consists of putting a sheet of paper in the typewriter and sitting down before you start your writing for the day and just

*Robertiello, *Psychoanalytical Quarterly* 37 (1963): 462-5.
†Rosen, "The Pen Is a Heavy Oar," *New York Times Book Review*, April 12, 1981, p.32.

typing whatever comes to mind as quickly as you can, not paying attention to typos, spelling or grammar. Don't think. As soon as your fingers come to a stop, take the page out of the typewriter. Don't look at it. Just date it and put it away for a week. After a week look at it, and then put it back. When you have a pile of these, you can see some of the trends in your unconscious. This exercise works very much as a seismograph to detect rumblings in your psyche before they break into your conscious mind. It also seems to keep you a bit more fluent in your own inner language. Examining these exercises months or years later, you will be surprised at the quality of some of what you wrote.*†

- *Self-hypnosis,* as described in the last section of this chapter, is also useful in helping to remove blocks and uncover buried memories which might be causing the blocks. It is also possible to do the above exercise while hypnotized, and thus, perhaps, be able to delve even deeper than you ordinarily could.
- *Exercise.* See the section on exercise later in this chapter and also chapter 9 for a discussion of how running and other types of exercise can help you prevent blocks by keeping you in contact with your unconscious and helping you to discharge energy that might otherwise become anxiety.
- Other creative activity can often help you loosen up a block by taking away some of the building frustration at not being able to express yourself in your usual medium.

Just as the origins of blocks are all very individual, so must be the cures. You may find that some variation on the advice given here works to free your creative energies. If you feel you are making no headway, you probably need outside help. In more and more cities, it is possible to find psychologists and psychiatrists who specialize in treating artists.

Surprisingly, blocks were not a very common problem among the freelancers I interviewed. Whether this is because blocks exist more in the popular press than in the lives of artists or because blocks are a luxury that struggling freelancers can't afford, is impossible to say. Several had been confronted with blocks and learned how to cope. Here is some advice from them:

Once, when my writing was going nowhere, I began to paint and draw — something I had enjoyed and done continually as a child. While I was still agonized over my failure at the typewriter, I was able to feel some positive pleasure in my painting. A sort of double sublimation, I suppose. Eventually, I felt the pressure was off my writing and I was able to get back to work. Now I try to keep my artwork up, because it forces me to use my eyes more carefully, which is gratifying in itself but also a boon to my writing.
—Novelist

Endurance. I just sit there grunting and wait. The important part about

*Edmund Bergler, The Writer and Psychoanalysis (New York: Robert Brunner, 1954), p. 258.
†The Surrealist painters and writers used automatism, or automatic writing, a similar method, to tap the unconscious and produce free-associated images.

being a writer is to be very patient. Whatever it is that makes the juices flow sometimes withdraws its favors. Something helps you, and I don't think that thing works capriciously. I think you have to work with it. Valéry said that inspiration was applying the seat of the pants to the seat of the chair. Being available. Once you've started, you have to work very, very hard.
—Writer

Just read some good writing which is related to your work. You can't help but pick up the rhythm of the other writer and be carried along yourself.
—Writer

DEPRESSION

All extraordinary men distinguished in philosophy, politics, poetry, and the arts are evidently melancholic.   *—Aristotle*

Depression is a common condition in the world today no matter what your occupation. It is a debilitating and de-energizing condition, but one which can be controlled in a number of ways. Learning what it is and what causes it can be a major step toward loosening its hold over you, for depression like many psychic disorders responds very much to the sufferer's active attempt to defeat it.

SYMPTOMS

There are many theories as to what causes depression, but little debate as to what the depressive syndrome consists of. Feelings of sadness, lack of energy, sleep disturbances, appetite changes and changes in sex drive are all symptoms of depression. The person with mild to moderate depression feels deflated. The simplest tasks overwhelm. Depressed persons may feel listless and sleepy all the time and may or may not have difficulty in getting to sleep. Very often they withdraw and appear unable to cope with their friends and families.

DEGREES OF DEPRESSION

Depression, like many psychological disorders, is a matter of degree. The aforementioned symptoms may be present to a mild degree that causes a lowered capacity for activity but is not incapacitating as more severe depression usually is. We have all experienced a temporary, downward change of mood in response to a rejection letter or the loss of an important relationship. But while this is physiologically related to true clinical depression, it is nowhere near as serious.

Depression is usually a realistic reaction to a loss. A depressive reaction can be adaptive, because it helps you express your need for comfort and relief in a way which your family and friends can perceive and perhaps satisfy. However, when it persists to the point where it disrupts your ability to function, it becomes neurotic. When it is so severe that you lose all hold upon your environment and become delusioned, it has gone beyond neurosis to psychosis.

This section is addressed to people who occasionally suffer from mild depression. If your depressed feelings persist in spite of your attempts to get yourself moving again, you probably need outside help—perhaps as little as a few hours with a therapist who can help you find out why you are depressed and teach you how to cope with depression.

THEORIES OF DEPRESSION

A theory of depression which is particularly relevant to discouraged freelancers says that the depressed person becomes overwhelmed by feelings of being unable to cope. In studies with rats, Dr. Jay Weiss of Rockefeller University has shown that it is the rat that has no control over its environment (in the form of not being able to escape from or avoid shocks given to its tail) which shows the biochemical changes normally associated with depression. Rats forced to work continually to escape shocks by turning a wheel show no such drop. Translated to the human context, this experiment indicates that it is the person who feels helpless to control his own situation who will become depressed—not the person who is literally run off his own feet trying to and succeeding in controlling it.* As we will see, activity and initiative are death to depression as well as vice versa. A lowering of your general activity level can't help but reduce your chances of initiating some new activity which will help pull you out of your depression. For example, if you are very depressed your initiative may be less and you don't bother to go out and get new work which might, if you succeeded in finding it, make you feel less worthless and less fatigued. If you are really depressed you won't even be able to get yourself away for a weekend or out to the movies—both of which ordinarily might help. Depression thus appears to be an interplay of both biological and motivational factors.

An analytical explanation of depression which is applicable here is that depression is precipitated by a threat to a person's dependencies on others, and by a lack of self-esteem. Many things can lead to this state: death, divorce, failure at work, overwhelming new responsibilities. One specific dynamic proposed by the psychoanalytical explanation of depression is that the Ego is overwhelmed by a sudden attack by the Superego. The Superego, as you will remember from Psychology 201, is that part of the personality which represents the internalized voices of your parents. It gives you your first taste of guilt as a child in the throes of the Oedipal complex and continues to stand for authority and discipline. What this can be to freelancers is the voice of the disapproving world—the business world or your family—which treats freelancers as second-class citizens or even as goof-offs. When you are met with this sort of deprecation and lack of understanding at every turn, you unconsciously begin to feel guilty for falling short of the unrealistically high standards your sadistic Superego sets for you.

Failure can precipitate depression, and feelings of failure and extreme self-criticism for not achieving unrealistically high goals are typical of all creative

*J. M. Weiss, "Psychological Factors in Stress and Disease," *Scientific American*, 226 (1972): 104.

people to some extent. Add to this the feelings of uselessness and failure to live up to the external requirements of the puritan work ethic that so many freelancers are made to feel, and you have another entree to depression. Using these theories of depression, we can understand why freelancers seem to be particularly prone.

DEPRESSION AND FREELANCERS

Guilt and lack of self-esteem are common to all sorts of artists simply because in a country where art is not considered particularly important and where importance and esteem are so tied to economic worth and conformity, people who live by different standards quickly perceive their inferior place. Damaging stereotypes abound: the irresponsible performer, the alcoholic writer, the dopey painter with his beret. This cause is mediated by the outer world, but there are other causes of depression which arise directly because of the nature of freelance work.

Postpartum depression is a term normally used to describe the typical depression which follows childbirth. This depression is said to result from the letdown or loss that one feels after so many months of intense involvement and anticipation. This situation is very similar to the feeling of being at loose ends that an artist has when the book or painting is finished or the play's run is over. Many artists have an extremely close attachment to the work they are gestating. When at last it is out in the world, the separation from it, along with the cessation of the activities associated with it, can trigger terrible periods of emptiness and loss. This happens for a number of reasons. You may have unrealistic expectations connected with the completion of the work: the story you have been working on will be picked up for the movies, the big break will come. When it doesn't, you forget about the work itself and feel only the disappointment of failing to attain unconscious, unrealistic goals. As an artist, you can learn to take pleasure in the creation of your work for its own sake and avoid the depression that comes when you fail to realize all of your pie-in-the-sky expectations.

According to Dr. Fred Ephrain, this type of depressive reaction is a sort of identity crisis. During the striving for a goal, your identity is bound up for so long with the task that when you finish you have lost something which has grown to be an important part of your identity.

Another cause of depression is the feeling of not having control over one's life. This is particularly prevalent among performers who must wait to be chosen before they can work. Large blocks of time from these people's lives can be spent just waiting without any idea as to when they will work again. Not only can the waiting be depressing, but the economic problems associated with sporadic and often underpaid work can add to the depression because often the person can't even afford to buy solace in the form of meals with friends, small vacations or new clothes. The frustration of poverty coupled with the frustration of not feeling in control of one's future can be paralyzing.

According to New York psychiatrist and depression specialist Dr. Frederic Flach, freelancers commonly doubt their control over situations when they feel taken advantage of, or even ripped-off, by a publisher, a gallery or some other party involved in the commissioning, buying or publication of their work. Even some of the best, most solvent publishers seem to regard biannual royalty statements as mere technicalities in the contract. Others have the same feelings about parting with money. Even when everything is on the level, artists may well feel a sense of paranoia about the whole process of making money off their work. The contracts can be difficult to understand, and you somehow always seem to wind up with less money than you had expected after advances or commissions or agents' fees are deducted. Unless you have a good sense of the business side of your art, you may be prone to paranoia and depression over your lack of control and your fears of being ripped-off. For this reason, as well as for the more practical one of not getting ripped-off, the wise freelancer will protect herself with a good business sense for her field and a good legal adviser or agent who knows the ropes and can intervene on her behalf.

WHAT AM I DOING HERE?

This is a question every freelancer, even the most successful, asks every now and again. Sometimes you forget the rewards and can only think of how much easier employees seem to have it. When things are going well, you wouldn't want to be doing anything else, but when you are poor, out of work and unappreciated, you wonder why you don't just acquire a job skill and stop beating your head against the wall. It is next to impossible to get down to work when you are feeling like this, so what do you do to snap yourself out of it?

• Do something that makes you feel proud again to be an artist: go to a museum, a film, a performance, or read a book. When you expose yourself to perfection or near-perfection, your own creativity is stirred. Once again, you will find yourself driven from within to attain goals that you set.

• Look at some of your own best work. You're pretty good sometimes, aren't you? It would be a shame if you just gave up with a whimper, wouldn't it?

• Show your work to someone else, a friend or an interested acquaintance. Freelancers often feel frustrated when they can't sell, publish or perform their work. At times like this, an audience and some feedback may help you realize all over again that you are special, with something valuable and unique to contribute to this world.

• If you can't stop wondering whether you'd be better off doing something else, maybe you should go do it for a while and see for yourself. You may find that a little exposure to the nine-to-five world is all the impetus you need to get you back to your drawing board or your typewriter. On the other hand, maybe you're happier in a more structured work environment.

• Perhaps you need to do both. You may find that you don't like to be poor or frustrated due to the lack of work, but still want to freelance. A part-time job may be a perfect solution, because it enables you to do your freelancing and yet be independent rather than at the mercy of the market all the time.

• Take a day or a weekend off. You may be browning out from overwork.
• Read an artist's biography or autobiography. Good ones are:

Laurie Lisle: *Georgia O'Keeffe* (Washington Square Press/Pocket Books 1987).
Louise Nevelson: *Dawns and Dusks* (Scribner, 1976).
Anne Truitt: *Daybook: The Journal of an Artist* (Pantheon, 1982).
James Lord: *A Giacometti Portrait* (Farrar, Staus, 1980).

As you can see from the following quotations, you aren't alone among freelancers in asking yourself this question:

Sometimes I just want it to be normal. I want to stop having the struggle every day when I get up, thinking, "OK, today I have to put this out, and this out." It's all coming from me. I think we all have the tendency to think life must be easier in the straight world, but intellectually I know that each of us is engaged in his own struggle. But I still can't help feeling that there has to be an easier way. —Writer-Director

I would love to work nine-to-five right now! I think there is a genius lurking behind the system. Everything that I revolted against I actually think is right. So what if you go and you hate your job? First of all, when you leave it, you leave it completely. You never think about it at home. You don't even have to think about it when you're there—you just kind of do it by rote. You have your weekends free, you have your two-week paid vacation. It makes a lot of sense, I want to tell you. America, I was wrong. It's great! Whereas when you're freelancing, you get up, you're worried, you make your phone calls, you go to meetings, you come back, it's seven o'clock and you haven't done any work on your novel. You're anxious, you forget about going to unemployment. You're a complete wreck. You can't have any relationships at all. You're lonely, because you're living by yourself. You're eating food stamps. It's no good. I think everyone should move to Westchester right now and work for IBM. —Television Writer

What do you do to keep yourself together when you really half want to quit? Oh, wait till tomorrow. I can always make myself feel better when I feel I've put out an effort and it's had an effect. Sometimes it helps to go see somebody else's work. If I go see a play or read a book that was wonderfully executed, I find that very inspiring, and I say, "Yes, you are doing the right thing." That validates my life when I can think, "That's what I'm after and eventually I can be there too." —Director

WHO DO YOU THINK YOU ARE?

The other side of "What am I doing here?" is "Who do you think you are?" Paranoia replaces despair in this query. It is both the voice of the world addressing the artist and the artist's own inner voice. Artists are most definitely considered low-priority, low-class citizens, particularly in capitalist societies such as ours. If you pay too much attention to your position in society, you will begin to internalize society's assessment of you and become depressed, or at the very least wonder why you're doing what you are doing.

- It is important not to get bitter about society's treatment of you, because you can distort this and use it as a rationale for flouting society in ways that can only hurt you (e.g., not learning about taxes or lousing up your credit rating).
- There is a strength in numbers when you feel like this. Go talk to a friend in the same field and realize that you're not alone in your boat.
- Or go to a meeting of a guild, union or arts council to which you belong. Sometimes for me, it is only the Authors Guild's annual meeting that makes me feel respectable when I have been feeling unsure about myself as a writer.
- In New York City, the Foundation for the Community of Artists sponsors a forum for artists of all disciplines called Artists Talk on Art. (For further information, contact Artists Talk on Art, Inc., 15 East 10th Street, New York, NY 10003.) Similar groups undoubtedly exist in other cities and can be located through the arts council which serves the area.
- Call or go visit your mentor or your agent or rep. This should help restore your sense of pride in yourself. When you see that someone of such high caliber believes in you, you don't have to care so much what the rest of society thinks.

Almost all of the freelancers I interviewed had something to say about society's low regard for and lack of support to artists:

This is the only country in the world in which the government really shows no desire at all to cultivate artists.   —*Actress*

Every time I have had a chance to write something in art magazines, I have tried to impress on the public that they have an absolutely different view of our life. We are really lower-class in the community—in every country from Libya to the U.S.   —*Painter*

I used to feel ashamed that I was still so poor when my friends were moving so glitteringly up the young-couples ladder, but I turned my back on the ones who really couldn't understand. I remember one of my friends saying to my mother that I just couldn't seem to hold down a job, and I wanted to strangle her. But now that we're in our mid-thirties, my career is going strong. Half of them are divorced and just catching on to what I've already learned about life, love, money. You just have to believe in yourself.
    —*Writer*

Always be aware that you are an artist and most people don't understand that. Everyone's got an idea what an artist is, and don't bother trying to explain it to them. Don't defend yourself.   —*Illustrator*

Don't ever apologize. In a given set of circumstances you may have to look as though you're apologizing to get away with it. Sneak your way through. Be as much of what you are as you can be. —Writer

REJECTION

Rejection is a fact of life for even the most talented professional freelancers. In situations where there may be five hundred actors auditioning for one part or several hundred manuscripts sent for one slot in a magazine, you obviously can't win all the time. Also in the arts, where so much of what is done is a matter of subjective tastes and needs, you can't be right for every art director, producer, editor, etc. This is something freelancers who are professional in outlook (even if not in income) learn very quickly. Although you may feel very close to your creations, you must learn to stand back from them enough to realize that they are being judged—not you personally. Most people who are in a position to accept or reject your work are nice people with a job to do. They have to make sure each piece of work fits into the whole under their direction. Most of them hate to turn down as many talented people as they have to do each time they choose one out of the crowd.

Constant rejection is discouraging. Sometimes you wonder whether your stories will ever stop coming back in the mail or whether you will ever be chosen for a part or sell a photograph. The answer is emphatically yes! If you hang in there long enough, you'll eventually start working.

"It's a game of tenacity," says one actress. "In the acting business if you stick it out long enough, you'll work. There are a lot of schloggs out there who work all the time. They just work their pants off, and they're no good, but they're good on the telephone, good at making the rounds."

Rejection is something you must learn to rationalize in the business of freelancing. You must figure out how you can shake it off and keep right on going without missing a beat.

- If your story has just come back in the mail, don't let the sun rise with it on your desk: slip it right into a fresh envelope (which you will have on hand) and send it elsewhere. A good way to implement this is to keep a list of other suitable publishers and their addresses with your filed copy of each story.
- If you are an actor, make sure to get to the next audition you are suited for.
- If you're an artist, try to have another gallery or art director to visit.

Remember, keeping the ball rolling is the only way to survive as a freelancer—whether it be bouncing back from rejection or hustling names of new people to show your work to. Here are some further thoughts about rejection:

I think it's very important to go in, do your best, and then shut the door even if it wasn't a day when you did do your very best. Just forget about it, and if it happens, it happens; and if it doesn't, it doesn't.
—Actress

You're going to get rejected a hundred times for every acceptance you get, and the acceptance may be a hundred-dollar mechanical job. It's not all just kids. It's fifty years of pros who are all hanging out in this town. They can knock off in two hours a job that may take you ten.
                                                                    —*Commercial Artist-Author*

You have to understand that rejections are done purely on the basis of personal judgment, and people make mistakes. A manuscript of Steps *by Kosinski was circulated among New York publishers several years after it was published, and they all turned it down. Stories like that really make you stop and wonder who all those goons are anyway, and why they're worth $25,000 a year. If a reader gets a foot cramp while she's reading your story, that may prompt her to put it down and send it back. You never know, but you can't let it slow you down.*   —*Writer*

Rejection? So what. It's the name of the game when you're any kind of artist. You just can't let their assessment sway you—whether they're rejecting you or lauding you. Fuck 'em. Those who can, do; those who can't get a job passing their judgments on the work of others.
                                                                    —*Painter*

You have to realize that if you aren't cast it's not because you're bad. A director has his needs, and for an actor that's something you have to learn—not to take it personally. The rejection that you meet all the time is not a personal affront.   —*Actress*

ANXIETY

Freelancers are subject to anxiety as well as depression, either concurrently or by itself. Anxiety is expressed by feelings of apprehension or fear and a sort of constant alertness against unknown danger. Physically, anxiety translates into sleep disturbances, tension, rapid pulse, dry mouth, sweating and nervous nonpurposeful movements such as nail-biting and foot-tapping. Perhaps the most distressing aspect of anxiety is that it hugs you closely and occupies your mind no matter what you are doing. There are degrees of anxiety, from the severe, free-floating variety where you begin each day with a terrible, inexplicable sense of dread, to the milder sort which may be a response to a stressful or frightening situation which you feel you can't handle. This sort of anxiety can be an everyday occurrence for the freelancer who truly has an insecure future and who has no way of dealing with it.

Basically, anxiety, like depression, is an adaptive response, though far from the best or the only adaptive response. What anxiety does is to effect the release of excess tension through bodily activity. This release helps prevent the tension from building up to unmanageable levels and really causing you to go off the deep end.

THE ANXIETY OF FREELANCING

Fear in a freelancer's life may be caused by money worries, lack of work or artistic problems related to the creation of work itself. Says one freelancer: "I'm always scared on New Year's, especially the first two or three years I was freelancing. New Year's is not a very enjoyable holiday for freelancers—you worry for the year, how it's going to be this year!"

Freelancing can be frightening, particularly if you support others besides yourself. If you let anxiety overwhelm you, you will become incapable of working. The working freelancer, perhaps more than anyone else who works for a living, must have ways of neutralizing her anxiety.

HELP FOR DEPRESSION AND ANXIETY

One of the first steps to take in learning to control anxiety or depression is to realize that it comes from you. It is your choice among a number of other possible responses to fear or anger. This is true of any anxiety from chronic dread to a momentary attack of fear, and of depression from mild to severe. You might try thinking that all perception is your projection upon the world anyway, and that you can make those perceptions as threatening or as manageable as you choose. Just realizing this alone will not rid you totally of anxiety or depression, but it will help. It is then up to you to find an effective method for coping with it. (See also chapter 9, Stress Management.)

EXERCISE

Recently, much has been written about the role of exercise in relieving depression; and for mild to moderate depression, daily hard exercise may be all that is needed to bring your mood up. Many psychiatrists are now making a daily run or swim or set of tennis part of their prescription for helping depressed or anxious patients. Dr. John H. Griest of the University of Wisconsin put eight depressed patients on a ten-week walking and jogging program. He found that six of the patients improved markedly within the time allotted, and more importantly, they maintained their improvement.

Dr. Herbert DeVries, a Los Angeles physiologist, tested tranquilizers against vigorous fifteen-minute walks for treatment of anxiety and found that the patients who exercised were far less tense. Physiologists know that muscles relax most deeply after increased muscular tension, and it is probably for this reason that exercise is so helpful in treating the physical tension which accompanies anxiety. Once the body is more relaxed, the mind can follow.

It is not known exactly why exercise helps, but it does seem to relieve some of the sleep difficulties, such as trouble falling asleep, which are typical of depression, or awakenings during the night or early morning, which are more typical of anxiety. This may be simply due to the fact that exercise is tiring and thus induces relaxation. Improvements in sleep can help, in turn, in coping with anxiety and depression. Depressed patients often get onto day-night cycles which are reversed from whatever is usual for them. Exercise during the waking hours can help regulate sleep times. Typically, depressed people feel sluggish and sad. The last thing they feel they want to do is go out and run a mile, but a mile run can be very energizing, particularly if done every day or at least four times a week. The feeling of well-being that hard exercise can produce can help to break the cycle of inertia and helplessness of depression.

For those whose response to stress is anxiety and tension rather than depression, exercise helps rid your body of some of the harmful chemical by-products of stress, such as high levels of adrenaline in your blood, which can cause high blood pressure if maintained year in and year out without release. Exercise provides an outlet for all the pent-up feelings of fight or flight which result from a stressful life-style.

COUNSELING

Many people hesitate to seek counseling from a psychiatrist or psychologist, because they are afraid of getting caught up in an expensive, lengthy process that will search their souls but not get to the real problem. This is certainly a fair assessment of many but not all therapists' work. Obviously if you have such severe emotional problems that you can't function, you may need to spend several years undergoing therapy, but this is not always the case. Increasingly, mental health professionals are offering short, goal-directed therapy designed to treat your symptoms and teach you new ways of coping. This focus on outer behavior rather than historic cause is often very effective as a therapeutic method, and changes can be seen over the course of a short, inexpensive treatment. This sort of short-term approach is practiced particularly by cognitive therapists, behavioral therapists and by hypnotherapists. It is particularly suitable for freelancers on a tight budget, since therapy may consist of only ten to twenty sessions.

If you feel you need a therapist, here are some sources from which you can get help: psychiatric clinics in major hospitals, local community mental-health centers, the psychiatry department of a nearby medical school, the psychology department of a university in your area and referrals from your own physician. If none of these is available, you should contact one of the following organizations:

AMERICAN PSYCHIATRIC ASSOCIATION
1400 K Street, NW
Washington, DC 20005
(202) 682-6000

AMERICAN PSYCHOLOGICAL ASSOCIATION
1200 17th Street, NW
Washington, DC 20036
(202) 955-7600

ASSOCIATION FOR ADVANCEMENT OF BEHAVIOR THERAPY
15 West 36th Street
New York, NY 10018
(212) 279-7970

MEDICATION

If your depression or anxiety is so severe that none of the aforementioned methods aimed at attacking it nonchemically is effective, you need psychiatric help.

Antidepressant medications are extremely powerful drugs which are sometimes brought in to counteract the changes in brain chemistry associated with depression. These drugs have side effects, and for less severe depressions they may not be indicated. While there was an explosion in the use of antidepressants in the late '60's and early '70's, many psychiatrists are cutting back and are trying instead to help their patients overcome depression in other ways.

More recently some psychiatrists have been using lithium with patients who are not true manic-depressives. Unlike people who simply become depressed, manic-depressives experience cycles of mood swing—from deepest depression to wild manic celebration and back again. Lithium was found to flatten out the peaks in these cycles and sometimes to help prevent wild fluctuations of mood altogether. Manic-depressive behavior is really a continuum in the same way that high and low blood sugar are. Neither extreme is optimum, and there is great individual variation as to what point in the continuum is typical and normal. There is a state just short of full mania which is called *hypomania*. Hypomanics are characterized by their manic energy, excitability and flights of ideas. They differ from manics in the degree of their excitability as well as in their firmer grip on reality. Hypomanics may or may not experience corresponding lows. Some people function best at a level which might be judged by a psychiatrist as mildly hypomanic. Throughout history many creative people have been manic-depressive or hypomanic: notable examples are Emily Dickinson and Joshua Logan, the producer.

Some psychiatrists are now finding that very small doses of lithium—far below the normal therapeutic range—can help prevent depression even in those who are not manic depressives and can keep some people in a state of mild hypomania. One New York psychiatrist who uses this therapy has noted that his patients who are in the arts, many of whom do have mild but not true manic-depressive mood swings, benefit from this moderate dose of lithium. Such patients can often stay in a mildly hypomanic state—without having to live through the down side of the cycle.

While anti-anxiety medications, such as the minor tranquilizers Valium and Librium, can be given, they are at best psychic Band-Aids which do little more than mask the underlying causes of anxiety. The use of these drugs has risen steadily over the past decade, and it is becoming apparent that many people are dependent on them to the point where they need them to function. This is particularly dangerous to freelancers, whose art can't afford the dulling of sensitivity that prolonged use of these drugs brings. Tranquilizers tend to deaden your sensitivity to experience when used in place of some less artificial way of coping with anxiety that allows you to feel the full range of emotions connected to an experience without becoming overwhelmed.

If you do suffer from the physical manifestations of anxiety and feel you need something to calm you down, inositol, a B-vitamin, and L-tryptophan, an amino acid, will probably work as well as any tranquilizer with no potential for addiction. Both can be bought in drug and health food stores. However, check with your doctor before experimenting with either.

WITH "GLASS IN HAND!"

"With glass in hand" could equally be "with joint in hand" for the purposes of this section, but the speech of Jack London from which it was taken perfectly explains the glamour so many artists find in drink and drugs:

*Glass in hand! There is magic in the phrase. It means more than all the words in the dictionary can be made to mean. It is a habit of mind to which I have been trained all my life. I like the bubbling play of wit, the chesty laughs, the resonant voices of men, when, glass in hand, they shut the grey world outside and prod their brains with the fun and folly of an accelerated pulse. ***

It is undeniable that many of the greatest artists were lushes: Poe, Utrillo, Jackson Pollock, Frank O'Hara and Billie Holiday are only a few. But in spite of much folklore, many of our very greatest did not indulge at all. This list includes Willa Cather, Edith Wharton, André Breton and René Magritte. Many of those who were addicted to drink or drugs wished bitterly that they weren't. Scott Fitzgerald felt that any line that he had written when he was drunk could have been done better had he been sober. Fitzgerald managed to keep producing in spite of his drinking problem—at least in the early part of his life. Hemingway was able to handle the problem by not letting himself have a drink until he had done his day's work. This is quite common among working artists, writers and performers who also indulge heavily, but even this restraint requires a high level of discipline. For those who enjoy drinking or drug-taking it can be inordinately tempting to ease creative frustrations with a draught of one's poison. Unfortunately, the average freelancer may find that discipline comes hard. It takes a lot more presence of mind and steady effort to break into the creative world of today than it does to supply a world already in love with your talent. The contemporary artist who must have a pint or five joints a day may find the doors to success closed to her if she can't get a handle on her habit.

The high incidence of drug and alcohol abuse among creative people is usually attributed to the loneliness of many creative occupations and the isolating pain of seeing and feeling more than most people are called upon to do on a daily basis. Just as blocks may be viewed as ways of protecting the artist from "the violence of the creative experience," as Rank calls it, overuse of alcohol and drugs may be an attempt at the same effect. According to novelist Irving Wallace, writers drink to ". . . relieve tension generated by the creative process—by hard thinking, being alone, being without discipline, keeping irregular hours."†

---

*Quoted in Barnaby Conrad, "Genius and Intemperance," *Horizon*, December, 1980, p. 40.
†Conrad, "Genius and Intemperance," p. 39.

Other theories center around artists' need to escape from the constant exposure to public scrutiny of their most private selves. In some cases, destructive as their habits may be, drink or drugs are the only way artists can allay their anxieties and produce at all.* Unfortunately, this attempt at self-medication is often where troubles begin. The mixing of drugs and work is not always the best step, for from there it is easy to forge a permanent connection between the two so that soon enough it is impossible to produce without the companion shot or joint. The tragic irony of it is that many artists can trace their substance abuse to an attempt to oil their own machinery when they were blocked.

Generally, drugs are not a free ride. They may give you roller skates for a while, but at some point you almost always pay with your work, your health or your energy.

A glass or two of wine, or a joint, at the end of the day will not ruin you as an artist. If you've worked hard, such a reward may be in order. And some freelancers do manage to have the best of both worlds in this respect: it is perfectly possible to allow yourself this indulgence without losing all control. A moderate intake of wine or pot can relax you and help prepare you for the next day's assault. But most freelancers, including those who at some time took great quantities of drugs or drink, learn that if you want to create as much as you are capable of, you have to be abstemious for the most part. Most of the freelancers interviewed below found drugs and alcohol incompatible with their work on a regular basis, although a few of them felt it all right to smoke a joint when they run out of steam:

I think it's usually very bad to attempt to smoke pot while writing. Sometimes if you have come to a snag it doesn't hurt to smoke a joint before you leave your desk, in case you get any spurts of imagination which you decide to write down. Many of these, however, are just too flighty and have to be culled from the work the next day. —Writer

It's not unusual for me to go through a bottle of wine in a day. I never keep it here. When I want it, I make myself go out and buy it bottle by bottle. If I just had a case under the sink, forget it. I know that's childish, but it's true about myself. I think it's OK if you allow for such things and have little plans. Otherwise I don't think there's anything wrong with having a glass of wine for breakfast if you want it. —Television Writer-Lyricist

Sometimes you get good ideas when stoned, but for the actual designing everything has to be dead on. Even for ideation I don't think it's always good. You get so excited, and then next time you look at it you see it's not so good. Sometimes you reach a point when you just can't go any more, and that's when it's time for a joint. Then you create a second burst of energy. That is better than doing it first thing in the morning the way I used to do. Acid was great that way also, although I haven't done any of that in about three years. —Graphic Designer

*Ann Roe, "Alcohol and Creative Work," *Quarterly Journal of Studies of Alcohol* 6 (1946): 401.

HOW TO CUT DOWN OR STOP

You will have to find your own way on the question of taking drugs to work, or even whether to take drugs at all. If you are having any problems avoiding taking drugs or drinking, even when you want to, you need professional help. The following methods should be helpful to those who want to cut out drugs or alcohol altogether, or to those who want to slow down. Another serious problem can arise for people who have stopped and find that they can't work. If these people can replace their chemical addiction with a positive addiction such as running or meditation, they may be able to fill the gap and get back to work.

- *Exercise* is one positive addiction which can replace a less healthy addiction. As you will see, many freelancers, even those with no bad habits, feel that heavy, regular exercise, particularly the rhythmic sort such as rowing or running, enhances creativity and aids concentration. (See the section on Exercise on page 126, and see also chapter 9.)
- *Hypnosis* can be an excellent way to overcome addictive difficulties, and it also can be used to enhance creativity by those people who rely on drugs or drink to do this. (See the section on Hypnosis page 132.)
- *Acupuncture* can be highly effective for ending addiction. It is painless, usually not prohibitively expensive and very effective according to people who have had acupuncture for addictions to drugs, cigarettes, food and alcohol.
- *Alcoholics Anonymous.* AA is probably the most effective method for overcoming drinking problems. There is an enormous network of AAs, and small rural towns are likely to have chapters in a local church. Even if you don't think you can cope with AA's somewhat religious overtones, try attending a meeting and see whether the atmosphere of support and care generated there doesn't inspire you to stick with it. Many very high-powered people have been saved by AA, and you are likely to come across plenty of savvy, sophisticated people who will have enough familiarity with your situation as an artist to give you the sort of empathy you need to stop drinking. You can locate the nearest AA by looking in your telephone book or the Yellow Pages, or by writing to Alcoholics Anonymous, P.O. Box 459, Grand Central Station, New York, NY 10017.
- Many large teaching hospitals have chemical-dependency units which often have out-patient clinics that handle both alcoholics and soft-drug takers.
- Many communities have alcoholic treatment centers, although they may not be inexpensive. The best way to find these is by looking in your local Yellow Pages under "Alcoholism Information and Treatment Centers." Since awareness of the frequency of alcohol abuse is growing, you will find that almost every county of the U.S. is served by AA or by a treatment center hotline. You can also get information through the National Council on Alcoholism, 12 West 21st Street, New York, NY 10010.

• Another place to get help is from the Association of Drinkwatchers International, Inc. This is a nonprofit, self-help program for people who wish to put their drinking into perspective—whether that involves stopping it altogether or just cutting down. Contact the Association of Drinkwatchers International, Inc. P.O. Box 179, Haverstraw, NY 10927.

As for help in controlling drug problems, the situation is better now than it used to be. Since heavy marijuana and cocaine use is so common nowadays, no longer are pot smokers and coke users lumped together with heroin addicts at treatment facilities. The trend is more and more in the direction of treating alcoholics and drug users at the same facilities, since there is more resemblance between these addictions than there is between heroin and marijuana or cocaine use. If there is no facility in your area specifically geared towards soft-drug abusers, approach alcoholism programs. If they don't handle marijuana and cocaine problems they may be able to refer you to one of the new marijuana treatment programs that are slowly springing up in large cities.

One excellent organization is Narc-Anon (no relation to AA), which counsels all drug and alcohol abusers, provides drug education and, at some centers, provides drug detoxification. You can get information on Narc-Anon from: Narc-Anon, 227 West 46th Street, New York, NY 10036; (212) 921-5374.

Also, the Odyssey Institute provides information on drug abuse and has direct drug abuse programs in Louisiana, New Hampshire, New York, and Utah. Contact: Odyssey House Public Information, 309 East 6th Street, New York, NY 10003; (212) 477-9630.

HYPNOSIS: AN IMPORTANT TOOL FOR FREELANCERS

Hypnosis has been the subject of so much misunderstanding over the years that it's just now beginning to seem respectable to all those who were frightened away. Say "hypnosis," and the average person unfortunately still thinks about parlor games in which people are made to squawk like chickens or scary Russian experiments in which people can learn languages overnight or crime dramas in which grisly murders are reconstructed under hypnosis. But all hypnosis really is is a technique for relaxing and focusing your mind.

Hypnosis is a natural state. You don't go off on some weird trip or enter any strange realms in the usual hypnotic session, although you can if you want to. You're actually probably hypnotized more often than you realize. For instance, when you're engrossed in a good movie, you are hypnotized. Someone could steal your coat from the next seat, and you wouldn't notice because you are concentrating so hard on the movie. Hypnosis can also occur spontaneously. Runners and other athletes often fall into a hypnotic trance.

Although the history of hypnosis goes back to Freud who used it extensively, hypnosis is now being explored as a tool for controlling bad habits and addictions, overcoming blocks and phobias and anxiety, improving concentration and, most recently, for helping your body to fight diseases such as cancer.

Hypnosis is really a method of enhancing two-way communication. Not only can suggestions go into your unconscious, but also buried memories and feelings can come up into awareness. For this reason, hypnosis can be a useful short-term psychotherapy. However, here I must caution you that not every qualified hypnotist is a good psychotherapist. If you are interested in the possibility of using hypnosis as part of your therapy you should look for a psychologist or psychiatrist who believes in using it as a tool.

I use self-hypnosis every day to help myself overcome work blocks. My hypnosis teacher emphasized that extreme caution was necessary when using this method to treat blocks until it was understood why the block existed. As stated earlier, blocks may be formed as a valid way of protecting an artist's psyche from material that is too painful or frightening to confront directly— almost like a psychic blister. Hypnosis permits you to delve very deeply into the unconscious in a very short time. In my case, blocks are due to laziness and, when I am working on assignment, often to a conflict about having to work for my money at all. So it is safe for me to blast through those blocks with self-hypnosis and hypnotic suggestions to get to work and finish that assignment before I starve.

Blocks often occur because of some sort of conflict. For instance, although you may think you really want to proceed full steam ahead in your career, unconsciously you may not. (Perhaps you harbor resentment at your parents for pushing you into an artistic career, perhaps you think you'd rather be a musician, and you may be subtly sabotaging yourself every step of the way until you figure this out.) This conflict might show up during a session with a hypnotherapist. So hypnotherapy for blocks can either be helpful or open a big can of worms, depending upon how much you want to work through your block. However, since many of us don't get our work done not because of blocks but rather because of laziness or disorganization, self-hypnosis can really help us cut away the nonessentials and get deeply involved in our work.

An interesting way of using hypnosis is rehearsing. This technique can be an excellent way to psych yourself up for something. It can be helpful, for instance, when preparing for a job interview or for actually rehearsing something that you are going to be performing. I use it often when I am going to speak somewhere, when preparing myself for a horse trial and very often for tackling assignments that seem to be beyond my capability. When I rehearse, I hypnotize myself and then create a vivid mental image of myself performing the action as I want to be able to. I take myself step by step through the whole interview or assignment or whatever, concentrating on feeling competent, happy and generally positive. You can really set your mind up for winning. This works because your central nervous system can't really distinguish between an event that you have actually lived through and one which you have just imagined vividly. By putting into your mind the picture and the feeling of you as you want to be, you have made that picture true—at least as far as your mind is concerned. Many experts feel that the best way to introduce this sort of positive imagery into your mind is to make yourself a tape that you can play back to yourself when you need reinforcement. It will probably help to write yourself some sort of script when you do this and record from that. Remember to write in a very positive tone of voice. Instead of making a tape that says,

"I'm not going to louse up this assignment, I'm not, I'm not, I'm not." Make one that says something more like: "I am exactly the right person for this assignment. I enjoy doing it, I find it interesting, and it is what I am good at. It will give me a chance to show what I can do. As I begin the job, I feel alert and confident. I will work calmly and smoothly until it is finished."

Although you may feel a little silly at first both recording and listening to this sort of self-boosterism, remember that it's a way to get things across to your unconscious mind. Be positive, use short sentences and use as many visual images as you can. Include images of the desired result, of yourself producing that result and, if you like, of people responding positively to you.

A hypnotherapist I know works similarly with performers who suffer from stage fright. First he asks them to locate the fear in their bodies, then he asks them to remember a time when they first felt that way. Quite often such feelings go back to some childhood trauma, such as being forced to perform or being laughed at while doing so. So much of what haunts us in our adult lives is imprinted in childhood. Next, the person is asked to visualize a time when she felt very relaxed and comfortable performing, and then a posthypnotic suggestion is given to the effect that she will feel like that when performing in general.

Believe it or not, this sort of imaging technique is being used very successfully in the treatment of cancer patients, who are taught to image their various immune system components fighting off the cancerous cells.

You don't necessarily even need to know self-hypnosis in order to use imaging techniques. The key is being really relaxed and concentrating deeply. People who meditate have a good idea of the level they need to reach when using techniques like this. I think it's a good idea to go to a hypnotherapist to really learn the standard ways of getting yourself into a hypnotic trance just because it's a surer, faster way of really concentrating, and you are likely to reach a deeper level of concentration.

Not everyone is equally hypnotizable. Artists are often very easy to hypnotize. Good subjects are imaginative, able to let go and temporarily give up control, trusting and suggestible. People who have to know exactly where they are at all times generally take longer to teach and may never be able to get into a very deep trance. As you practice, you can learn to hypnotize yourself in a matter of seconds and to get to very deep unconscious levels. It's a subtle state. You are in a condition of relaxed awareness, but you don't really feel any different. It's often hard to tell whether you have actually succeeded in hypnotizing yourself. In fact, the best proof is really whether it helps you accomplish what you want with it.

Hypnosis can be used to give yourself a suggestion that you will do something or feel a certain way after you have come out of the trance. You can also put yourself in a hypnotic trance and then stay under while you do your work or whatever you want to use it for. Only you shouldn't drive in an altered state, even such a mild and natural one as hypnosis. I often work while hypnotized. I put myself under, imagine myself hard and happily at work and then I give myself a post-hypnotic suggestion that when I come out of the trance I will continue to work. Or I may continue to work while in a trance. In both cases, the results are truly miraculous. The work just seems to fly by. I really find that it helps me to get hold of myself and defeat my procrastination problems.

I know the use of the word *trance* makes the whole thing seem a bit unreal. It's not so arcane as all that. You've all had the experience of working really well, being truly centered. When we work in that state, work becomes totally absorbing. Hours may fly by without our even knowing it. Self-hypnosis can make that state seem more attainable. Instead of just stumbling into it, you can evoke it every time.

My hypnosis teacher became especially interested in working with artists. He had already given a couple of workshops for visual artists to teach them how to use self-hypnosis to bring out their creativity to its fullest expression and even to improve technique by helping them to relax. He felt that uses of hypnosis like this were the wave of the future, and he was training other people to work with artists and writers. If you're interested in that sort of approach or just in learning self-hypnosis, you can get a referral from the American Society for Clinical Hypnosis at 2250 East Devon Avenue, Des Plaines, IL 60018 or (312) 297-3317.

CHAPTER NINE
STRESS MANAGEMENT

WHAT IS STRESS?

These days we hear a lot about stress, and much of what we hear is wrong. Stress, according to Dr. Hans Selye,* the man who first introduced the engineering term *stress* to medicine, is "the rate of wear and tear in the body caused by life at any one moment." Stress is really about adaptation to changes. All change, good or bad, can take its toll. Every body is a map of the adaptations it has made over a lifetime. Psychological defenses, skin blisters and suntans are all examples of the body or mind adapting to stress. Although too much stress, requiring too many adjustments, can be harmful, so can too little. Without some stress, we wouldn't be impelled to change or grow.

When we are forced to adjust our behavior in some way, we react to the very core of our most primitive selves. No matter what the stressor, we react with some degree of fight or flight response which you may remember from high school biology. It's a response that we share with other animals. Physiologically it's the same for all of us and for all of us involuntary. We pump adrenaline and cortisone-like substances. Our heart rate and blood pressure increase as do our breathing and the rate at which we burn food. All this is to prepare us to fight or flee what we perceive as danger. This sort of automatic response was highly appropriate in the lives of our ancestors a million years ago, but for the most part, it's excessive in this world of constant but hardly life-threatening stressors. In fact, the body and mind's response to stress can be far more life-threatening than the situation that triggered the response. Civilization has changed faster than our bodies have, and this lag is apparent in many other ways. In ancient times, we usually did end up either fighting or fleeing and so worked off all the adrenaline that we had pumped up. Nowadays we usually have the opportunity neither to fight nor to flee but have to swallow our emotions instead. So here your body is doing hundreds of times a day what was actually developed for emergencies: the driver in front of you

*For a detailed explanation of the relationship between the fight or flight response and stress diseases, I highly recommend *The Stress of Life*, by Dr. Hans Selye. His book (published by McGraw-Hill, 1978) is well written and not difficult for interested laymen.

slams on his brakes and your adrenals pump as though you had been jumped by a mountain lion, an art director doesn't like what you turned in, you burn your hand on a stove, the neighbor's dog barks day and night. Such are the petty stressors of everyday life. But unless you learn how to counteract their effects on your mind and body you may be setting yourself up for health problems.

The good news about stress is that study after study has shown that stress is far less likely to harm us if we feel in control and have some ways of coping with stress. Specifically, one psychologist at the University of Chicago made a study to determine why some people under a lot of stress became ill while others bearing similar types and amounts of stress stay well over years. The difference she found was a personality characteristic that she called hardiness. Hardy people viewed life and its changes as challenges and chances to learn and develop new potentials—not as things to avoid. These people had a strong sense of commitment to themselves and to their talent. When problems arose, they felt sure of their ability to make the best of a bad situation.

Other studies have shown that stressors affect us less if we feel we have some measure of control. A study of Swedish train commuters demonstrated that commuters who were able to board the train at the beginning of the line, enabling them to get the seats they liked and to arrange their parcels suffered far less stress from commuting than commuters who got on nearer the city, had a shorter ride but couldn't get the seat that they wanted or really exert much control over the situation. What this should say to you is: try to make the best of bad situations when they arise. Even if you can't change much, maybe you can make small symbolic changes that will make you feel better.

EXERCISE

There are several benefits to hard exercise. The ones that are most relevant to a freelancer's needs are (1) protection against stress-induced diseases, (2) increased ability to concentrate and achieve goals, and (3) enhancement of creativity.

PROTECTION AGAINST
STRESS-INDUCED DISEASES

The typical freelancer's life is plagued by ups and downs and uncertainty of all sorts. Such upsets cause corresponding physiological changes as parts of the body's reaction to arousal. It is unfortunate for our health when we do not work off the tension caused by the chemical processes triggered during such arousal.

Exercise is something that I consider almost a miracle cure for just about anything that ails you from depression to procrastination as well as an important way of staying balanced and healthy. As a society, we've become very sedentary. At some point earlier in the century we crossed a line where the stressors of everyday life multiplied more and more rapidly, and we used our bodies less and less, meaning that we had fewer outlets for working off the stress hormones that get churned up in our bodies. As artists, it's important that you not lose the connections between your mind and body, that you stay healthy and energetic to do your work, that you have a reliable way of coping with stress and that you be able to concentrate and create. I am positive that exercise and sports can help you do all these things and more, and more good research is appearing to back up what I have learned for myself over the years.

Being in a constant fight or flight state, mobilized for action, is eventually exhausting to all systems of our bodies. If this sort of stress is kept up day after day without release, we are likely to set ourselves up for disease. It's becoming evident that high blood pressure, heart disease, strokes and ulcers are often already stewing along by our twenties. The right kind of exercise done regularly can help prevent these diseases by giving you an outlet for muscular tension caused by stress and increasing your body's efficiency in using oxygen, thus allowing your heart to work less hard to nourish your cells. And it can lower cholesterol levels and blood pressure. Exercise, if done faithfully, will also help keep your weight under control, which is very important to your health.

The newest thing that is known about exercise is that it causes the release of a class of hormones called endorphins. This group of substances is chemically similar to morphine and occurs naturally in the body. They are like our own built-in pain killers, and their release is associated with highly pleasant feelings. Hard exercise also causes the release of adrenaline which paradoxically, like amphetamine, can make us feel tense and anxious or energetic and happy. Released during times of stress, it has a negative effect. It makes our blood pressure rise and our hearts pound, but released during exercise we're working off the physical effects but still feeling the euphoric psychological side effects. After hard exercise, adrenaline release drops way back. In order to be effective and especially to cause endorphin release, exercise should be aerobic, and you should exercise hard and often. Aerobic exercise is the kind that gets you out of breath and makes your heart and lungs work hard. Combining this with periods of rest and repair conditions us so that our heart and lungs are strong and ultra-efficient at pumping oxygen. Good aerobic exercises are fast walking, running, cycling, rowing, swimming, canoeing and cross-country skiing. Sports like windsurfing, tennis and downhill skiing may help tone your body and release tension which is, of course, beneficial, but you need the sustained oxygen shortage and recovery of the "out-of-breath" sports really to get the benefits of exercise. The key may be that you have to feel some pain or fatigue to get the benefits. It is known that the endorphins are released when there's some pain—when you push past fatigue and get your second wind.

So find some sort of exercise that you like and do it at least three times a week for at least half an hour. I think artists have a tendency to stay cloistered with their work and to feel that hearty exercise somehow doesn't fit their image. I know I certainly felt that way for a long time as my muscles languished, and I became flabby and easily fatigued. Then I started running, and I was amazed at the difference in how I felt after several months of really making that effort to get out there and move.

EXERCISE AS AN AID TO
CONCENTRATION AND CREATIVITY

Exercise in this instance means running, and perhaps other long-distance, individual aerobic sports. Most of the literature on the psychological benefits of exercise discusses running, but there is no reason that walking, skating, canoeing, swimming and other such exercises should not produce the same results. While all exercise can promote cardiovascular fitness, it seems to be the combination of inner quiet and deep breathing over long periods of exercise that produces the psychological benefits.

Some experts claim that the increased ability to concentrate and accomplish what you want is due to the imprinting of goal attainment and success that comes from distance running. Running can be as grueling and as painful as creating artworks. You may even recall that a painter interviewed earlier in this book compared the discipline needed to produce art to that needed to power a runner through a long-distance race. Many times along the way you feel like stopping and giving up, but the rewards are yours if you don't. It is certainly possible that running creates a parallel within your mind to whatever you are trying to do in your work. Once you have established a pattern of pushing yourself beyond the first reproaches of fatigue when you run, you have initiated a behavior which can be applied to your mental work as well.

A New York Academy of Sciences conference concluded by stating that long-distance runners are more stable and more independent than nonrunners. Since stability and independence are so necessary for freelancers, perhaps you really should investigate running as a way of protecting yourself against stress and improving your abilities to function as a freelancer.

Many artists who run feel that it makes them more creative. It has been proposed that this is simply due to the unusually long time runners dwell in their unconscious as they run. While it's difficult to hold problems in your mind as you run, you may find that flashes of insight come to you. It is also possible that problems get turned over to the unconscious, just as they do in sleep, where they are worked on, solved and allowed to resurface in your conscious mind. Some runners who are particularly interested in the meditative, creative aspects of running have developed methods for encouraging this effect. Further information on this subject can be found in the following books:

Glover, Bob, and Sheperd, Jack. *The Runner's Handbook*. Penguin, 1978.

Henderson, Joe. *Long Run*. World Publications, 1976.

Jackson, Ian. *Yoga and the Athlete*. World Publications, 1975.

Kostrubala, Thaddeus. *The Joy of Running*. Lippincott, 1976.

Rohe, Fred. *The Zen of Running*. Random House, 1974.

Spino, Mike. *Beyond Jogging*. Berkley Books, 1976.

BREATHING

The simplest way to control anxiety as it occurs is to breathe deeply. Deep breathing is a way of counteracting the fast shallow breaths of the stress response. By deep breathing, I mean three-part breathing where you inhale from your stomach, letting it swell out as you draw air into every part of your lungs. Breathe in slowly and think about getting air from the tops of your lungs up near your shoulders to the very bottom near the bottom of your rib cage. If you feel a particular area of tension, try to direct the air you are breathing in to go to that place. Hold this nourishing air in and then let it out as slowly as you took it in, letting your stomach muscles push every last bit of air out. Then repeat until you're breathing in a calm, three-point rhythm. As you breathe in, think about all the energy and nourishment that you are taking in; as you breathe out, think of all the tensions exiting your body. No matter what is going on, if you can just mentally step aside and take a few breaths you'll find that you can think more calmly and feel more in control. When we are upset, we are apt to take quick, shallow breaths which don't properly oxygenate our blood, or we don't breathe at all. This can make us feel dizzy and tired. As you do your deep breathing, you might try telling yourself that all your perceptions are really things that you have projected on the world. You can make these perceptions as threatening or as manageable as you choose. This alone won't solve your problems, but it's a good way to change your mind-set and say, "Hey, lighten up!"

I've found singing to be an excellent stress reducer for this same reason: breath control. Singing is both pleasurable and rhythmical, and it forces you to take deep breaths which help rid you of tension.

In any case, do learn how to breathe properly and then practice breathing when things go wrong. It really does work. I used to get very irritated when an actor friend, who first introduced me to this idea, used to urge me to "take a deep breath" when the world was falling apart at my feet. But when I actually began to make these couple of deep breaths part of my response to a stressful situation, I began to see what all those thousands of years of Yogis meant.

MEDITATION

Meditation is another curative and preventive technique of use to freelancers and anyone else who is under pressure. It will help you relax your mind and body and let go of your anxieties.

Many people associate meditation with Eastern religions. Actually, just about every religion, Catholicism included, has some provision for contemplation as a way to self-knowledge. No matter what the foundation of thought behind each type of meditation, the beneficial bodily changes associated with it are pretty much the same. For that reason, I'll base this discussion on Transcendental Meditation or TM, a form of meditation for Westerners developed by the Beatles' friend, the Maharishi Mahesh Yogi. TM is really a revised form of yogic meditation which has eliminated some of the elements of intense concentration and superhuman physical control and is easy to learn. It's probably the most common form of meditation in this country.

Dr. Herbert Benson, a hypertension and heart specialist at the Harvard Medical School, developed his own form of meditation after doing extensive studies on the Maharishi and his followers to see what meditation really did to the body. He found that meditators enter a state where their bodies consume less oxygen almost as though they are hibernating. They produce alpha brain waves which are indicative of deep relaxation. Blood levels of lactate, a substance produced by the muscles, which is associated with anxiety, are lowered. Heart rate and breathing are likewise slowed down. The meditators themselves claimed to have better concentration and discipline, increased physical and mental energy and general centeredness in all aspects of their lives.

Getting into TM nowadays is expensive. It costs a couple of hundred dollars. You have to go to a TM center, have instruction and receive your mantra, a Sanskrit word which supposedly has great meaning for you personally and which you are to intone as you meditate. Dr. Benson was so impressed by TM's benefits that he developed an even more Westernized version which can be learned without paying more than the price of his excellent paperback, *The Relaxation Response*, and without getting tangled up with mantras and incense which some people may shy away from—especially since the sixties are so far in our past.

Of his Relaxation Response (RR), Dr. Benson says: "Our Western society is oriented only in the direction of eliciting the fight or flight response which is repeatedly brought forth as a response to our difficult everyday situations and is elicited without conscious effort. The relaxation response can be evoked only if time is set aside and a conscious effort is made." Dr. Benson feels that the relaxation response is as natural to us as the fight or flight response, that we have the ability to call on it to counteract the effects of fight or flight. It produces the same bodily changes that TM does. It involves sitting quietly in a comfortable position (you don't have to crank yourself into a Lotus position!), closing your eyes and progressively relaxing your muscles from your toes to your face. Then you become aware of your breathing. As you breathe out you silently say to yourself the word *one* or anything else that is simple and soothing. You continue this for ten to twenty minutes. When distracting thoughts come, you don't get upset and you don't dwell on them, just let them float away. Let your mind be passive. Dr. Benson suggests that you practice the RR twice a day, perhaps using it as a substitute for a coffee break. He cautions you not to do this within two hours of a meal, because the digestive process seems to interfere with the RR. The same is true, by the way, of self-hypnosis.

So I think it is possible that meditation in some form offers us more than just health benefits. It may put us on a level of consciousness where we're more open to the magic of synchronicity and the forces that bind the universe together. It's certainly worth a try.

FLOTATION TANKS

It is now possible to float your cares away inside a tank of body-temperature water. These tanks, which are like oversize bathtubs, large enough for you to stretch out in without touching the sides, are designed to put you into a state of sensory deprivation.

Their proponents say that they do everything that meditation does for you and more. They help you relax and tune out your troubles; they help you get a sense of the universe around you; they help you focus and concentrate in daily life.

The tanks are about the size of a double bed so that you have plenty of room to float around freely without continually banging against the sides. The water is at 93.5 degrees which is skin temperature, so you really do lose track of your body boundaries. You are buoyed up by several hundred pounds of dissolved Epsom salts so that you float quite far out of the water with no effort at all. All the tanks I've seen are entered somewhat like tombs. You go down a couple of steps and then close a door behind you. It's very black in there. The one time I floated, I had definite grave fantasies which the manager told me was a common fear of first-timers. So I shut the door and stretched out in the tank, but I really wasn't able to relax completely and derive any great benefit from that first session. My husband, an artist, on the other hand, swears by tanks. No sooner had he lain down than he was off on some trip through the galaxies as a particle of light. When his time was up, he didn't even hear the manager pounding on his door. I thought he had drowned, although they assured me that it was next to impossible to do in that dense water. Finally, they had to go in and actually open up his door and tell him to get out. For the next few days he said he felt distinctly calmer, all stimuli were more intense as though his receptors had been amplified—colors, sounds, smells all came across more strongly.

Many top stress management people say that for certain types of people tanks may be a real answer for stopping smoking, coping with stress and generally being clearer. Floating, like hard aerobic exercise and also like cigarette smoking and other stressors, stimulates endorphin release. Endorphins, as you remember, are those morphine-like substances that our bodies produce in response to pain or stress. That's why hard exercise can often substitute for smoking, because the addictive component in smoking may be those endorphins, and as long as you get them, you don't care whether they come from running or floating or smoking. Unfortunately, many smokers find it so unpleasant to exercise hard enough to achieve this effect that they never really make the substitution. Such people may find that floating works better, because although it provokes endorphin release for some reason, it is also effortless. Also, while endorphins are increased during floating, other stress hormones drop off.

I think tanks are the coming thing. Most cities now have several tank establishments. A hospital in Wisconsin did a study and found that float tanks are helpful in a wide variety of problems: headaches, chronic pain, anxiety, ulcers and heart problems, to name a few. If you want more information on floating or where to do it, you should contact The Flotation Tank Association: (213) 264-7960. Currently, it costs about $15 or $20 a session, which is steep, but the effect is said to last for days, and it's certainly cheaper than other types of therapy. Probably more and more health clubs will be getting tanks as well. Even the Dallas Cowboys and other football teams have gotten them for the deep relaxation of their players.

YOGA

The word Yoga comes from a Sanskrit root that means to join, to concentrate on, to apply. It is an excellent way to integrate the mind and the body and is therefore an excellent method by which freelancers (and everyone else) can reduce the impact of a stressful existence. Hatha Yoga works from the inside out by working on the nervous system, muscles and ligaments. Its purpose is to stretch, strengthen and realign bodies which have become weakened and distorted in response to daily stresses.

Several of the freelancers who contributed to this book were students of Hatha Yoga. I was very impressed with their enthusiasm for this method of harmonizing their minds and bodies. According to them, Yoga, practiced for twenty or thirty minutes each day, can make one feel relaxed yet full of energy and very clearheaded.

Hatha Yoga is taught in many places, from health clubs to religious centers. Be sure to inquire about the teacher's training. Many unqualified instructors throw a few Yoga poses into an exercise routine and call it Yoga, and this won't do you as much good. A knowledgeable teacher will be able to help you much more and will know how to correct your specific problems. It is in this way that your mind and body will derive the fullest benefits from Yoga.

AROMATHERAPY

Aromatherapy—the use of aromatic oils and essences to induce different moods and even to heal—has an ancient history. Recently, however, aromatherapy has come to be studied in more accredited medical circles. Gary Schwartz, MD, professor of psychiatry and psychology at Yale, uses the healing power of scent in the treatment of many diseases and disorders. Of all the scents he has tested to reduce stress, a spicy apple scent seems to work best. In one of his studies, exposure to this fragrance caused his subjects systolic blood pressure (the upper figure) to fall by three to four points.

You might want to experiment with other scents that work for you whether you are trying to lift your spirits (try lavender or peppermint oil) or trying to put yourself to sleep (try rose oil or hops). Small amounts of oils can be added to your bath water, or you can even carry around little vials of scents that you need for various purposes. Certain perfumes can even do the trick. When I am unable to get to sleep in a strange hotel room, I can put myself to sleep just by putting on some Joy, which has a rose oil base.

NUTRITION

The subject of proper nutrition is large enough for several books. Everyone should eat well for maximum performance from themselves, but freelancing as a way of life can affect your diet in several ways. You have chosen one of the most demanding life-styles. You need a great deal of energy and resilience. Your senses have to function at their highest level at all times, and your body must be able to bounce back daily from the stress of freelancing. Optimum nutrition is needed to achieve this. And this requirement is complicated by the fact that many freelancers have cash flow problems and can't afford enormous meals and plenty of supplemental vitamins. Also, many hardworking freelancers don't have a great deal of extra time on a regular basis in which to cook. Bearing all these needs and restrictions in mind, how can freelancers nourish themselves adequately? First, you should understand that the majority of foods manufactured and promoted by the large American food companies passes none of the requirements for nutrition for freelancers. Although it is quick to prepare (in some cases), it is neither nourishing nor inexpensive.

NUTRITION AGAINST STRESS

The basis of eating to counteract stress is avoiding those foods which compound the ill effects and eating those which give back some of the vitamins, minerals and amino acids which the body loses under stress.

Simple carbohydrates such as sugar (sucrose) and glucose are important to avoid. Sugar, which people have been brainwashed to think of as energy food, is not that at all. It causes spikes and drops in your blood sugar level which are associated with sluggishness, fatigue and mood changes. Furthermore, as we have seen, carbohydrates act as a natural sedative, and so eating starches and sugars to excess or eating them at the wrong times is counterproductive if you're facing a long day.

Carbohydrates *are* necessary for energy, but just in a different form. The kind of complex carbohydrates that the body can use without undergoing too violent blood-sugar changes are found in nuts, grains, fruits and some vegetables. These carbohydrates provide a steady supply of energy without provoking the great flood of insulin that causes unstable blood-sugar levels associated with simple sugars.

Salt can compound the ill effects of stress by causing the blood pressure to remain high and thus placing unnecessary strain on the heart, blood vessels and kidneys. It has recently been implicated in premenstrual tension, mood swings and migraines. The typical American diet contains up to twenty times the salt actually required by the body. This is due mostly to the "hidden" salt put in foods as a preservative and flavoring. You might not expect it, but there is excessive salt in cookies, canned soup and frozen macaroni. In many cases, you don't taste a lot of this salt because certain sodium compounds don't taste salty even though they contain more sodium than table salt (sodium chloride). These include monosodium glutamate, sodium benzoate and sodium nitrite (which is also carcinogenic).

You can save a lot of wear on your body and probably prolong your life by cutting out table salt and not eating processed foods except in emergencies. The human need for sodium is very low, and unless you are a nonlacto vegetarian, you don't need any salt added to your food even in hot weather. Your body will take the salt that you require from dairy products, bread, meat and even such vegetables as spinach and kale.

Protein is needed for growth and repair of tissues. As we have seen, the neurotransmitters norepinephrine and dopamine, which give you mental energy and increase alertness, derive from tyrosine, an amino acid found in proteins. Proteins are made of up to twenty-two amino acids, eight of which cannot be synthesized in the body and so must be provided in your diet. Protein is found in eggs, milk, cheese, fish and red meat. Grains, nuts and seeds also contain protein, but in less complete forms. If you decide to get your protein from these sources alone, you should eat proteins which are complementary, i.e., that together provide a more complete protein. Rice and beans and wheat and beans, both food combinations common in poorer countries, are excellent complementary proteins.

Both stress and smoking can drive up your cholesterol levels. Since high cholesterol is associated with atherosclerosis and heart disease, it is desirable to keep your cholesterol level near normal. The most important way to do this is by being active—not by eliminating eggs from your diet. Exercise lowers cholesterol levels while eggs, according to nutritionists Dr. Carl Pfeiffer of the Princeton Brain Bio Center and Dr. Roger Williams of the University of Texas, are not the dangerous source of cholesterol that the Heart Association says they are. However, animal fat such as that found particularly in beef, lamb and pork is an important source of fat and cholesterol overload and should be restricted in your diet. Better choices are veal, chicken and fish.

There is currently much controversy concerning the effects of certain other dietary fats on our cardiovascular health. While it used to be thought that polyunsaturates, such as safflower oil reduced cholesterol levels while monounsaturates, such as olive oil, didn't, now there is evidence that olive oil actually has the more salutory effect on the levels of various fats in our blood. The omega 3 fatty acids found in the flesh of oily fish such as salmon and bluefish is also much touted as a treatment for high cholesterol levels. All these ideas require more analysis, using large numbers of people and following them over time. However, you can steer your way through the maze of conflicting, fluctuating opinions by following these broad suggestions and trying to change the whole way you feed yourself to reflect them.

- De-emphasize red meats to two or three servings per week. Eat more fish, veal, game and poultry.
- Don't feel you have to have some sort of flesh at each meal. A salad made of grains and vegetables can be every bit as filling and both cheaper and healthier.
- Only eat when you're hungry.
- Drink less alcohol (two of anything per day is enough) and more water.
- Eat plenty of roughage in the form of vegetables and fruits and whole grains.
- Cut way back on sweets.
- Savor what you eat and eat it in moderation.

CHEAP NUTRITION

Fortunately, the best nourishment is often not the most expensive. These days, starving people aren't always thin—they're often fat, because the only cheap foods that most people know about are high in salt, sugar and fat. This is particularly noticeable when you have to eat away from home. I have often been in the situation of being on the street with only a dollar in my pocket and frogs in my stomach. And what did I find to eat at that price? Prepackaged cakes, pizza, candy, hot dogs and, only if I was very lucky, yogurt or fruit. If yogurt and fruit are not available, peanuts bought at a candy store are at least high in protein, even though they are also high in fat and salt. Fortunately, more and more different nut and dried-fruit snacks are becoming available at the sort of candy stands you might find in an office building where you are freelancing. But unfortunately these snacks are quite expensive, and the time is in sight when a dollar will not even buy you one bag. If you choose yogurt, try to get the kind that is plain, rather than sitting atop an inch of sugared preserves. Yogurt is not the manna it has been made out to be, but it does provide you with calcium and protein. To be avoided are hot dogs, which are nothing but animal offal stuffed into a length of gut and preserved and flavored with sodium nitrite, a known carcinogen. Cakes and cookies are just empty calories which give you nothing but blood sugar problems and cavities.

SOURCES

The following books are recommended for people who don't have a great deal to spend on food but still want to maintain a delectable and varied diet:

Courter, Gay. *The Bean-Sprout Book*. Fireside, 1977.

Gregory, Dick. *Dick Gregory's Natural Diet for Folks Who Eat: Cooking with Mother Nature*. Harper and Row, 1973.

Lappe, Frances M. *Diet for a Small Planet*. Ballantine Books, 1975. This book is excellent on sources of complementary proteins.

Shurtless, William, and Aoyagi, Akiko. *The Book of Tofu*. Autumn Press, 1975.

Ungerer, Miriam. *Good Cheap Food*. Viking Press, 1972.

WHAT ABOUT FOOD STAMPS?

Food stamps are an example of a program which is ostensibly for the benefit of those who rarely receive its assistance. The program is administered slightly differently in each state. The average per person benefit is currently about $45 per month. For the number of your closest food stamp office call (800) 453-4000; Utah (800) 535-2100; Alaska (800) 982-1500.

CHAPTER TEN
TIME OUT

GETTING TO SLEEP

You must sleep. While it won't harm you to stay up one or even two whole nights in order to make a deadline, this should never become a habit.

Besides the fact that your body must rest in order to repair, it is widely held that the daily descent into the unconscious that occurs when you dream is responsible for much creative thinking, especially for work that is symbolic and deeply in touch with the submerged, collective unconscious that Jung wrote of. In his story "Master Miscry," Truman Capote says, "Dreams are the thoughts of the soul."

As we learn about the action and persistence in the body of most soporifics, it is becoming apparent that these drugs are not optimal sleep drugs. Barbiturates depress the central nervous system and act more to anesthetize you than to induce true sleep. REM sleep, the period of rapid eye movement, is necessary to beneficial rest, and barbiturates inhibit the REM state. Barbiturates also have a synergistic effect with alcohol and are often the object of abuse. More recent and less devastating sleep drugs are minor tranquilizers such as Librium, Valium and their analogue, Dalmane. These drugs are far more satisfactory, but even these can be addictive, and they double in strength in the presence of alcohol.

So, realistically, what are you supposed to do when you've been up for two nights sweating caffeine and your eyelids feel like sandpaper with each faltering blow that they inflict upon your raw corneas? You turn off the light and sink into the comforting embrace of your bedclothes, but you can't get your mind off your deadline, your exhaustion, your fears for the inadequacy of what you have just finished. You lie there awake, unable to stop obsessively ruminating about the job. You catch sight of your clock; the three has just flipped into the hour position, and you sit bolt upright, nearly in tears. You'll be hopeless at nine if you don't sleep, but you'll be a zombie if you take a sleeping pill this close to the morning. Five and a half hours' sleep is what you need. Here is how to get it naturally:

Baths. There are several recipes for aquatic soporifics that have been imparted to me. The first I owe to Dr. Karen Dorros: sit on an expendable stool or chair* in the shower and run the water as hot and hard as you can comfortably

---

*Remember not to use one whose joints are glued together, or it may collapse in the humidity.

bear it. The heat of the water forces your muscles to relax. Remain there for twenty minutes, then go from the shower directly to bed.

In her very useful book, *You Are Not the Target*, Laura Archera Huxley, who is Aldous Huxley's widow, gives a recipe for a sleep-inducing bath. In her version, you have a long, warm soak, with your night garment handy in the bathroom. Upon completion of the bath, you rise from the tub, dress yourself in the night garment without drying off, dash headlong into the bedroom and slide between soothing, dry sheets and plenty of blankets. Hold these tightly up to your chin to avoid a chill. The next thing you'll know it will be morning, and you'll awaken dry and refreshed. This works because your circulation rises to dry you, and when your blood is drawn from your head to your body you feel drowsy. For further exercises to help put you to sleep, see her book (Avon Books, 1976).

Drinks. The next class of readily available soporifics is sleep-inducing beverages. They include the following:

Camomile tea, or Celestial Seasonings' Sleepytime tea

Hot Ovaltine, or hot skimmed milk with honey and cinnamon. This is not just an old wives' remedy. It works because of the high amount of L-tryptophan in these drinks (while it is not yet known why it puts you to sleep, L-tryptophan is the amino acid precursor to serotonin, the brain transmitter associated with sleep).

Nonprescription pills. The two best sedative substances are both sold over the counter, seem to be free of side effects and are actually nutritive. One, inositol, is a B-vitamin; the other, L-tryptophan, is an amino acid which occurs naturally in the brain. They should be available at any health food store or drugstore which carries an extensive range of vitamins. Both L-tryptophan and inositol are useful in relieving anxiety and can often serve well instead of Valium. They will induce deep, refreshing sleep, but dreaming is unaffected and you awaken feeling alert and ready to face the day. (See also Aromatherapy, page 143.)

VACATIONS

Many freelancers never know when to take a vacation. This is because many of them can't separate their work from their lives, since their work is what they like to do best. We were brought up to believe that work is supposed to be a drag, and when it isn't we keep wondering whether we are working enough. Others tell you how easy your work is compared with theirs, and you feel guilty even to be contemplating a vacation.

What those others don't know is that the freelance life-style takes a physical and emotional toll that you may not even be aware of until you get away somewhere and realize how much unraveling has to be done before you are really unwound. As one freelancer says, "It's all coming from your own energy. Whatever is going to come in is going to be the result of what you put out. If you stop putting out you'll starve."

This situation is clearly very different from that of the employee, who can often dawdle and put out very little without starving. He is only a cog; you are the whole wheel, and the motor and the rest of the machinery as well. The typical freelancer has all the woes of a banker, a lawyer, a debtor and a hard laborer—on top of the struggle to think and create. While this is possible, it requires far more energy and adaptation than anyone, including you, realizes. You, more than any employee, need your vacation.

Looking at it from a strictly practical point of view, you won't even be able to maintain your efficiency if you can't let yourself take a deserved and needed vacation. Vacations serve the function of giving you breathing space and the opportunity to stand back from your work and perhaps be more objective about what needs to be done than you would be if you just kept on slogging away relentlessly. While this may seem dedicated, it is the sort of dedication that is out of place once you leave university—and even there it doesn't always get you as far as you think it will, and for the same reason. People who can't look at their work through both ends of the telescope are not as likely to do worthwhile work as those who have the discipline to concentrate while they are working, but who can also let fresh breezes blow through their brains. So many of the great breakthroughs in science and art have come during these periods of standing back, when the unconscious has hold of the problem but the conscious mind is doing something unrelated, just daydreaming perhaps. This concept is one you will come across in many forms; *reculer pour mieux sauter*, Buddha going into the desert, Arnold Toynbee's "withdrawal and return." You can also just call it a vacation and let your mind use the time as it needs to.

The need for frequent short vacations is one that I was aware of in my own case, and I was extremely heartened to have this instinct corroborated for me by so many of the freelancers I spoke to:

When you get the most frustrated it is time to take the day off. Go back to it fresh.   *—Photographer*

Sometimes you really have to go off—preferably alone—and let the silence descend. After you've done that long enough, suddenly everything becomes clear, and the right way to do whatever you were stymied by before just appears fully formed in your mind. I've found that distance is the best editor. It helps you let go and be objective enough to make changes that only weeks before tore you apart.   *—Novelist*

CHEAP VACATIONS FOR FREELANCERS

How many times have you wished that you could just find a little country rooming house, or what's known in the British Isles as a bed-and-breakfast? The available guides to country inns tend to focus mainly on chic little gems, many of which are beyond your budget (though not always, if you go off-season). Now, Nancy and Jon Kugelman, a couple from Hartford, Connecticut, have reintroduced the small U.S. tourist home as a friendly, inexpensive solution for people who want to take a cheap vacation without sleeping in a tent.

Rooms at the establishments they list usually cost $10 to $20, and for a few dollars more, you can get breakfast. Accommodations are simple—the bathroom is down the hall, and the beds may not be exactly "posturepedic"—but these little places tend to be clean and cheerful. The Kugelmans' directory includes 1,262 tourist homes in the East, South, Midwest and Canada. It is called *Sleep Cheap* and is available from McBride Publishers, 157 Sisson Avenue, Hartford, CT 06105; (203) 523-1622.

One way to get cheap airfare is by hooking up with one of the smaller courier companies that don't have their own fleets of planes and instead use individual freelancers traveling on commercial flights. You generally have to let the courier company use part or all of your baggage allowance, but they also pay at least 50 percent and sometimes 100 percent of your round-trip fare. You merely drop off your package on arrival at your destination airport.

You can find out about traveling this way by writing Stratus Transportation (P.O. Box 8235, San Francisco International Airport, San Francisco, CA 94128: [800] 872-8700) or Archer Courier Systems (855 Avenue of the Americas, New York, NY 10001: [212] 563-8899). Sandman Express of Los Angeles acts as a referral service for members who frequently travel this way: (213) 397-8100. You can also find air courier companies in the Yellow Pages.

You might also consider joining a discount travel club for an annual fee of $35 to $50. These sell unsold space on airplanes, ships and hotels at enormous savings—sometimes as much as 70 percent off full fare. You generally have to leave soon after booking; supplies are limited; and tickets aren't usually refundable. Still, the savings may be well worth these limitations. For further information try:

Encore:
(800) 638-0930.

Vacations to Go:
(800) 624-7338.

Stand Buys
311 West Superior Street
Chicago, IL 60610
(312) 943-5737

If you have a nice dwelling that you'd be willing to swap, contact Holiday Exchange (P.O. Box 878, Belen, NM 87002).

CHAPTER ELEVEN

FREELANCING AND YOUR RELATIONSHIPS

As in just about every other realm, freelancers (and those who love them) are confronted by problems peculiar to their way of life as well as by all the usual romantic problems. This is not to say that freelancers have double the romantic problems of employees. In fact, freelancing by one or both partners can enhance certain relationships, depending upon the individual situations. For instance, some freelancers may have an advantage in their more flexible schedules or greater free time. In some cases busy freelancers find partners who also need a great deal of time away from the relationship and are quite content with the freelancer's long hours. On the other hand, the partner who needs a lot of contact may find the presence of the freelancer at home all the time reassuring, and some freelancers may work better with a loved one close by. In other words, there are many ways of looking at it all.

However, there are some common issues that freelancers should be aware of beforehand so that they can work them out fairly when and if they arise.

RELATIONSHIP PROBLEMS COMMON TO FREELANCERS

WORK VS. LOVE

Anyone who has tried knows how tough it can be to strike a balance between work and love. One often feels that when work is going well one either doesn't need love or it doesn't work out. Conversely, when love is going well, work often goes to hell in a hat for its duration. A balance can be achieved, but the mercurial nature of artisitc work itself means that this balance will always be shifting.

An artist's more intimate connection to her work (as compared with a non-artist) is a fact that both people should be aware of. This can be threatening to partners who are jealous or who like their work but aren't in love with it and can't understand why you are with yours. Sometimes you will be misread as cold, because your work gives you so much that you appear to have less need of a relationship than others. As Otto Rank said in *Art and Artist* in a chapter entitled "The Artist's Fight with Art," "His calling is not a means of livelihood, but life itself . . . He does not practice his calling but *is* it."*

*Otto Rank, *Art and Artist* (New York: Tudor Publishing, 1932), p. 386.

Most freelancers, even commercial artists not so deeply tied to their work, have times when they have to pull their heads into their shells and focus only on their job. Tired freelancers working against deadlines are not the most personable creatures. They can be cranky, withdrawn, hostile, paranoid or simply exhausted. Some drone on at every opportunity about the difficulties they are having. Others refuse to communicate at all.

Other freelancers may be more understanding in such situations, although you hear equally often of ones who choose just such times to throw a scene. Particularly between partners who work in the same area there can be a lot of subtle undermining going on. Competition and professional jealousy can be devastating to two people who love one another. Professional counseling may be needed to keep jealousy from destroying the relationship.

Naturally, needs shift in relationships. You who spend fifteen hours a day painting and think you're complete may need a shoulder to cry on during a crisis not related to your work. It is possible to become so involved with your work that you feel you don't need anything else. Many relationships have been thrown away thanks to this belief. Sometimes it's true, but often artists realize too late that they cannot bear to live an unshared life, even though the alternative complicates their work. A painting is only fair comfort at your father's funeral. Two published books may not make up for a life with no children. Therefore, it usually ends up that you have to balance love and work, shifting continually to give both yourself and your partner a fair deal.

Here are some of the problems you may have to confront:

Time problems. The time squeeze for freelancers can be as bad as that for doctors, with none of the financial rewards guaranteed. And nothing can be as hard on a relationship as chronically spending too little time together, not talking enough and often not making love enough due to exhaustion. The beginning freelancer may be grossly overworked. Often the only way to stay alive is to take on two or more projects, meaning that eighteen hours a day and weekends are full.

Again, communication is important. If your partner can be made to understand how important the work is to you and to know that some day you expect to be more relaxed, he will be more willing to stick it out. It is hard for some people to sit by every night while you work or to always go to parties alone, and you should acknowledge this.

You must also come to an understanding about your responsibilities to your home if you are married or live together. Few women anymore are content to pander to irascible artistic geniuses who are too intense to help with the housework. Sometimes, when a big push is on in your work, it is permissible to let your responsibilities slide, but in general you must find a way to do your share of housework, child care or grounds maintenance. Your partner should never have to pay for your being a freelancer by taking on all the domestic work.

It's a good idea to allow a few days between jobs in which you can become reacquainted. Working under the pressure of a deadline or being in a show for weeks can pull you further apart than you'd like to think. It's preferable not to go on to the next project without having a little undiluted time together.

Living, loving and working in a small space. Another complication that freelancing can bring to your romantic life is the problem of being unable to separate your work from the rest of your life. This does not have to be so difficult to solve if one of you leaves the house for a set period every day, or if the freelancer has a truly separate work space, or if you live apart.

What is most important in any case is that your partner realize when to back off and ignore your existence, so that you do not feel quite so pressured by having all the important parts of your life together under the same roof.

If I'm working, there is an area of me that is sated, so I'm not as needful of people to fill me. I don't have the feeling of "Oh, God, I'm not working, so you've got to be more than what you are to me." I'm much easier to be with when I'm working. There are also times when you have to do your homework and you really have to cut off. If I'm living with a man it's cut-off time in the relationship. He can only get so much of my attention, and not the full picture. But, for me to be able to go through my own work process and get fulfillment from what I'm doing makes me a fuller person.
—Actress

Freelancing has improved my relationship with my wife—with a bit of scheduling just so we all know when we can be together and when Daddy is working. My being home attending the house while the kids are in school has enabled my wife to go back to school, and somehow I feel more like a father—participating in almost every part of my family's life—than I did when all I was was just a tired person who was at home for seven or eight hours and usually fagged out on the bed. —Cartoonist

One of your greatest resources is time. When you have two freelancers under the same roof, this may become one of your greatest problems. My wife is a freelance writer and also likes to play the guitar. These activities take time. We also have a child and another on the way. This parenting stuff really takes time! An agreement necessarily has to take place in order to make the arrangement work. Only commitment to each other totally and unconditionally can work. I get excited when my wife writes, because I believe in her work, but this means that I may have to take care of our daughter for a number of days so that my wife can work undisturbed. Naturally, this means that my plans are back-burnered for a while, which can crimp my deadline time and force me to work later hours. All in all, I think it is worth the sacrifice of my time, since I believe in my wife's work as she believes in mine.

The important thing to remember is that these agreements must be made ahead of time or you will have a volatile situation on your hands. Our primary commitment is to each other and our family first. Everything else gets second billing, including careers. This actually produces a kind of security in our home for all the parties involved. Nothing will get in the way of our relationship. —Commercial Artist

I think writers should either live with people who are willing to cater to them and understand exactly how to, or else they should live with another

writer who at least understands the pain of being a writer. Though, if your novel gets published first, look out! —*Writer*

Erratic schedules make relationships more difficult. Actors tend to flock together, because most people don't understand what they go through, especially during those long periods of unemployment. Normal, well-adjusted people should stay away from actors and they know that. I remember talking to a guy in a bar and after I told him what I did he said, "God, you're beautiful, but I can't even talk to you because you're an actress." And he turned away from me. I understood that he obviously had real life experience with performers. Either they can't give, or sometimes when they're giving a lot you wish they'd shut up and not pull their performing seal routine on you. —*Actress*

It's very dangerous to have affairs with other freelancers. It's very dangerous. In fact, I don't do it if I can avoid it. It takes all your time. The people I'm seeing now all have to be at work at nine o'clock; which is great, because either they're all out of here, or I have to be out of their house early. You know what happens if you sleep with other freelancers: you make breakfast and lie around half the morning with the papers. The only problem is the occasional resentment on the part of those who have to go to work—because they think that what writers do is easy. —*Screenwriter-Lyricist*

Going on the road. Sooner or later most performers or technicians have to go on the road, and this can play havoc with those you leave behind unless they are prepared for it. If the person left behind is overly dependent, your going on the road can be a traumatic, angering event. On the other hand, more independent and trusting people can view their partner's going on the road as an opportunity to have some time alone.

Men I talked to usually seemed more secure about going on the road than did women. None of the men I questioned said he would give up a tour because of family or romantic reasons unless it was a question of acute illness or a child's graduation. Women, on the other hand, were far more likely to forego a tour in order to keep a man. Needless to say, the kind of person who is always making you feel guilty for leaving on tour may be the wrong person for a performer to be with. Male or female, they usually have pretty much the same views on it.

The minute you mention the phrase "going on the road" all some people can think of is you lying in bed in a dingy hotel room with another member of the company or crew (to whom you supposedly have unlimited access) nestled against you. To these people, every little bus and truck tour of New England conjures up lurid visions of Mick Jagger acrawl with females. Still, it isn't completely in their heads. It's well known that musicians don't have to be Mick Jagger to attract hordes of women, and that pretty female thespians get propositioned, but it is only in the absence of trust and reassurance by you that fears of these sirens and satyrs really persist.

Sometimes another difficulty in the eyes of the stay-behind is *their* sex life. They may resent your leaving them high and dry to go (as they view it) on an extended party across America. Or they may be threatened mainly by the loss of support and communication.

It's not your fault that your work requires you to go on the road, so don't feel guilty, but do try to empathize. Your partner's feelings should be easy to understand, and they can certainly be allayed if you are just willing to talk them out and assure your partner of her or his place in your life. A secure, trusting relationship should be able to survive one person's going on the road if that is how he makes a living. There are steps you can take to make this whole experience less traumatic:

Shared expenses. First of all, discuss the arrangements for your shared living quarters, if any. Will you continue to pay your share of the expenses? (I believe in agreeing on this issue on paper at the time you sign the lease if one or both of you will go on the road for extended periods.) Unless you have made arrangements to the contrary which cause no financial hardship to your partner, you probably should continue to pay your share of the rent or mortgage, but not utilities. You should split your phone calls back and forth. Touring companies and some regional gigs aren't always fabulously well paid, and you may not be able to pay your share from your salary. If your partner is willing, could you sublet part of your present quarters, or could you rent it to someone as a half-day work space? If your partner doesn't take to this, and you live in an intimate space, you would be unfair to insist. You may have to borrow some money to cover your costs. An understanding partner with flexible finances might be willing to contribute more temporarily.

Another expense may be the cost of child care during the hours when you would normally do this. If the person going on tour can pay for his substitute, he should. Otherwise, both parents should chip in for some sort of day care or baby-sitter when needed.

Staying in touch. You can also reassure your partner by discussing beforehand how you can keep in contact. You should give the other person the most complete itinerary you can, with addresses and phone numbers, even if you end up doing the major part of the telephoning whenever you have the time. It always makes the person left behind feel more secure if he knows he can contact you in an emergency.

You should ascertain whether there's any way the other person can join you for part of the time. Can he get a vacation? Is there room for another traveler on the tour? The thought of being able to spend a day off or a few days on the road together may make your partner feel less dismal.

Here are the comments of some freelancers and their partners with regard to going on the road. As you can see, some of them found successful ways to cope with touring, while others didn't talk it out and were sorry:

I guess I didn't realize how much the whole idea of the tour upset her until I came back a month later and found that she hadn't been home for a week, because she had left me and moved in with some friends. I just didn't think about it at the time. I was having a great time hanging out with the band. I

*could have gone to see her on a couple of weekends, but somehow I didn't.
I guess I just never expected her to leave.* —Musician

*His going on the road used to be the thing I dreaded the most. I remember
once even tearing a page out of* Backstage *because it had a casting call for a
nine-month tour of his favorite play. I felt terribly ashamed, but we were
young, and I was afraid to be left alone, afraid he'd find some amoral little
actress, and afraid he was so anxious to go out on the road because he didn't
love me. But finally one day it did happen; he got a part on a three-month
tour of the West Coast. I cried for half a day and then we sat down and
talked. We made a deal that we would talk on the telephone every few days
and write, and that I'd come out for the last two weeks and we'd drive
home.*

   *I found that I got on fine without him, although I was about as sad as
I've ever been during those first couple of days. Each subsequent tour gave
me confidence, and now I look forward to his getting a seven-week job at a
dinner theater in Alabama.* —Wife of Actor-Director

*I couldn't understand his tours. He never tried to make it work for us. He
got mad that I got upset, but he never said anything except, "This is what
my life is. My music means more to me than you do. You'd better get used
to it, because I'd ideally like to be on the road half the year." Never did he
say that we could make arrangements to see one another, to talk, to write.
So I figured, "Well, I can't live like this, never knowing when he'll just split
and expect me to understand." So I left him.* —Drummer's Ex-girlfriend

   Never forget that your work imposes upon your partner's life more than just
about any other type of work would do—often with little financial reward. It
takes a resourceful, independent person to cope with your life-style. If you are
lucky enough to find such a person, remember that the tougher the going gets
for you, the tougher it gets for her. There's no need to feel guilty, but there
is room to be grateful to the person who shares your life as a freelancer.

   Although the main orientation of this chapter has been romantic relationships, freelancers should realize that their work can impose a strain on their
platonic and even their business relationships too. Most of the advice given to
help you maintain romantic relationships can be applied to these parts of your
life as well.

   Friends need to be clued in about your work and your schedules. After you
have slammed down the phone for the fifth time because a friend called during
your practice or your work time, she may become unsure of when to try to
reach you and may cease trying. Let people know what your general work
hours are, and be sure to let them know when your work is going to prevent
your socializing for an extended period. Friends often feel dropped if you don't
keep in touch, but they will be less likely to if you've warned them about your
deadline. Your friends are important. They need not become the enemies of
your work.

CHAPTER TWELVE
THE FREELANCER PARENT

Freelancing and parenting are two enormous jobs. Many who haven't tried it mistakenly assume that freelancing during a child's preschool years is less grueling than working away from home at a steady job. As any serious freelancer who has tried it knows working odd hours at home is about the most difficult thing for a parent to do when there are young children to be cared for at the same time. Freelancing on top of being a parent is probably the most demanding combination of jobs there is. There are few parents alive today who wouldn't agree that parenting is a hard job—often a joy, but also a job, and freelancing is two jobs: getting the work and then doing it.

This chapter is addressed to *parents*—not just to mothers. In many households only one of the parents works freelance at home, and increasingly often it is the freelancer father who tends the children while the mother works elsewhere and may even be the principal breadwinner. Pediatric literature in general has been directed toward the stay-at-home mother, with little credit given to the father and his capabilities and problems as an active parent. I intend this chapter as a guide to how to juggle these several jobs and how to cope with the typical problems that arise for freelance parents. While some of the problems are common to both sexes, fathers and mothers also face some different sets of problems in their duties as freelancers and parents.

It can be the best of both worlds when both parents are freelancers with flexible hours. This way each parent can have a really good chunk of uninterrupted work time every day without feeling a moment's guilt about leaving the child in uncaring or incompetent hands. It gives the child the benefit of a close observance of both sexes performing both their nurturing and their productive roles, and it allows both parents to develop fully as parents and as freelancers. The major snags come, as in so many situations, with a lack of income or at least cash flow. Although this certainly doesn't *have* to change anything, it can lead to everybody's being cooped up in too small a space or to a lack of mobility. However, in this case, stressful as it can become with two freelancers pushing themselves to produce and coping with children, it is certainly the cheapest child-care arrangement.

Most often, the father is an employee, and the freelancer mother is left to care for the children, the house, and somehow do her work. But increasingly, the mother works elsewhere, and the father minds the nest and does his work from home. Here are some of the major complaints of stuck-at-home freelance parents of both sexes. In some cases, mothers and fathers have different views of the same problem. They have each contributed to the solutions presented here.

PROBLEMS AND SOLUTIONS

GUILT

Any psychiatrist will tell you that guilt is the major problem of all working mothers, except those whose income is essential to the support of the family. But guilt is even stronger for freelance mothers, because, as Dr. Ruth Moulton of the William Alanson White Institute says, "The family of the woman who is a psychiatrist or lawyer or artist knows she's doing it because she *enjoys* that kind of work. The woman who takes a job because she needs money . . . is not nearly as likely to be *blamed* for working. She will feel less guilty about her job and in some ways is freer than the professional woman, who may feel terribly guilty about not being with her children all day."

Guilt arises for some from breaking out of the traditional role and perhaps neglecting some essential aspect of the children's lives in the process. This is not just the guilt that derives from not being with the child. Rather, it is the guilt which comes with insisting on independence in a society where independent women are still seen as a threat. Though it is difficult to make a single woman feel guilty about this nowadays, it is still easy to press those buttons to keep young mothers in line.

The duty of providing for the family is a male tradition that binds freelance fathers as much as antiworking sentiments do mothers. One musician said, "One night I looked into our baby's eyes and I thought to myself, 'What are you thinking about, man, gigging for free with this helpless baby depending on you?' "

Most stereotypes are built around a grain of truth, and certainly the negligent working mother and libertine artist father do exist as parents of unfortunate children. But truly most parents don't fit these images and shouldn't have to shoulder the guilt more properly directed at a few bad eggs. The only answer is to keep reminding yourself that your guilt is due to your failing to live up to prejudices dreamed up by unenlightened, outdated people with nothing better to do. It is possible to arrive at creative solutions for child rearing, and in situations where this is done with sensitivity towards the children, they can greatly profit from something other than the prescribed "Father Knows Best" approach that is commonly held up.

ISOLATION

Parents of either sex who care for children at home feel isolated during the early years of their children's lives. This is true even of nonworking mothers who are isolated from coffee klatches and shopping sprees. It is intensified for men and women who are used to going out and interacting with the work world in their field. Such parents, when they are shut in with a demanding, babbling two-year-old, often become frustrated because of their isolation from their colleagues and the lack of intellectual stimulation. They become anxious that they are being left behind during their sabbatical. Since freelancing is a business of personal contacts, parents who are stuck at home become doubly frustrated unless they develop some plan for coping with the situation.

The best way to avoid the frustrations of being cooped up with a young child is to be aware of the situation and decide how to cope with it before you have the baby. Basically, your choices are to accept isolation and use it constructively or to refuse it altogether. Some parents refuse to be isolated from their careers and decide to leave even very young babies in ancillary hands. While some experts deplore this, others say that a young baby needs someone, preferably the same person, to interact with all the time, but that this person doesn't necessarily have to be the natural mother or father. It just has to be a nurturing, responsive human. This could equally be a grandparent, or a baby-sitter of some sort. What is important is that the person be enthusiastic about the baby. With this sort of setup you are more likely to want to cuddle the baby after work than throw it at the wall as you might if you were chained to its side all day long. (I will discuss some of the possibilities for child care further along.)

One mother told me of a group of other artist mothers which meets at a set time and a set place where no one has to play hostess, so that its members can talk about the problems of being a woman and an artist. Such a support group goes a long way toward ending the isolation of being a mother and an artist. You may be able to organize or join a similar one. You'd be surprised at how many others may be itching to talk over the problems of melding the two jobs of parenting and freelancing. You may already know plenty of others in your boat who would be interested in joining a group with these objectives. If not, try contacting an arts council in your area for the names of other parent-freelancers. Another way to reach potential group members is to advertise in the publications of any professional associations to which you might belong.

PRIVACY

Lack of privacy can be one of the most pressing problems to the parent who works at home. It is very difficult to put across to young children that just because you don't leave the house to go to work doesn't mean that your work is any the less important. It is even harder to communicate to the children that even though their parent is sitting in a corner of the living room, he can't be bothered during certain hours.

Getting privacy in which to work is extremely difficult if you are broke, because generally it involves having a large enough living space for you to be able to isolate yourself and have the children cared for in some other part of the house where their cries are inaudible to you. But while it is absolutely necessary that you have a work area to call your own, even if it's just a closet (see the section Home or Outside Work Space? in chapter 3), you must understand that when you are home alone with the children and wish to work, your privacy cannot be total. Like it or not, you have to be close enough to hear an infant's cries or the sounds of a hurt child. The only alternative is to arrange for an outside studio plus child care or to place the child in some sort of child care outside the home. In any case, these alternatives require having money at a time when you quite possibly don't have enough to spare.

Another way of handling the privacy problem is to give it up altogether during certain hours, or even to adapt to working with a mild level of childish activity. I must stress that only parents with temperaments considerably more placid than mine can manage this. It is unrealistic to expect that everyone can handle it. If you are an artist, you may be able to interest your child in doing what you do. Children love to imitate their parents. Try bringing your crayons, paints or clay and letting them sit with you as you work. Children who are really drawn into such activities are capable of sustained, quiet concentration if given half a chance.

If you need more privacy than this, one way in which you might get it is by making rules in advance that you are never to be disturbed when you are working. One mother said that she had been able to make this concept more meaningful to her ten-year-old by extending the same privilege to her. No matter how you try to do it, the principle of "do not disturb" is a hard one to teach to children. Naturally, it is far easier when someone else is caring for the child and can handle most of the child's needs himself. One writer made a rule that she was only to be disturbed at five minutes to each hour, except in emergencies. She admits that this rule isn't always heeded, but she feels that it has lessened her children's resentment of her work.

Another way to get privacy for your work is to do it during hours when everyone else is sleeping—either after dinner if the children are young enough to go to bed early, or early in the morning. A schedule like this can be grueling unless your partner is willing to pull his own weight. In effect, it means that you are working a double shift every day.

EXHAUSTION

Freelancing and parenting are, separately, two of the most demanding jobs. Combined, they are staggering. As one painter said, "You do it because you have a very strong desire, but you're not aware of the toll. Most people deny the amount of energy that is required, and they don't realize until later how drained they are."

Some exhaustion is inevitable, particularly when the children are babies and you must get up ever four hours to feed them. It's wise, for the mother's health at this stage, to go slow on freelancing, so that there is not a major confluence of deadlines and 2 A.M. feedings. Preferably, as you wean the baby, you should begin to resume your normal freelancing schedule. Fathers who freelance during these early months have it less bad, since their bodies are not subjected to the exhaustion that often accompanies nursing. But even they will probably not totally escape being woken up in the night and being on call during their work hours. Freelancer fathers can alleviate the strain of this grueling schedule by having some definite work hours when they are not on call. Most mothers have difficulty relinquishing responsibility at this time, but those who wish to work seriously must learn how to do so. This may be accomplished by paying someone to come in during your work hours or by working at a time when your husband can take charge. What is important is that you have a break. In this way it is possible to prevent the extreme stress and exhaustion of caring for an infant plus splitting your concentration between him and your work.

As the child grows older, your problems are reduced in some ways: you tend to worry less about him; if you're a woman, your body isn't exhausted from nursing; and other helpers can begin to play a more significant child-care role.

Naturally, if you can afford outside help, you won't have to shoulder two jobs quite as fully, but if this isn't economically feasible, here are some things to consider to help reduce exhaustion:

- Lower some of your standards. You can't be Superparent, Superfreelancer *and* Superhousekeeper. Settle for a slightly dirty house, let the children sleep in sleeping bags, eat less complicated meals.
- Let your children help out. It's not exploitative to let children pull some of their own weight. If you can accept their best efforts and not be over-critical, children can help you wash dishes, sweep, vacuum, prepare vegetables and feed the animals.
- Older children should be allowed to take more responsibility for their lives. Give them clocks and put *them* in charge of getting themselves up for school. Show them how to run the washer, cook breakfast or care for the pets. It will take a lot of the pressure off you, and they will be more competent adults for it.
- Plan your time better by choosing your priorities. Do you really have time to be in the PTA? Let some other mother who isn't finishing a book do it. Try not to let anyone make you feel guilty for weeding out lower priorities. They may not know what it's really like to care about their work.
- Make sure that at least part of your work time is completely uninterrupted. Even if you have to stay up late or arise at dawn, it's still less strain than always doing two things at once.
- Make sure to eat well and get plenty of exercise (see the sections on Exercise in chapters 8 and 9).
- If possible, have one totally free day every week, or at least every two weeks.

FATHERING

Husbands of freelance mothers have to do more than just be verbally encouraging. They have to make sacrifices and take care of themselves and their children more than the average father does. A good husband is perhaps the single most important factor making it possible for a mother to freelance. Husbands who grew up expecting to be taken care of by women are positively *dangerous* to women artists.

One of the main reasons that many fathers do not pull their own weight is that our society does not value a father's participation in the rearing of his children except as the breadwinner. Men are so often painted as incompetent with babies and children that this belief has become deeply ingrained. Doctors, schools, the family—all tend to consider the mother as the primary parent. Then of course there are the stupid prejudices that nurturing men are somehow not "masculine." Yet a study by Drs. Greenberg and Morris* revealed that most men are innately nurturing and that this potential can be released with enough exposure to a baby. They found that fathers as well as mothers demonstrate a strong bonding with their infants.

So don't be swayed by the prejudice that your husband can't and thus won't assume some real responsibility for the children. You must be willing to teach him what to do and to be patient at first. Men are not geared to assuming major child-care responsibility, but many men can make up for this.

You must never lose sight of the fact that a baby is the equal responsibility of both of you. Just "helping out" isn't enough. In a strong, supportive relationship, your husband should be willing to take equal responsibility so that you have time to devote to your work just as he does to his.

CHILD CARE

The hardest part of trying to freelance at home when you don't have much money is arranging child care of some sort to allow you the time to do your work. Even if you are not completely destitute, finding a child-care solution that you feel comfortable with is not always easy. Cheap and super-reliable child care is essential for freelancing parents, but unfortunately our society has not yet advanced very far in the realm of national day care of some sort.

Here is a compendium of some of the most workable inexpensive methods:

DAY-CARE CENTERS

What day care does exist in the United States is of two sorts: private within a licensed or unlicensed mother's home, and either privately or publicly run in a center.

Family day-care centers in individual homes are not usually well thought of. They consist of a mother or other untrained person taking care of up to six children in a home. Most of the centers are unlicensed, and the facilities are usually nil. The "program" generally is centered around naps, snacks and television. This is not to say that all such centers should be avoided at all costs. If it's all that is available to you, you may decide that it's better than nothing— at least until you can get enough work to pay for something better. And not every at-home day-care center is substandard. If the person in charge is known to you, this may be an excellent solution. Particularly in rural areas where individual enterprise is the main subsistence, you may find some very qualified women (or men), some even with relevant training, running such a service from home. In cities, though, beware. There have been chilling reports of addict mothers and health and safety violations at these places.

*Martin Greenberg, M.D., and Norman Morris, M.D., "Engrossment: The Newborn's Impact Upon the Father," *The American Journal of Orthopsychiatry*, Volume 44, Issue #4, July, 1944.

Public day-care centers are usually funded, licensed and run by either the state or city department of health or welfare. Typically they are housed in churches, public schools or other public buildings. The staff is usually adequate to excellent, and children receive quality attention and nutritious meals. The fee is usually nominal or nonexistent. You should be able to get a listing of centers in your neighborhood by contacting one of the above-mentioned agencies in your state or city.

There are also licensed, private day-care centers of all sorts and degrees of quality. Usually these have trained, competent professional on the staff, sufficient equipment, materials and play space and nutritious meals. If you are lucky, you will be able to locate one where the hours that your child spends there will be enriching and contribute vastly to his socialization and emotional growth.

But you must view *all* centers carefully. Some of the best centers may look like sloppy, chaotic places until you investigate further and find a warm, responsive staff backed by a group of involved parents. Other centers may have wonderful facilities but provide no more than regimented custodial care, with little thought as to bringing along the individual child according to his needs. This sort of attitude may particularly be a problem at one of the large, chain day-care centers such as Kindercare, Alphabetland, etc.

Finding the right day-care center is essential to your child's success with it. Here are some important considerations to bear in mind when choosing one.

- Are the hours suitable? Some centers provide half-day care; others allow you to drop the child off only when you need to rather than at a set time every day.
- Can you afford the program?
- Is the atmosphere one that your child could be happy in: neither bedlam nor overly suppressed?
- Do the staff members respond to the children, or only to the parents? Is there such a turnover that children can't establish a bond with the same person over a long period?
- Do the other children seem interested and involved in their activities, or have they merely been disciplined into submission?
- Are there sufficient supplies and play equipment for the children? Are these things of a type that encourages exploration and creativity?
- Is the center run as a business? If so, are corners cut to widen the profit margin? Is parental involvement encouraged?

Once you have answered these questions to your satisfaction on visits without your child, take her along and get her opinion. Spend an hour or two there together—perhaps at different times of day. Sometimes a child will be able to sense things about the other children's level of contentment that you might not pick up. Of course, some children are dead set against leaving home under any circumstances, and then you must decide whether to push or to seek an alternative. In any case, make your child understand that you are always open to discussion if things are not working out happily. When children know they aren't trapped, they tend to be more open to new situations.

CO-OPS

Co-ops exist at all levels, ranging from a small group of mothers taking turns providing day care in their homes to a larger group which pools its resources and rents a facility and hires a staff. In the former case, each set of parents must be on duty for a few days every week or two.

If you are interested in organizing a co-op, here are some sources which may be helpful in this endeavor: The Women's Action Alliance (370 Lexington Avenue, New York, NY 10017; [212] 532-8330) will send you their information kit, "How to Organize a Child Care Center." The Bank Street College of Education (610 West 112th Street, New York, NY 10025; [212] 663-7200) offers a consultation service and information on setting up a child-care center.

BABY-SITTING POOLS

Sitting pools serve less for day care on a regular basis than for special-occasion baby-sitting. A group of parents will usually form one, each parent taking his turn as the group's secretary. The secretary will have an active list of which parents are available to sit and when. You receive credits for each hour that you sit. For freelancers who need free baby-sitters and have time to contribute, this is a useful system. It is not hard to find other willing parents if you ask at your day-care center, in the park or at parties. This system is a bonus for children in that they have a chance to meet peers instead of being abandoned to a strange adult.

AU PAIRS

A fairly inexpensive solution with many bonuses is an *au pair*. An au pair is traditionally a girl, though I have known one male au pair, who is given room and board, and sometimes a small amount of pocket money, in return for tending the children part of the day. Au pairs are not slaves—they are usually young students who want to live in another country. They are treated as part of the family on most occasions, and they are given a fair amount of time off to justify the small remuneration that they get. Many au pairs go to university while their charges are in school.

If you have a spare room and a little cash, an au pair can be an excellent solution. One who speaks another language offers a great education for any child. Children are much better at picking up languages than their elders, and if you are lucky, you may end up with bi- or trilingual children.

Hiring someone, sight unseen, from overseas can be risky. It is also illegal, since these people do not necessarily qualify for work permits. (Usually this is gotten around by having the au pair obtain a student visa and even enroll at a local college to keep up the appearance. However, it is illegal for people on student or tourist visas to work. Under the old law, only the foreigner was liable if caught. Under the new law, people who knowingly employ illegal aliens, even for au pair jobs at prices that no American would work for, face fines ranging from $250 to $2,000. It is not likely that this would be enforced for first-time offenders, particularly two hard-working parents who can't get by any other way. Nevertheless, if you do get caught, you will lose your au pair.)

In order to reduce the chance of an unpleasant surprise, correspond plentifully with the au pair candidate. Get references and a photo. It is very important to ascertain for sure how good her English is. You don't want your child in the hands of someone who really doesn't know what is being said. Other questions to ask include the following:

1. Does she plan to go to college while in your employ?
2. What sort of home does she come from?
3. Has she come from a home with lots of children?
4. Has she ever had much to do with children in some other way?

You should come to some understanding in advance, on paper, about what the procedure will be if the arrangement does not work out. Does the person plan to come to America anyway, or is she coming specifically to fill your job? If this is the case, you should probably offer to split the airfare in the event you are dissatisfied.

To find an au pair, buy a copy of the *International Herald Tribune*, where many prospective au pairs advertise. Also, ask any friends from abroad for children of friends or their own family members who might be interested in the job. When you have had one good au pair who is returning home, be sure to ask if she has any friends or relatives who might be interested in taking over the job.

There is still a legal, although not boundless, source of au pairs. This is the American Institute for Foreign Study, which brings in several thousand au pairs each year under a cultural exchange program run by the United States Information Agency and Experiment in International Living. Contact the American Institute for Foreign Study, 102 Greenwich Avenue, Greenwich, CT; (212) 219-0744.

Another source of fairly inexpensive live-in child care is colleges in remote parts of the country where students are often dying to come to a bigger city or another part of the country. You can often locate candidates who are willing to work as au pairs by mailing notices to be put on bulletin boards and also by contacting the university's employment office. Naturally, you can also do this at a local college; but remember, au pairs whom you feed and lodge far from home are going to be cheaper than local kids trying to pick up some money.

If you don't have to have a live-in helper, you have more flexibility in finding a local college student who can work on an hourly basis. Another good choice is to find a pleasant, intelligent dropout who is taking some time off from college and who needs cash. Such individuals may provide superior care, much more on your child's level than the ministrations of an older, stodgier person. Try putting an ad in local student and counterculture newspapers. Naturally, as with all such guardians, screen applicants carefully.

FAMILY MEMBERS

Grandparents and other older (or younger) family members can sometimes be helpful. Even if they can't take the children every day, it can be comforting to know that they're available should you suddenly have to drop everything to do an assignment.

To reiterate: freelancing while you are bringing up children is a very demanding task—one which you should consider carefully before you undertake it in the first place. Not every parent can cope with the tremendous pressures of both these jobs. There is no disgrace in stopping work temporarily while you either take care of your children or work in a slightly more stable job so that you can afford to pay for child care and have a more predictable schedule. There is no disgrace in simply not having children. Artists are different from others. For many of them, their work fills the need that other people can only fill by becoming parents.

REFERENCES

Breithart, Vicki. *The Day Care Book*. Knopf, 1974. A useful compendium of day-care solutions.

Caplan, Frank. *Parents' Yellow Pages*. Doubleday, 1977. Put out by the Princeton Center for Infancy, this book gives extensive resources to help you deal with almost every aspect of parenting.

Curtis, Jean. *Working Mothers*. Touchstone, 1977. A useful, reassuring book based on interviews with working mothers.

Greenleaf, Barbara, and Schaffer, Lewis. *Help: A Handbook for Working Mothers*. T.Y. Crowell, 1978.

Kids Day In Day Out. Christopher Cerf, ed. Doubleday, 1979. This gigantic book is filled with practical first-person advice given by hundreds of parents who were interviewed for the project.

Laury, Jean Ray. *The Creative Woman's Getting It Together at Home Handbook*. Van Nostrand Reinhold, 1977. An excellent book crammed with first-person advice from scores of women fiber artists. Such topics as coping with the mess, and the playpen in the studio are covered better here than anywhere else.

Liman, Ellen. *Babyspace: A Guide for Growing Families with Shrinking Space*. Putnam, 1984.

Norris, Gloria, and Miller, JoAnn. *The Working Mother's Complete Handbook*. Dutton, 1979.

Skelsey, Alice. *The Working Mother's Guide to Her Home, Her Family and Herself*. Random House, 1970 (currently out of print). Many people's favorite handbook of humorous, practical advice for coping.

PART THREE

MONEY MATTERS

CHAPTER THIRTEEN

HOW TO MAKE MONEY AND STILL DO YOUR WORK

Freelancers, particularly in years when work and cash flow are sporadic, must learn to be nimble about making money when it's needed without getting hopelessly ensnared in other careers. Check any classified section and you'll see that part-time and temporary jobs are at a premium. More and more people are catching on that nine to five does not constitute a life, and they are clawing to get at the few decent jobs that require less than forty hours' commitment. For this reason, you may become unnecessarily discouraged if you go the classified/temp agency route. The ideal job for you is one that (a) you can leave at any time without feeling guilty, (b) you work at only when you need cash, (c) lets you decide your hours, and (d) enables you to pick up contacts or other inside information.

With a little luck and a lot of energy you can survive even the longest hiatus between jobs, but in order to do so you must become comfortable with the patchwork approach of part-time work, unemployment checks if you're eligible, loans and even an occasional stint as a full-time employee. Some people find this constant need to be on the lookout for work draining and demeaning. Generally these people end up working nine to five. Other people find that the direct barter of time and energy for money that exists when you approach employment in this manner makes them feel more independent and in control of their own time.

WORKING OUTSIDE YOUR FIELD VS. STAYING WITHIN IT

There are two schools of thought concerning what you should do if you need to work to supplement your freelance income. Some people think it's best to stay within your field and do commercial work or something that is on the production end but still related to what you do as a freelancer. Others feel that the integrity of their own work fares better if they do something completely unrelated, perhaps even menial, so that they do not confuse the boundaries of their own work with vulgarized versions of their own creative ideas.

The first school argues that by staying within your own field, you make contacts and gain knowledge that will be helpful to you in your own work. Proponents of this strategy say that you don't necessarily have to lose the integrity of your work by doing this. They say if you're good you should be able to do anything you're called upon to do. This sort of thinking makes sense in the performing arts, where great work can often depend as much on virtuosity and range as on individual creative vision. And many theater people in particular seem to feel that it is important and desirable to work in the theater even if that means doing box office or being a gofer. A lot of them believe that a constant contact with the theater world is the only way to know the inside scoop and to get work. But a few believe that, on the contrary, it is the kiss of death to appear in any capacity but actor, if that is what you are trying to be. Still, this would allow you some range: no one I talked to felt that it can harm an actor to make television commercials, because an actor is not in the position of having to create his own scripts. Theoretically, developing the ability to act in any situation should strengthen an actor, who is an interpreter and an instrument rather than an originator in the same sense that an artist or writer is. One producer had this to say: "A lot of actors make commercials to make money, but they don't realize how much it helps them—because it gives them a certain stature. To come across in a thirty-second commercial takes talent: a talent which may or may not apply to theater. However, it changes people's first impressions of you, and first impressions are so important in this business."

Several writers also felt that there is nothing wrong with doing many types of writing as long as you know your own style, too. Many artists working in both commercial and fine arts felt that it is possible to benefit financially without one's own work being seriously affected. However, almost as many said they prefer poverty to commercial art—because of the effect on their work and their creative energy.

Those who say that it is best to do something unrelated say so mainly for two reasons: first, you feel less urgency to do your own work if you are doing a watered-down version of it all day long; second, working at something else, especially something mindless, frees your mind for the problems of your own work. The variety of your two lives can be useful in keeping your thoughts from getting deeply rutted around what you do. If you work commercially for any significant length of time, they say, your work will undergo changes for the worse.

My own advice on the matter: if you do choose to do commercial work, realize that you have been hired to do a client's job as well as you possibly can. Every job you do is a step in your career. Doing some commercial work won't turn your art to stone nor ruin you for "serious" art, and it may prove to be not only profitable but fun as well. Remember too that it isn't intrinsically harmful to do things someone else's way. If you're lucky, you may learn something. I believe that artists depend on serendipity and odd chance juxtapositions to develop their artistic personae. I see no universal virtue in staying pure in your ivory tower, doing only your own work—particularly if you are starving yourself to keep up your self-image of "real artist." Many people make the decision that they would rather live comfortably and so go into commercial work while continuing to press on in their own work on the side. Talent is something that you should be able to go out and use rather than worry about keeping it pure in a vacuum bottle.

You will see by what the following freelancers have to say that the decision on how to earn money is highly individual. You have to experiment a bit to see with what amount and at what sort of outside work you prosper best. It depends as much on your own preferences as on any subtle effects you think it might have on your own style.

I always tell younger people to go get dopey jobs. Lots of times you can read. You can use the time very well if you're clever. A lot of these jobs involve just having a body to sit there, and they don't care if you simultaneously read or learn lines or sketch. —Painter

If you need to get part-time work, find something that's related to your own work. Although you may not make a lot of money, you get the psychological satisfaction of being in the right place. Also, being in the right place at the right time may be a cliché, but we all know people get work for that reason every day in this city. That's very much how things work here. Teaching runs second. It probably doesn't hold as much opportunity for you to advance in your career, but at least it's satisfying in some small way, and at least you're not subjected to the unutterable squalor of driving a cab or handing out leaflets. —Actor

A full-time job allows one to have the courage of one's convictions. —Poet

A day in a commercial art studio is as much fun as a day in a bank, but you have nothing to do. Sometimes you sit there drinking coffee (or something stronger) for the whole day. You must stay there because they are paying you. It was one of the most difficult chapters of my life. I fought with myself to make myself go there. After two months I was out of energy, because I was so sure that I had to be active during the working day. If I had an idea it was absolutely at a different time. Thus I decided to freelance while I was still a student.
Artist and freelance are the same for me. To be an artist means being able to survive freelance. When an artist is pressed to live like a daily worker I think he has so much less chance to be somebody in the future. It's easy to say "OK, I can work five days a week and then have weekends." Absolutely crazy. After a forty-hour week you are so tired you dream only about TV, a good restaurant or a small trip to Long Island. —Painter–Editorial Artist

Sometimes people have their feeling of failure too wrapped up with their jobs. If they have to take an outside job they feel—"Oh, I'm not good enough to be working constantly in theater." It's not that at all. You never know when that experience will come in handy other than for survival money. It's important to get out of the house and go do something. It gets your momentum going. —Actress

JOBS UNRELATED TO THE ARTS

Jobs unrelated to the arts may be divided into *skilled, semiskilled* and *unskilled.* Skilled jobs are those which require some specific knowledge or talent. Semi-skilled jobs are open to more people. They entail responsibilities which require a lesser degree of training or skills which can be picked up on the job. Unskilled jobs are those which can be done with no particular training or skills at all.

The jobs proposed in this section are not the only enterprising jobs that you can find for yourself. They are ones that my interview subjects had done themselves or had heard of others doing. This list is by no means exhaustive: it is simply to show you the diversity of jobs artists often have to take to support their art.

UNSKILLED WORK

Circularizing
Department store employee
Door-to-door sales
Medical research
Messenger
Moving business

Night work
Taxi driver
Telephone sales
Test panels
Waiting and kitchen help

Circularizing. This classic job of down-and-outs is enjoying a large-scale revival in cities. Banks, restaurants, new stores, health clubs and massage parlors are the best sources for this sort of work. You will often find advertisements in the classifieds. Pay is normally between $3.50 and $5 per hour.

If you decide to hand out circulars, be sure to wear your most comfortable shoes—and a truss if you are at all prone to lower back pain.

Department store employee. Even two weeks' work at a department store can help you out, and you can work part-time: Many stores have a shift that consists of two evenings and Saturdays. It's tiring for your feet and fatiguing for your spirit, but it is definitely something to consider when you need clothes, as employee discounts sometimes go as high as 25 to 40 percent off. You generally begin to get some sort of discount after two weeks of employment.

You can often find work through the personnel department by just walking in. Start a month before Thanksgiving to get Christmas jobs, because these are popular. Large department stores often make you take a couple of classes in which you learn the history of the store, how to frank a cash register, how to handle voids, and all the other details of retail life. You are always paid for attending these.

One of the more interesting department store jobs I heard about was that of a musician who was the store Santa at a large department store in Hartford, Connecticut. His downfall came when he was unable to name all of his reindeer for a suspicious child who then loudly proclaimed him a fraud.

Door-to-door sales. A small fortune can be made if you happen to have a talent for selling door-to-door. The best companies to work for are the recognized ones such as Fuller Brush and Avon, since customers trust their products. Usually a regional manager will place ads in the newspaper when looking for new salespeople. You work on a commission basis, so that you have plenty of room for initiative. You can expect to earn in the neighborhood of 40 percent of your gross sales.

According to one actor who smashed all Fuller Brush sales records for a summer of work:

Fertile areas for selling include new housing developments and summer resorts in early June. One of the tricks is to get neighbors' names from each person you sell to. Then you go ring their bell and say, "Mrs. X thought you might be interested in some mops." She will ask what Mrs. X bought, which you tell her. They always want to keep up with the Joneses where Fuller Brush is concerned.

Medical research. Research laboratories often need paid volunteers. Pay is usually about $4 to $5 per hour for participating in an interview, but if you are called upon to give samples of blood, urine, spinal fluid or bone marrow, the pay rises. Some experiments require that you live in the hospital. This can, of course, be a real help if you have nowhere to live and nothing to eat. If you're lucky, you may even get into marijuana research or sleep studies, which can be both fun and interesting. This sort of work is morally permissible, but selling blood to profit-making blood banks is really not. Participating in research as a subject is noble and essential to scientific advancement. Selling blood is the worst sort of prostitution, and many people have been repaid for doing so by contracting hepatitis, which is *no joke*. You should *donate* blood only at hospitals or at large blood banks such as Red Cross. The profit-making blood banks are generally in the slums, and much of the equipment used is dirty. With the additional threat of AIDS, you should need no further convincing to stay away.

The best way to find out about legitimate guinea-pig jobs is to look on university and hospital bulletin boards. Newspapers often carry advertisements in their Public Notices columns.

You will almost always have to sign an informed consent form, so do be sure you know what you are getting into. You might not be happy submitting to a spinal tap when you thought they were just going to draw blood.

Messenger. Especially in cities, there is a plethora of messenger jobs. There are foot messengers, motorcycle messengers, bicycle messengers and auto messengers. The best ways to find openings are either to look in the classifieds, particularly in counterculture newspapers, or to look the companies up in the Yellow Pages and apply directly. Because messengering is a common way of making emergency money, there is a fairly high turnover at these outfits, and if you list yourself with several companies your phone will soon ring with job offers.

If you live in an area less heavily saturated with messenger services, you should put an ad offering your services in your local paper and on bulletin boards. People who live outside cities are often in desperate need of couriers who will pick up and deliver items in the city. In setting fees, count on charging $5 to $10 an hour for your time, plus gas.

Some messenger services work on the incentive system where you, as an independent contractor, split fifty-fifty on the fee with the company.

A musician I talked with who has recently paid for his studio time by working as a messenger says, "You have your mind for yourself. You're allowed all that time to think about your projects as you move about, instead of being in the house trying to fight off the magnetic waves coming from the drug box. You're outside getting exercise in the sun and fresh air, and that can really stimulate your mind."

Moving business. If you own a motor vehicle you have an excellent source of income standing right at the curb. A car or van can be used to move objects and people for very adequate remuneration. If you plan to get into the moving business, you will need a truck or van and some reliable helpers. In order to do a professional job and not wreck anyone's valuables, you will also need moving pads or old quilts. You can ask that your clients do their own crating, or you can charge more and supply crates and padding and do that also.

Remember that your moving vehicle and other equipment is at least partially tax-deductible, depending on how much you use it for personal driving.

In order to protect yourself when moving valuables, you should go over each item in the owner's presence and record any scratches or other imperfections—such as missing drawers or feet. In addition, inventory each piece and record the number of boxes. Have the owner sign and retain a copy of this itemized inventory. (Note that this sort of informal arrangement works if your business stays small and your clients are not in possession of extremely valuable items. Should you expand and start competing with larger movers, you should buy liability insurance to cover yourself in case you accidentally lose or damage someone's possessions.)

You are free to set your own hours. Remember that many people who work during the day are delighted to be moved in the evening or on weekends.

Here are some tips from a musician who has had his own moving company for several years:

It's good to advertise in colleges around May and June, when people are so happy to be splitting for good that they'll do anything to get their stuff out of the dorm. Since college kids often don't have much to move, we offered a special deal of a flat price per van-load so that they could get a bunch of friends and make it even cheaper.

Night work. People whose creative energies come forth most strongly during the day may find that a night job is the best way to support themselves. Any establishment which runs twenty-four hours a day is a good bet. Among these are hotels (Nathanael West worked as a night desk clerk in a hotel on Twenty-third Street while he wrote *Miss Lonelyhearts*), restaurants, hospitals, nursing homes and some university libraries. Many large law firms hire a late shift of stenographers and word processor operators, a good opportunity if you have these skills. Many artists also find work as night doormen and security guards.

While many people hate the so-called graveyard shift, from midnight until morning, it is quite popular with artistic types, and you may find that you have interesting colleagues at these jobs.

Taxi driver. Taxi driving is a mindless job that can give you a sense of freedom and up to $150 per shift in busy cities. You must obtain a chauffeur's license, which you usually do by taking your old operator's license to the Motor Vehicle Department along with one or two photos. You then take your license and apply to one of the hack companies that you will find in either the classifieds or the Yellow Pages. You will then be sent to the Taxi and Limousine Commission to take the geography test for your hack license. In New York City, at least, the test is ridiculously easy and involves more the simple skills of reading and writing than any knowledge of the city's streets. Armed with your chauffeur's license and your hack license, you are now ready to hit the streets. Several freelancers I spoke with had tried taxi driving, but most had become discouraged. The following is a typical response from a painter who tried it and found he didn't like it:

I thought: "Oh, drive a taxi. That will be fun to just cruise around the city all day. I can drive fast in this traffic and I'll makes some tips." Wrong! First of all, I made something like $3.75 in tips the first day; but worse than that, there are all kinds of unwritten, unspoken rules. I sat there for three hours the second day, and not only wouldn't they give me a cab, but they also wouldn't tell me why. Finally it turned out that they thought I had too many miles on the cab for not enough fares. When the boss finally came in, I told him I had been going to the airport a lot, and he said, "So stop going to the airport." It was a nightmare from the beginning to the end three days later. They expect you to drive around all day in these terrible pollution-spewing vehicles, the tips are either feast or famine, and the bosses are extremely unpleasant.

These words, however, were spoken by a quite high-strung young man who had recently moved to New York. If you know your city well and have endurance at the wheel, you may like hacking.

A more relaxed sort of driving job can sometimes be lined up by applying to any of the car-rental companies which allow the customer to drop the car at his destination. These companies employ drivers to fetch and return these automobiles, and they pay very nicely. In New York there is a waiting list at each of the car rental companies for this plum work, but it might save your neck at some future point to get yourself on the list and wait for your name to come up.

Private chauffeurs make good money, particularly if they work for movie moguls or recording companies. For this (as for driving a taxi) you need a chauffeur's license. Once you have that, you can look in the classifieds for work. If you want to be a private chauffeur, go to employment agencies for domestics. Also, look in the Yellow Pages for the names of limousine services and apply to them. Some of these also work on the independent-contractor system and thus allow you to drive when you are free. If your work, or some facet of it, is portable, you will be glad of the free time you will have while waiting at the curb for passengers.

Telephone sales. Telephone solicitation is sleazy, depressing work which takes a certain knack and an obtrusive personality. I have never met another freelancer who had anything good to say about it. It can tide you over if you can stand to do it full-time. You usually can find it in the classifieds. You will generally sell light bulbs, encyclopedias or magazine subscriptions.

I once had the disturbing experience of selling light bulbs over the telephone for a company which employed the handicapped in its warehouses. The job site was a depressing second-floor suite in a side street of downtown Hartford. Six of us sat at two long tables, each with a WATS (pre-paid long-distance dialing) telephone and an out-of-state directory. Our job was to try to sell packages of light bulbs to small businesses. We were paid $3.25 an hour plus commissions up to a certain point, after which we were given commissions only. I don't know what that point was, as neither I nor any of the other people who started with me that week attained such a level.

Test panels. My favorite spare-time work is being a member of the test panels or focus groups (as they are often called) held at advertising agencies. These panels test the reaction of a carefully chosen population to a new product, concept or occasionally even a new law. Agencies often are very specific as to whom they need: WASPs, or women only, or people who eat breakfast cereal more than three times per week, or cat owners. They assemble a panel, then someone from the ad agency leads a discussion or gives samples to try while your reactions are recorded or evaluated from a viewing room. There are many bonuses to participation in test panels. You often get a meal out of them, or at least coffee and carbohydrate-laden snacks. They usually pay $15 to $20 for an hour or two of participation.

One agency that recruits respondents for focus groups in New York is Quality Respondents (which can be reached at [212] 877–7577). While you are not supposed to go to more than one panel per month, I know plenty of New York theater people who make the circuit with far more frequency than that under assumed names and invented domiciles.

Waiting and kitchen help. Waiting on tables is a classic tide-over job of starving artists, and with good reason, because for the time you put in, the remuneration can be fabulous. Unlike many well-paying jobs, this is one you don't need any particular talent for, and one which you can leave with no qualms the minute your ship comes in.

Most restaurant help is hired through word of mouth. Those advertised in classified often turn out to be unusually unpleasant (e.d., topless jobs and all-night diners). In order to land a better waiting job, hang out at the bars and restaurants in your area and see which ones appeal to you. Then tell the owner, or whoever is in charge, that you are available. Even if there is no opening, most places are happy to take your name. Often, if some of the regular help is absent, you will be given a trial run. Always look for new places opening up. If you hit them at the right time, you can often walk right into a job.

If you are hired, be sure to clarify the terms. Some places pay you a small salary (often as low as $10 per shift) on top of tips which are 100 percent yours to keep. Others require you to pool your tips and divide them with the other waiters. (See page 191, Working off the Books: Pro and Con, for a discussion of tips and tax liability.)

One of the freelancers I interviewed had found a job in an executive dining room through the want ads. She earned a steady weekly salary of $150, plus benefits, and had only to show up for three hours every day to wait on the company big shots in a small, genteel dining room high over Wall Street. This type of job requires more of a steady time commitment, but if you can give it, the pay and hours are superb.

Kitchen help is needed to chop, peel and otherwise assist the chef. Pay is usually around the legal minimum, but the job can be convivial if your co-workers are, and you may be able to realize some fringe benefits in the form of leftovers.

One actress sounded an interesting caution to other thespians which I will repeat here:

Waitressing is all right, but honestly, you have to be careful not to let it distance you from your real work. I don't know why this happens, but I have seen so many actors and actresses get caught in this rut of waiting on tables to pay for more and more training, but they never go to auditions. You ask them why they're not looking for acting work and they say, "I'm not ready." You have to guard against this, because eventually it builds up. A performer's fears can be very self-reinforcing.

SEMISKILLED WORK

Au pair	Modeling
Bartending	Polling
Extra work	Substitute teaching
Game show contestant	Tour guide
Gardening	

Au pair. This is a European term for a live-in lion tamer for the children, who gets free room and board, and sometimes pocket money on top. While this might not be your cup of tea at home, it's not a bad way to get by abroad, or even in a city like New York. Au pairs generally have quite a lot of time to themselves when their charges are in school. You can use this time to work or locate a place to live in a new city. To get au pair jobs in Europe, look in the international edition of the *Herald Tribune* and in the classifieds of foreign papers.

If you do find a position in a foreign country, make sure that all your visas are in order *before* you leave. You might also call the consulate of the country in question to clarify matters. In almost every country of the world you will need something more than a tourist visa in order to work as an au pair. However, since most European countries are now members of the Common Market, it is very difficult for Americans to get working papers in those countries. In many cases this problem can be solved by your enrolling in language or civilization courses for foreigners given at a university, so that you become eligible for a student visa. Your prospective employer should find out this information from her end. Again, call the consulate of the country to clarify matters. (See also the section Au Pairs in chapter 12.)

Bartending. The requirements for bartending vary according to where you work and how big a volume the bar does. In busy city bars, you will be expected to have gone to bartenders' school—so that you know how to mix, serve and garnish drinks. Smaller bars, those catering to students, and country bars will usually be less stringent in their requirements. But you should still know what you are doing, and you should keep a copy of one of the bartenders' guides handy in case someone comes in and orders a Rusty Nail or a Pink Squirrel.

Bartenders, like waiters, may depend upon tips only, or in some bars be also paid the minimum wage. Bartenders' school usually costs around $500 and runs for forty hours—which can be spread out over a couple of weeks. You can usually find a school in your locality through the Yellow Pages.

Extra work. To get extra work you can register at certain casting agencies which are under the jurisdiction of SAG (Screen Actors Guild) in New York and Los Angeles, and SEG (Screen Extras Guild) in Los Angeles. Regular agents don't handle extras, because they are prohibited from taking a commission from an extra's wages. You must be a member of SAG or SEG, or join within thirty days of your first job as an extra. This rule is to keep producers from hiring friends at nonunion wages. There are set wages for general extras, special-ability extras, and those who have "silent bits." Addresses you need to know:

SCREEN ACTORS GUILD
1700 Broadway
New York, NY 10019
(212) 957–5370

SCREEN EXTRAS GUILD
3629 Cahuegna
West Hollywood, CA 90068
(213) 851-4301

SCREEN ACTORS GUILD
7750 Sunset Boulevard
Hollywood, CA 90046
(213) 876–3030

Game show contestant. An actor and writer I know went from deepest poverty to having $18,000 in the bank a week later after cleaning up on the "Match Game." The trick is to watch the game shows until you know what sort of contestants a show has and how to play. At the end of the credits you will see the name of the contestant coordinator. Technically you are supposed to write him for tickets. My friend got his by saying that he was from out of town and was leaving Los Angeles soon. Since they usually have many locals, they were thrilled to get an out-of-towner. At his audition he was asked to play the game and then simulate winning in the house style. According to my friend, "Some shows want hysteria, which I can't do. They want to see you getting a heart attack. I chose the "Match Game" because the emphasis is on the celebrities."

If you are considering this route to riches, there are a couple of cautions that you should not ignore. First of all, don't underestimate the amount of frustration and wasted time that a stint on a game show may cost you. Some shows put you through an arduous selection process, in which you are auditioned several times and then left hanging for weeks before it is determined whether or not you will actually be used.

Secondly, unless you remember to sign a form that is often thrust beneath your nose at an inopportune moment, you will be stuck receiving a load of useless junk that you might win instead of money (*and* paying tax on its value). Money or goods that you earn will be severely taxed, because they are considered unearned income.

Still and all, game shows do work for some people who have the right combination of skill, luck and personality. If this idea appeals to you, start deciding which show suits you best, but *don't* spend any more time than that in front of your television. Those interested in learning more about how to get on game shows might want to look at one of the following:

Muntean, Greg. *How to Become a Game Show Contestant: An Insider's Guide.* Fawcett Books.

Schwartz, Maria S. *How to Be a TV Game Show Winner.* Harmony.

Gardening. If you are good with plants and have some knowledge and experience, you can make decent money maintaining gardens. Many people are too busy to care for their gardens adequately and are only too happy to hire someone else to weed, cultivate, stake and perhaps water.

Gardening was one of my major sources of income during the summer doldrums of my early career.

This job can even be done by city freelancers since many townhouses and stores have landscaping. Professional landscapers usually charge a great deal to maintain these plantings, and owners are delighted to have it done by someone less overqualified.

Modeling. While serious advertising and fashion modeling is skilled work, there are other sorts of modeling jobs open to people who feel comfortable making money this way.

Many performers get jobs modeling, particularly on a temporary basis at conventions and promotions of various sorts. Pay for working at information booths or handing out samples at trade shows can be fabulous—occasionally as much as $175 per day. You will probably be asked to supply a picture when you apply at these agencies. Many times personnel for this sort of promotion are acquired directly through newspaper ads. Generally they are looking for rather wholesome types, so leave your punk jewelry at home and put on your whitest smile.

Department stores also use models to hand out samples. Particularly in smaller cities, you can get this work directly from the stores' personnel offices. A new trend in the advertising world is to use more natural types, so that you don't always have to be extremely attractive in a conventional way to model. However, most people in this field are either performers or people who model full-time. Particularly for television, it takes real ability to come across as a particular character in thirty seconds. If you want to try this work, approach

theatrical agents for television work. Larger cities have special agents for character models. If your city doesn't, see whether a fashion-model agency won't
represent you.

People of my acquaintance have made as much as $150 a day modeling for
porn rags. One was busted and had made nowhere near enough to pay the
$1,000 worth of legal fees that she ran up.

Polling. Polling work can often be obtained through major networks and newspapers whenever there is a big controversy, such as Irangate or an election. It
can be good work to tide you over, because it is usually temporary; but there
is also a good chance that, should you want to, you *can* stay on longer if you
have worked out. The definition of working out is simply making people keep
answering time-consuming questions of opinion. Such a job can be a gold
mine of characters, dialects and stories for actors and writers.

To find jobs, apply directly to large television networks and newspapers in
your area or else to one of the national opinion polls, such as:

THE GALLUP ORGANIZATION
63 Bank Street
Princeton, NJ 08540
(609) 924-9600

BURKE MARKETING RESEARCH
7 Corporate Park Drive
White Plains, NY 10640
(914) 694–2000

LOUIS HARRIS AND ASSOCIATES
630 Fifth Avenue
New York, NY 10022
(212) 541–6430

In census years (1990, 2000) you can apply to the Bureau of the Census for
jobs interviewing the citizenry.

The pay for polling work varies from organization to organization and according to whether you work from their office, from your home, or go door-
to-door.

Here is the experience of an actor who worked successfully as an interviewer:

*I got a job working for the Harris Poll. You are given a long list of questions
and a list of telephone numbers. During the first few days they monitor
some of your calls just to observe your technique. If you don't have a high
rate of getting the full questionnaire answered they let you go. I found it
absolutely fascinating to talk to people all over the country about breakfast
sausage one night, Nixon the next, and abortion the third. I really got into
it and didn't have any problems keeping them talking. The other thing they
monitor is whether you make any personal calls, which is something that
you should* not *do.*

Substitute teaching. Substitute teaching ("subbing") can be excellent work if
you are good at handling children or adolescents. A college degree is usually
not necessary for subs, though some college experience is desirable. The pay
is usually $30 to $50 per day, although subs in dangerous inner-city schools
usually make more. Subs who are willing to cross picket lines can often make
$75 per day even in small communities.

To get a job subbing, list yourself with either the superintendent of schools or with the office of the principal of a particular school. If you register with the superintendent of schools, your name is made available to all the schools of the district unless you make restrictions as to how far you will travel. On the application you will be asked to indicate which subjects you can teach and which age groups. Don't worry if you were once an A student in History and can now barely remember what the Magna Carta is. Usually the regular teacher will try to prepare the material for the sub in advance, or else the class will be asked to write or read and your main task will be supervising them. Do think carefully about what age groups you feel comfortable with. High school students nowadays are far more ill-behaved, and even dangerous, than they probably were in your day. It's not much fun to try to conduct an English class if you can't control the rowdy seventeen-year-olds who are taller than you and won't break up their card game in the back of the room. After being intimidated by such a class (in rural Connecticut—not in a ghetto), I realized that junior high school was my limit, except for the occasional librarian job that I accept from the regional high school.

Tour guide. If you like showing people around and have something to show them, you can make good money and have a pleasant time. The key is to have a special angle so that you can get a good hold on the market. Examples of this are the actors who give tours of Broadway and the Italian writer who organizes custom-made tours (the Porno tour, the Museum tour, the Architecture tour, the Dope tour) for fellow Italians who come to New York. If you live in the country but have something of a tourist trade, you may be able to give tours of local wonders or take visitors on climbing or cross-country skiing expeditions if you are expert enough in these areas to take on other people safely.

Generally the best way to set up this sort of business is to advertise in local papers and in the home papers of your target customers. The Italian writer advertises his off-beat tours in Roman underground newspapers. Small hotels may be willing to post notices or keep a pile of your flyers at the front desk.

You will have to gear your prices to the going rate in your area. In the city you can expect to get $35 to $50 per customer for a five-hour tour. They should pay separately for any refreshments.

Because this business involves other people who will be in your custody, you need to be very careful about limiting your personal liability should one of your tourists twist an ankle while rock climbing or be mugged on Broadway and decide to go after you. One way to do this is to get a lawyer to draw up a release form that your customers should sign before departing. You may want to go even further than this and incorporate your business so that any suits are brought against the corporation for its assets, not against you for yours. It is essential that you get legal guidance before you set up this kind of business.

If you are good at languages and can cope with shepherding groups through foreign countries without breaking down like Richard Burton in *Night of the Iguana*, you might be interested in looking for regular employment as a tour guide.

There are many tour companies throughout the country that offer packaged tours to groups. Get as many of their brochures as you can from a travel agent and pick ones whose itineraries appeal to you. Then apply directly to the companies that you have chosen. You will be particularly appealing to them if you speak any relevant foreign languages or are a native of the area you will be traveling to.

SKILLED WORK

Carpentry
Catering and cooking
Teaching and tutoring

Carpentry. Good carpenters make good money (upwards of $10 per hour, depending upon locale). Wherever you live, there is always a demand for people with building and carpentry skills, and you should have no trouble freelancing in this area should you decide to.

The way to get freelance work is to advertise via the classifieds and local bulletin boards. When you see construction going on, you should always check to see if any more hands are needed.

Catering and cooking. Catering and cooking can be an excellent solution to your money problems if you are a competent cook and have a decent business sense. Probably most freelancers who are trying to do their work at the same time they bring home the bacon as a caterer will want to keep their catering business manageable and small and private. You can make good money this way without getting so involved in your catering that you never go back to that novel or that film.

If you go public, you will need to acquire an outside kitchen that meets the Department of Health standards of hygiene. A home kitchen, where you prepare your own meals and cats stalk the counters, will emphatically not pass muster for the department. So the freelancer who wants to make some living money as a cook or caterer does best to work within a small network of satisfied customers or to advertise in small local papers and on neighborhood bulletin boards. By keeping a fairly low profile, you may be able to stay anonymous to the authorities. However, don't count on this. Two freelance film makers who live in my town tell me that the first catering advertisement they ran in our local paper brought them a phone call from the doctor who serves as health inspector here. One way of avoiding this situation is to offer your services as a cook and prepare your customers' food in their own kitchens.

When cooking at other people's houses, make sure to scout the kitchens in advance and have everything in writing—from whether there are any diabetics in the group to the fact that the soup tureen is chipped. Although this may sound picayune, it can save you grief in the long run.

It is hard to generalize about how to set your prices. The best advice seems to be to talk to other caterers in your area and find out how they charge. Some people charge an all-inclusive set fee per person; others charge for the cost of the food plus an hourly rate for their work. Others say that your price should be three times the cost of the raw ingredients. However you decide to do it, don't forget to take into account the cost of any cooking equipment you bought, its depreciation if applicable, and also your gasoline and driving time. These will add considerably to your costs and you shouldn't ignore them when figuring out your fees.

A very handy book for persons interested in making money this way is *How to Turn a Passion for Food into Profit* by Elayne J. Kleeman and Jeanne Voltz (Rawson-Wade, 1979).

Teaching and tutoring. Many freelancers like to teach—either their own art or something unrelated in which they are proficient. If you enjoy teaching and have something to teach, you may be able to attract enough students on a freelance basis to get you by.

Schools occasionally have need of tutors to work at home with long-absent students. Because this job is more professional than subbing, pay is usually a few dollars higher than it is for subbing in your area. If you are interested, contact the superintendent of schools in your area.

If it is something else that you want to teach, local advertising (bulletin boards, small papers) is your most efficient way of reaching potential students.

Of the freelancers I interviewed, there were varying opinions about teaching one's own art form:

I rather enjoy working with young writers, but I find it very time-consuming to be as effective a teacher as they deserve. I teach at a local college, because I need the money, and I am not one of those lucky people who have some other totally unrelated talent. My hat is certainly off to the writer who can go program computers when he needs to. You have to read each student's manuscript very carefully and thoughtfully, and this can involve quite a commitment when there are twenty or thirty students in your class.
—Writer

Any time you give something like that it saps your energy. I think teaching is wonderful. I love teaching, passing on to younger people both the business experience and the experience of an eye. If you like doing it, it's fine. Some people have to teach, and they've had it to the point where it sticks in their craw and they're jaded and tired. For me— I can't take two full days out of the studio. I work six days now. The work is something that demands constant attention. It's not something you can take up and leave off. It demands continuous concern and focus, and I can't stop and go teach and get back into it.
—Painter

SOURCES OF SATISFYING WORK

Here are some further leads to help you find decent autonomous work outside your art to help pay the bills:

Freed, Dolly. *Possum Living (How to Live without a Job and Almost No Money)*. Universe Books, 1978.

Handbook of Home Business Ideas and Plans (by Mother Earth News). Bantam Books, 1976.

Hewitt, Geof. *Working for Yourself.* Rodale Books, 1977.

Kahm, H.S. *101 Businesses You Can Start and Run with Less than a Thousand Dollars.* Dolphin Books, 1973.

Levinson, Jay Conrad. *Earning Money without a Job.* Holt, Rinehart & Winston, 1979.

Levinson, Jay Conrad. *550 Ways to Earn Extra Money.* Owl Books, 1981.

Polking, Kirk, ed. *Freelance Jobs for Writers.* Writer's Digest Books, 1984.

TEMP AGENCIES

If you don't mind dipping into the nine-to-five life every now and then and also have what are called "skills" (typing, with or without shorthand), you may be well served by temporary employment agencies. Sometimes temp agencies even have jobs that don't require "skills." During my prepublishing years I utilized these services heavily. My jobs included: doing census-type surveys of workers on designated city blocks, handing out free cigarette samples, handing out circulars in front of Grand Central Station and counting bank customers arriving at an all-night machine.

Temp agencies can be found in the Yellow Pages or the classifieds of your newspaper. Sometimes the trades such as *Backstage* and *Variety* have ads. Also look in whatever counterculture papers there may be in your town, because sometimes agencies with a high number of reasonably interesting jobs have the savvy to try to attract that readership.

When you register with the agency, you go in, take a typing test and have an interview. If they think they can ever place you, you are listed and they call you when they have something suitable, or you check in with them a couple of times a week. The best times for this temporary office work are the vacation transitions: summer, early September, around Christmas, and anytime there's a flu going around. Also, if you work steadily for a number of weeks, some agencies offer cash bonuses. You might shop around with this perk in mind. Don't limit yourself to only one agency. One poet I know was listed with eleven agencies simultaneously.

MAKING YOUR OUTSIDE JOB PAY OFF

Unskilled, semiskilled and temporary jobs rarely provide the fringe benefits that skilled, permanent jobs do unless you are opportunistic enough to go after them. You should be certain to grab some of these fringe benefits before you leave the job. Many of them are things that most people wouldn't even consider as fringe benefits, but which are gold nuggets for freelancers. Here are some which should not be overlooked:

1. Always apply for credit cards when you have a job.
2. Copy relevant names from office Rolodexes.
3. Xerox any publicity lists that you can get your hands on. You never know when you might have something urgent to ask Bianca Jagger. Sometimes you can even sell these lists to fund-raisers or new groups starting up.

4. Be sure to stock up on stationery: letterheads, envelopes, labels, etc. You never know when you may need these.
5. Keep every ID card that you are ever given. Again, you never know when they'll come in handy; but if they could be useful, and you don't have them, you'll feel very frustrated. You can always disguise the dates with scissors, bleach or the holder you display them in.
6. Make as many friends as you can where you work. If you always have a friend there, you may be able to get favors done even after you've left. A co-conspirator who will handle landlords and credit checks for you makes your situation optimum. But even more straight-arrow types could unexpectedly come in handy.

WORK RELATED TO YOUR ART

WORK OPPORTUNITIES FOR VISUAL ARTISTS

Doing freelance paste-up and mechanicals. If you know how to do this sort of commercial work, you should be able to pick it up through ads and through the grapevine.

Taking in darkroom work or renting out your darkroom.

Photographing weddings, bar mitzvahs and christenings. Satisfied customers are your biggest source of continuing work. And don't forget to come to the party with plenty of business cards.

Stringing for newspapers. If you happen to be on the scene and no photographers from the papers or wires are around to scoop you, you can often sell them your photos. For this sort of thing, it always helps to have some sort of press pass. Even a phony one that you can buy in penny arcades can be doctored to pass when you flip it at the site of some disaster.

Photographing accidents. According to one savvy photographer, if you're on the spot at an accident you can often cash in by selling photographs to the victims for use in making insurance claims. Be sure to get all license-plate numbers and other pertinent data so that you can contact them later if they are unavailable on the spot. If a cab company is involved, contact it. While this may seem a ghoulish pastime, you're actually helping the victim greatly increase his chances of collecting damages.

Doing head shots and portfolios for performers and aspiring models.

Working in an art supply or photographic store. This can pay off dividends in discounted supplies and connections with people who might be able to help you in some way.

Audiovisual work. Often freelancers (photographers, artists, designers) can find work in the audiovisual departments of large companies doing such things as putting slide presentations together for training, marketing and fund-raising. Usually a staff person does the optical bench work, but freelancers are engaged for location work.

WORK OPPORTUNITIES FOR WRITERS

Reading. If you have a friend at a publishing company, you may be able to get a job as a reader of unsolicited manuscripts on a freelance basis. You will usually be expected to make a short report describing what you read.

Copy editing. Again, if you know some in-house editors who can help you to be selected, you may be able to get work copy editing or fact checking. You will be required to take a test showing that you really do know your English well enough to be doing this. The word is that economics are causing more houses to use freelancers for jobs like this.

Ghost writing. Ghost writing is all right if you can get along with whomever you're ghosting for and can imitate what their style would be if they could write. Just make sure your personalities fit and that you have a detailed collaboration agreement telling how much each of you is going to make, your responsibilities, your rights and what to do if the relationship must be terminated.

Copywriting. For this sort of work you should approach publishers and ad agencies.

Running a workshop. If you can get participants (you really need to have been published to have sufficient authority) you can run writing workshops in your house. You might also try approaching prisons, nursing homes, and hospitals to see if you can start out on a volunteer basis, but often these workshops become so popular that an institution will decide to budget a bit of pay for you.

A very useful source, loaded with ideas, is *How You Can Make $20,000 a Year Writing (From Where You Live)* by Nancy Edmonds Hanson (Writer's Digest Books, 1980).

ONE ARTIST'S GOOD ADVICE ON GHOSTING

One problem with ghosting is that you may not receive credit for work that you did that went out under someone else's name. If you have some clout, you may be able to get your name on the cover of a book that you have ghostwritten. However, on smaller jobs you may not really be able to get credit, and this can leave your portfolio or résumé looking a bit thin if you do a lot of it. Here is some very savvy advice from freelance artist, Russ Miller, that will help you enhance your reputation and take credit for work even if it appears under other people's names.

"Make sure that you keep a copy of some part of the project that no one else could possibly have unless they were closely involved with the production of the work. For instance, for logo designs I keep all the pencil workups and attach the publisher's notes to each. This way, people reviewing your work can see the exact stages that you went through in each instance if they have any doubts that 'the unknown artist' was really you.

"There's a cruel twist to all this. After doing thirteen issues of a comic for one publisher as a ghost, I sent my portfolio to them, and they rejected my work as not being up to their standards! Honest! I filed their letter in my 'ironic twist' file."

MONEY OPPORTUNITIES FOR PERFORMERS

Cruise ship jobs. This work heads the list for performers. What could combine the best of both worlds better than a job in which you get paid to perform and travel all over the world? All cruise ships have entertainment ranging from comedy acts, dancers, bands and variety show artists. Both performers and technical people are generally needed. Occasionally you may have cruise staff duties as well. An actor friend of mine who originally signed on to be director of the ship's theater, found that he was also expected to hold shuffleboard clinics, choreograph shows for septuagenarian dowagers and dance with them at dinner. In return he traveled from New York to Sydney and back via Fiji, Easter Island and many other enviable ports of call. Bed and food were provided and good beer cost 15¢ a bottle, and he was given $1,000 on top for the ten-week trip.

You can run these jobs down by looking in the trades, by calling the ship lines directly or by contacting the following producers:

BRAMSON'S ENTERTAINMENT
BUREAU
1440 Broadway
New York, NY 10018
(212) 354–9575

FIRST RUN PRODUCTIONS
306 West 40th Street
New York, NY 10118
(212) 760–9310

SEASCAPE LTD.
1080 Port Boulevard
Port of Miami
Miami, FL 33132
(305) 372–9000
Attn: Manager of Entertainment

Guide to Cruise Ship Jobs, which you can get from Pilot Books (103 Cooper Street, Babylon, NY 11702) for $4.95 will give you more detailed information on these jobs.

Street performing. This can be lucrative if you pick a good spot. Make sure you're not invading someone else's accustomed stage. New York street performers are said to be among the most territorial. It's also a good way for bands, clowns, magicians and the like to meet future employers. In addition, many out-of-work performers like street performing because it gives them a chance to keep in practice and also to work when nothing else is happening:

I performed everywhere there were people: crafts festivals, concerts, open-air stuff. Go to where there are 5,000 people lined up to get into a concert and don't forget to hand out cards. People would come up and say "can you do X?" (I never turned down a gig. I never had a set act, so I improvised at formal dinner parties, insurance company dinners, grand openings of banks, and I also did a lot of volunteer work at children's hospitals.

—Member of Mummenschanz Mimes

Teaching. Many performers get by teaching dance or voice or their musical instrument.

Party work. You can get work ranging from telling stories at a kids' party to playing rock 'n' roll at college dances and debutante parties. One clever magician managed to get some class lists and sent out flyers to all the parents in a local school.

Backstage and front-of-house work. This includes sewing costumes, painting scenery, doing box office or press work, being a gofer and being a technical assistant, house manager, etc.

Porn-related jobs. If it doesn't make you feel that you are contributing to something ugly and destructive rather than creative, there are pornographic jobs to be had, some milder than others. One actress found work with some friends doing loud breathing and ecstatic cries on a pornographic record. I was once invited by an actor I lived with to be his partner in a film intended for medical students about how to have sexual intercourse. This choice call was from *Backstage*, where occasionally others of its ilk can be found. Be *very* wary before accepting one of these jobs. There have been some very ugly incidents involving women performers, which is only to be expected considering the ugliness of the minds which produce and consume most pornography. If you are a woman, try to have a male friend accompany you. Also, know the law in your area. One actress I know was busted for obscenity and wound up with a Class E felony on her record.

Speech lessons. If you speak well and have an aptitude for teaching, you can give lessons to people who want to rid themselves of various accents or speech impediments.

Music for parties. It isn't all rock that's in demand. One string quartet in New York gets by nicely playing at dinner parties. It's an idea which could be promoted into a rage by an enterprising freelancer.

Studio work. This can be a good option for musicians who are better players than entertainers. Most of the available work is commercial. Television and radio work adds residuals to your pay. Singers can get work as background singers. You must sight-read music for studio work.

Scoring. This is a good option for musicians with a good "hand." Much scoring from orchestral music to jazz is done by independent contractors. One musician suggests placing an ad offering to do charts for copyright purposes, since musicians need charts with the music written out, and many can't do it for themselves. He charges $25 per chart for rock songs.

Music reviews. Small papers and music magazines are your best bet for selling record reviews. The average pay is $10 to $25 per piece. Approach music editors or record review editors with a couple of sample reviews.

EMERGENCY FUNDS AVAILABLE TO ARTISTS

Any artist may run into temporary but desperate financial trouble and may qualify to receive money from one of the emergency funds listed below. Financial hardship due to illness, acts of God or long periods of unemployment are considered valid reasons for an artist to receive money from these sources. If your financial troubles are due to frivolous overspending, perhaps you should consider taking a part-time job instead of taking money from these institutions. The funds are usually founded by individual advocates of artists such as Rubin Gorewitz's Change, Inc., or else they are set up by such membership organizations as the Authors League, which administers the Authors League Fund from donations from its members. In most cases, you do not have to be a member of the organization to receive its philanthropy, but it is hoped that you will return the money when you get back on your feet, so that others may avail themselves of these limited resources.

The emergency funds are:

EMERGENCY FUNDS

THE ACTORS FUND OF AMERICA
1501 Broadway
New York, NY 10036
(212) 221-7300.

ARTISTS EMERGENCY LOAN FUND
The Artists Foundation
110 Broad Street
Boston, MA 02110
No- or low-interest funds for up to six months.

ARTISTS' FELLOWSHIP INC.
47 Fifth Avenue
New York, NY 10003
(212) 255-7740
Emergency funds to professional visual artists.

THE ARTISTS' WELFARE FUND
32 Union Square East Suite 1103

New York, NY 10003
(212) 477-8795.
This organization occasionally offers an arts awards program with prize money.

THE AUTHORS LEAGUE FUND
234 West 44th Street
New York, NY 10036
(212) 391-3966.
Any professional writer who is a citizen may apply.

CARNEGIE FUND FOR AUTHORS
330 Sunrise Highway
Rockville Center, NY 11570
Open to authors who've had at least one book of reasonable length published commercially. Grants are available to cover financial emergencies arising from illness, fire or other acts of God.

CHANGE, INC.
c/o Rubin Gorewitz
Box 705
Cooper Station
New York, NY 10276
(212) 473-3742.
*This organization was established by
Robert Rauschenberg. It gives grants to
professional artists in all disciplines
undergoing health, fire or housing emergencies.*

EMERGENCY MATERIALS FUND
Committee for the Visual Arts
223 West Broadway
New York, NY 10013
(212) 226-3970
*Small grants are available to artists with
shows in nonprofit galleries who need
funds to finish work or for preparations
for the exhibition.*

KRASNER—POLLOCK FOUNDATION
P.O. Box 4957
New York, NY 10185
*Any painter, sculptor, mixed media artist
or graphic artist may apply. There is no
limit as to term or amount of loan.*

MUSICIAN'S EMERGENCY FUND
16 East 64th Street
New York, NY 10021
(212) 758-2450
*This fund has limited amounts to lend to
musicians in trouble. If you can, you
will be asked to perform in hospitals and
nursing homes.*

MUSICIAN'S FOUNDATION
200 West 55th Street
New York, NY 10010
(212) 247-5332.

P.E.N. FUND FOR WRITERS
P.E.N. American Center
568 Broadway
New York, NY 10013
(212) 334-1660
*Emergency grants and loans are avail-
able to help established writers through
financial crises.*

MARK ROTHKO FOUNDATION
1133 Broadway
New York, NY 10010
(212) 253-6662
*Emergency grants from $500 to $5,000.
This fund is particularly interested in
providing funds for older artists. Applications are accepted any time by letter describing your situation. A résumé should
be sent with your application.*

BARTER

An idea whose time has really rolled around again after twenty centuries is
bartering. Barter is merely an exchange system which doesn't utilize money.
It relies on the swapping of goods and services. The University of Wisconsin
Extension Service made an analysis of the barter system and concluded that it
was a system with many advantages. For one thing, barter is a value for value
exchange that is untouched by inflation. In situations where cash is scarce,
barter can increase your cash flow and your buying power by freeing your cash.
For example, if you can barter for your food, the cash that you would ordinarily
have spent on food can be saved and used for something else without putting
you in debt. The analysts also concluded that barter encourages an involved,
self-reliant life-style, helps to build trust, and takes the emphasis off money
and places it on a more human level of existence.

In order for barter really to work to any significant degree in your life, you
should probably try to join a skills exchange, barter bank or clearing house.

There are numerous such organizations springing up across the country. To begin with, you join and pay a small monthly membership fee which entitles you to receive a catalogue of goods and services being offered by other members and in which you yourself may advertise. If you are interested in making a trade, you then contact the individual who has advertised. Other organizations work on a system of credits and debits which are kept track of by a central office.

Finding such a group, or organizing one yourself, is a good idea if you really want to make barter a significant part of your life, since otherwise the biggest problem is hooking up with others to deal with.

The IRS is attempting increasingly to intervene in these sorts of cashless exchanges. There is a $13 billion barter business in the United States. If your bartering is mainly on the level of swapping favors such as baby-sitting or house-sitting, you needn't worry. If, however, you are bartering objects or more skilled services (e.g., trading a drawing for a doctor's services), be aware that you are supposed to declare the fair market value of the goods and services given you as part of your income. Now, of course, you can probably get away without reporting this, but be aware that IRS agents are particularly alert to this possibility among freelancers—especially among those who show very little income.

To find out more about this growing trend, read *Barter* by Constance Stapleton and Phyllis Richman (Scribners, 1978); *Let's Try Barter* by Charles Morrow Wilson (Davin, 1980); or *How Much Will You Take for It?* by Annie Proulx (Garden Way, 1981).

The following organizations offer barter services:

BUSINESS EXCHANGE, INC.
4716 Vineland Avenue
North Hollywood, CA 91602
(213) 877–2161; (818) 761–2085

ATWOOD RICHARDS, INC.
99 Park Avenue
New York, NY 10016
(212) 490–1414

PFEISTER BARTER
274 Madison Avenue
New York, NY 10017
(212) 683–1500

Some barter magazines are:

Barter Communiqué (Full Circle Marketing Corp., Box 2527, Sarasota, FL 34230; [813] 349-3300)

The Great Exchange (655 Madison Avenue, New York, NY 10021)

WORKING OFF THE BOOKS: PRO AND CON

Freelancers are often given the opportunity to work off the books. Users of your artwork may pay you under the table, or you may decide not to report your tips from a waiting job, or not to report the income you make as a part-time gardener. At times you may be so poor that you need every penny you make and then some, and you can't afford to have money withheld. There are points in favor of working off the books; but for the most part, these pros are overridden by cons.

PROS

- You have more take-home cash.
- You won't have to pay any taxes on it.

CONS

- The IRS may catch up with you without even auditing you. What if they decide to audit the restaurant and find that you earned $3,000 waiting on tables?
- If you're not paying Social Security taxes you may not be getting credit (see the section Social Security Benefits in chapter 19). The more you earn, the higher your Social Security payments will be upon your retirement.
- Even though you may pay slightly higher taxes, the higher your gross income the better when it comes time to borrow money. Many freelancers who've shaved their figures at tax time wish that they had padded them when they apply for credit.
- You may think you're being given a good deal, but actually your employer is benefitting more than you are. She doesn't have to bother with a lot of bookkeeping regarding withholding taxes and paying Social Security, and she doesn't have to make unemployment or worker's compensation payments on your behalf. Should you get badly hurt on the job (as a freelance graphic designer friend of mine recently did), you would have to rely on your own insurance for medical and disability coverage. Do you have such a policy? If you are laid off, you won't get unemployment.

As with most points of freelance survival, there is no unbendable rule. Sometimes you will be too broke not to work off the books if you have a chance to, but if you don't have to go this route, it is better to avoid lying about your income. It is illegal, remember.

MAGIC

You may want to try a less concrete way of filling your coffer. It is a performer's good luck charm taught me by the actress Fiddle Viracola, and I enter it here not to be precious but because it has worked. Buy a sansevieria (or snake plant), which costs about $2 at cut-rate plant stores. Sansevierias are those pointed jade and celadon plants which look like upended artichoke leaves and seemed to predominate in 1950's decoration. Take a silver coin (a dollar was recommended, though a dime or a leftover foreign coin will do fine) and press it down into the earth so that it disappears. Then water the plant. I have added an additional step to this procedure which I feel potentiates the magic. I add any coins I happen to find on the street to the pot. If you're not inclined to believe in this sort of thing it probably won't work for you, but it has worked astonishingly well for me and several other artists I know.

CHAPTER FOURTEEN
GRANTS

I was very surprised at the small number of freelancers who had ever considered applying for a grant.* Certainly grant money isn't just doled out like welfare, but millions of dollars are given to artists and art groups every year by the government and by foundations, public and private. The time spent in applying for grants, though not insignificant, is time well spent. If your project is a worthy one, and you can get this across to the grant committee, you have a decent chance of receiving funding for the creation or the finishing of a work.

Many artists seem to feel demeaned at accepting "charity." To me, this is an unrealistically squeamish attitude: it seems to me that if the creation of your work is really important to you, you shouldn't care where the necessary money comes from as long as it comes legally. There is a limit to how much an individual can do. If your work is making experimental films, for instance, which are expensive to produce and not yet particularly profitable, you have little hope of earning enough in an outside job to support yourself and your work and still have time left to film. A grant isn't welfare; it is financial recognition that your work is important and deserves to be created even if you yourself can't afford to, and even if the work ultimately earns no money.

AID TO INDIVIDUALS

Since 1969, the number of grants to individuals has greatly decreased because of changes in tax laws governing the foundations' deductions of such grants. Also, nowadays it is far less important for a rich person's public image to be known as a patron of the arts. In the days when fortunes were being made very rapidly, the newly rich took great pains to show their cultivation by becoming patrons of the arts. In these times it is, unfortunately, equally prestigious to own a football team or to simply give a lot of parties.

It is much easier to come by a grant if you are a not-for-profit, tax-exempt corporation such as a theater group or a dance company. There is still hope for individuals, though to tell the truth, it is very limited. The most important sources of money for individuals are:

*For the purposes of this book, a grant is a subsidy given to an individual or a nonprofit, tax-exempt organization to create or complete a work or program.

Prizes   *Foundation grants*
Fellowships and scholarships   *Private donors*
Federal grants

Prizes are given out by many different types of institutions—including educational institutions, foundations, professional associations, government affiliates here and abroad—and by individuals. Prize money is usually obtained either by entering your work in a contest or by being chosen by a committee on the basis of your contribution as an artist. Prize money that you win through an application is usually taxed, but prizes for which you are selected without applying usually are not taxable. If you do win a prize you will want to check with its donor as to its status with the IRS.

Fellowships are generally given by educational and professional societies. Fellowships usually consist of the use of facilities such as editing rooms or sound studios. Occasionally a living stipend is also paid. The dollar value of a fellowship is not normally tax-deductible. A *scholarship*, as the name implies, is given for the purpose of study. Educational institutions, professional societies, government sources, foreign governments, foundations and individual patrons are the usual sources of scholarship money.

Federal grants are given by the government. Normally, the best way for an individual to gain access to these funds is by applying through a local arts council or other umbrella organization. (An umbrella organization is a group which is empowered to receive tax-exempt monies. Your local or state arts council is the best place to find out about such groups and find to which of them you might be able to attach yourself.) Recently, many states have cut back, or dropped altogether, their programs of aid to individual artists. The same is even more true regarding *foundation grants*. However, one hope in this area is for you to find a foundation or a company with a very specific interest which your individual project suits. For instance, an individual wishing to make a documentary on noise may not be able to get a foundation grant from those foundations which normally fund groups unless he goes to one with a parent company in some way related to the project—such as a company that makes acoustical products.

Individual donors have accounted for much of the aid to artists over past centuries. And during the middle part of this century there were tax advantages to individuals who became patrons. Unfortunately, these tax breaks are no longer in effect when the object of philanthropy is an individual artist: nowadays you can get a deduction for donating money to an opera or ballet company but not to a painter or filmmaker.

SOURCEBOOKS

The best sources of aid to individuals can be found by consulting the following:

Awards List. Available from Poets and Writers, 201 West 54th Street, New York, NY 10019. A listing of 100 grants, fellowships and prizes available to writers.

Encyclopedia of Associations. Available from Gale Research Co., Book Tower, Detroit, MI 48226. This volume gives information on U.S. nonprofit organizations. Excellent source on grant-giving organizations which are not foundations.

Foundation Grants to Individuals. Available from the Foundation Center, 79 Fifth Avenue, New York, NY 10003. This volume has five indexes to help locate 1,041 foundations that award grants of $2,000 or more to individuals. Information includes: contact names, size, assets and number of individuals receiving grants from a particular foundation.

Grants and Awards Available to American Writers. Available from P.E.N. American Center, 568 Broadway, New York, NY 10012. A thorough listing of grants and prizes offered to writers.

Grants and Awards in Music. Chaddie B. Kruger. Available from Music Educators National Conference, 8150 Leesburg Pike, Vienna, VA 22180.

Grants in Photography: How to Get Them. L. Mosher. Available from Amphoto, 750 Zeckendorf Blvd., New York, NY 11530.

The Grants Register. Roland Turner, ed. St. Martin's Press. Information on awards, fellowships and the like, for individuals in all fields.

Money Business: Grants and Awards for Creative Artists. Available from the Artists Foundation, Inc., 10 Park Plaza, Boston, MA 02116.

Money for Artists: A Guide to Grants and Awards for Individual Artists. Rebecca Lewis and Rita K. Roosevelt, eds. Available from the American Council for the Arts, 1285 Avenue of the Americas, New York, NY 10019 ($9.95 paper). This book is an exhaustive guide to grants, awards, fellowships and residencies available to individual artists.

National Directory of Arts Internships. Warren Christenson. California Institute of the Arts. Available from the American Council for the Arts, 1285 Avenue of the Americas, New York, NY 10019 ($25.00). This book describes nationwide opportunities for individuals who wish to become interns in the fields of dance, theater, music, art, design, film and video.

The National Directory of Grants and Aid to Individuals in the Arts. Available from Washington International Arts Letter, P.O. Box 9005, Washington, DC 20003. This book is a very complete listing of grants, scholarships and prizes to individuals.

Sponsors: A Guide for Video and Filmmakers 1987. Available from the American Council for the Arts, 1285 Avenue of the Americas, New York, NY 10019.

Supporting Yourself as an Artist: A Practical Guide. Deborah A. Hoover. Oxford University Press ($13.95). Available from the American Council for the Arts, 1285 Avenue of the Americas, New York, NY 10019. This book, written by a fund-raiser and grant-giver, advises you on how to approach funding organizations.

APPLICATION PROCEDURES
FOR INDIVIDUALS

Application procedures vary depending upon the source of the potential funding. You should send for the organization's brochure or bulletin and study it well. It should clue you in on application procedures, deadlines and other important information that you need.

Normally, your first step is to make contact via a preliminary letter which briefly outlines your proposal, tells who you are (some grantors request a résumé at this stage of the process) and gives a ballpark estimate of how much money you will need from them. It is important that you study the brochure of the organization's entry in one of the references listed above in order to determine the ceiling on what they will give. If the maximum paid out for a project in the past was $4,000, don't ask for $6,500. Your preliminary letter should result in your being sent an application form or given the go-ahead to apply. If you are provided with a form, read it carefully at least *twice*, then write out your answers on a separate page, edit them, make sure they fit into the space allotted (some forms tell you that you may add pages; others say not to) and then type out the application obsessively neatly. If you haven't already been asked for a résumé, it goes off with the application. The budget also goes off at this time. Your budget should be accurate and well researched. Many grantors make their decisions not on artistic merit, but upon clarity of purpose, your letters and evidence of good financial planning.

LETTERS OF REFERENCE

You will be asked to supply letters, or references, and this step is crucial. Many grantors rely on these recommendations when choosing recipients. It is therefore to your advantage to get the best references you possibly can. This is another reason for you to groom connections and make sure your work is widely seen (see the section Connections in chapter 2). The best references are prominent people, particularly those in your field, who know and like you. Next are former teachers, followed by your agent or rep. You should make contact with references well before their letters are due. Some grantors provide forms and questionnaires for this purpose; others simply ask for letters.

The letter writer should tell how long she has known you and in what capacity. She should also tell what she thinks of your work, your professional commitment and your potential. Details should be given, but two or three typed pages should suffice. Be sure she knows when the letter must arrive at the grantor's office. It is a courtesy for you to provide stamps and an envelope for the mailing of the letter. If the mails in your area are unreliable or if you are close to your deadline, take no chances: spend the money to send your references' letters to the grantor by Express Mail. Don't forget to thank your references for their efforts.

OTHER PROCEDURES

Not all grants to individuals are applied for in this way. For some, you merely send the names and addresses of your references. For others, you must be nominated by someone important in the field. In many cases you may go through an abbreviation of the procedure for nonprofit groups (see page 202, Aid to Nonprofit Groups).

ARTISTS' COLONIES

While not exactly vacation spots, artists' colonies provide the very important service to creative people of making a quiet, bucolic setting available to those who need it most. To be able to work under ideal conditions, away from the usual pressures of your life, can help you to organize yourself and give you a sense of direction for months afterwards.

Several of the colonies, such as MacDowell, Yaddo and Millay, are former estates with lovely old-fashioned rooms and commodious grounds. Unlike the popular image of the artists' colony as part resident psychiatric hospital and part summer camp for grown-ups, these retreats really provide a peaceful setting for those who need to find some quiet. Generally, the only rule is that no one disturbs anyone else or takes up an undue amount of space.

Each colony has a deadline for applications. Some are completely free of charge. Others charge a small fee per day, although even these colonies will occasionally waive or substantially reduce this for needy but promising artists. Others provide free accommodation but expect you to supply food.

Escaping from one's family is often what is most needed, and accordingly, some of the colonies do not allow mates and children during a residency.

It is hard to predict in advance just how you will do in one of these colonies. Some artists thrive, finding their productivity greatly enhanced. Others find that they are distracted by the beauty of the setting, the other artists' silent presence or the absence of their families.

One painter I spoke with said, "For me, there's nothing like it—the solitude, the clean living, the utter peace that comes when the ringing phones and the footsteps in the hall are not for you. When I'm at Millay, I feel as though I'm alone in the world, and for me that's the best way to create."

On the other hand, a young woman writer who had just been to Cummington had this to say: "Though I found it very helpful for my work, it was just a little bit too long to be without my husband. I got terribly lonely and spent the last week trying to force myself to work instead of pining for him."

I myself share that first artist's view to such an extreme that I do my best work alone in the wilderness, in a remote area where no one but the FBI or Interpol could find me. My personal version of a retreat to an artists' colony is to travel out of season to some country that I want to see, carrying a manuscript and paper. I find that I have to move around every week or so. Other people who work this way find that they prefer to rent undistinguished digs in the country for very little money. You will probably have to go a bit farther afield these days to find a rural area where you can still rent cheaply, and zealous development is worsening the situation daily.

Costs have risen so abruptly that most colonies have changed their fees. A few still offer free room and board, but most ask that you pay what you can. This is normally arranged *after* you arrive so that no one deserving is turned away for lack of money.

Here is a sampling of artists' colonies which accept general applications. It is not exhaustive. A call to your state arts council might turn up a similar retreat that is open only to residents of your state.

ARTISTS FOR ENVIRONMENT FOUNDATION
Box 44
Walpack Center, NJ 07881
(201) 948-3630.
Visual artists are accepted here to serve residencies within the Delaware Water Gap National Recreation Area, on a semester basis coinciding with Delaware Water Gap College's program. Residencies are for three months: September to December or February to May. Artists are provided with a house, utilities included. The application deadline for both sessions is November 15.

ARTPARK
Box 371
Lewiston, NY 14092
(716) 745-3377.
This colony accepts visual artists, architects, performers and craftspeople. The season is June through Labor Day, and applications are due October 1. A stipend and room and board are provided.

ATLANTIC CENTER FOR THE ARTS
1414 Art Center Avenue
New Smyrna Beach, FL 32069
(904) 427-6975.
The center holds 4 three-week residencies per year for visual, literary and performing artists. There is a "master artist" for each discipline and about thirty fellows.

BLUE MOUNTAIN CENTER
Blue Mountain, NY 12812
(518) 352-7391.
Choreographers, composers, visual artists and writers may apply for residencies. The season runs June 15 through February.

CENTRUM FOUNDATION
Box 1158
Fort Warden State Park
Port Townsend, WA 98368.
This colony accepts all artists including performers. A room and studio space, as needed, are provided. The season is September through May.

CREEKWOOD COLONY FOR THE ARTS
204 West Linwood Drive
Homewood, AL 35209
(205) 870-4261
All artists, including performers, are invited to apply to this nineteenth-century working farm. No application deadline. Send a S.A.S.E. for an application.

CUMMINGTON COMMUNITY OF THE ARTS
Cummington, MA 01026
(413) 634-2172
All artists, performers included, are eligible for a full two-month summer residency or a one- to eight-month residency October through May. Families with children are welcome in July and August. The fee, which covers room and full board, varies depending upon the season. Some financial aid is available. Cummington is especially interested in disadvantaged artists. In addition to the fee, you are asked to donate five hours of work each week for the good of the community. The application deadline for summer is April 1.

CURRY HILL PLANTATION WRITERS RETREAT
Bainbridge, GA
Mailing Address: 404 Crestmont Avenue
Hattiesburgh, MS 39401
(601) 264-7034.
Writers may come for a one-week session in the spring.

DJERASSI FOUNDATION RESIDENT ARTIST PROGRAM
235 Bear Gulch Road
Woodside, CA 94062
(415) 851-8395.
Musicians, choreographers and composers may apply for one- to three-month residencies. Offered are room, board and studio space.

DOBIE-PAISANO FELLOWSHIP PROJECT
University of Texas, Main Bldg. 101
Office of Graduate Studies
Austin, TX 78712
(512) 471-7213.
This situation is open only to writers.

DORLAND MOUNTAIN COLONY
Box 6
Temecula, CA 92390
(714) 676-5039.
This colony is open year-round to choreographers, composers, media artists, musicians, visual artists and writers. Your stay is in exchange for a certain amount of work.

DORSET COLONY HOUSE
Box 519, Church Street
Dorset, VT 05251
(802) 867-2223.
Visual artists and writers may live and work here. The season runs from September 15 to May 15. A contribution is requested.

ALDEN B. DOW CREATIVITY CENTER
Northwood Institute
Midland, MI 48640
(517) 832-4403.
All artists including musicians and performers are invited here. The season runs mid-June through mid-August.

FINE ARTS WORK CENTER
24 Pearl Street, Box 565
Provincetown, MA 02657
(617) 487-9960.
Ten writers and ten visual artists are each awarded a seven-month fellowship which runs from October 1 to May 1. Living space and studios are provided. Some financial aid is available, but funds are limited. Apply prior to February 1 of the year in which you want to go.

THE WILLIAM FLANAGAN MEMORIAL CREATIVE PERSONS CENTER
c/o The Edward F. Albee Foundation, Inc.
14 Harrison Street
New York, NY 10013
(212) 226-2020.
The center, founded in 1968, is in Montauk, New York. It is open from May 1 to October 15 for writers and painters. There is space for six artists at a time. Residencies are for one month. Artists share the kitchen and pay for their own food. Applications are reviewed between January 1 and April 1 and should include work samples, a biography and two recommendations. Please send a S.A.S.E. for the return of your materials.

HAMBRIDGE CENTER
P.O. Box 8
Rabun Gap, GA 39568
(404) 746-5718
All artists including weavers, potters and architects are invited to apply for residencies of two weeks to three months. Families are not invited. No financial aid is available. Apply two months in advance of your intended stay.

INSTITUTE FOR ART AND URBAN RESOURCES (P.S.1)
46-01 21 Street
Long Island City, NY 11101
(718) 784-2084.
Open to visual artists and sculptors.

KALANI HONUA INTERCULTURAL AND RETREAT CENTER
Box 4500
Kalapana, HI 96778
(808) 965-7828.
All artists are welcomed here and should apply one month prior to their intended visit. Financial aid is available. Room, board and work space are provided.

JOHN MICHAEL KOHLER ARTS CENTER
608 New York Avenue
Sheboygan, WI 53081
(414) 458-6144.
This colony is open year-round to writers. A stipend is offered along with a room.

THE D. H. LAWRENCE SUMMER FELLOWSHIP
D. H. Lawrence Committee
English Department
University of New Mexico
Albuquerque, NM 87131
(505) 277-6347.
This fellowship is awarded annually to one writer who spends the summer at D. H. Lawrence's former ranch. Families are welcome. Application deadline is January 31.

THE MACDOWELL COLONY
100 High Street
Peterborough, NH 03458
(603) 924-3886 or
163 East 81st Street
New York, NY 10021
(212) 966-4860.
Each resident receives room, board and exclusive use of a work space. Limits: thirty persons in summer and fifteen to

twenty at other times. The colony accepts professional writers, visual artists and composers. You must apply at least six months in advance. Fees are set according to ability to pay.

MAITLAND ART CENTER
231 Packwood Avenue
Maitland, FL 32751
(305) 645-2181.
Visual artists including craftspeople are invited.

THE MILLAY COLONY
Steepletop
Austerlitz, NY 12017
(518) 392-3103.
This colony accepts writers, artists and composers. Write or call for an application.

NETHERS FARM RETREAT FOR POETS AND CLASSICAL MUSICIANS
Box 41
Woodville, VA 22749
(703) 987-8913.
This twenty-seven-acre informal farm retreat in the Blue Ridge foothills is open year-round to poets and classical musicians. A limited number of one- to four-week residencies are available. Others may come for $45 per week or $160 per month or in exchange for labor. Guests purchase and prepare their own food. Write for information and application. There is no deadline for applying.

NIANGUA COLONY
Route 1
Stoutland, MO 65567
No telephone.
Residencies of two weeks to two months are offered to architects, choreographers, composers, musicians, sculptors, visual artists and writers.

EUGENE O'NEILL THEATER CENTER
Opera Musical Theater Conference
305 Greatneck Road
Waterford, CT 06385
(203) 443-5378.
Composers and writers may apply to come to this conference in August. A stipend, room, board and travel expenses are provided.

EUGENE O'NEILL THEATER CENTER NATIONAL CRITICS INSTITUTE
234 West 44th Street
New York, NY 10036
(212) 382-2790.
This program is open to writers during the month of July. Apply by April 15. Financial aid is given.

PALENVILLE INTERARTS COLONY
Box 59
Palenville, NY 12463
(518) 678-9021 or (212) 206-7564.
This colony is open to all artists. Application deadline is April 1 for June through September residencies. The usual fee is waived for those who want to work in exchange for their stay.

RAGDALE FOUNDATION
1260 North Green Bay Road
Lake Forest, IL 60045
(312) 234-1063.
Residencies of two weeks to two months are available for performers, visual artists, composers, writers and architects in this charming nineteenth-century house on the prairie. The fee includes room and board. Some financial assistance may be available.

MILDRED I. REID WRITERS COLONY
Penacook Road
Contoocook, NH 03229
(603) 746-3625.
The colony is open in July and August. Residencies are had in exchange for work.

ROCKLAND CENTER FOR THE ARTS
27 South Greenbush Road
West Nyack, NY 10994
(914) 358-0877.
While not a colony, nearby writers in search of work space in quiet, rural surroundings may apply here. Call for applications.

ROSWELL MUSEUM AND ARTS CENTER
100 West 11 Street
Roswell, NM 88201
(505) 624-6744.
This colony is open all year for visual artists and craftspeople. A stipend, room, board, studio and materials are offered.

SCULPTURE SPACE
12 Gates Street
Utica, NY 13502
(315) 724-8381.

This colony is open all year to visual artists and writers. There is a limited amount of financial assistance for which you must apply by December 15. Otherwise there is no application deadline for nonfunded residencies.

SQUAW VALLEY COMMUNITY OF WRITERS
Box 2352
Olympic Valley, CA 95730
(916) 583-5200.
Writers should apply by June 1 for the month-long residency in August. A fellowship is offered to those chosen.

UCROSS FOUNDATION
Ucross Route, Box 19
Ucross, WY 82835
(307) 737-2291.
Architects, composers, media artists, visual artists and writers are invited to apply. The season is August through May.

VILLA MONTALVO CENTER FOR THE ARTS
Box 158
Saratoga, CA 95071
(408) 741-3421.
This colony is open year-round to architects, composers, musicians, visual artists and writers.

THE VIRGINIA CENTER FOR THE CREATIVE ARTS
Sweet Briar, VA 24595
(804) 946-7236.
Twenty-one residencies of one to three months are open to writers, visual artists and composers at Mount San Angelo, an estate adjacent to the Sweet Briar College campus. College facilities are available to fellows. The fee of $15 per day includes room, board and studio. Financial aid is available. Write to William Smart, Director, for an application form and further information.

FRIENDS OF WEYMOUTH INC.
Weymouth Center
Box 839

Southern Pines, NC 28387
(919) 692-6261.
Composers, musicians, performers, sculptors and writers are accepted here year-round.

THE HELENE WURLITZER FOUNDATION OF NEW MEXICO
P.O. Box 545
Taos, NM 87571
(505) 758-2413.
Twelve studios are available to artists in all media.

YADDO
Box 395
Saratoga Springs, NY 12866
(518) 584-0746.
Yaddo, a beautiful turn-of-the-century estate, is open to writers, composers and visual artists. Residencies are usually for one to two months. Applications are due by January 15, but spaces remaining for the winter period are assigned during a second admissions period in August. There is no fixed fee, but artists are expected to make a contribution. Yaddo is planning a summer residency program for printmakers and metalworkers at the Hand Hollow Foundation in East Chatham, NY. Write to Yaddo for details.

THE YARD
Box 405
Chilmark, MA 02535
(617) 645-9662.
Performers and musicians should apply by January 1. The colony is open May through September.

YELLOWSPRINGS INSTITUTE
Art School Rd.
Chester Springs, PA 19425
(215) 827-9117.
Performers, choreographers, musicians are invited to apply for residencies by December 1. Stipend, room and board are provided to those who are chosen.

FOREIGN COLONIES

ALTOS DE CHAVON
1 Gulf and Western Plaza
New York, NY 10023
(212) 333-3388.

All artists may apply by July 30 for three-month residencies from September to June.

AMERICAN ACADEMY IN ROME
41 East 65th Street
New York, NY 10021
(212) 535-4250.
Architects, media artists, sculptors and visual artists can apply for fellowships. Application deadline is November 15.

**BELLAGIO STUDY AND CONFER-
ENCE CENTER**
The Rockefeller Foundation
11333 Avenue of the Americas
New York, NY 10036
(212) 869-8500.
Composers, musicians, visual artists and writers may apply ten months prior to the time they would like to visit.

LEIGHTON ARTIST COLONY
c/o Banff Centre
Box 1020
Banff, Alberta, Canada T0L 0C0
(403) 762-6216.
All artists except performers may attend. The center is open year-round, and a fellowship is offered.

**SASKATCHEWAN WRITERS/ARTIST
COLONY**
Box 3986
Regina, Saskatchewan
Canada M5S 1T6
(306) 757-6310.
Visual artists, writers and composers are invited. Room and board are provided.

SCOTTISH SCULPTURE WORKSHOP
1 Main Street
Lumsden, Aberdeenshire
Scotland, AB5 4JN
Tel: Lumsden 04648 372.

THE TYRONE GUTHRIE CENTER
Annaghmakerrig, Newbliss
County Monaghan, Ireland
Tel. 047-54003.
Three-month residencies for choreographers, composers, musicians, visual artists and writers. Financial aid is available only to Irish artists.

AID TO NONPROFIT GROUPS

Before a foundation or any other donor will contribute money to your organization, you must be certified not-for-profit and you must be tax-exempt.

NOT-FOR-PROFIT CORPORATIONS

It is generally easier to get your tax-exempt status if you are incorporated. You will also find that banks, landlords and others you have financial dealings with will be more cooperative if you are a corporation. Psychologically, it makes you seem more responsible if you have gone to the trouble and expense involved in incorporating. In fact, incorporation is to your advantage as an officer or member of the group, since one of the major advantages of incorporation is the limited liability of its members no matter what happens to the corporation. A corporation is a separate entity from its members, and they can't be held personally responsible when it is in financial trouble. While the underlying concepts are the same, this sort of not-for-profit corporation and the sort of profit-making business corporation an individual freelancer may form as a businessperson should not be confused. An arts group hoping to get funded generally incorporates as a not-for-profit corporation in order to get the necessary tax-exempt status.

You will need a lawyer to help you incorporate. Volunteer Lawyers for the Arts will do this for you (see chapter 20, Legal Matters, for addresses). Otherwise, you can often find lawyers' ads (in states where they're allowed) which show their fees for incorporation. You can probably get it done for $500 to

$1,000. In order to incorporate as a Type B not-for-profit corporation under the laws of New York State, you must satisfy the following two requirements:

1. Your primary, though not necessarily exclusive, purpose must be nonpecuniary (not-for-profit) although you may engage in profit-making activities to further your non-profit activities (e.g., you may sell refreshments at performances if you plow the money gained back into your organization).
2. No part of your assets, income or profits may be distributed to members, directors or officers except as salary for services rendered.

Many corporations are chartered in the state of Delaware, because the process of incorporation is quicker there. However, no matter where you incorporate, you will have to secure authority to do business in your home state.

You will need legal advice when incorporating, so I will limit this discussion to the matters you must take care of before you can receive funds. A very complete and informative treatment of incorporating and obtaining tax exemption is published by Volunteer Lawyers for the Arts. It is called *To Be or Not to Be: An Artist's Guide to Not-for-Profit Incorporation* and is available from Volunteer Lawyers for the Arts, 1285 Avenue of the Americas, New York, NY 10019. While it cannot replace the personalized guidance of a lawyer, it is simply written and well worth reading.

TAX-EXEMPT STATUS

Once you have successfully incorporated as a Type B not-for-profit corporation, you must then apply for exemption from tax both on the income you receive and on contributions. You will also want to get sales tax exemption through your state department of finance and taxation.

You apply for federal tax exemption by writing: Internal Revenue Service, 1111 Constitution Avenue, Washington, DC 20224.

Request IRS Publications #557 and Form 1023. You should probably retain the same lawyer or legal service to help you file. If your group qualifies, you will be given the code number 501 (C)(3).

If you are a new group, or a small one, and you are not yet tax-exempt, you will need an umbrella organization to help receive monies for you and to help with your accounting. The first step toward locating such a sponsoring organization in your area is to contact the nearest office of Volunteer Lawyers for the Arts. This organization will be supremely helpful when you are setting yourself up, and it has branches all over the country.

The Cultural Council Foundation (625 Broadway, New York, NY 10012; [212] 473-5660) handles grant money for numerous nonprofit, unincorporated arts organizations. While they work with groups at the moment, they are discussing working with individuals in the future. In addition, CCF will help train new arts groups in survival tactics such as basic grantsmanship and accounting.

PERSONNEL

While the law requires only that you have two officers, a president and a secretary, you may also want to add a financial director, who is in charge of receiving and disbursing money. Both the financial director and the director of the whole project should have the power to sign checks. Since corporate officers are considered employees and are thus entitled to workers compensation and unemployment benefits, it is a good idea for everyone's sake to choose directors who are otherwise employed and receive these benefits elsewhere.

You may also decide to have a board of directors which can have voting privileges or not, as you choose. Try to select a few names which are prominent and recognized in your field. It certainly adds clout to your letterhead and may be a positive benefit in your quest for philanthropy.

GOALS

Once you have chosen your key personnel and have your application for tax-exempt status in the mail, it is time to sit down and get a consensus as to the organization's goals and image. Don't waste time talking about whom to apply to for funds until you know exactly what it is you have to offer, what results you will show, and who will benefit. One of the main reasons for rejections is applications which look as though the organization had not thought out its goals. So take some time to hash out just who you are and what you are trying to do.

BUDGET

During this time you must also come up with an operating budget. Your budget will be divided into direct and indirect costs. Direct costs include wages and salaries, personnel benefits, travel costs, supplies, communications costs and anything else directly connected with the expense of operating your organization.

Indirect costs include salaries for such outside personnel as accountants, plant operating expenses and depreciation of equipment.

GOVERNMENT OR CORPORATE FUNDING?

Government grants are generally awarded to projects which are considered valuable enough to subsidize with the taxpayers' money. This means that the project must either have far-reaching implications for the public or must explore a totally new area. In addition, you must have been a tax-exempt, nonprofit corporation (or under some sort of nonprofit umbrella) for two years or more before the government will touch you. Occasionally a nonprofit organization will propose a project that will benefit the government in some way, such as creating a training program, producing audiovisual materials or making a survey. In such cases, the government may decide to award a contract to the organization. But don't hold your breath waiting for this to happen to your group: government contracts to arts organizations are scarce.

Here are some differences between private and government funding:

1. Foundations are usually judged to be more flexible and open to innovation and experimental projects, although some artists dispute this judgment, saying that foundations, too, only like you if your message is right.
2. Applications for government grants are almost always done on printed forms; applications to foundations rarely are.

3. Foundation proposals are usually shorter.
4. Foundations are not subject to the Public Information Act and thus don't have to provide you with a reason for a turndown.
5. Recipients of National Endowment for the Arts grants must comply with parts 3, 5 and 505 of Title 29 of the Code of Federal Regulations, which specifies that all professional personnel and technical and mechanical labor be compensated according to the standards of their unions.

   Recipients of all government grants are required to comply with the Civil Rights Act of 1964 and with the Rehabilitation Act of 1973. Together, these bar discrimination on the basis of race, color, national origin or personal handicap. You must file an "Assurance of Compliance" form when you apply for a government grant. This form will serve for all future applications to the same agency.
6. The government has much stricter standards for your keeping track of money they give you, and they will audit your financial records.
7. All recipients of federal grants have to assume at least 5 percent of the operating costs, either in the form of equipment bought, services paid for by the organization or staff overtime donated.

WHERE TO APPLY FOR GOVERNMENT GRANTS

Probably most arts-related projects will gravitate toward the National Endowment for the Arts or the National Endowment for the Humanities or, possibly, toward the Department of Health and Human Services. You should send for their program guides to get an idea as to what their interests are in relation to your group's special area.

NATIONAL ENDOWMENT FOR THE ARTS
1100 Pennsylvania Avenue, NW
Washington, DC 20506
(202) 682-5400

NATIONAL ENDOWMENT FOR THE HUMANITIES
1100 Pennsylvania Avenue, NW
Washington, DC 20506
(202) 786-0438

U.S. DEPARTMENT OF HEALTH AND HUMAN SERVICES
200 Independence Avenue, SW
Washington, DC 20201
(202) 475-0257

If, after consideration, you decide that it would be appropriate for your project to seek government funding, you should take these steps.

First, you need information. You should obtain a catalogue from the government agency (or agencies) you have targeted. And the following publications will also be helpful:

The Catalogue of Federal Domestic Assistance. Available at the nearest Foundation Center Collection. This is considered the best source of information on government grants. It lists and describes all federal programs which offer funds.

Des Marais, Phillip. How to Get Government Grants. Public Service Materials Center, 1975.

Encyclopedia of U.S. Government Benefits. Roy A. Grisham, Jr. and Paul D. McConaughy, eds. T. Y. Crowell, 1977.

The Federal Register. Available at the nearest Foundation Center Collection (see the list of regional collections on page 208). This is published two or three times a year and contains guidelines and regulations for government grant programs.

Hillman, Howard. *The Art of Winning Government Grants.* Vanguard Press, 1977.

Since government grant applications are generally made on forms supplied by them, your next step is to send off to the targeted agencies for their application forms. The information they will need will be:

1. The title of your project.
2. The name of the project director.
3. The time period for which aid is requested.
4. A statement of total direct costs.
5. The name of the organization's government liaison.
6. The name of the person responsible for accounting.
7. The organization's objective.
8. A detailed budget.

SOME POINTERS ON FEDERAL FUNDING

Often a good strategy for small organizations to use is to apply for federal funds which are routed through state and local arts councils and agencies. The waiting and application procedure will probably be less onerous this way.

It never hurts to stay in touch with local government officials, congressmen and senators. Find out what their interests are: perhaps one of them is on a relevant committee. Ask to have your organization put on the mailing list for *The Congressional Record.* Keep them informed via press releases or an occasional letter of what you're doing and of what effect it will have on their constituencies.

When all of your applications are complete you will have to sit and wait for six to nine months—about the length of time it takes them to act on these applications. Also, you may have to host a site visit in which the prospective grantors will come around to see your project's facilities and operations.

Sometimes, when the money comes, it is given to you as matching funds or as a challenge grant which you match with contributions from other sources each dollar, or every other dollar, the government gives you.

Federal money is paid once a year, either as a letter of credit or as a Treasury check. Because of this delay, organizations have sprung up which lend money to nonprofit recipients of grants until the actual grant money comes in. Funding is for one year at a time, with applications renewable annually. Once you have gotten your federal money, you must submit expenditure reports which basically tell how the government's investment in your project is being used, what people or institutions are being served and the outcome of this. These must be submitted according to certain deadlines which vary from agency to agency. You should also include any items you have published or which have appeared about your organization. Bear in mind that it never hurts, when seeking continuing support, to publish as much as possible on what you are doing. This keeps you in the public eye: if the government decided to drop your funding they would have to answer to the people. Many of the materials that you use, such as photo offprints of published articles, can be used equally profitably in press kits and other sorts of publicity and fund-raising.

FOUNDATION GRANTS

If you decide that a private foundation or a corporation would be more appropriate as a source of funds, then you will have a larger task, for more will depend on your ability to sell yourself. There are many more foundations to choose from, and since there are no printed forms you will have a lot more writing to do. On the other hand, the large number of foundations, some of them with quite specific interests, makes for a higher probability of actually getting funded. "A foundation is a nonprofit organization in business to give away money," as Patricia and Daniel Gaby point out in their book, *Nonprofit Organization Handbook*, and if you approach the right organizations in the right tone, they won't go out of their way to deny you funds. In fact, they need you as much as you need them—your existence keeps them in business and vice versa. All you must do to get a foundation to support you is be able to sell yourself in such a way that you can prove you are working within its area of interest and can produce a good product.

As soon as you have organized the personnel who will be involved in the fund-raising effort, you should hold a meeting and get it straight as to exactly who you are, what you have to offer, how much money you'll need in order to function and what results you can promise for that money in a year's time. The following questions should probably be part of your agenda:

1. What is unique about our project? How does it differ from similar ones?
2. What do we expect to accomplish in a year? (Be specific about your goals.)
3. What do we offer? (In one sentence.)
4. Who will be served?
5. What credible authorities will endorse us?
6. How long will the project last?
7. What will become of us when our funding expires?

Spend as many meetings as you must to arrive at answers you all agree on and which you can communicate effectively to others, for these answers are really the germ of a proposal.

Researching Potential Donors. Your next step is to go to a library, preferably to one of the reference collections which have been organized in every state by the Foundation Center, which is an independent, nonprofit organization supported by foundations. Its purpose is to disseminate information on private giving through programs to the public, nationwide reference collections and numerous publications. A visit to one of the centers, or to one of the regional collections they have set up, is imperative for any individual or organization seeking philanthropy. Using this library, you can research the most appropriate organizations to approach so that you don't waste your time and that of the potential donor by applying to foundations which don't support your particular field, don't serve your geographic area or don't have sufficient money available for your needs. At the branches in New York, Washington, Cleveland and

San Francisco, trained librarians are on hand to answer questions, and orientations are held. An Associates Program is offered to fund-raisers who need frequent and immediate access to recently updated information by toll-free telephone. A $325 annual membership fee pays for ten toll-free calls per month. For more information on this and other Foundation Center offerings, call (800) 424-9836. The addresses of the main branches and regional cooperating collections follow.

THE FOUNDATION CENTER NETWORK

The Foundation Center is an independent national service organization established by foundations to provide an authoritative source of information on private philanthropic giving. In fulfilling its mission, The Center disseminates information on private giving through public service programs, publications and through a national network of library reference collections for free public use. The New York, Washington, DC, Cleveland and San Francisco reference collections operated by The Foundation Center offer a wide variety of services and comprehensive collections of information on foundations and grants. The Cooperating Collections are libraries, community foundations and other non-profit agencies that provide a core collection of Foundation Center publications and a variety of supplementary materials and services in subject areas useful to grantseekers.

Over 100 of the network members have sets of private foundation information returns (IRS Form 990PF) for their states or regions which are available for public use. These collections are indicated by a • next to their names. A complete set of U.S. foundation returns can be found at the New York and Washington, DC, collections. The Cleveland and San Francisco offices contain IRS returns for those foundations in the midwestern and western states respectively.

Because the collections vary in their hours, materials and services, **IT IS RECOMMENDED THAT YOU CALL EACH COLLECTION IN ADVANCE.** To check on new locations or current information, call toll-free 1-800-424-9836.

Reference Collections Operated by
the Foundation Center

• **THE FOUNDATION CENTER**
79 Fifth Avenue
New York, New York 10003
212-620-4230

• **THE FOUNDATION CENTER**
1001 Connecticut Avenue, NW
Washington, DC 20036
202-331-1400

• **THE FOUNDATION CENTER**
Kent H. Smith Library
1442 Hanna Building
1422 Euclid Avenue
Cleveland, Ohio 44115
216-861-1933

• **THE FOUNDATION CENTER**
312 Sutter Street
San Francisco, California 94108
415-397-0902

COOPERATING COLLECTIONS

Those collections marked with a bullet (•) have sets of private foundation information returns (IRS Form 990-PF) for their states or regions, available for public reference.

Alabama

• BIRMINGHAM PUBLIC LIBRARY
2020 Park Place
Birmingham 35203
205-226-3600

HUNTSVILLE–MADISON COUNTY
PUBLIC LIBRARY
108 Fountain Circle
P.O. Box 443
Huntsville 35804
205-536-0021

• AUBURN UNIVERSITY AT
MONTGOMERY LIBRARY
Montgomery 36193-0401
205-271-9649

Alaska

• UNIVERSITY OF ALASKA
Anchorage Library
3211 Providence Drive
Anchorage 99508
907-786-1848

Arizona

• PHOENIX PUBLIC LIBRARY
Business and Sciences Department
12 East McDowell Road
Phoenix 85004
602-262-4636

• TUCSON PUBLIC LIBRARY
Main Library
200 South Sixth Avenue
Tucson 85701
607-791-4393

Arkansas

• WESTARK COMMUNITY COLLEGE
LIBRARY
Grand Avenue at Waldron Road
Fort Smith 72913
501-785-4241

• LITTLE ROCK PUBLIC LIBRARY
Reference Department
700 Louisiana Street
Little Rock 72201
501-370-5950

California

• CALIFORNIA COMMUNITY
FOUNDATION FUNDING
INFORMATION CENTER
3580 Wilshire Blvd., Suite 1660
Los Angeles 90010
213-413-4042

• COMMUNITY FOUNDATION FOR
MONTEREY COUNTY
420 Pacific Street
Monterey 93940
408-375-9712

CALIFORNIA COMMUNITY
FOUNDATION
4050 Metropolitan Drive #300
Orange 92668
714-937-9077

RIVERSIDE PUBLIC LIBRARY
3581 7th Street
Riverside 92501
714-787-7201

CALIFORNIA STATE LIBRARY
Reference Services, Rm. 309
914 Capital Mall
Sacramento 95814
916-322-4570

• SAN DIEGO COMMUNITY
FOUNDATION
625 Broadway, Suite 1015
San Diego 92101
619-239-8815

• THE FOUNDATION CENTER
312 Sutter Street
San Francisco 94108
415-397-0902

• GRANTSMANSHIP RESOURCE
CENTER
Junior League of San Jose, Inc.
Community Foundation of Santa
Clara County
960 West Hedding, Suite 220
San Jose 95126
408-244-5280

• ORANGE COUNTY COMMUNITY
DEVELOPMENTAL COUNCIL
1440 East First Street, 4th Floor
Santa Ana 92701
714-547-6801

• PENINSULA COMMUNITY
FOUNDATION
1204 Burlingame Avenue
Burlingame, 94011-0627
415-342-2505

• SANTA BARBARA PUBLIC
LIBRARY
Reference Section
40 East Anapamu
P.O. Box 1019
Santa Barbara 93102
805-962-7653

SANTA MONICA PUBLIC LIBRARY
1343 Sixth Street
Santa Monica 90401-1603
213-458-8603

TUOLOMNE COUNTY LIBRARY
465 S. Washington Street
Sonora 95370
209-533-5707

Colorado

PIKES PEAK LIBRARY DISTRICT
20 North Cascade Avenue
Colorado Springs 80901
303-473-2080

• **DENVER PUBLIC LIBRARY**
Sociology Division
1357 Broadway
Denver 80203
303-571-2190

Connecticut

DANBURY PUBLIC LIBRARY
155 Deer Hill Avenue
Danbury 06810
203-797-4505

• **HARTFORD PUBLIC LIBRARY**
Reference Department
500 Main Street
Hartford 06103
203-525-9121

D.A.T.A.
880 Asylum Avenue
Hartford 06105
203-278-2477

D.A.T.A.
25 Science Park
Suite 502
New Haven 06513
203-786-5225

Delaware

• **HUGH MORRIS LIBRARY**
University of Delaware
Newark 19717-5267
302-451-2965

District of Columbia

• **THE FOUNDATION CENTER**
1001 Connecticut Avenue, NW
Washington, DC 20036
202-331-1400

Florida

VOLUSIA COUNTY PUBLIC LIBRARY
City Island
Daytona Beach 32014
904-252-8374

• **JACKSONVILLE PUBLIC LIBRARY**
Business, Science, and Industry Department
122 North Ocean Street
Jacksonville 32202
904-633-3926

• **MIAMI—DADE PUBLIC LIBRARY**
Humanities Dept.
101 W. Flagler St.
Miami 33132
305-375-2665

• **ORLANDO PUBLIC LIBRARY**
10 North Rosalind
Orlando 32801
305-425-4694

• **UNIVERSITY OF WEST FLORIDA**
John C. Pace Library
Pensacola 32514
904-474-2412

SELBY PUBLIC LIBRARY
1001 Boulevard of the Arts
Sarasota 33577
813-366-7303

• **LEON COUNTY PUBLIC LIBRARY**
Community Funding Resources Center
1940 North Monroe Street
Tallahassee 32303
904-478-2665

PALM BEACH COUNTY COMMUNITY FOUNDATION
324 Datura Street, Suite 340
West Palm Beach 33401
305-659-6800

Georgia

• **ATLANTA—FULTON PUBLIC LIBRARY**
Ivan Allen Department
1 Margaret Mitchell Square
Atlanta 30303
404-688-4636

Hawaii

• **THOMAS HALE HAMILTON LIBRARY**
General Reference
University of Hawaii

2550 The Mall
Honolulu 96822
808-948-7214

COMMUNITY RESOURCE
CENTER
The Hawaiian Foundation
Financial Plaza of the Pacific
111 South King Street
Honolulu 96813
808-525-8548

Idaho

• CALDWELL PUBLIC LIBRARY
1010 Dearborn Street
Caldwell 83605
208-459-3242

Illinois

• BELLEVILLE PUBLIC LIBRARY
121 East Washington Street
Belleville 62220
618-234-0441

DUPAGE TOWNSHIP
300 Briarcliff Road
Bolingbrook 60439
312-759-1317

• DONORS FORUM OF CHICAGO
53 W. Jackson Blvd. Rm 430
Chicago 60604
312-726-4882

• EVANSTON PUBLIC LIBRARY
1703 Orrington Avenue
Evanston 60201
312-866-0305

• SANGAMON STATE UNIVERSITY
LIBRARY
Shepherd Road
Springfield 62708
217-786-6633

Indiana

ALLEN COUNTY PUBLIC
LIBRARY
900 Webster Street
Fort Wayne 46802
219-424-7241

INDIANA UNIVERSITY NORTH-
WEST LIBRARY
3400 Broadway
Gary 46408
219-980-6580

• INDIANAPOLIS—MARION
COUNTY PUBLIC LIBRARY
40 East St. Clair Street

Indianapolis 46204
317-269-1733

Iowa

• PUBLIC LIBRARY OF
DES MOINES
100 Locust Street
Des Moines 50308
515-283-4259

Kansas

• TOPEKA PUBLIC LIBRARY
Adult Services Department
1515 West Tenth Street
Topeka 66604
913-233-2040

• WICHITA PUBLIC LIBRARY
223 South Main
Wichita 67202
316-262-0611

Kentucky

WESTERN KENTUCKY
UNIVERSITY
Division of Library Services
Helm-Cravens Library
Bowling Green 42101
502-745-3951

• LOUISVILLE FREE PUBLIC
LIBRARY
Fourth and York Streets
Louisville 40203
503-223-7201

Louisiana

• EAST BATON ROUGE PARISH
LIBRARY
Centroplex Library
120 St. Louis Street
Baton Rouge 70821
504-389-4960

• NEW ORLEANS PUBLIC LIBRARY
Business and Science Division
219 Loyola Avenue
New Orleans 70140
504-596-2583

• SHREVE MEMORIAL LIBRARY
424 Texas Street
Shreveport 71101
318-226-5894

Maine

• UNIVERSITY OF SOUTHERN
MAINE
Center for Research and Advanced
Study

246 Deering Avenue
Portland 04102
207-780-4411

Maryland

• ENOCH PRATT FREE LIBRARY
Social Science and History Department
400 Cathedral Street
Baltimore 21201
301-396-5320

Massachusetts

• ASSOCIATED GRANTMAKERS OF MASSACHUSETTS
294 Washington Street
Suite 501
Boston 02108
617-426-2608

• BOSTON PUBLIC LIBRARY
Copley Square
Boston 02117
617-536-5400

WALPOLE PUBLIC LIBRARY
Common Street
Walpole 02081
617-668-5497 ext. 340

WESTERN MASSACHUSETTS FUNDING RESOURCE CENTER
Campaign for Human Development
Chancery Annex
73 Chestnut Street
Springfield 01103
413-732-3175 ext. 67

• GRANTS RESOURCE CENTER
Worcester Public Library
Salem Square
Worcester 01608
617-799-1655

Michigan

• ALPENA COUNTY LIBRARY
211 North First Avenue
Alpena 49707
517-356-6188

UNIVERSITY OF MICHIGAN— ANN ARBOR
Reference Department
209 Hatcher Graduate Library
Ann Arbor 48109-1205
313-764-1149

• HENRY FORD CENTENNIAL LIBRARY
16301 Michigan Avenue
Dearborn 48126
313-943-2337

• PURDY LIBRARY
Wayne State University
Detroit 48202
313-577-4040

• MICHIGAN STATE UNIVERSITY LIBRARIES
Reference Library
East Lansing 48824
517-353-9184

• FARMINGTON COMMUNITY LIBRARY
32737 West 12 Mile Road
Farmington Hills 48018
313-553-0300

• UNIVERSITY OF MICHIGAN— FLINT LIBRARY
Reference Department
Flint 48503
313-762-3408

• GRAND RAPIDS PUBLIC LIBRARY
Sociology and Education Dept.
Library Plaza
Grand Rapids 49502
616-456-4411

• MICHIGAN TECHNOLOGICAL UNIVERSITY LIBRARY
Highway U.S. 41
Houghton 49931
906-487-2507

Minnesota

• DULUTH PUBLIC LIBRARY
520 Superior Street
Duluth 55802
218-723-3802

• SOUTHWEST STATE UNIVERSITY LIBRARY
Marshall 56258
507-537-7278

• MINNEAPOLIS PUBLIC LIBRARY
Sociology Department
300 Nicollet Mall
Minneapolis 55401
612-372-6555

ROCHESTER PUBLIC LIBRARY
Broadway at First Street, SE
Rochester 55901
507-285-8002

SAINT PAUL PUBLIC LIBRARY
90 West Fourth Street
Saint Paul 55102
612-292-6311

Mississippi

JACKSON METROPOLITAN LIBRARY
301 North State Street
Jackson 39201
601-944-1120

Missouri

• **CLEARINGHOUSE FOR MIDCONTI-
NENT FOUNDATIONS**
P.O. Box 22680
Univ. of Missouri, Kansas City
Law School, Suite 1-300
52nd Street and Oak
Kansas City 64113
816-276-1176

• **KANSAS CITY PUBLIC LIBRARY**
311 East 12th Street
Kansas City 64106
816-221-2685

• **METROPOLITAN ASSOCIATION
FOR PHILANTHROPY, INC.**
5585 Pershing Avenue
Suite 150
St. Louis 63112
314-361-3900

• **SPRINGFIELD–GREENE COUNTY
LIBRARY**
397 East Central Street
Springfield 65801
417-866-4636

Montana

• **EASTERN MONTANA COLLEGE
LIBRARY**
Reference Department
1500 N. 30th Street
Billings 59101-0298
406-657-2262

• **MONTANA STATE LIBRARY**
Reference Department
1515 E. 6th Avenue
Helena 59620
406-444-3004

Nebraska

**UNIVERSITY OF NEBRASKA,
LINCOLN**
106 Love Library

Lincoln 68588-0410
402-472-2526

• **W. DALE CLARK LIBRARY**
Social Sciences Department
215 South 15th Street
Omaha 68102
402-444-4826

Nevada

• **LAS VEGAS–CLARK COUNTY
LIBRARY DISTRICT**
1401 East Flamingo Road
Las Vegas 89109
702-733-7810

• **WASHOE COUNTY LIBRARY**
301 South Center Street
Reno 89505
702-785-4190

New Hampshire

• **THE NEW HAMPSHIRE
CHARITABLE FUND**
One South Street
Concord 03301
603-225-6641

LITTLETON PUBLIC LIBRARY
109 Main Street
Littleton 03561
603-444-5741

New Jersey

**CUMBERLAND COUNTY
LIBRARY**
800 E. Commerce Street
Bridgeton 08302
609-455-0080

THE SUPPORT CENTER
17 Academy Street, Suite 1101
Newark 07102
201-643-5774

COUNTY COLLEGE OF MORRIS
Masten Learning Resource Center
Route 10 and Center Grove Road
Randolph 07869
201-361-5000 x470

• **NEW JERSEY STATE LIBRARY**
Governmental Reference
185 West State Street
Trenton 08625
609-292-6220

New Mexico

ALBUQUERQUE COMMUNITY FOUNDATION
6400 Uptown Boulevard N.E.
Suite 500-W
Albuquerque 87110
505-883-6240

• **NEW MEXICO STATE LIBRARY**
325 Don Gaspar Street
Santa Fe 87503
505-827-3824

New York

• **NEW YORK STATE LIBRARY**
Cultural Education Center
Humanities Section
Empire State Plaza
Albany 12230
518-474-7645

BRONX REFERENCE CENTER
New York Public Library
2556 Bainbridge Avenue
Bronx 10458
212-220-6575

BROOKLYN IN TOUCH
101 Willoughby Street
Room 1508
Brooklyn 11201
718-237-9300

• **BUFFALO AND ERIE COUNTY PUBLIC LIBRARY**
Lafayette Square
Buffalo 14203
716-856-7525

HUNTINGTON PUBLIC LIBRARY
338 Main Street
Huntington 11743
516-427-5165

• **LEVITTOWN PUBLIC LIBRARY**
Reference Department
One Bluegrass Lane
Levittown 11756
516-731-5728

• **THE FOUNDATION CENTER**
79 Fifth Avenue
New York, New York 10003
212-620-4230

SUNY/COLLEGE AT OLD WESTBURY LIBRARY
223 Store Hill Road
Old Westbury 11568
516-876-3201

• **PLATTSBURGH PUBLIC LIBRARY**
Reference Department
15 Oak Street
Plattsburgh 12901
518-563-0921

ADRIANCE MEMORIAL LIBRARY
93 Market Street
Poughkeepsie 12601
914-485-4790

QUEENS BOROUGH PUBLIC LIBRARY
89-11 Merrick Boulevard
Jamaica 11432
718-990-0700

• **ROCHESTER PUBLIC LIBRARY**
Business and Social Sciences Division
115 South Avenue
Rochester 14604
716-428-7328

STATEN ISLAND COUNCIL ON THE ARTS
One Edgewater Plaza Rm. 311
Staten Island 10305
718-447-4485

• **ONONDAGA COUNTY PUBLIC LIBRARY**
335 Montgomery Street
Syracuse 13202
315-473-4491

• **WHITE PLAINS PUBLIC LIBRARY**
100 Martine Avenue
White Plains 10601
914-682-4488

• **SUFFOLK COOPERATIVE LIBRARY SYSTEM**
627 North Sunrise Service Road
Bellport 11713
516-286-1600

North Carolina

• **THE DUKE ENDOWMENT**
200 S. Tryon Street, Suite 1100
Charlotte 28202
704-376-0291

DURHAM COUNTY LIBRARY
300 N. Roxboro Street
Durham 27701
919-683-2626

• **NORTH CAROLINA STATE LIBRARY**
109 East Jones Street
Raleigh 27611
919-733-3270

• THE WINSTON-SALEM
FOUNDATION
229 First Union National Bank Building
Winston-Salem 27101
919-725-2382

North Dakota

WESTERN DAKOTA GRANTS
RESOURCE CENTER
Bismarck Junior College Library
Bismarck 58501
701-224-5450

• THE LIBRARY
North Dakota State University
Fargo 58105
701-237-8876

Ohio

PUBLIC LIBRARY OF CINCINNATI
AND HAMILTON COUNTY
Education Department
800 Vine Street
Cincinnati 45202
513-369-6940

• THE FOUNDATION CENTER
Kent H. Smith Library
1442 Hanna Building
1422 Euclid Avenue
Cleveland 44115
216-861-1933

• THE PUBLIC LIBRARY OF
COLUMBUS AND FRANKLIN
COUNTY
Main Library
96 S. Grant Ave.
Columbus 43215
614-222-7151

• DAYTON AND MONTGOMERY
COUNTY PUBLIC LIBRARY
Social Sciences Division
215 E. Third Street
Dayton 45402-2103
513-224-1651

• TOLEDO—LUCAS COUNTY PUBLIC
LIBRARY
Social Science Department
325 Michigan Street
Toledo 43624
419-255-7055 ext. 221

OHIO UNIVERSITY—ZANESVILLE
Community Education and Development
1425 Newark Road

Zanesville 43701
614-453-0762

• STARK COUNTY DISTRICT
LIBRARY
715 Market Avenue North
Canton 44702-1080
216-452-0665

Oklahoma

• OKLAHOMA CITY UNIVERSITY
LIBRARY
NW 23rd at North Blackwelder
Oklahoma City 73106
405-521-5072

• TULSA CITY—COUNTY LIBRARY
SYSTEM
400 Civic Center
Tulsa 74103
918-592-7944

Oregon

• LIBRARY ASSOCIATION OF
PORTLAND
Government Documents Room
801 S.W. Tenth Avenue
Portland 97205
503-223-7201

OREGON STATE LIBRARY
State Library Building
Salem 97310
503-378-4243

Pennsylvania

NORTHAMPTON COUNTY AREA
COMMUNITY COLLEGE
Learning Resources Center
3835 Green Pond Road
Bethlehem 18017
215-865-5358

• ERIE COUNTY PUBLIC LIBRARY
3 South Perry Square
Erie 16501
814-452-2333 ext. 54

• DAUPHIN COUNTY LIBRARY
SYSTEM
Central Library
101 Walnut Street
Harrisburg 17101
717-234-4961

LANCASTER COUNTY PUBLIC
LIBRARY
125 North Duke Street
Lancaster 17602
717-394-2651

• THE FREE LIBRARY OF
PHILADELPHIA
Logan Square
Philadelphia 19103
215-686-5423

• HILLMAN LIBRARY
University of Pittsburgh
Pittsburgh 15260
412-624-4423

• ECONOMIC DEVELOPMENT
COUNCIL OF NORTHEASTERN
PENNSYLVANIA
1151 Oak Street
Pittston 18640
717-655-5581

JAMES V. BROWN LIBRARY
12 E. 4th Street
Williamsport 17701
717-326-0536

Rhode Island

• PROVIDENCE PUBLIC LIBRARY
Reference Department
150 Empire Street
Providence 02903
401-521-7722

South Carolina

• CHARLESTON COUNTY PUBLIC
LIBRARY
404 King Street
Charleston 29403
803-723-1645

• SOUTH CAROLINA STATE
LIBRARY
Reader Services Department
1500 Senate Street
Columbia 29201
803-734-8666

South Dakota

• SOUTH DAKOTA STATE LIBRARY
State Library Building
800 North Illinois Street
Pierre 57501
605-773-3131

SIOUX FALLS AREA FOUNDATION
404 Boyce Greeley Building
321 South Phillips Avenue
Sioux Falls 57102-0781
605-336-7055

Tennessee

• KNOXVILLE–KNOX COUNTY
PUBLIC LIBRARY
500 West Church Avenue
Knoxville 37902
615-523-0781

• MEMPHIS SHELBY COUNTY PUBLIC
LIBRARY
1850 Peabody Avenue
Memphis 38104
901-725-8876

• PUBLIC LIBRARY OF NASHVILLE
AND DAVIDSON COUNTY
8th Avenue, North and Union Street
Nashville 37203
615-244-4700

Texas

AMARILLO AREA FOUNDATION
1000 Polk
P.O. Box 25569
Amarillo 79105-269
806-376-4521

• THE HOGG FOUNDATION FOR
MENTAL HEALTH
The University of Texas
Austin 78712
512-471-5041

• CORPUS CHRISTI STATE UNIVER-
SITY LIBRARY
6300 Ocean Drive
Corpus Christi 78412
512-991-6810

• EL PASO COMMUNITY
FOUNDATION
El Paso National Bank Building
Suite 1616
El Paso 79901
915-533-4020

• FUNDING INFORMATION CENTER
Texas Christian University Library
Ft. Worth 76129
817-921-7664

• HOUSTON PUBLIC
LIBRARY
Bibliographic & Information Center
500 McKinney Avenue
Houston 77002
713-224-5441 ext.265

• FUNDING INFORMATION LIBRARY
507 Brooklyn
San Antonio 78215
512-227-4333

- **DALLAS PUBLIC LIBRARY**
Grants Information Service
1515 Young Street
Dallas 75201
214-749-4100

- **PAN AMERICAN UNIVERSITY**
Learning Resource Center
1201 W. University Drive
Edinburg 78539
512-381-3304

Utah

- **SALT LAKE CITY PUBLIC LIBRARY**
Business and Science Department
209 East Fifth South
Salt Lake City 84111
801-363-5733

Vermont

- **STATE OF VERMONT DEPART-MENT OF LIBRARIES**
Reference Services Unit
111 State Street
Montpelier 05602
802-828-3261

Virginia

- **GRANTS RESOURCES LIBRARY**
Hampton City Hall
22 Lincoln Street, Ninth Floor
Hampton 23669
804-727-6496

- **RICHMOND PUBLIC LIBRARY**
Business, Science, & Technology Department
101 East Franklin Street
Richmond 23219
804-780-8223

Washington

- **SEATTLE PUBLIC LIBRARY**
1000 Fourth Avenue
Seattle 98104
206-625-4881

- **SPOKANE PUBLIC LIBRARY**
Funding Information Center
West 906 Main Avenue
Spokane 99201
509-838-3361

West Virginia

- **KANAWHA COUNTY PUBLIC LIBRARY**
123 Capital Street
Charleston 25301
304-343-4646

Wisconsin

- **MARQUETTE UNIVERSITY MEMORIAL LIBRARY**
1415 West Wisconsin Avenue
Milwaukee 53233
414-224-1515

- **UNIVERSITY OF WISCONSIN– MADISON**
Memorial Library
728 State Street
Madison 53706
608-262-3647

Wyoming

- **LARAMIE COUNTY COMMUNITY COLLEGE LIBRARY**
1400 East College Drive
Cheyenne 82007
307-634-5853

Canada

CANADIAN CENTER FOR PHILANTHROPY
3080 Yonge Street
Suite 4080
Toronto, Ontario M4N3N1
416-484-4118

England

CHARITIES AID FOUNDATION
14 Bloomsbury Square
London WC1A 2LP
01-430-1798

Mexico

BIBLIOTECA BENJAMIN FRANKLIN
Londres 16
Mexico City 6, D.F.
525-591-0244

Puerto Rico

UNIVERSIDAD DEL SAGRADO CORAZON
M.M.T. Guevarra Library
Correo Calle Loiza
Santurce 00914
809-728-1515 ext.274

Virgin Islands
COLLEGE OF THE VIRGIN
ISLANDS LIBRARY
Saint Thomas
U.S. Virgin Islands 00801
809-774-9200 ext.487

There are several publications which will aid you in identifying those foundations which might have an interest in funding your project. What you must look for are those institutions which have given money to related projects in the recent past. Remember that certain areas go in and out of fashion. The smallest percentage of foundation support goes to the arts; education, health and science are all more favored. It is also true that foundations are most likely to favor projects in areas which are already heavily funded. This is because they don't want to be saddled supporting a perpetually barefoot project which has no support from anyone else. Nor do they want to have to be forced to choose, when the grant expires, between continuing to support a project and killing it. Approach large foundations in your area. It doesn't hurt to be away from the large, concentrated urban areas where everyone has a palm extended. With regard to grant getting, it helps to be regional.

The person in charge of fund-raising should expect to put in at least a couple of days in the library going through these volumes:

The Foundation Center National Data Book. Available from: The Foundation Center, 79 Fifth Avenue, New York, NY 10003. This is an extremely thorough book that lists 24,859 active U.S. foundations by state, assets and grant size. It is particularly useful for identifying foundations of all sizes within your area.

The Foundation Grants Index. Available from: The Foundation Center, 79 Fifth Avenue, New York, NY 10003. This is a valuable cross-referenced guide to over 30,000 grants reported to the Foundation Center. You can locate grantors by location, subject, type of recipients and by name.

Useful reference books from other sources are:

Annual Register of Grant Support. Published by Marquis Academic Media, 200 East Ohio Street, Chicago, IL 60611. This useful book is indexed by interest, organization and area. It includes both government and private programs.

The Bread Game (The Realities of Foundation Fundraising). Herb Allen, ed. New Guide Publications, 330 Ellis Street, San Francisco, CA 94102. A clearly written guide to fund-raising in all of its aspects.

Gaby, Patricia V., and Daniel M. *Nonprofit Organization Handbook.* Prentice-Hall. This extremely valuable book gives tips on fund-raising, grants, lobbying, public relations and publicity.

Hall, Mary. *Developing Skills in Proposal Writing.* Available from Continuing Education Publications, Waldo 100, Corvallis, OR 97331. A well-written manual of proposal writing worth a thorough reading.

Hillman, Howard. *The Art of Winning Corporate Grants*. Vanguard Press, 1980.

Seltzer, Michael. *Securing Your Organization's Future: A Complete Guide to Fundraising Strategies*. The Foundation Center ($19.95). A useful guide to securing funding, fund-raising strategies and emerging new funding opportunities.

Users Guide to Funding Resources. Published by Human Resources Network. A guide to grants by areas funded. Included are chapters on proposal writing.

Through the Foundation Center you may also buy a printout of foundations' funding projects in key areas. These are called Comsearch Printouts. They cost $17.50 per subject ($6 on microfilm) and give the foundation's name and location, the names and locations of recipients, and how much money the foundation gave the recipients and for what purpose.

With the aid of these sources, you should be able to select ten to twelve likely targets whose funding interests and geographical area served match your project. You and your fund-raisers should then attempt to refine this list of possible donors further by discussing the following questions:

1. Is there a trend apparent in this foundation's donations?
2. Does it support one phase of a project more than another?
3. Does it have a regional preference?
4. What about the duration of support? Does the foundation give money to continuing projects, or to one-shot situations?
5. Are any stipulations made as to the use of the money or the number of times you may apply for funding?
6. Can your organization afford the costs of visiting the foundation?
7. Does anyone in your group know any of the foundation's officers or board members?

This list of questions may help you eliminate a few potential donors. You should then begin gathering facts on those which remain.

Initial contacts. It is now time to contact within your narrowed field. The first contact should be a letter expressing interest and requesting a meeting. This initial letter should be concise. With it you are trying to ascertain their degree of interest in you, as well as request a meeting. It should incorporate your understanding of the foundation's concerns, the project's suitability in the light of those concerns, the project's specific objectives and its means for reaching them, and a brief mention of your resources and personnel.

Address the letter to the officer in charge of grant solicitations, the name of whom one of the reference volumes you use should provide (if no name is specified, approach the principal officer). Always check that any names you find in directories are still current by calling the foundation. Your project head should sign the initial correspondence unless someone else in your organization has a contact in the foundation.

Keep this exploratory letter under three pages. The point of it is to give them just enough information to entice them into seeing you, but not so much that they can eliminate you.

Alternatively, your initial contact can be made by telephone, although it is much easier to work face to face. Many experienced grant getters discourage the telephone approach as being too pushy. If you do decide to call, make sure you know the name of the right person to talk to. And, as you should in any situation involving an executive and a secretary, *be sure to get the secretary's name.* You never know when you'll need it, and it is always a good idea to cultivate a spirit of familiarity and cooperation between yourself and key secretaries and receptionists.

When you get the officer on the line, request a very brief meeting. At this point he will most probably say that you should send something in writing first. To this you can try replying that your project is very new, and that you just don't have sufficient printed materials yet. Stress the brevity of the meeting requested. If he still refuses, don't make a fool of yourself by being too insistent.

If you get a tentative meeting date, thank him and hang up. Confirm the appointment by mail or with your friend the secretary. Do not speak to the officer again—he might have a change of heart.

At the meeting. Before the meeting you should rehearse your presentation, as well as the answers to very probing questions as to the importance of your project, the credentials of its personnel, its ability to provide what it promises. You must be able to radiate enthusiasm and knowledge without appearing canned. In order to come off well at this initial meeting you should rehearse. Many projects are turned down because their directors appear, by their rambling answers, not to have really thought about their objectives. Nobody is going to give $30,000 to a group which appears disorganized, for such groups have a tendency not to know how to organize spending, and consequently dollars given to them don't go far.

The more money you are requesting, the more people you should bring to the meeting and the more important they should be in your organization. Bring along an articulate expert if you plan to present technical material.

As long as you're asking for money, you have to play the game their way. People who give grants to the arts have to wear suits and ties, and so should you in their presence. To show up looking like the Living Theatre on stage may amuse you, but if you want the money to have a real theater season, play it straight (see page 49, Dressing for Success).

Also, don't overstay your welcome. Give your presentation, answer any questions and then leave. The meeting should take up no more than an hour. Do be sure to find out when the committee on grants meets, so that you have your proposal in on time.

The proposal. A proposal should be no longer than ten typed, double-spaced pages; four to eight pages is preferable. Etiquette dictates that you type each proposal on good white bond: do not simply photocopy your applications. As with your presentation of your person, be sure the copy you send is clean and well proofread. While a few typos or smears on a page may not bother you, remember that you must think like the grantor in the grey flannel suit: this sort of bilinguality must be developed by the artist. Make the proposal easy on the eyes: use wide margins, indent the paragraphs and break up large bodies of print. Never use erasable paper: those whose professions call for a great deal of reading are driven mad by the poor contrast and smeared words which result when this type of paper is used. (See also in chapter 6 the sections Appearances, Stationery and Copying.)

A proposal describes a need and proposes a program to meet it. Break the proposal down into paragraphs by a method such as the following:

I. *The Introduction, or Overture.* This is really a summation, and you'll do best to write it last.

II. *Documentation of the Need.* This describes what is lacking and the relation of your proposal to similar ones. Use persuasive facts and statistics as well as the opinions of respected individuals in the field.

III. *Objectives.* This is a statement of your goals, in descending order of importance.

IV. *Methods of Implementation.* Show you know your stuff here, but don't use jargon. It makes people feel stupid. It often looks good to make a timetable of just which steps will be accomplished when.

V. *Your Organization's Credentials.* Here emphasize your past accomplishments, both as an organization and as individuals. Give a brief biography of key personnel. Describe your resources, such as your space, special equipment, access to volunteers, and so on.

VI. *Procedure for Evaluation.* Try to introduce a third party who will monitor your program and make evaluations. Explain who this person will be and what criteria he will use for the evaluation.

VII. *Your Budget.* Take time to work this out properly. It is stupid to ask for too little in an effort to appeal. If you don't get enough, you won't be able to deliver what you promise. On the other hand, don't pad, either (although you should consider the rate of inflation in your figures). Be very specific as to amounts and intended uses. And don't forget that a proposal is a legally binding document. This section should include figures on:

1. Wages, salaries and benefits. Don't forget to include cost-of-living increases if you are budgeting for more than a year of salaries.

2. Outside services (legal, accounting, etc.). Only list those that will definitely be used. Foundations are more and more insistent on seeing proof that you actually received such services.

3. Rent. You can defend this figure, if you haven't yet got a space, by getting a letter from a local real estate agent estimating the cost of what you will need.

4. Utilities (phone bills, gas, water and electricity). If any of these are included in your rent, list them anyway and put $00.00 as cost.

5. Supplies. List only big ones: a Xerox machine, a camera, lights, etc. Put stamps, paper and other such items together in a lump sum under *General Office.*

6. Travel. Itemize and explain these expenses *most carefully.*

7. Miscellaneous. These are expenses that you can't categorize elsewhere. Itemize these.

8. Reserve. Five percent of your total budget should be added in as general reserve cash.

VIII. *The Future of the Project.* Foundations prefer projects which won't become albatrosses around their neck. They see their support as giving you a start, a momentum, which you must then maintain. Will you become self-supporting? Are you requesting money for only a one-shot project? Will someone else take up some of the funding? Give a realistic plan for raising additional funds.

The following addenda may be included with the proposal:

1. References from well-known people in the field.
2. Names and bios of board members and personnel.
3. Supporting facts (clippings, statistics, etc.).
4. Your IRS 501 (C)(3) (proof of tax exempt status).
5. Your annual report.

Do not attach these addenda to the body of the proposal, but put them in a ring binder, preferably with acetate protecting each page.

The proposal should have a title page and cover letter. A sample format for a title page is on the opposite page.

Many grant seekers feel that it is better to bury the amount needed in the text rather than to put it right out on the title page. But the people I spoke with at foundations all agreed that this is silly, since everyone knows that your quest for philanthropy is the reason you are communicating in the first place.

Your covering letter should be short—less than a full page. Its only function is to refresh your potential donor's mind as to your program.

Follow-up. Now is the time for letters from your board members to those of the foundation. They should state confidence in the project or offer assistance.

You may also invite the potential donors to your establishment for a site visit so that you can introduce your staff and review the facilities. It goes without saying that you should handle requests for more information promptly.

After all this is done, you must sit back and wait patiently for three to six months.

If you are rejected. It's going to happen at some point, so be prepared to shrug off your failures. Don't give up. Even if you don't get funded this year, hang in and apply again. The money is out there, if you can just convince a donor that your program is tailor-made to his interests. It is permissible to ask why you were turned down, though foundations, unlike the government, don't have to tell you. You can also, at this point, try asking for half of the money in the form of a matching grant, and then approaching another grantor. This may make them both happy. Foundations like to feel that their contributions are going further than they really are.

Even if you are turned down once by a foundation, it doesn't mean that you always will be. It pays to keep them abreast of your progress. Perhaps, as you move into more advanced stages, their interest may grow. As with any relationship, you're least attractive when you're neediest. If you are rejected, write a polite letter thanking them for their consideration and mentioning that you will keep them informed and will get in touch with them again.

If you are accepted. If you do get the grant your relationship with your grantor continues. Your director should acknowledge the award immediately.

When the last champagne bottle has been drained you must sit down and read the instructions and responsibilities that come with your award. Are there any stipulations regarding publicity or spending? When are your reports due? Is anything else expected of you? Some grants, such as CAPS Grants, require you to devote a certain number of days to public service before you receive all of your money.

A Proposal for a
$50,000 Grant
to Aid
The Poets' Consortium

Submitted to
The Buck Foundation
on
November 10, 1987
by
Martha Rhodes, Director
The Poets' Consortium
143 Jay Street
New York, NY   10013

Reports. You should be honest about both your successes and your failures in your reports. Enclose any favorable press that you have received. Mention public and professional reaction to your program. Invite your donors to performances or even to meetings: some of the people like to feel that they're involved on the ground level of a growing young project.

SERVICES FOR GRANTSPEOPLE

If you are going to be responsible for a lot of fund-raising, you may want to avail yourself of some of the following services:

The Foundation Center, 79 Fifth Avenue, New York, NY 10003; (800) 424-9836.

The Grantsmanship Center, 650 South Spring Street, Los Angeles, CA 90014; (213) 689-9222. This center offers a forty-hour course in grantsmanship. It also publishes a news bulletin eight times a year.

Carroll Michaels, 491 Broadway, New York, NY 10012; (212) 966-0713. Ms. Michaels offers a consulting service for artists and arts organizations regarding grants proposals and publicity.

New York Foundation for the Arts, 5 Beekman Street, New York, NY 10038; (212) 233-3900. This organization offers interest-free loans of up to $5,000 to organizations which have received confirmations of grant support but which need immediate cash.

STATE ARTS COUNCILS

ALABAMA STATE COUNCIL ON THE ARTS & HUMANITIES
Al Head, Executive Director
323 Adams Avenue
Montgomery, AL 36130-5801
(205) 261-4076

ALASKA STATE COUNCIL ON THE ARTS
Chris D'Arcy, Executive Director
619 Warehouse Avenue, Suite 220
Anchorage, AK 99501
(907) 279-1558

AMERICAN SAMOA COUNCIL ON CULTURE, ART AND HUMANITIES
Matil da Lolotai, Executive Director
P.O. Box 1540
Office of the Governor
Pago Pago, AS 96799
(684) 633-4347

ARIZONA COMMISSION ON THE ARTS
Shelley Cohn, Executive Director
417 West Roosevelt Avenue
Phoenix, AZ 85003
(602) 255-5882

ARKANSAS ARTS COUNCIL
Amy Aspell, Executive Director
Heritage Center, Suite 200
225 E. Markham
Little Rock, AR 72201
(501) 371-2539

CALIFORNIA ARTS COUNCIL
Robert H. Reid, Executive Director
1901 Broadway, Suite A
Sacramento, CA 95818
(916) 445-1530

COLORADO COUNCIL ON THE ARTS & HUMANITIES
Ellen Sollod, Executive Director
770 Pennsylvania Street
Denver, CO 80203
(303) 866-2617

CONNECTICUT COMMISSION ON THE ARTS
Gary Young, Executive Director
190 Trumbull Street
Hartford, CT 06103
(203) 566-4770

DELAWARE STATE ARTS COUNCIL
Cecilia Fitzgibbon, Executive Director
820 North French Street
Wilmington, DE 19801
(302) 571-3540

DISTRICT OF COLUMBIA (DC) COMMISSION ON THE ARTS & HUMANITIES
Barbara Nicholson, Acting Executive
Director
420 7th Street, NW, 2nd Floor
Washington, DC 20004
(202) 724-5613

FLORIDA ARTS COUNCIL
Chris Doolin, Executive Director
Department of State, The Capitol
Tallahassee, FL 32301
(904) 487-2980

GEORGIA COUNCIL FOR THE ARTS & HUMANITIES
Frank Ratka, Executive Director
2082 East Exchange Place, Suite 100
Tucker, GA 30084
(404) 493-5780

INSULAR ARTS COUNCIL (GUAM)
Linda Tiatano Reyes, Executive Director
Office of the Governor
P.O. Box 2950
Agana, GU 96910
011-671-477-7413

STATE FOUNDATION ON CULTURE AND THE ARTS (HAWAII)
Sarah Richards, Executive Director
335 Merchant Street, Suite 202
Honolulu, HI 96813
(808) 548-4145

IDAHO COMMISSION ON THE ARTS
Michael Reinbold, Executive Director
304 West State Street
Boise, ID 83720
(208) 334-2119

ILLINOIS ARTS COUNCIL
Adrienne Nescott Hirsch, Executive Director
State of Illinois Center
100 W. Randolph Street, Suite 10-500
Chicago, IL 60601
(312) 917-6750

INDIANA ARTS COMMISSION
Thomas Schorgl, Executive Director
47 S. Pennsylvania
Indianapolis, IN 46204
(317) 232-1268

IOWA ARTS COUNCIL
Jeanann Celli, Executive Director
State Capitol Complex
1223 East Court Avenue
Des Moines, IA 50319
(515) 281-4451

KANSAS ARTS COMMISSION
John Carey, Executive Director
112 West 6th Street
Topeka, KS 66603
(913) 296-3335

KENTUCKY ARTS COUNCIL
Roger Paige, Executive Director
Berry Hill
Frankfort, KY 40601
(502) 564-3757

LOUISIANA STATE ARTS COUNCIL
Derek Gordon, Executive Director
P.O. Box 44247
Baton Rouge, LA 70804
(504) 925-3930

MAINE STATE COMMISSION ON THE ARTS & HUMANITIES
Alden C. Wilson, Executive Director
55 Capitol Street
State House Station 25
Augusta, ME 04333
(207) 289-2724

MARYLAND STATE ARTS COUNCIL
Jim Backas, Executive Director
15 West Mulberry Street
Baltimore, MD 21201
(301) 685-6740

MASSACHUSETTS COUNCIL ON THE ARTS & HUMANITIES
Anne Hawley, Executive Director
80 Boylston Street, 10th Floor
Boston, MA 02116
(617) 727-3668

MICHIGAN COUNCIL FOR THE ARTS
Barbara Goldman, Executive Director
1200 6th Avenue, Executive Plaza
Detroit, MI 48226
(313) 256-3735

MINNESOTA STATE ARTS BOARD
Sam Grabarski, Executive Director
432 Summit Avenue
St. Paul, MN 55102
(612) 297-2603

MISSISSIPPI ARTS COMMISSION
Nancy Gilbert, Executive Director
301 North Lamar Street
P.O. Box 400

Jackson, MS 39201
(601) 354-7336

MISSOURI ARTS COUNCIL
Ms. Wally Weil, Executive Director
111 North 7th Street, Suite 105
St. Louis, MO 63101
(314) 444-6845

MONTANA ARTS COUNCIL
David Nelson, Executive Director
35 South Last Chance Gulch
Helena, MT 59620
(406) 444-6430

NEBRASKA ARTS COUNCIL
Robin Tryloff, Executive Director
1313 Farnam-on-the-Mall
Omaha, NE 68102
(402) 554-2122

NEVADA STATE COUNCIL ON THE ARTS
Bill Fox, Executive Director
329 Flint Street
Reno, NV 89501
(702) 789-0225

NEW HAMPSHIRE COMMISSION ON THE ARTS
Robb Hankins, Executive Director
Phenix Hall
40 North Main Street
Concord, NH 03301
(603) 271-2789

NEW JERSEY STATE COUNCIL ON THE ARTS
Jeffrey Kesper, Executive Director
109 West State Street
Trenton, NJ 08625
(609) 292-6130

NEW MEXICO ARTS DIVISION
Patrice Gabriel, Executive Director
224 E. Palace Avenue
Santa Fe, NM 87501
(505) 827-6490

NEW YORK STATE COUNCIL ON THE ARTS
Mary Hays, Executive Director
915 Broadway
New York, NY 10010
(212) 614-2909

NORTH CAROLINA ARTS COUNCIL
Mary Regan, Executive Director
Department of Cultural Resources
Raleigh, NC 27611
(919) 733-2821

NORTH DAKOTA COUNCIL ON THE ARTS
Donna Evenson, Executive Director
Black Building, Suite 606
Fargo, ND 58102
(701) 237-8962

COMMONWEALTH COUNCIL FOR ARTS AND CULTURE (NORTHERN MARIANAS ISLANDS)
Ana Teregeyo, Executive Director
P.O. Box 553, CHRB
Saipan, CM 96950
011-670-9982, 9983, FAX 9028

OHIO ARTS COUNCIL
Wayne Lawson, Executive Director
727 East Main Street
Columbus, OH 43205
(614) 466-2613

STATE ARTS COUNCIL OF OKLAHOMA
Betty Price, Executive Director
Jim Thorpe Building, #640
Oklahoma City, OK 73105
(405) 521-2931

OREGON ARTS COMMISSION
Peter deC. Hero, Executive Director
835 Summer Street, NE
Salem, OR 97301
(503) 378-3625

PENNSYLVANIA COUNCIL ON THE ARTS
June Arey, Executive Director
Finance Building
Harrisburg, PA 17120
(717) 787-6883

INSTITUTE OF PUERTO RICAN CULTURE
Elias Lopez Soba, Executive Director
P.O. Box 4184
San Juan, PR 00905
(809) 723-2115

RHODE ISLAND STATE COUNCIL ON THE ARTS
Iona Dobbins, Executive Director
312 Wickenden Street
Providence, RI 02903-4494
(401) 277-3880

SOUTH CAROLINA ARTS COMMISSION
Scott Sanders, Executive Director
1800 Gervais Street
Columbia, SC 29201
(803) 758-3442

SOUTH DAKOTA ARTS COUNCIL
Charlotte Carver, Executive Director
108 West 11th Street
Sioux Falls, SD 57102
(605) 339-6646

TENNESSEE ARTS COMMISSION
C. Bennett Tarleton, Jr., Executive Director
320 6th Avenue, North, Suite 100
Nashville, TN 37219
(615) 741-1701

TEXAS COMMISSION ON THE ARTS
Richard Huff, Executive Director
P.O. Box 13406, Capitol Station
Austin, TX 78711
(512) 475-6593

UTAH ARTS COUNCIL
Carol Nixon, Executive Director
617 E. South Temple Street
Salt Lake City, UT 84102
(801) 533-5895

VERMONT COUNCIL ON THE ARTS
Andrea Escher, Acting Executive Director
136 State Street
Montpelier, VT 05602
(802) 828-3291

VIRGINIA COMMISSION FOR THE ARTS
Peggy Baggett, Executive Director
James Monroe Building
101 No. 14th Street, 17th Floor
Richmond, VA 23219
(804) 225-3132

VIRGIN ISLANDS COUNCIL ON THE ARTS
John Jowers, Executive Director
P.O. Box 6732
St. Thomas, VI 00801
(809) 774-5984

WASHINGTON STATE ARTS COMMISSION
Michael Croman, Executive Director
Mail Stop GH-11
Olympia, WA 98504
(206) 753-3860

WEST VIRGINIA ARTS & HUMANITIES DIVISION
James Andrews, Executive Director
Dept. of Culture & History
Capitol Complex
Charleston, WV 25305
(304) 348-0240

WISCONSIN ARTS BOARD
Arley G. Curtz, Executive Director
107 South Butler Street
Madison, WI 53703
(608) 266-0190

WYOMING COUNCIL ON THE ARTS
Joy Thompson, Executive Director
2320 Capitol Avenue
Cheyenne, WY 82002
(307) 777-7742

REGIONAL ARTS ORGANIZATIONS

ARTS MIDWEST (IA, MN, ND, SD, WI, IL, IN, MI, OH)
David Fraher, Executive Director
Hennepin Center for the Arts
528 Hennepin Avenue, Suite 302
Minneapolis, MN 55403
(612) 341-0755

CONSORTIUM FOR PACIFIC ARTS & CULTURES (AS, CM, GU)
Bernie Lopez, Executive Director
2141-C Atherton Road
Honolulu, HI 96822
(808) 946-7381

MID-AMERICA ARTS ALLIANCE (AR, KS, OK, MO, NE)
Henry Moran, Executive Director
20 West 9th Street, Suite 550
Kansas City, MO 64105
(816) 421-1388

MID-ATLANTIC STATES ARTS CONSORTIUM (DC, DE, MD, NJ, NY, PA, VA, WV)
Michael Braun, Executive Director
11 East Chase Street, Suite 1-A
Baltimore, MD 21202
(301) 539-6656

NEW ENGLAND FOUNDATION FOR THE ARTS (CT, MA, ME, NH, RI, VT)
Marcia Noebels, Executive Director
678 Massachusetts Avenue, 8th Floor
Cambridge, MA 02139
(617) 492-2414

SOUTHERN ARTS FEDERATION (AL, FL, GA, KY, LA, MS, NC, SC, TN)
Sharon Donahue, Executive Director
1401 Peachtree Street, NE, Suite 122
Atlanta, GA 30309
(404) 874-7244

WESTERN STATES ARTS FOUNDA-TION (AK, AZ, CO, HI, ID, MT, NM, NV, OR, UT, WA, WY)
Terry Melton, Executive Director
207 Shelby Street, Suite 200
Santa Fe, NM 87501
(505) 988-1166

SOME ADDITIONAL GRANT DIRECTORIES

American Art Directory. Jacques Cottell Press/R. R. Bowker Co. (Includes section on scholarships and fellowships.)

Moser, Lida. *Photography Contests.* Amphoto. (Includes listing of contests and interviews with judges and competitors.)

Pavlakis, Christopher. *The American Music Handbook.* The Free Press, 866 Third Avenue, New York, NY 10022. (Includes U.S. musical contests, awards, grants, fellowships and honors.)

Scholarship and Grant Programs: Film. American Film Institution, JFK Center for the Performing Arts, Washington, DC 20566.

Scholarships in Radio and Television. National Association of Broadcasters, 1771 N Street, NW, Washington, DC 20036.

CHAPTER FIFTEEN

WHAT'S IT WORTH?

In my freelancing seminars, one of the most frequently asked questions concerns how to price one's work. Naturally the answer to this depends upon the type of work you do, your geographical location, your level of skill, your competition and your client's ability or willingness to pay. In this chapter, I will give you some general guidelines and refer you to sources of more specific information according to profession.

NEGOTIATING PRICES AND PAYMENTS

QUOTING JOBS

In cases where your client asks you for a quote, there are various factors you should consider. A job should pay for all the time you put into it, plus any expenses you incurred, and should give you something on top to apply towards taxes and overhead. You can arrive at this figure in several ways.

One formula you can use as a guideline for quoting on a per job basis involves adding up your annual operating costs: rent on your work space, utilities, telephone, salaries and other costs of doing business. Dividing this figure by various estimates of your number of jobs per year (hard to do until you're established) will give you a number equal to the minimum amount you can charge per job according to how many jobs you expect to have each year. Really this figure just gives you your base rate per job. Any profit to you must be added on top. Obviously this formula is just a desirable guideline, because you may be willing to or forced to make less on some jobs in order to snag a client or because you will get such good experience or exposure, or because you are new on the block. All of these factors must be considered.

You can also divide your annual operating costs by twelve which gives you the overhead figure you need to cover each month. This method actually gives you a bit more leeway in how you apportion your operating costs so that you can add a higher percentage on to your bigger jobs or to jobs for richer clients and less to smaller clients.

Another way to charge for a job is on an hourly basis. You should get an idea of the going rate in your area when deciding what to charge. You can do this by asking other freelancers in your line of work what they charge or by asking art directors or editors or other users of your type of work how much they are currently paying. You can also ask clients to show you invoices from other freelancers for similar jobs. If you're new in town or inexperienced, you might want to start by cutting 25 percent off the going rate. There are certain caveats when charging by the hour. First of all, in your efforts to attract clients don't price yourself ridiculously low. Clients want quality work and a freelancer whose rates are too far below the going rate may be met with suspicion and ultimately closed doors. The beginning freelancer is safer to assume a middle-of-the-road pricing policy.

Secondly, get a sense of how fast other freelancers turn around similar jobs. This is harder to find out if only because of the difficulty of comparing the complexity of different jobs. Again, try asking freelancer friends who do similar work for similar clients and ask art directors, editors and other clients' representatives. It's important that you know how quickly you work in comparison to other freelancers. If you work faster than the average, you should be aware that you may be cheating yourself out of money if you're basing your charges on the going hourly rate. Fast workers may do better to charge on a per job basis according to how long you think it would take a freelancer who worked at a more average pace. Alternatively, you can pad your hours and charge on an hourly basis.

In some cases, your client will have a vastly inflated idea of how long a project takes and will grossly overpay you. I'm usually willing to let that go by if the job is being paid for by a large, rich corporation. One reason not to accept a ridiculous overpayment is that at some point the client may wise up and realize that you are taking gross advantage which obviously doesn't reflect well. I chance this when I am working for a large company, because in such cases I can always respond with, "Well, I thought it was a little high by smaller companies' standards, but I figured that your pay scale was higher."

If your client underestimates the time and difficulty of a job, you must ask for more money. Politely explain that although the job looks easy enough, certain steps take longer than the observer might expect. Be prepared to explain things to them without feeling attacked and defensive.

Sometimes you will be asked to do rush jobs. This should usually cost a client extra. I generally charge an extra 50 percent on top. Other people even get away with doubling the price. However, if you have an old client you want to keep happy or if you are new and have just started building your clientele, it is to your advantage to sometimes do rush jobs for your regular price. If you do give such a break, be sure to tell them that normally you would charge a supplement but that this time you aren't, because you would like their business and value your long working relationship.

Be sure that you and your client know exactly what you are being paid to do so that if more tasks are added on or if you run overtime, you can charge more. Try not to lock yourself in, because employers often do try to sleaze in more hassles to the dollar. When you have agreed upon price and duties, you should be sure to detail these in your contract or letter of agreement. (See chapter 18, Collecting What's Owed You.)

When quoting a price, you must be very certain what rights you are giving away. One-time rights to use a piece of work should cost a client less than if he buys all rights to the work. Illustrators, photographers and writers generally sell the right to use an image or a piece of writing in a single specific instance. The Graphic Artists Guild urges designers to work similarly and sell one-time rights and charge for the reuse or extended use of such products as logos, letterheads and book covers which may, by their nature, be used over and over for many years.

Some users of your work may require you to transfer all rights to them as a condition of doing the job. This arrangement is known as "work for hire." In some cases, you may not mind functioning as a hired gun and selling all future rights to a piece you have done on assignment. Just remember two things: you have to agree that a piece is a work made for hire and sign away your rights in writing. Remember that you are forever giving up any future claim to the piece and charge accordingly. The Copyright Justice Coalition, an alliance of various artist and writer groups, is currently trying to have work for hire eliminated from the Copyright Law except in the case of screenplays.

Your job acceptance form or letter should spell out very clearly just which rights you are selling. Don't forget to specify how and when your original artwork or negatives should be returned to you, because this gives you important control over whether or not your work can be reused without your permission or knowledge. Sometimes the other side of the coin can become an issue, and clients who have bought all rights may try to hold on to your original to prevent you from reusing it. Nevertheless, try negotiating for the return of your work by offering to sign an agreement specifying that you won't reuse the work.

We feel it works best to customize your prices for each client. What I tell new clients is that we are going to charge them a standard rate until we get to know them (and find out just how much of a hassle they are to work with), but that as we get to know their needs, we will be able to customize the prices according to their situation. Clients like this. They like to feel that they are special and that you are working with them and not cheating them. —*Graphic Designer*

The vice-president of a busy print shop offers these suggestions for overcoming clients' objections to your prices.

- Explain that you get what you pay for. Of course the client can always find somebody to do the work cheaper, but they may be taking a big chance. With you they may have to pay extra, but they will lessen their risk of disappointment and can depend on a quality product.
- Explain to your prospective client that good quality vendors are reliable, experienced, and can anticipate problems that could jeopardize the project. They are financially stable, unlikely to go out of business and have modern equipment. Low-ball vendors are often rookies. Their production materials may be old or second quality, their equipment outmoded. Their unstable financial picture can cause problems for the client, and they may not be reliably able to deliver what they promise.

PAYMENT SCHEDULES

It's also important to settle on how you are to receive your payment. Is it to be a lump sum plus expenses after you turn in an acceptable assignment? Or will you be paid a percentage up front with expenses reimbursed monthly or by some other arrangement? There is no single acceptable solution here. How you choose to receive your money depends upon your needs and your feelings about the financial status of the outfit you're working for.

If you are embarking on a project that will take several months to complete, ask for half or a third on signing and a third upon presentation of the first half of the job. This advice is especially true if your expenses for the job will be high. Even if your client is reimbursing your expenses on top, you will need cash in hand to get the job started and to buy what you need as you go along. If your cash flow is good this won't be as much of a problem. Some people actually prefer, as long as they have enough cash saved, to receive the money as a lump sum at the end. There's something more psychologically satisfying about getting one check for $3,000 rather than three checks for $1,000 over several months. However, there are pitfalls to this preference. Those partial payments could be earning interest. Secondly, if the client turns out to have a payment problem, you have collected nothing to sustain you in case you have an eight- or ten-week wait for their accounting system to spit out a check. In a worse case—that the company hits upon hard times before they pay you— the more money you got up front, the less you will now be missing. I have learned, in my own business, to take some money up front—particularly from small clients. Most of the large companies that I work for are refreshingly professional about paying. If a client is reluctant to pay you half up front for even a small job, you should beware of getting involved.

PRICING GUIDELINES BY PROFESSION

WRITERS

Writers working for publications such as magazines or newspapers with a set rate per word or per page don't have much of a problem. Basically, you can either take or leave what they offer. Since very few literary agents will be bothered handling articles for their clients, you will be on your own to negotiate. If the publication particularly wants your piece or wants you as a contributor, then you may be able to negotiate a higher fee. Generally, as you get to be a frequent contributor to a publication, your work should be more highly re- munerated. If, after two pieces, your rate hasn't gone up, ask your editor whether a 10 to 20 percent increase can be arranged. If it's a small or new publication they may turn you down, but a well-established magazine will generally start to pay you more.

If you are engaged in your own freelance writing business you will have no publication guidelines as to how much a job is worth. You can charge on a per job or a per hour basis. Sometimes a potential client will make you an offer based on what her company would like to pay you. It's your job to have an idea of the going rates in your line of work. To do this, you should consult with other writers of similar material, discuss it with editors who aren't involved with the job in question and check in *Writer's Market*. This book, which is updated annually, is a useful listing of magazines, book publishers, newspapers and other outlets for freelance writing. One useful section in the back tells you the going rates for various types of writing jobs, ranging from speech writing to creating ad copy. Occasionally, the Editorial Freelancers Association or the Authors Guild publishes information on the average prices paid for different types of writing and editing.

Typically, writing jobs involve additional expenses over and above the cost of your time. These might include telephone expenses, transportation, copying, typing and mailing expenses. In your agreement or contract indicate that these expenses will be billed separately whether you charge by the hour or by the job. This saves your having to estimate your expenses when setting the price for the job and miscalculating to your disadvantage.

COMMERCIAL VISUAL ARTISTS

Graphic designers usually charge for the work plus expenses, and they generally mark up expenses from 10 to 25 percent. Illustrators generally have lower expenses than graphic designers and in the past did not mark them up when billing clients. Now, however, some illustrators are marking up expenses before passing them on to clients.

While it is a common practice for commercial artists to deal directly with print shops and make big money on the markup to their client, one commercial artist voiced a loud caveat, particularly to small-time operators. Sometimes clients disappear, abandoning the work in your lap. If you have contracted with the print shop on your client's job, and the job is a large one, you could lose your shirt in one rip. One artist's policy is to present the client with camera-ready work and to let them make a separate arrangement with the printer. He is willing to act as liaison between the client and the print shop, which he does at an hourly rate, but this way although the client gets his services, he is not financially at risk. This way of operating loses some good money and even results in the derision of other freelancers, but he prefers to sleep comfortably at night.

The must-have reference on pricing for both illustrators and designers is the *Graphic Artists Guild Handbook: Pricing and Ethical Guidelines*, which is available free to their members and can be purchased by the public. *Selling Your Graphic Design and Illustration* by Tad Crawford and Arie Kopelman also gives some useful guidance.

Professional Business Practices in Photography and *Stock Photography Handbook* are available from ASMP (205 Lexington Avenue, New York, NY 10016; (212) 889-9144. Information included is based on surveys of working photographers.

PERFORMERS

Many musicians and actors are members of unions whose pay scales dictate what they will be paid. In cases where musicians are playing non-union gigs such as weddings or private parties, they will determine a price per musician based on the going rate in the area. A band will add expenses that they must pay out of pocket, such as rental of the PA system and travel. Generally the band leader, even if he or she is also getting paid to play, will get a decent sum for being the leader and organizing the gig, doing the charts and managing the rest of the band members. Under union rules, the band leader is paid almost double.

Most young musicians trying to get started find that the union is of limited benefit for them since the majority of the clubs where they can get dates aren't unionized. Although members are told not to play at such establishments, most musicians cannot afford to obey this dictum. Instead, many find themselves guaranteeing a certain door at their gigs or else paying the difference. While the union is adamantly opposed to members' playing under such circumstances and blacklist clubs where this goes on, many musicians take a more pragmatic view if it might pay off in terms of getting a contract. At the higher end of the scale, at large clubs, the union can make a player's life very pleasant indeed by guaranteeing that members will be decently remunerated and will work under tolerable and safe conditions (for lists of these unions, see page 277).

Nonunion actors and dancers will generally have to take what is offered by small theater and dance companies that they work with. However, occasionally actors and dancers hire themselves out for private performances at parties and other occasions. In this case, they follow the same basic guidelines as stated above.

CHAPTER SIXTEEN

BUDGETING AN UNPREDICTABLE INCOME

*B*udget. Now there's a thoroughly unappealing word in most people's minds. Whether it dredges up visions of blue-haired high school accounting teachers or painful childhood memories of your parents fighting behind closed doors on Sunday afternoons, it is probably not a pleasant thing to think about. Most freelancers don't bother to budget because they figure that their income is so sporadic, so feast or famine, that budgeting is one unpleasant duty that they may sidestep. In the words of one frustrated actress, "One of the hardest things about freelancing is that you can't plan. You can't budget because you have no idea how much money is going to be coming in."

But actually, a flexible budget can go far toward making your life more pleasant, because it can help relieve some of the draining financial crises that you will probably find that you go through every week otherwise. This is not to say that budgeting can substitute for income, or even regulate your cash flow (though it can help). The more of your financial dealings that you can make automatic the better, and a proper budget can make certain monthly and quarterly disbursements of money systematic and thereby far less attention-consuming to you.

HOW TO MAKE A BUDGET

To begin the simplest budgeting method you can adopt, get an accountant's ledger or just a large piece of paper. This page will represent one month's income and outflow. First, enter any fixed expense, such as rent and loan or pension payments, making a separate line for each and recording their monthly amounts.

No matter how hungry you are, these expenses have to come off the top. They are the bills which you know you have to pay no matter what. Dustin Hoffman is reputed to have taken this idea so seriously that, when he was an unemployed actor and stage manager, he kept separate glass jars for rent, food, lights, etc. He put a certain amount of whatever he made into each jar and never permitted himself to borrow money from one to spend on something other than what he had it earmarked for.

The vital thing to remember about these fixed expenses is that the only excuse you have for not paying them is that you're not eating. In that case, you should make a partial payment of each one and send an explanatory note stating when you hope to be able to send the balance. (Do this even if you honestly don't know yourself when money will come in. Particularly in the case of loans, they like to see that you *intend* to pay. The best thing to say is that you will pay them when you are paid for a job you are owed for. This is really all you can do, but it still comes across better than a sort of shamed disregard.)

Now make lines for the usual amounts you spend for ordinary and necessary business expenses such as paper, paint, stamps and lessons. While defaulting on these won't get you in trouble with anybody else, it will make it hard for you to produce income in most cases.

Next come slightly more flexible expenses such as food, telephone, utilities and transportation. These are flexible because you know you can adjust them somewhat when you are broke. You can eat tofu and vegetables for about $3 a day, and you can walk or ride a bicycle for cheaper transportation. You can definitely cut your phone bill by trying to use it only for business calls, and by taking advantage of the evening and weekend off-peak hours whenever possible. Utility bills can be cut if you start turning out lights behind you, taking advantage of off-peak hours, and lowering your use of energy-consuming appliances, if you have any. These are merely suggestions for cutting back if your cash flow isn't flowing. Everyone wastes money on different things, so only you will know where you can best cut back without feeling the pinch.

Now, while an employee could take this whole process further and subtract these expenses from his monthly income to find out what was left over for fun, you more or less have to stop. You should add up your fixed expenses to come out with the bedrock figure that you need to come up with once a month to keep from being evicted, cut off, foreclosed upon or any of the other vicious-sounding things that banks, utilities and landlords can do to you if you don't pay them. Always know what this amount is and strive never to default on it, no matter how you have to rustle up the money. Naturally, most people prefer to have more money than this, but it isn't *always* possible when you are starting out; and if that information dismays you, you should probably reconsider your decision to freelance.

Once you know how much bare survival costs, and how much automatically gets paid out to others each month, you can then figure out about how much extra you can spend on your work. Anything above and beyond necessities can be apportioned for daily spending money—for clothes, entertainment and unexpected expenses.

Monthly payments to a savings account are important enough to consider a fixed expense as soon as you have the wherewithal. You need some sort of emergency cushion to pay for unexpected expenses, which can range from a broken typewriter to a broken arm.

But I never know how much I'll be getting each month, you say. Usually, only performers have *no* idea what their income will be for the next month, and they often have outside jobs for just this reason. Artists and writers can often estimate their accounts receivable a month ahead—if they are fortunate enough to be paid on time. Publishing royalties and performing residuals are usually reported in twice-yearly statements, followed thirty to sixty days later by payment if all goes well.

If all goes smoothly and you get your money, royalties and residual income can make your budgeting a bit more meaningful. When you have worked widely, you will be able to stagger royalty payments so that you have an actual cash flow, rather than scattered payments with arid months in between. Until that time, your best bet is to try to build up a bit of a cushion before you go freelance. If you already are freelancing, you should ferret away at least a little bit every time you have something left over, until you have enough to float you for a few months in case of disaster.

MANAGING YOUR BILLS

Although their arrival may come well after you have forgotten or used up the items they refer to, you can be quite certain that bills will arrive. People often tend to ignore this and act as though they have more money than they actually do have. It is tempting to use credit to double your buying power, but nothing gets you into financial trouble faster. If, according to your budget, you have $25 per month to spend on professional supplies, you should not routinely be spending $25 cash and charging another $25 worth (although obviously there will be occasional situations in which you must use your credit in this way in order to do a particular job). If you do charge something you must subtract that amount from what you have left to spend—not just ignore it. Otherwise, when the bill comes in, you will have nothing left to pay it with and will then have to dip into what you have budgeted for essentials or the next month's supplies. Such a system is a surefire way to defeat your budget and put yourself behind.

Here are some general hints which will help you keep your bills from unbalancing your budget:

• Try to stay on your creditors' good side by paying promptly when you *do* have money. Then when you don't, they are more likely to be lenient with you if you point out your good record.

• If you don't have the full amount, pay what you can toward bills. This at least helps you to keep in good standing, and it ensures that you don't waste what money you have. A common tendency is to squander money that comes in if the amount is too small to pay off what you owe. If you owe $75 for your telephone, $20 for your electricity, and $37 to the art supplies store, but only $75 of what you are owed comes in, pay each creditor a large part of what you owe, because otherwise it is too easy to spend the $75 and still not have decreased your debt.

• Keeping all your bills in one place makes it easier to keep track of what you owe.

• Mark on your calendar any due dates for bills which carry service charges for late payment, such as credit card, loan and department store bills. To give yourself longer to pay, you might mark down closing dates in department store and credit card billing cycles. If you make purchases as soon as possible after the closing date, you will not get a bill for almost a month, and you will have a second whole month before the payment is due (see also chapter 17, Credit).

CONTROLLING YOUR SPENDING

A very important part of budgeting is controlling your spending. The poorer you are, the harder it is to control your spending, because money and purchases assume a more central position in your mind when you are broke. Many people's worst sprees come when they have nothing in their pockets but their credit cards. Buying brings you comfort when nothing else does—rather like an addiction. And, like any sort of fix, it merely worsens the problem when the high of spending money and getting something new in your life wears off. You still have no money, and now you need even more to pay the new bills.

On the other hand, there can be trouble when you have been making lots of money. Suddenly, as the jobs keep rolling in and you find yourself even turning down jobs (something that you would have thought impossible two years ago), you decide that you have moved permanently into a higher echelon and begin to spend as though you had an inherited income to count on. Be chary! While you may have hit a new level, chances are that you will still experience slow periods when you are going to need a cushion in the bank. If you spend every penny that comes in, you will have inflated your monthly obligations to the point that you may have serious trouble if all your clients take ninety days to pay or things slack off. Here are some pointers that may help you control your spending.

- Don't walk around with much extra cash on you. Have enough for an emergency ($10 will usually tide you over) but not enough to accommodate overspending:
- Don't buy anything when you are feeling emotional about something in your life.
- Ask yourself whether you *need* something or merely want it. Of course, once in a while you should buy something you want but don't need, but wait until you're a little ahead. If you're *too* rigid and puritanical about saving your money, you can make yourself resent the idea of saving altogether.
- Do not make any major purchase without first sleeping on it for at least a day, and preferably a week.
- Not everything you own or consume needs to be imported. If you're broke, remember you can switch back to Maxwell House from Celebes Kalossi, from San Pelligrino to seltzer.

BUDGETING FOR TWO

Nothing can end a relationship faster than constant fighting about money. A well-designed budget will reduce the likelihood of this happening.

Finances are likely to be quite variable in the typical freelance household, and this necessitates flexibility. First, you should decide whether you are both making enough to split everything exactly in half, and whether you want to make that arrangement. This may not appeal to you if certain expenses are mainly run up by one of you. Another problem with this method is that it often involves a great deal of time and nit-picking to divvy everything up. You may be tempted to let small expenses slide by without splitting them, and that is when resentment does begin to build. It might be more sensible to divide major monthly expenses, such as rent, utilities and basic charges for the telephone. This is simple since it only requires sitting down and dividing things up once a month. Food can be paid out of a central fund (a jam jar will do fine) to which you each contribute a set amount monthly. The rest of your expenses, such as transportation, clothes and work necessities, should really be the responsibility of each of you. Particularly in young households, where you both freelance, this arrangement will ensure that no one gets penalized for having a less costly career, as often happens when one of you has a high overhead (e.g., a photographer with a studio) and the other has almost no overhead at all (e.g., a novelist).

This is only one possibility. There will be times when one of you is making far more than the other, and you need a contingency plan for this. How you decide to deal with this eventuality will be a highly individualized matter which depends on your relationship. In some cases, the higher-earning partner is willing to assume more of the costs during this time, so that the broke one can get on with essential work. I have met other couples who have agreed not to do this even if one partner is forced to hold down an outside job to make ends meet. Says one freelancer: "I consider my work almost as one would a child from an earlier marriage. I feel that I am responsible for it just as Charles is for his work. We each make sacrifices for our own work at times, but we have an agreement that our partner doesn't involuntarily sacrifice for our work. Of course that still leaves it open for us to bail one another out if we feel able. Cold-blooded, but it keeps us friends. It evolved mutually."

In cases where one partner consistently earns more money (e.g., the wife's a lawyer and the husband a freelancer) you may decide to let the higher-earning partner automatically assume the large bills while the freelancer takes care of himself and some of the smaller expenses; or the freelancer's earnings can go into a savings account as a nest egg.

I urge you not to open a joint checking account. It is more time-consuming to balance, and it opens the way to arguments over spending. Another point to consider is that, in the event of one of your deaths, the account could be frozen until the estate was settled, and you know how long that could take. It is a better plan to have separate accounts, even if you divide your income exactly in half. Another possibility is to have a household account into which you both put money that is to be spent jointly.

BANKING

While it may seem condescending for me to urge you to go out and open a savings account and a checking account, you'd be surprised at the number of freelancers I interviewed who didn't have any sort of bank account—or who had only a savings account. Dumb! If you don't have a place to put your money so that you don't have unlimited access to it, your top drawer or your cookie jar ends up being your bank. This is foolish for the following reasons:

• It makes impulse spending too easily within the realm of the possible. Even if you are thrifty during the day, it is often irresistibly tempting if you are stoned or drunk to break one of the twenties from your "bank." And, once broken, it's as good as gone. Do this a few times and you'll go to make a legitimate withdrawal and find but $12 left.
• You have no record of your payments for tax purposes. If all your money is in your drawer and you are robbed, you'll be sorry. At least money in the bank is safe and insured.
• You'll never be able to get credit, and in most places you'll have trouble finding landlords who will rent to you.
• You collect no interest on savings sewn into your mattress.
• It's inconvenient always to have to carry cash.
• You'll have to go stand in line at the bank and pay an extra 50¢ or 75¢ fee to get a money order every time you want to pay for something by mail.

So go out and start up two accounts, checking and savings, preferably in different banks, so that if you get a credit card or overdraft checking with one bank, it cannot dip into an in-house savings account of yours in order to pay itself what you owe. Unfortunately, this is cleverly made less simple for you by banks which will give you free checking if you keep a minimum balance in a savings account at the same institution. If practical, you should put any savings over and beyond this minimum in a second savings or money market account in another bank, preferably one which will pay higher interest than a commercial bank.

You may even decide to double your number of bank accounts by having separate business and personal accounts. Although this isn't technically necessary for a sole proprietor, unless you do business under another name, it may make your accounting easier, because you don't have to waste time sorting out your own money and that of your business for the IRS. Also, if you are an impulse spender, it may be safer and less tempting for your business assets not to be in your personal checking account. Such a system probably doesn't make much sense, however, unless you have enough cash flow to keep reasonable amounts in your accounts.

Never keep more than you need to in your checking account. Keep the rest in some liquid interest-bearing account where it can be readily transfused into your checking account. If you decide to separate your personal and business banking, you can pay yourself a salary which you move monthly or weekly from your business account to your own savings or checking. Also transfer into your business checking whatever you need to pay your bills and run your business for the month or week.

Get into the habit of shopping around for the best deal any time you have business to do with a bank. Although the outer limits are set by the state and federal governments, banks are in competition with one another for clients and so the deals that they offer can vary considerably. This is true of interest on loans, cost of checking accounts, prices of safe deposit boxes, interest rates on savings accounts, even banking hours. You don't have to exhaust yourself going to every bank in the city, but it is worth your time to check with the banks convenient to your home or workplace.

Besides a bank account, a small businessperson needs a good relationship with a banker. Banks do not have to be monolithic edifices with deaf ears when you have a problem. The way around such treatment is to have a personal relationship with a banker whom you can call upon as needed. Many of the individuals and small businesses I talked to mentioned how useful it can be to have a friendly banker who likes your business and will go to bat for you.

The way to begin this relationship is to make out a business plan. This needn't be a formal Harvard Business School sort of document. You can actually just present the information in a letter. Be sure to include the following information:

- A brief description of your business. Tell what it is that you make or do. Not everyone understands what a graphic designer or a copy editor does, so explain your role in such a way that your potential banker will see what a useful function you fulfill. If you are a fine artist, you obviously don't need to discourse on the important function of art in society. Instead, mention anything that will distinguish you in the banker's mind's eye from the stereotypical picture she may have of an "artist" or "writer." This would include shows, publications, reviews of your work or even a strong statement from a rep or teacher.
- Identify the market and your place in it. If you have impressive clients, even if they are just local, by all means drop their names (with their permission).
- Tell how much you made last year and how much you have made so far this year.
- List your business assets (equipment, cash on hand, your home or workplace if you own it, any other assets of your business).
- Likewise list your debts. Just discuss your business indebtedness here. No need to volunteer that you owe $1,000 to Visa unless you spent the money on a new camera or other business equipment. Of course, since you are a sole proprietor, you may be asked to supply information on your personal credit history.
- Describe your future objectives. Tell where you are trying to go with your work, why you have a chance in the marketplace and how you plan to get there.
- Lay out your cash needs. Probably you're going to need money to get there from here. Tell what it is needed for and how it will add to your business. Tell any other potential sources you have, if any, for some of the money. This might include grants that you have applied for, big jobs that you have been promised or loans from personal sources.

Making out a business plan is a useful exercise as it helps you define who you are, where you want to go and what you need in order to accomplish your goals. Once you've done it, call the bank and ask for an appointment with one of the officers so that you can introduce yourself and your business. It doesn't hurt to mention in advance what it is that you do and ask whether there's an officer with a particular interest in small business or in the arts. Plenty of bankers started out wanting to be artists, plenty still dream about one day quitting the bank and becoming an artist. You may get lucky and find a banker who'll enjoy the vicarious pleasure of getting your business going and for whom you can do a good turn by telling him about art schools or hot young painters he might want to collect or the names of some literary agents.

You may also want to get hold of a book called *Practical Financial Guide for Small Business* by a former banker named Richard L. Duffy. It is available through Appletree Enterprises (Box 4939, Foster City, CA 94404) and has very useful advice on making out a business plan and approaching lenders.

Be aware that all the figures mentioned for interest rates and service charges can (and do) change at the drop of a hat. Likewise, banks are constantly developing new packages. The following sections are intended as general guides. Your bank may not offer the exact services described here, and interest rates differ from bank to bank.

TYPES OF CHECKING ACCOUNTS

There are numerous types of checking accounts available. Some pay interest, some charge you for each check that you use, and for overdrafts, and also levy a service charge. Some are free, requiring only that you pay for the printing of your checks and for overdrafts, and others are "free," meaning that you pay no per check charge or service charge unless your balance falls below a certain minimum (although again you do pay for check printing). A variation on the latter deal entitles you to maintain your minimum balance in a savings account at the same bank, and as long as the sum of the two accounts or of the savings account alone doesn't fall below that, your checking is free of service or per check charges.

Since 1981 banks have been able to pay interest on checking accounts called NOW accounts. NOW (negotiated order of withdrawal) accounts are offered nationwide by savings banks, savings and loan associations and commercial banks. Generally they have a catch—if your balance drops below a certain minimum, even for a millisecond during the month, either you will receive a lower rate of interest or you will be made to pay a service charge.

Many banks now offer money market accounts which pay you higher interest than you would receive on a regular savings account, although interest rates fluctuate weekly. As with NOW accounts, you must maintain a minimum balance in order to get full interest. You are allowed to write a limited number of checks to other parties although generally you may withdraw money yourself without penalty.

To get the best checking deal, you must shop around and see which bank allows you to keep the lowest minimum balance in order to get free checking. You may not want to put much money in beyond this minimum, since other plans such as money market funds or time deposit accounts will pay you more interest on your money.

Checks can give rise to some of the same complications that credit cards do if you are prone to overspending. Even if you don't have the cash to buy that unnecessary item, you can always pull out your checkbook. If your finances are at all shaky, you should probably not make a habit of carrying your checkbook with you. I only take mine when I know I will need it, but I do carry one or two spare checks in my wallet in case of emergency. (If you do this, just make sure to note the number of the check and its amount when you finally use one.)

CASH MACHINES

If your bank has a mechanized teller you can do all your banking by inserting a plastic card into a machine and punching buttons, and you can keep only as much as you need for a few days in your checking account and let the rest earn interest in a savings account. When you need to cover some checks, you simply transfer the money from your savings.

Here are a few things to bear in mind when banking by machine:

- *Always* count the money you get from the machine. Mine was once short by $80, which I didn't notice until hours later when I pulled out my wad and found I was short. Fortunately for me, the lost money had fallen back on the floor behind the machine's brain, and an honest teller reported it to the bank so that they were able to verify my story and reimburse me!
- Depending on the program, some automatic teller machines make it easy for someone to come in seconds after you've left, when some of your account information is still on the screen, and tap into your account. So never leave one of these machines until it dismisses you.
- Always take your receipt; it is the only record of your transaction that you will get.
- Beware of spending more than you can afford when you withdraw money from these machines. Most are programmed so that the least amount you can take out is $20. You can have a deposit slip ready and redeposit on the spot what you don't need, so that you don't end up squandering the $20, when all you needed was $5 for the movies.

Even newer than the automatic teller is a rather Brave New World concept of using the same sort of magnetized debit card to make purchases from co-operating merchants. Merchants have terminals into which you insert your bank card, and the money is transferred from your account to the merchants'.

The disadvantage of this system is its potential for invading your privacy. The bank's computer has a record of the purchases you made which could be used in many ways ranging from the annoying (use by marketing experts) to the sinister (use by who knows whom?). Computers are vulnerable to electronic whizzes who may be able to steal money from your account or simply to get information about you. As the computer age advances in the hands of the profit-motivated sector, the citizens of this country would do well to keep very close watch on what develops.

From a more immediately practical standpoint, this system will eliminate your ability to float checks—i.e., it will eliminate those days of grace before a check clears when you may not actually have any funds to draw against.

GETTING THE HIGHEST
INTEREST ON YOUR SAVINGS

The amount of interest you can earn is tied to how long you can give your money to the bank to play with. Not only is your money working for the bank, it is working for you, so make it go as far as you can by being informed about the ins and outs of savings. Points to consider are:

The interest rate.
How the interest is compounded.
How often it is compounded.
The type of account.

Interest rates are tied to the general price of money, and they fluctuate. I will not quote any figures in this section because, chances are, by the time you read this book the interest rates will have changed again. In general, savings and loan associations and mutual banks can pay slightly higher rates than commercial banks.

Although the rate of interest is the most important determinant of how much money you can earn from your savings, the frequency of *compounding* also makes a difference. Compounding is the process of calculating interest on your money. The more frequently your bank compounds interest, the more you will earn. This is because each time it is compounded, a little more is added to the principal, and you are subsequently paid interest on your principal *plus* the interest that has already accrued. *Daily compounding* is obviously most desirable, followed by *quarterly*, then *annual compounding*. With interest compounded daily, the principal grows a little each day, and therefore so does the base amount on which your subsequent interest is calculated; so you gain daily what seems to be an infinitesimal amount. Actually, over the years, the frequency of compounding can make a staggering difference in what you earn.

The final consideration when shopping for a savings account is the *computation method* they use for calculating interest. If you make frequent deposits or withdrawals, this may make a difference. Traditionally, these are three in number. The *low-balance method* is least favorable to you, since you are paid interest only on the lowest amount in your account. Make sure to check whether your bank uses this method. If it does, try hard to find a better deal. What you should look for is *day of deposit to day of withdrawal*, which means that you will be paid prorated interest (interest on your money for the number of days the money was actually in the bank) for whatever amounts you had in your account. Banks often give *grace* days: a variable number of days (e.g., four) at the beginning or end of a quarter during which you can withdraw money but still earn interest on it to the end of the quarter.

While you may not be able to find a bank that is favorable in interest rate paid, frequency of compounding, *and* method of computation, it is worth a try. Banks are in competition with one another for depositors, and of course the more consumer-oriented they are, the better they do. Particularly in large cities, you will find this sort of war going on to your advantage.

The type of account you decide to open will determine, to some extent, the amount of interest you are paid. The most liquid account would be a *passbook savings* or a *statement savings account.* Here you have complete flexibility as to when and how much you can deposit or withdraw. Banks are trying to push statement savings accounts, in which you get a monthly or quarterly statement like that of a checking account, and so they offer an extra ¼ percent or so of interest for these.

Remember that funds in passbook or statement savings accounts can be used as collateral for personal loans. This type of loan is usually quite inexpensive and can be a good option for freelancers who are having trouble borrowing.

You can earn higher interest by putting your money into a *time deposit account* or *Certificate of Deposit* (CD). This type of account is less liquid. You agree not to touch your principal for a specified period of time, ranging from seven days to several years. The longer the term you agree to, the higher the interest rate. If you withdraw early, you are penalized by having your interest reduced. Usually, but not always, you lose the interest on the part of the principal which you withdrew for the quarter in which you withdrew it. This is not a terrible loss, considering that you are probably earning at least 1 percent more than you would if you'd had your money in a straight savings account. Many people don't realize that you are entitled to withdraw interest you have earned without any penalty. Time deposits are a good deal if you feel reasonably sure that you won't need the money, but even if an emergency arises and you have to withdraw early, you may still come out ahead.

Share draft accounts are offered by credit unions (see also chapter 17, Credit). Interest rates on these accounts compare favorably with those paid by savings and loan associations and mutual banks. If the credit union has had a good year, you may even get a little bonus interest, since these organizations are cooperatives. On the other hand, if the union's manager is not skillful and it has a bad year, you may not earn as much interest as you would with a passbook account. On the balance, well-run credit unions are bargains and offer a wide range of financial services at favorable prices. If you are eligible for one, do join.

Money market funds have been in existence since the mid-70's. They were developed so that small investors could pool their money and buy CDs and government bonds in higher denominations than would be possible for them to purchase individually. At the time of this writing there is a minimum initial investment in these funds, but you can reinvest in amounts of $100 or more. You can receive checks from your fund which you can write for amounts of $500 or more. In general, whenever the prime rate is high, so are money market yields. You can find the names of the funds in the *Wall Street Journal,* and *Money* magazine carries a table of their recent yields so that you can see which fund seems most active. The business section of the Sunday *New York Times* also gives a chart of recent money market yields. If you have enough money to get into one of these funds, do. Not only will you earn the highest no-risk interest, but your funds will also be extremely liquid.

Money market funds have cut into banks' business so dramatically that many of them are scrambling to better their offerings to depositors and retrieve some of the lost business. Many savings and loan associations and banks are now offering a new type of account designed specifically to compete with money market funds.

FURTHER READING

You will find all of the following books very helpful. I urge every freelancer to have at least one of these reference books on the shelf:

Blodgett, Richard E. *The New York Times Book of Money*. Quadrangle Books, 1978. This is a good basic book. My only reservation is that it is slightly out-of-date and oversimplified in places. For those who can barely stand to read about money, this won't make you o.d.

Clair, Bernard E., and Daniele, Anthony R. *Love Pact*. Grove Press, 1980. This book, written by two lawyers, is indispensable for people who are living together. It discusses joint vs. separate accounts, the legal aspects of living together, who pays for what, and a contingency plan for dividing your shared belongings should the relationship fail.

Phalon, Richard. *Your Money*. St. Martin's Press, 1981. The author is an editor at *Forbes*, and the book is entertaining and iconoclastic. Although some of the advice may be debatable, the book may amuse you enough to make learning about money a bit more palatable.

Porter, Sylvia. *Sylvia Porter's New Money Book for the 80s*. Avon, 1980. This great tome is best described as an economic encyclopedia. If I had to choose one reference book on this subject, it would be this one. It goes into banking, money management, insurance, education, divorce, funerals and other such matters germane to everyone's life. Porter has an excellent section on investing, and a superlative one on consumer rights and how to complain effectively.

Quinn, Jane Bryant. *Everyone's Money Book*. Dell, 1980.

Schlayer, Mary Elizabeth, with Cooley, Merilyn. *How to Be a Financially Secure Woman*. Ballantine, 1978. This is a succinct and easily comprehensible book that focuses on the special money problems of women, particularly those who are newly on their own.

Van Caspel, Venita. *The New Money Dynamics*. Reston Publishing Co., 1978. This book is excellent on investing and fairly advanced money management. Ms. Van Caspel's advice is sharp and useful. If you can comprehend it, you can pick up some savvy tips from this book.

CHAPTER SEVENTEEN

CREDIT

For all but the most celebrated freelancers, there will always be times when the wolf is at the door or only a month away, when there is no work in sight and a world recession threatening. This is a fact about which you must adopt a realistic attitude right from the start, or you will wake up one morning to find you have only half of next month's rent. You will waste the next three days biting your nails, making phone calls, and chemically assuaging your pain at night.

If handled methodically, these bleak periods can actually serve as springboards in your life, for they will force you to do your utmost to find work and do it well. You may surprise yourself at just how much your utmost is.

There will be times when even your utmost isn't enough to procure any work or grant money in time. These periods can best be survived by concentrating on the fact that at least you are in control of your fate. You can either borrow money or take a job. While not the most savory alternatives to many people, at least one of them can alleviate your immediate problem.

WHY FREELANCERS DEPEND ON CREDIT

Because of the unpredictable nature of their cash flow, freelancers often need to borrow in order to keep functioning. This is true particularly at the beginning of your career, when you often have to spend a lot more money than you make. Most creditors look at both ability and intent to repay when considering lending you money. When they receive an application from an actor who makes $30,000 one year and $6,375 the next and who changes addresses frequently, they assume he is a shiftless person and do not generally extend credit unless he knows how to play their game.

By now most freelancers have come to accept catch-22 as a way of life, and nowhere is catch-22 more the rule than in the confusing world of credit. So it shouldn't surprise you that to a lender the best person to loan money to is someone who already owes money. In fact, if you have never borrowed you may have to struggle to establish credit. Obtaining the first loan will be the greatest challenge.

Before you even think of going out and getting any credit card or loan, there are some things you should know to keep from getting burned. Some types of credit are better than others. The kind which the financial world most wants to foist on you is the worst: bank credit cards such as Visa and MasterCard.

CREDIT CARDS ARE NOT CHARGE CARDS

Credit cards are charge cards, but not in the way the bank would have you believe. Contrary to what you may think, when you go out and charge $75 worth of drawing supplies or take a client out for a drink, you are not charging the goods or the services directly to an account with a merchant. You are taking out a loan of money, and unless you pay your bill right away, interest on this loan can cost you upwards of 18 percent per year, which isn't cheap. When you buy goods or services with a bank credit card, what you are actually doing is borrowing money from the bank—money which they pay to the merchant or purveyor of services. Unless you are able to pay off your bills at once, you should think of credit-card purchases as cash loans with interest. And, since the banks are lending you depositors' money, they are far more insistent about getting it back than corporations working with their own money. You make a purchase and "charge" it with your card. The bank then credits the money to the merchant while charging you interest on the amount loaned you.

When you charge a purchase to an account with a merchant, if the merchandise proves shoddy you are in a better position to complain since your creditor is also the seller and you can withhold payment from him. If you have used a bank credit card such as MasterCard or Visa, you have very little recourse unless you haven't yet paid your bill. Since October of 1975, it has been a federal law that you are entitled to withhold payment on a purchase of more than $50 made within one hundred miles of your residence with a bank credit card if you can prove that the goods were not satisfactory and that you did complain to the seller and attempted to obtain satisfaction.

DO YOU REALLY NEED A CREDIT CARD?

"But I *need* a credit card," you say. The last time you tried to rent a car you were turned down even though you offered a $500 cash deposit; the manager at the Hilton forced you to come down to the lobby and pay a quarter for phone calls because you were paying for your room in cash; the airline treated you like a hijacker because you paid cash. Ours is becoming a credit world, and people tend to regard you with hostility and condescension if you don't have plastic cards.

But you don't need a bank credit card. You will be better off having a car-rental card and an airline card, a travel and entertainment card, and a store charge or two. That way you aren't borrowing money but are rather charging goods or services.

Also, by having cards good only for fairly specific services, you probably won't squander quite as much of your money. People who have cards spend more money, possibly as much as 35 percent more money.* It's easy to see why, especially in the case of people who don't really have the money in the first place. If you're living in a fifth-floor walkup full of starving cats and half-

*Ralph George, *The New Consumer Survival Kit* (Boston: Little, Brown, 1978), p. 179.

finished manuscripts, and during better days you somehow managed to obtain a credit card, you'll always be able to get to some cheery, well-lighted store or restaurant and charge up all sorts of impractical things. For freelancers this sort of spending is lethal, because they don't have the security of knowing that if they have been extravagant more money will be coming next week or next quarter. The card fools you into thinking that you have money to spend, but you don't. You have only the card. A good rule of thumb is not to buy anything on credit that will not be there when the bill comes, or to buy only things that are directly related to the production of income. If you can exercise this kind of control, then you can defeat the odds and make your credit card work for you. (For pointers on controlling your spending, see chapter 16, Budgeting an Unpredictable Income.)

WHICH CREDIT CARDS TO GET
AND WHICH TO AVOID

There are several different kinds of plastic credit cards: travel and entertainment cards, bank cards and store charge accounts. Banks try to make it desirable for you to obtain Visa or MasterCard. You get the card free, or for a small fee, and you don't have to pay off your balance. Travel and entertainment cards, on the other hand, seem expensive and undesirable because you are expected to pay off the balance when you are billed. However, as a freelancer on a tight budget, this is the kind of credit you should be getting. While bank credit cards help you to fantasize that you have plenty of money to spend by allowing you to pay back in tiny bits with a bit of interest added, travel and entertainment cards do not lend themselves as easily to extravagance. Once you have been forced to pay up in full for an evening's indiscretion, you will think twice the next time about going out to an expensive restaurant or flying to the coast to escape your woes. A travel and entertainment card will serve to identify you in situations where you are looked upon askance if you do not have plastic, and you can use it for essential travel and entertaining, but it won't tempt you to such buying sprees as Visa and MasterCard, which are currency in every sort of establishment nowadays.

If you have a car you might want to apply for an oil company credit card, just so that you aren't stranded without the money to get to a job. On the other hand, you may not have the self-control to use it only for emergencies, and gas bills can add up very quickly. My own experience has taught me that I squander gas when the money for it isn't coming immediately out of my pocket.

It is a very good idea to have a car-rental card, since the rental companies now require that you have some sort of credit card to identify yourself even if you are paying in cash. It can be next to impossible to rent a car quickly if you have no card.

For the occasional emergency garment or household item that you need immediately and can't pay cash for, open an account in a good department store.

The way to manage your cards is to keep them in a file so that you are not tempted to just whip them out whenever you need a psychological lift. Try to pay off the balance due completely, even when you are not required to do so. While the bank or other creditor doesn't make as much this way, you waste less.

GETTING THE BEST CREDIT CARD DEAL

Although most credit card interest rates are still several percentage points over the national average for an unsecured personal loan, there is beginning to be increasing competition for customers. Banks which offer Visa and MasterCard are now going as low as 12 percent in their advertisements, but unless you know how to decode the often mystifying fine print, you may be paying more than you know. This is due to different schemes for calculating the balance on which you are charged interest. It's all rather complicated. Your best bet is to call the issuer of the card or cards that you have and ask them some questions. First, do you have an interest-free grace period for each new purchase during which you are not being assessed interest for these items? Some banks do not give you any grace period at all but begin charging you interest from the day the purchase is recorded so that by the time you get your statement you have wracked up several weeks worth of interest charges on each of that month's charges. This is the worst possible deal and will cost you the most in interest charges. Some banks still offer deals whereby you are not charged interest if you pay the balance off in full. (If you are lucky, even if you don't pay off the total bill each month, interest is still levied only on the unpaid balance and on any new purchases you make that month. This is the best possible deal presently being offered.) Some banks will cancel this free ride in the future if you don't pay your balance off in full each month. Others mention in small print that if you do not pay off the next month's balance in full you will be charged interest *retroactively* on the previous month where you actually did pay off your balance in full. California, Texas, Florida and Illinois are among the states where interest can be charged retroactively.

If you already have a card or are shopping for one you might want to check and find out just what the bank is offering you. They do have to disclose this information to you in terms that you can understand (not the small print on the back of your monthly statement). If they don't do this to your satisfaction, don't do business with them.

Perhaps the best way to decide which card is the best deal for you is according to your payment habits. If you pay off your balance in full each month, you should look for cards with the lowest annual fee and the longest grace period before you are charged interest on new purchases. If you tend to carry a balance from month to month the grace period is less important because you generally *don't* get a grace period unless you pay up in full each month. So you should be on the lookout for the lowest interest rate you can find. If you take out a lot of cash advances check to make sure the interest rate on these transactions isn't higher than that on purchases and that there are no extra fees.

You can get lists of credit card issuers and the deals they offer by writing Bankcard Holders of America, 333 Pennsylvania Avenue, SE, Washington, DC 20003.

CREDIT WITH SUPPLIERS

If you work in a field such as commercial art, photography or journalism, which calls for fairly frequent purchases of supplies, you should also open accounts with a couple of suppliers. The standard terms for such accounts are 2/10, net 30: you get a 2 percent discount for payments made within ten days, and payment in full is expected within thirty days. These figures may vary (e.g., 3/15, net 60), but you generally get a reward for early payment. You might want to open accounts with several suppliers at a time, so that if you owe one of them money to the point where they won't accept orders until you pay, you can still buy what you need from a competitor to get the next job done.

Generally, suppliers want credit references from other people with whom you've done business. If you haven't yet had other accounts, you'll probably have to shop around for a while until you find someone who will take a chance on you. If you have a friend at the bank (if you don't, make one), put his or her name down as a credit reference.

Don't forget to obtain a resale license if you buy a lot of materials. This will save you a bit of money (see Resale License, page 325).

It doesn't hurt to go into a store that you plan to patronize, with your portfolio, introduce yourself to the manager and let them know that you will be using their services regularly. I have had two businesses carry me monthly on their books with no trial period after such an introduction. Often you will even get a slight discount if a business is sure that you will become a regular customer. It is, of course, crucial that you keep up with your payments, otherwise your credit and your reputation will go downhill fast.
—Commercial Artist

OTHER KINDS OF CREDIT

Instead of having a credit card, with its high interest rates and the constant temptation to overspend, you may prefer to take out a lower-cost loan to finance a necessary expenditure. This approach gives you the double safeguard of having to justify the purchase to a lender as well as to yourself. Commercial banks will make you a personal loan which you can repay in one lump or in installments over the term of the loan.

It is generally easier to request a *personal loan*, even if you are planning to use the money in your business. You will be asked why you need the money, so go into the bank with a good story even if you actually intend to use the money on something else. The bank officer will be more favorably impressed if you have a budget detailing the costs of what you intend to buy, rather than just a vague notion that you would like to borrow $1,000.

If your credit rating is satisfactory, you should have no trouble borrowing from a bank. However, if the bank isn't confident about you as a credit risk, it may ask you to take out a chattel loan, which means that the bank puts a lien on some valuable item that you own, so that you have extra motivation to pay off your debt.

If you have no credit rating, or an insufficient one, the bank may ask you to find a co-signer who does qualify for the loan.

If you do not make your payments, you are hit with a delinquency charge, usually about 5 percent of your monthly installment. If you still don't pay, you receive a series of increasingly disturbing reminders and warnings. At this point you should really contact the bank and discuss the situation; because these late payments *are* recorded (as I was dismayed to learn when applying for a personal loan after having fallen very slightly behind on payments on my car loan).

HOME EQUITY LOANS

Under the old tax law, people were encouraged to overspend on credit purchases, because consumer interest charges were fully tax deductible. This deduction is being phased out under the new law and will soon be gone. The new law is somewhat discriminatory as it allows homeowners (but not renters) to take out home equity loans up to the purchase price of their home, plus the value of any improvements they have put into it, and deduct 100 percent of the interest. If you use the borrowed money for educational costs, home improvements or medical costs you may borrow an amount equal to a percentage of your equity in your home (the appreciated value of the property minus any money that you still owe on it). Most lenders will let you borrow 75 to 80 percent of your equity.

When you take out this sort of loan, you are given a credit line which you can draw checks against until you run out of money. There are several repayment schemes. You may pay only interest and then have a balloon amount due in ten or so years. Or you may be asked to pay both interest and a bit of principal on a monthly or quarterly basis. This at least forces you to reduce your loan balance on a regular basis.

I think that these loans are dangerous for anyone, but particularly disastrous for freelancers who can find themselves in especially serious debt problems because of their sporadic cash flow. The radio ads I hear urging people to use the value of their homes to start writing checks to fuel their fondest desires turn my stomach. Because what you're being so blithely encouraged to put at risk is your home. If you don't keep up on your payments you lose your home and your place of business in one stab. All your new furniture won't mean a thing when the marshals come pile it up in front of your house. If you can't control impulse spending on your $1,000 Visa credit line what makes you think you will with the $50,000 credit line you got by hocking your loft?

STRATEGIES FOR GETTING CREDIT

Now that you know how to differentiate between different sorts of credit, you need to learn how bank credit departments work and think. What are the banks' criteria for deciding whom to lend money to?

WHO IS CREDITWORTHY?

The real question, of course, is who *seems* creditworthy? The whole credit world is heavily skewed in favor of those who have the *ability* to pay, whether or not they have the intent. This is really a major miscalculation, because it's often much simpler to collect from an $8,000-a-year artist than from a person with an income of a million dollars a year. In fact, bill collection systems are set up to deal with people who can't easily pay and are thus more easily intimidated, as opposed to the spoiled and fearless rich (some of whom manage to run up a tab over decades just because they are immune to threats).

Right from the start of your interview with the bank officer, remember that the impression you make can be important. This is not to say that a bad impression will ruin your chances if everything else about your loan is acceptable, but since freelancers tend not to be favorites of the loan departments, a bad first impression can do you more harm than it might do someone with a more conventional life and financial background. As in any situation in which you are asking for money, don't arrive at the bank in a paint-smeared smock or some other eccentric costume. Look and act as though you are used to dealing with money, not as though you're going to blow it all and then come back asking for more.

When reviewing your credit application, prospective lenders look for a steady job, an income above $10,000 for at least three years, and evidence of stability, such as having a spouse or having lived in the same place for more than three years. At least the first two items may present problems to the average freelancer. Anyone who has tried knows that most banks and credit departments just don't quite know how to deal with freelancers and their unreliable incomes. So what does one do? You lie and you act, and then, if you get it, you manage your credit very well, at least until you have built up a more extensive credit history.

Never put "actor" or any sort of performer under "occupation" unless there is no question of your satisfying the income requirement. There is real discrimination against performers in the business world. Artists aren't exactly met with open arms either, unless they are employed commercial artists. Although creditors seem to trust journalists, they consider poets and novelists poor risks. If you have any sort of steady part-time work, list it, and pad the amount you say you earn from it in order to show a respectable annual income. Obviously, you can only do this if you're friendly with your employers and they will go along with you if called upon as references. If you marginally satisfy the income requirement you will probably be able to get credit, but you may have to show proof of income. Lenders often ask for your 1040 forms from the previous year or two to establish this, but you do not have to show them your tax returns if you don't want to. Sometimes a letter from your agent or representative with your earnings and accounts receivable will pass; sometimes you can type out a financial statement of your own earnings, accounts receivable, assets and outstanding debts listed, along with a couple of references from businesses which have extended you credit.

If you don't satisfy the income requirements as an artist, you'll have to put down whatever occupation you engage in to augment your income, or go the street route presented in the next paragraph.

One dishonest strategy centers on the job requirement. If you have any sort of job, even if *you* know it's only until after Christmas or until you get a part in a play, apply *at once* for credit cards, bank loans or charge cards. If you don't have a job and don't plan to get one, perhaps you have a friend with a business who will vouch for you when the credit department calls to ask about you. List yourself as his or her employee, but make sure that anyone who might answer the phone number you give is aware of the particulars you put on your application. This method is fraudulent, but it is widely used by free-lancers, and I have never heard of anyone getting busted for it. A businessman of my acquaintance tells of a pimp, newly released from prison, who was able to get credit sufficient to purchase a brand new pimpmobile by saying that he was an engineer at a friend's recording studio, even though the studio itself could not qualify for a corporate American Express card!

If you can work it out with your parents or some other person who believes in you, they can order an extra card for you to use. Your purchases will be billed to their account, and you will have to keep things straight with them. Adult artist-children who don't qualify for credit cards on the basis of their income should probably draw up a contract with their parents about how soon they have to pay them back for each month's purchases and what happens if they can't pay them back for a while.

You may also be able to find a bank that will give you a credit card secured by a passbook savings account. You'll be given a credit limit less than or equal to your account balance, and you'll have to tie up some cash, but if you make your payments and stay within your credit limit, you can ask in six or twelve months that they drop the collateral requirement.

HOW TO APPEAR CREDITWORTHY

I must now introduce tactics described in an indispensable book for anyone who incurs debts: *Your Check Is in the Mail: How to Stay Legally and Profitably in Debt.** This book is revolutionary—as subversive as something written by the Yippies—yet one of its authors is a lawyer. Do not fail to buy it and read it. You will find it helpful and highly entertaining.

One of the authors' suggestions is that a corporation is inherently more respectable than an individual in the eyes of prospective lenders. Where a bank might question your ability to handle modest debts which you as an individual may incur as normal and necessary business expenses, it tends to assume that

*Bruce Goldman, Robert Franklin and Kenneth Pepper, Esq. (New York: Warner, 1984).

a corporation will be able to cover those same sums. Also, if you incorporate you have the advantage of limited liability—legally you and your corporation are two separate entities. Many such corporations exist only on paper, and 100 percent of the stock may be owned by the same person. If your corporation gets into financial trouble, its creditors cannot take your personal assets or garnishee your salary. However, incorporation isn't cheap. You need a lawyer to draw up the papers, your own paperwork increases and you will have to pay a couple of hundred dollars to charter the corporation. A prolonged discussion of the benefits and costs of incorporation is beyond the scope of this book. You should take up that matter with an accountant dealing in your field. One can be found through guilds, unions or local arts councils. As a rule of thumb, you should have a fairly steady income in the five-figure range before incorporation will really be cost effective for you as an individual freelancer.

If you do incorporate, you can use Dun & Bradstreet to your advantage. Dun & Bradstreet is an organization which functions as a sort of credit bureau for corporations. Subscribers have access to their extensive files on the creditworthiness of corporations with which they (the subscribers) are contemplating doing business. If any prospective creditor who is a Dun & Bradstreet subscriber requests a report on you and there has never been a report, Dun & Bradstreet will call and ask if they can send someone by to get information. The information you give is not given under oath, so that if you don't want to give out current information, you can give projections based on what you *hope* your business for the year will be, along with a couple of personal references. These references will be checked, so don't give any who are going to say that you're a deadbeat. But aside from that, they probably won't check any further. As long as you don't say anything that you *know* to be false, there's nothing wrong with being optimistic in your projection of the year's business. It's not hard to come out with a very impressive-sounding Dun & Bradstreet report, which can be worth quite a lot in credit. Remember, your prospective creditors do want your business, and a good D & B report is all you need to convince them.

You can acquire some of the added respectability of incorporation without going to all that expense by applying for a Certificate of Doing Business at the County Clerk's office and paying about $35. You are then registered as Farrah Freelancer, doing business as Hole-in-the-Wall Graphics Company, and can put all your business ventures into this umbrella company. As the authors of *Your Check Is in the Mail* point out, this sort of trick gives you a great psychological advantage. You immediately *seem* more businesslike and therefore more creditworthy. Incidentally, this is also worth remembering as a consumer: the word "Company" tagged on at the end of a name does not necessarily signal respectability.

BUILD UP YOUR CREDIT RATING, BUT DON'T PLAY THE GAME

However you manage to do it, once you have some credit you are well on your way to getting even more. It then becomes so easy that it seems like a game. Actually, it is a game—a very carefully planned game in which you face all of the dangers of playing roulette against a Vegas house. The point of the game is for you to get carried away and spend more than you have so that you have to spend even more, in the form of interest, to space out payments for what is often a lot of extravagant and unnecessary merchandise and services. So don't get caught up on the borrowing treadmill, but do build up your credit. The way to do this is by showing what a good borrower you are.

Being a good borrower in your creditor's eyes is not quite the same as being a good borrower in the eyes of a typical citizen. Creditors like to know that they are going to profit from you, and they won't be able to do this if you do not incur interest charges. I once borrowed a small amount from a bank to cover my rent until some royalties were paid me. The royalties arrived two weeks later, and so I went straight to the bank to pay off my loan. But the bank wasn't nearly so happy to see me as I had expected it would be. In fact, it slapped me with a penalty for paying off my loan ahead of schedule. I couldn't have been more confused, though I still insisted on paying off the loan while I had the money rather than squandering what I had just received and falling even further behind. I remained confused until an accountant explained to me that banks smile on those borrowers from whom they make money. If you pay off your whole loan at once, they don't make much interest. The way to get a good credit rating is actually to owe money first, and then pay it off, but not too quickly.

Lending institutions want to see that you will incur debt (thereby making you a potential customer) *and* pay it off (thereby making you profitable to them). Do this a couple of times, and you'll find that you have quite a good credit rating.

In fact, it can be a good idea to take out loans at times when you don't need them, put the money in a savings account and then pay them back all at once when the first payment is due. You should ask before doing this whether there is any penalty for paying off the loan ahead of schedule.

IF YOU ARE DENIED CREDIT

The first thing to do when you are denied credit is to find out why you were rejected. If your income is sufficient, and if whatever you put down as employment checked out, there may be a blot of which you are unaware in your credit file, or you may not have any credit history at all.

If your rejection was due to your not having any credit history, you are going to be hard pressed until you can prove yourself creditworthy. You may find it possible to start out by opening a charge account at a department store. Traditionally, the better stores do less extensive credit checks on you, and as long as you can put something down under "employer" and at least $10,000 in income, you have a fighting chance. Another way is to talk a creditworthy friend or relative into co-signing a loan note for you. (That way, the bank knows that it can nab your co-signer if you should confirm their impression of you as not creditworthy.) Then you pay off the loan, and you're on your way to establishing a credit history. Next, you will probably be allowed to take out a small loan in your own name. You do this a couple of times, and you will have built up a decent little credit history which can be used as a springboard to a much bigger line of credit.

If credit was denied you because of something in your credit file, find out which bureau the information came from. Usually the bank or store which turns you down will inform you of which credit bureau they used. If you go to a bureau within thirty days of being denied credit you are entitled to an explanation of what is in your file, free of charge. If you go after this thirty-day period, they may charge you a nominal sum. You may find a shocking error, such as their having listed you as a felon or in bankruptcy. This is particularly true if you have a common name, according to the authors of *Your Check Is in the Mail.* The reason for this is that credit bureaus often use public court records as information sources in an indiscriminate way: if a Sam Cohen is being sued in civil court and your name is also Sam Cohen, you may suffer—there is an excellent chance that the goon in charge of transcribing information from the court clerk's office will enter that lawsuit in every file bearing the name of Sam Cohen. Indeed, even the Sam Cohen who was involved in the suit may be unjustly treated: the credit bureau may never check back to see whether he won or lost the suit.

It is up to you to correct such errors, which is why it pays to check your credit file once a year even if you have to spend a little money to do so. If you find a mistake, the credit bureau must reinvestigate. And if they find you are right they must correct their records (always check back to make sure they have done so). If you and the credit bureau disagree, you have the right to enter your side of the story into your file.

The other sort of credit report is something out of *1984* called an "investigative consumer report": it contains information on your general reputation, life-style, religious and political affiliations, and things that are even less anyone else's business such as your drinking habits and sexual preferences. If you have applied for medical insurance or an important job, it is quite possible that a credit-bureau snoop will have made the rounds of your friends, neighbors and business associates to check on you.

Under the Fair Credit Reporting Act, whoever requests such an investigation must notify you within three days that such a report has been ordered. You are entitled to be told the "nature and substance" of the report but not the sources of the information. A reinvestigation can be done at your request. Recently these investigative reports have come under criticism, since there is evidence that the investigators sometimes lie or even make up much of what is in them. It is in your interest to check the veracity of such reports if you have been notified that one is in progress. It's your only guarantee of there being any reality to the opinions they give out about you.

If you are rejected for a business loan, ask your bank officer for information on Small Business Administration loans, or contact the SBA directly.

U.S. Small Business Administration
1441 L. Street, NW
Washington, DC 20416
(202) 653-6365

SBA has a Loan Guarantee Program which can really save your life. If your loan application is very close to acceptable, your bank can send your application to SBA and ask them to review it. If they decide they can take a chance on you, they act as guarantors of the major part of the loan, and your bank will give you the money. Individuals may not apply directly to SBA.

If you are a member of a minority group you may be able to get help at the office of the Minority Business Development Agency. This agency can be found under U.S. Department of Commerce listings in your local directory.

WHEN YOU HAVE CREDIT

MANAGE IT WELL

If this is the first time you have been granted credit and you are a freelancer, you should feel very lucky; and you, more than anyone else, should be very, very good for the first year. Don't fall behind on your loan payments, no matter what you have to do to come up with the money. If you have a credit card, it is to your advantage to make a few charges, pay them and then file it away for emergencies and identification only.

When you use a credit card don't make the mistake of throwing away your copy of the transaction. First of all, you should keep it to check against your bill (they do make mistakes). Secondly, you may need it at tax time: better safe than sorry at the end of the year. Thirdly, thieves can and do retrieve these slips from garbage cans and merchant's floors, and then use your name, number and signature to fill out an application for a duplicate card with your name and any other address.

WHEN DOES IT PAY TO BUY ON CREDIT?

There are a couple of situations in which it is advantageous to buy something on credit even if you can't quite afford it. If you can be controlled enough to save your card for such situations, a credit card such as Visa or MasterCard can buy you a lot of flexibility. If the current political situation dictates that a certain commodity will become more expensive permanently (e.g., oil and its derivatives) or temporarily (e.g., paper, because of a strike at the mills), it is to your advantage to buy a large stock on credit. This is particularly true for artists and writers. I was very impressed to hear the following statement from a well-known young illustrator:

Economics is important. If there's an oil shortage the first person who's going to get hit by that is the commercial artist, because paper is going to go up, and oil paints are going to go up, and the first place that money is withdrawn is from the arts. Art is considered a luxury. You really have to have some idea of what's going on, because it affects you directly first and foremost. The last hired on a factory line is your position. But if you know, and if you cover yourself, you won't get left out in the cold. If you pay attention to the news you'll know three months beforehand to go out and stock up on supplies, because they will be going up 35 percent. It has become very expensive to be an artist. You can't afford to run by potluck.

Sad to say, I found this lady's hard-nosed attitude toward the economics of her work dishearteningly rare, if not unique, among the freelancers I interviewed.

It also makes sense to purchase major items—cameras, computers, home appliances—on credit during sales. If you take out a personal loan at 16.5 percent interest to buy a $700 camera at a 20 percent discount, you have saved more by taking advantage of the discount than you will lose in interest payments, even if you take a full year to pay. This may not be the case, however, if you use a credit card instead of taking out a less costly personal loan. If you get a below market loan, you can save even more (see below).

STRATEGIES FOR SAVING ON CREDIT COSTS

• If you have a passbook savings account, you can use it as collateral for a less expensive loan. You can usually borrow about 90 percent of the balance. These loans generally cost a couple of percentage points more than the account is earning, which is cheap, and even cheaper when you consider that you are making 5 percent or better on the money in the savings account, In effect, this sort of loan only costs you about 2 to 3 percent and enables you to have a cash reserve.
• Credit unions are cooperative organizations of people with a common affiliation—a union, a political philosophy, an employer, etc. These offer a way to save through the purchase of shares in the credit union. Members are called shareholders rather than depositors. Credit unions can also offer low-cost loans and other services, such as Visa and Master-Card, occasionally at lower interest rates than those offered when you obtain them through a bank.

  In addition to providing cheap loans, credit unions may also give out dividends from any monies left over after operating expenses have been met. Because credit unions are cooperatives, everything is done as much to the shareholders' advantage as possible.

  For information about federally insured credit unions in your area, contact The National Credit Union Administration, 1776 G Street, NW, Washington, DC 20456; (202) 357-1100.
• Several artists' and small business groups offer credit unions to members. These include Support Services Alliance, Actors Equity, the Graphic Arts Federal Credit Union in New York, the Boston Visual Artists Union, and the Foundation for the Community of Artists' Artists Community Federal Credit Union. The last also makes Working Assets Money Fund Visa cards available to members. Working Assests is a socially responsible credit card organization which donates a few cents from each purchase you make on your card to such deserving organizations as Amnesty International, the ACLU and Oxfam. Particularly

heartening about FCA's credit union is that the loan committee is made up mainly of artists who understand the particular needs of other artists and can examine credit applications through different glasses.

Check to see whether other organizations to which you already belong or for which you are eligible offer credit unions or other credit services to members.

• If you have life insurance you can often borrow against it at well below market rates. Just remember that if you die with the loan outstanding, the company will deduct the amount owed from what it pays your beneficiaries.

• You may be able to get a discount of up to 5 percent for paying in cash rather than with a card. Since it costs merchants 5 percent to have a card service, they will sometimes give you the discount. But you have to ask. They are not required by law to post notice of this policy.

HITTING THE HOCK SHOPS

Another possibility for the temporarily indigent freelancer is to pledge some item of appraisable value as collateral for a secured loan. A secured loan can run the gamut from a low-risk situation involving a bank or loan society to a transaction in a storefront pawnshop straight out of O. Henry.

There are several advantages to secured loans. First, usually you don't have to present a credit history or any information beyond some I.D. for loans under $1,000. (You should only get loans over $1,000 from reputable loan societies who have bank affidavits for you to sign asserting that you own what you are pledging and that there are no liens on it. It will be notorized on the spot, and you will get the money in a matter of hours.)

Also, you can keep hocking and redeeming something when you need to raise cash. A respectable institution, such as the Provident Loan Society of New York, will only accept jewelry, stamps, coins or silverware. Expect to get around 25 percent of value. The lowest echelon of pawnshops are those sad places with guitars hanging in the window and rows of watches and navy rings below them. Interest rates are high in them, and it is totally your responsibility to redeem your pledge before it is auctioned.

The disadvantages basically depend on what sort of institution you are dealing with. At a reputable one, the loan is usually good for a year. At this point you are sent a notice indicating how much interest you owe. You are generally given a grace period, with one more notice, in which to pay the interest. Then your pledge will be put up for auction. A rip-off or no-frills joint might make a "sewer service" (i.e., serve your notice into the trash) and then, not hearing from you, proceed straight to auction. If you pay up your interest, your loan is generally extended. If your pledge is auctioned by a reputable institution it will retain only the loan plus interest and 10 percent or so for the auctioneer. The rest, if any remains, will be sent to you. But you can't expect this from a pawnshop.

In order to take out a secured loan, ask a lawyer or accountant or banker to point you toward a reputable lender. If you have to look in the Yellow Pages, look under "Pawnshops" and try to go to the place with the best address. You can further check them out through the Better Business Bureau.

Secured loans save freelancers' lives, but don't go wildly hocking heirlooms unless you have a reasonable expectation of cash coming in to pay off the loans, or unless you are so desperate that you don't mind losing the family silver. If you're that desperate, it might be better to borrow money from your family. Don't extort, but many families suddenly find money to lend when heirlooms are on the block.

BORROWING MONEY FROM FRIENDS

When it's time to borrow money and you have no prayer of getting any from a bank or credit institution, you have no choice but to turn to family or friends. Try friends first, if you have any who have enough money to help you out without making you feel uneasy at causing them financial tension. Try to borrow from people who won't feel it.

Borrowing from family members is a time-honored institution for the fledgling artist. Whereas your parents may be fed up with supporting you, what about Uncle Warren, who always said if he could start again he'd be a painter? Or Aunt Laura, who used to be a dancer? It is to these second-tier relatives that you must appeal. They are often more sympathetic than your immediate family. Godparents may also be worth a try, and also friends of the family. Ask in a way that doesn't make you feel like a child asking for a handout. Invite your victim out for dinner, or make dinner at home. Talk about what you're doing and your enthusiasm for it, answer honestly any questions they ask about your financial straits, and then give them time (and perhaps some more wine) and hope they'll ask whether you need to borrow some money. If you feel you can, come right out and ask for what you need. If it makes you feel better, offer to pay the going rate for a commercial loan. In any event, do sign an agreement and keep copies. This is useful to them for tax purposes and to you for the same reasons, and also for your self-respect. A notarized letter should be drawn up stating the date, the term of the loan, the amount and any agreement about paying interest or payment scheduling.

IF YOU FALL INTO DEBT

If you get over your head in debt there are two things you can do. You can try to extricate yourself from it in a conventional fashion—by trying to make more money and controlling your spending—or you can apply creative debt management.

DEBT COUNSELING

If you go the first route you should start by locating a consumer credit counseling service. There are numerous such nonprofit clinics around the country to help people who have gotten so far into debt that they can no longer manage the sluice of debts they have accumulated. You can get a list of consumer credit counseling services nationwide through The National Foundation for Consumer Credit Inc., 8701 Georgia Avenue, Silver Spring, MD 20910; (301) 589-5600. The CCCS will have you in for a session with a counselor who will spend as long as is necessary with you to devise a budget that you can stick to and begin paying off your debts. If you are really in bad shape, you are a candidate for their debt management program. In order to be considered for this you have to agree to relinquish your credit cards. You will then be made to suffer the trauma of watching the counselor cut the cards in half with scissors and drop them into the wastebasket. The counselor will then help you break down your debts into manageable payments. Occasionally CCCS will ask creditors to waive interest charges or extend the deadline for payment so that the monthly payments are smaller. Generally, creditors are so happy to be paid anything at all that they will agree to this, particularly if you have made the effort to go to CCCS in the first place. Beware the "debt counseling" services offered by many lenders. These are often just further loans to pay off your existing ones—always a terrible idea. Make sure that the service you use, if not a branch office of CCCS, is a *nonprofit* service.

CREATIVE DEBT MANAGEMENT

Your second alternative is to become a creative debtor. If you decide on this— and it does have its advantages—you would be a fool to proceed without a copy of *Your Check Is in the Mail*. Let this book be your bible, encyclopedia and style manual, for this approach to debt requires a totally new outlook. Basically, the message of this book is that being in debt can be quite profitable if you come to think of the money you owe as an interest-free loan, and are not frightened by attempts to make you pay it back more quickly than is convenient for you. The two main types of strategy are delaying tactics and direct computer sabotage.

DELAYING TACTICS

Most large businesses and stores work on the hundred-day billing cycle. To take advantage of this you must first determine on what day of the month each billing cycle begins. Generally there is a line on your statement which will say "charges made as of ———— ," or something to that effect. To get the maximum ride, buy early in the billing cycle. Thirty days later your purchase will appear on your statement. If you don't pay it, all that happens is that in another thirty days it appears on your statement again—this time in the previous balance column. After ninety days you will begin to receive meek apologetic reminders that your payment is overdue. After this you can either hold out, hoping that the company will have crossed that line where it actually costs them more money to keep trying to collect and they write you off (usually about a year), or you can begin more direct tactics. Because you should have some understanding of the reasoning behind these tactics, I will go into some of the simplest tricks here. *Your Check Is in the Mail* should provide more detailed help for you.

COMPUTER SABOTAGE

- An X-Acto knife is the perfect instrument for adding a few holes to computer punch cards. Your holes won't be noticed by humans, yet the computer will be confused, so your card will be spat back on the floor and have to be reprocessed by hand, which gives you a few days' leeway.
- A fascinating suggestion from the same anonymous Englishman who invented the trick above is quoted in *Your Check Is in the Mail*: mail your punch card and payment check in an envelope which you have saturated with cheap perfume. The perfume molecules are said to knock the computer out of whack so that it can process neither your bill nor anyone else's.
- You can sometimes confound the computer by putting two conflicting amounts on your check.
- "Overlook" signing your check in your haste to pay your bill. Such a mistake can buy you a couple of days while they return it to you.

INTERVIEW WITH A MASTER DEBTOR

Here are some suggestions on creative debt management from a savvy New York businessman with a much-acclaimed knack for surviving:

If you have a postage meter you can roll back the date and then just chalk up the late delivery to an incompetent postal service. I use this one a lot around tax time. Speaking of tax time, it doesn't have to be so traumatic. Even if you don't pay your taxes on time, the government only charges you 6 percent interest on your unpaid balance—far cheaper, half as expensive, as a bank loan which you might take out to pay them.

You can also have out-of-town bank accounts from which checks take a long time to clear.

There are all kinds of harassment from collection agencies. This usually begins about three months after you have failed to pay. The collection agency threatens you for a while, and if you still don't pay they finally turn your case over to a lawyer as they have been threatening to do. But the lawyer is quite easy to deal with: he will give you a much better deal than they. You start giving them any kind of money and you're cool. The collection agency will say, "You have to have a certified check here by next Tuesday or we'll turn it over to the lawyers." So you say, "Well, I can't pay it all. I'll give you half this Tuesday and half the next." And the collection agency says, "No! We won't accept it. Pay us by Tuesday or we'll turn it over to lawyers." So Tuesday comes around and you speak to the lawyer. He will usually give you six months to pay, because from his point of view anything paid is a plus since he's getting a percentage of whatever is coming in.

If you get served with a summons, the most important thing to remember is that your creditor is counting on your simply ignoring it completely. Then he will get a default judgment. If you don't show up or put in a defense it's pretty swift: they get a default judgment and then they can attach your bank account or garnishee your salary. But if you put in an answer to the summons, you can knock the wind out of their sails. You simply enter a plea of General Denial, which means "I deny everything," and then it becomes a matter that has to go to trial. If they don't get a default judgment basically they're finished, because it costs them so much to proceed. So, keep them from getting a default judgment and you are in business. As soon as you put in an answer they are ready to negotiate. As long as you don't default, the ball is in your court.

You can't really go too far with Con Ed and the phone company. Of course you are entitled to go to the Public Service Commission, and they can't turn off your service until the hearing, but that only takes about ten days and then you're back where you started, only now the people you're dealing with have gotten more angry and are out to really screw you. With Con Ed, you can try to plug your stuff into the landlord's hall light.

Another thing is that it pays to have more than one bank account. You can really get a lot of leverage that way. Deposit checks from one account into the other. If you keep it sort of rolling around back and forth you can stay a few days ahead.

One of the main things a debtor should remember is that it is not against the law to owe money. There is no such thing as debtor's prison except for alimony cases; it was abolished in the early 1800's. A lot of times collection agencies will imply that you will go to jail, and I think a lot of people sometimes believe that they have committed a crime by not paying their bills. This is why a lot of times when people receive summonses they get so uptight about it that they just don't deal with it, and then there's a default judgment and basically they've lost. The game is over at that point.

No matter what the collection agency tells you about paying legal fees and exorbitant interest, there's a limit to what they can tack on. Usually, even if they threaten to put you out of business and totally wipe you out, it ends up being a negotiated settlement. Somehow, percentages are never in the direction of wiping people out. At that point they tend to lose interest. They usually end up compromising, because the lawyers say, 'Well, it's going to cost you more to fight it, and what's the point?'

Any freelancer needs to know about small claims court. It's really a people's court. Usually the magistrate will make some sort of compromise, because you are both swearing in opposite directions and he has no real way of knowing. You can also get a default judgment here. If you go against a corporation, a corporation has to have an attorney represent it, and it will cost more than it's worth to them. A lawyer might charge $500. The thing about small claims is that it pays to do about six cases at once. You wait until you have a bunch of cases and then you go down and file all of them at the same time. That's what all the landlords do—all the professionals. If you've *got six cases going, you'll probably get about $500 per case, and that's worth it to you. A corporation especially will usually default. Any of these potential adversaries really come on tough at first, but to an amazing degree they will settle.*

It's very good to have a corporate seal. The last time I was at a convention in Europe I just whipped out the corporate seal and the hotel people couldn't resist it. It looks so official. I remember going to the desk. They weren't taking checks of even the biggest companies, and I just signed the bill and stuck the corporate seal on it. I didn't even have to wait in line. I was able to leave the convention early. I've done that all over Europe. It's good to pay if they do bill you. Pay the first bill, and that will have a number on it, and then you have an account. Then, if you have an account at Claridge's, you can get an account at the Crillon. Just tell them, "I have an account at Claridge's." Many of them are part of a big association anyway; and although they don't exchange credit, they do have some interrelationship. And it's good to have credit at a hotel. You can always go to a hotel for a night to think up some new schemes. You can do the same thing at restaurants and hotels at home. Leave your business card when you get the check. Usually they will mail the bill to your office. You pay the first bill, then you have an account.

A FINAL WORD

Here I feel it is necessary to restate what I said at the beginning of this chapter. Credit is almost a sine qua non of freelancing, since the typical freelancer's cash flow is erratic no matter how great his yearly income. However, you must be extremely careful, more careful than an employee, not to turn this emergency source of cash into an albatross around your neck. Credit or borrowed money can lure you into thinking that you are in better financial shape than you really are. Then when the bills come, so does the truth, and you realize that you are even further in debt.

When trying to decide whether or not to make a purchase on credit, ask yourself if it is a necessity or a nicety. If it is really the latter, either set aside a little savings fund for it or ask for it for Christmas. If you aren't able to do this, you should consider getting rid of your card or getting a more limited one. Niceties are cold comfort when the heat's been turned off. And you are not in business to support your credit card.

CHAPTER EIGHTEEN
COLLECTING WHAT'S OWED YOU

After having waited for thirteen days I have at last received your letter in reply to mine. This delay has caused me much damage. You finally answer that you cannot make any decision about the panel which I should keep for you. By God, this is an ill-mannered way to tell me that even were I to die you could not give me a farthing. This has caused me much grief for various reasons, one of them being that I am, as is well known, one of the poorest monks in Florence. . . . If you could let me have on account from you a little corn and wine, it would be a great comfort to me.

—*Fra Filippo Lippi, 1439**

Without question, the major problem confronting a great many freelancers is how to collect money that is owed them for works already produced. The shocking truth is that some publishers, advertising firms, galleries and clients you may deal with are quite shameless in their attempts to rip-off the very people by whose talents much of their money is made. Somehow, once you have turned in your drawings or your galleys, you become a nuisance, always bothering them for your money. What you may not understand is that you are now expendable in their eyes. What it sometimes seems they really wish is that there were some way to run a magazine without artists or a publishing company without writers. All freelancers, even those who make out well, seem to have trouble collecting at least some of the money owed them. One graphic artist, who works at a very high level, estimates that you should expect to lose about 10 percent of what you have earned in this way. This doesn't mean that you shouldn't make every attempt to collect all of what is owed you—just don't be devastated if you don't succeed in every case.

The most important thing is to decide whether you want to work for free or not. If your answer is an indignant No!, then make sure you're just as emphatic about getting a full agreement in writing every time you lift up a pencil for somebody. This is where the beginning freelancer can be so easily ripped-off—and often is. In your gratitude for getting a job, you don't dare bring up the question of terms. That is your first big mistake: it is stupid not to ask how much you're getting paid. This brands you as an amateur who is so pathetically

*Quoted in Rudolf and Margaret Wittkower, *Born Under Saturn* (New York: W.W. Norton, 1969), p. 256.

grateful for work that just being used is reward enough. Some people say that you should *never* work for nothing: "No man but a blockhead," wrote Samuel Johnson, "ever wrote except for money."

Although I think there are occasions for which it is justifiable to work for free or at cost, these should be at your discretion and no one else's.

COLLECTION PROCEDURES*

GET IT ON PAPER

Once you and the person hiring you have come to a decision about pay, delivery date and other terms, such as right of refusal, get it on paper. This is standard, and you are a fool digging your own grave if you waive this step in your enthusiasm for getting the job or in your desire to please. It is standard procedure to state any sort of agreement in writing these days; anyone you're doing business with should be happy to sign an agreement with you. Refusal is a dead giveaway that you are dealing with a less-than-honest person, and you should probably refuse the job—or else make him pay up front before you lift a finger.

You won't be able to collect a penny in court unless you have a written agreement or purchase order. It doesn't have to be anything grand. Even an exchange of letters will stand up in court. The real point to having this written agreement is that it gives you something to sue on. People's memories are very capricious during disputes over money, and you will never agree on the particulars of a verbal agreement you made several months ago unless a piece of paper exists.

The paper should give as much detail as possible about the transaction: the more you specify in the agreement, the fewer loopholes you leave for unscrupulous users of your work. A basic agreement should give both parties' names and addresses, a description of the work, a delivery date, the work's title if any, its size or length, the fee and an enumeration of which expenses you will be reimbursed for if any (this is crucial), and of course which rights you are conveying. You should also include some provision for what happens if you can't perform what you have agreed to do. This document should be signed by both parties and witnessed if possible (though this is not strictly necessary).

Such an agreement will suffice in a pinch, but it is preferable that you make use of contracts that are more tailored to your specific situation. Many guilds and professional groups have developed standard letters of agreement and contracts, or guidelines to help you draw them up, which help their members protect themselves in situations common to their profession.

Visual artists will find many different sorts of sample contracts in Tad Crawford's *Legal Guide for the Visual Artist* (Dutton, 1980) and his *Selling Your Graphic Design and Illustration* (St. Martin's, 1981) or Robert M. Cavallo and Stuart Kahan's *Photography: What's the Law?* (Crown, 1976). The American Society of Journalists and Authors (1501 Broadway, New York, NY 10036;

---

*See also page 276, Special Collection Procedures for Performers.

[212] 997-0947) has developed a Standard Letter of Agreement for authors. The Authors Guild (234 West 44th Street, New York, NY 10036; [212] 398-0838) has developed a Standard Trade Book Contract and also a Standard Royalty Statement form. This information is given to members of these associations. You should also check with any organization to which you belong even if they do not offer standard agreement forms. They may havee a legal department which could help you draw up an agreement to use with your clients. It is advisable to keep a pile of agreement forms photocopied and ready to go when you receive assignments, so that you are never tempted to dispense with the contract when you are in a hurry.

If you are selling goods for $500 or more, the Uniform Commercial Code requires you to have written evidence *unless* the goods are created specifically on the purchaser's order. Also, contracts which cannot be performed within one year have to be in writing.

Now, if there is any unreasonable delay in your getting paid, at least you have something to show in court as evidence.

BILLING

An effective billing system goes a long way in helping you to collect what is owed you. Admittedly, billing is a bore when you're busy at work. but make time to do it or you'll never get paid. Depending upon how you work and what your product or service is, you may bill clients monthly or on a per job basis. If the latter, you and the client should decide on a payment schedule, and you should also agree on how expenses will be handled. (See chapter 15, What's It Worth?)

Billing requires some form of invoice whether you just send a simple typed letter or have pre-printed invoice forms. In either case, you should make things very explicit on your invoice so that you and your client know just what they are paying you to do. This is important so that neither party ends up feeling abused. If you don't use invoice forms, figure out a simple and clear format for your bills. Depending upon how you work, you may need to show expenses, the price of each job, and the client's previous balance. If your invoice is just a typed page be sure to state your terms as part of the description of the work done as shown in the sample invoice below:

INVOICE

6/27/87

Charts and illustrations to be used in series, "Divorce and Remarriage in the Eighties" only. Original artwork to be returned to the artist by August 15.	**$6000**
Telephone calls through June 1	**$30**
Payable Now	**$6030**

A more complicated pre-printed invoice form might include columns listing categories of expenses with space for you to fill in the dollar amount of any that you incurred on the job. The form might also state the terms and conditions regarding usage, reimbursement of expenses, return of artwork, notes or other materials used in preparation of the job, kill fee and settlement of disputes. These terms and conditions will be somewhat variable according to your profession. The book *Selling Your Graphic Design and Illustration* by Tad Crawford and Arie Kopelman gives examples of invoice forms for graphic designers and illustrators which can easily be adapted to use by photographers, writers and other types of freelancers.

When you send an invoice, make sure you date it and have a record so that you can send an identical copy to the accounting department if the first one gets "lost" (an all too frequent occurrence with some companies, I might add). There are several ways of making such records:

- Simple photocopying.
- Have a computer file or even a whole disk of invoices. Even if you do store this information on a disk, make sure that you have at least one printed copy of each invoice in a file.
- Use printed invoice forms that come with a carbon. Large stationery stores have blank invoice forms, or you can have some with your business name and/or logo printed up. Also, some computer programs, such as *My Office*, allow you to create business forms such as invoices.
- Always date your invoices and make copies for your records. You'll need them if you have to start sending out second and third notices. Keep a list or a file of unpaid invoices and check it on a regular basis (at two-week intervals is good) so that you can send out your reminders to pay up. These reminders should be marked in such a way that it is clear that you are on their case. You can make out an invoice that simply gives the date of the first bill, the words "previously billed" and the amount still due. To this you can add something like "payable immediately." You can also mark it "second notice" if you feel like leaning a little harder.
- One hot tip I've got to impart to you in the matter of billing is the extreme usefulness of starting a file of clients and their payment habits. In my file, I list how long the company generally takes to pay, the name of someone to talk to in their accounting department (very important and useful), how often they cut checks and any other information I can glean.

The most deadly danger for freelancers and small businesses is not billing. Many clients turn out to be slow payers which can be disastrous to your cash flow. A poor cash flow is the number one reason businesses fail.
—Printer/Designer

If a client is a consistently bad payer and has received multiple warnings, you may have to resort to holding on to a piece of work until you are paid. Try to do this politely so that you have a chance of keeping the client rather than in a hostile manner that will definitely lose you the business. Say, "I can't bankroll you. You are an important client and you get good service, but I can't deliver as well to you unless I am getting paid and can pay my suppliers. I have no choice but to hold up the work until I am paid."

—Graphic Designer

GETTING TOUGH

UNREASONABLE DELAY

After you have billed your client, how long should you have to wait for your money? Four weeks is reasonable although many companies seem to take about six weeks. One or two weeks would really be more fair, and eight weeks is outrageous and all too common. You as a hardworking businessperson, deserve your money within a month after you complete a job and your client accepts it. (And don't let them delay reviewing and accepting the work either. If they haven't given you their comments within two business weeks then they owe you a good explanation, and you should send a bill anyway to get it started in their "system.") Why should you wait longer? So that the company can have free use of your money a bit longer? For this is what happens when you don't get your money on time. You are, in effect, extending an interest-free loan to a company while you starve. It is also important as a matter of principle to stand up for your rights in this respect. The terribly unfair practice of paying writers and artists on publication rather than on acceptance is slowly being phased out. Most well-established publications have stopped this outrageous practice, and most of the writers' and artists' groups advise you to stay away from those that haven't. I would add that you should stay away loudly. The only way to force that sort of change is through boycott and pressure. If you have trouble getting paid by a company, tip off other freelancers, and perhaps also the relevant professional organization. Writers who have problems can report publishers to the National Writers Club (1450 South Havana Street, Denver, CO 80239; [303] 751-7844). Visual artists can contact the Graphic Artists Guild (11 West 20th Street, New York, NY 10011; [212] 463-7730) or the American Society of Magazine Photographers (ASMP), (205 Lexington Avenue, New York, NY 10016; [212] 889-9144).

If you haven't received your check within forty-five days, call up and ask where it is. It is courteous to call the person in the company you actually did the work for. Tell him that it's been six weeks and that you'd very much like a check. Generally the people you will be reporting to will have no idea that you haven't been paid, so don't get huffy yet. Offer at this point to deal directly with the accounting department if that makes things simpler for him. Some people are delighted for you to take this task over. Others feel that you have overstepped your boundaries in so doing.

Have your records handy when you deal with accounting departments so that you can back up what you are saying about how overdue the payment is. It's important to date your invoices so that when accounting pleads that they just received your invoice, you can reply with the exact date on which it was mailed so long ago.

If accounting pleads an honest delay such as a computer foul-up or that the person who needs to sign your check has been away, tell them politely but firmly that you would very much like to have your check within a week, pointing out that your payment has been owing for nearly two months. If, after two months have passed, you are still getting the runaround, tell them, if it's practical, that you'll come around and pick up a new check at a specified time. Now, if they still hedge, you can be pretty sure that you're getting the runaround. At this point you should explain calmly, but very firmly, that you will be going down to small claims court to file a claim against them unless you have your payment by the end of the week. If you're dealing with a deadbeat, you won't get your check come Friday. You may get a long diatribe about the company's fiscal woes, or you may hear nothing.

In the first instance, you must decide how far you want to humor them. In some cases it makes sense to. One such case is if you depend on a continuing relationship with such a company in order to collect royalties or to get other work. The first time they are late with your payment, you may not want to antagonize them to the point where you jeopardize your relationship later. On the other hand, you don't want to have them get the impression that you are a pushover. This is a situation to be played by ear. Stay on their case, just so they know you mean business. Learn how to be passive-aggressive, a coping behavior which, though unacceptable in daily life, is tailor-made for collecting from recalcitrant debtors. Call them at least twice a week, Monday and Friday, plus any other times in between that they indicate they *might* have money.

Don't be afraid of them. For some reason, many freelancers often don't dare stand up to the people who owe *them* money. Give them a little grace if you see fit to, but don't take any abuse. Some accounting departments seem to get a little mixed up and become testy when you call, even though it is they who are in your debt. At the first hint of sharpness in their tone, carry through your threat and march right into court. Nobody says they have to like you, but as long as there is a contract, the law says they have to hold to it and pay you.

If you are dealing with a small business, such as a small, independent publisher, PR company or graphics firm, it is possible that they are having the same sort of cash flow problems that you have periodically and do plan to pay you. It doesn't make you feel much better to hear this, but if you are hoping for a continuing relationship, it is often better to be understanding for another week or two. If, as they say, there really is no money, you won't succeed in collecting a penny any sooner and you'll probably make an enemy if you do sue.

This is a fine line to tread, because if they feel they have too much leeway they'll take advantage of you. What you have to do is gain as much knowledge of their financial picture as you can. Why is their payment late? Company accountants at small cliff-hanging businesses are the best actors you'll ever encounter, so this may be difficult. Try to get a definite date on which they *will* have the money and make it clear that you'll file if they don't pay by that time. If, on that day, they promise it for the next morning, tell them you will stop off on your way to small claims court and see if it's ready. If it's not, go ahead and sue.

TAKING THEM TO COURT

As a freelancer, you are most likely to be involved with small claims court and civil court. Which court your case is heard in depends on the amount of money involved. It varies from state to state, so check yours, but the ceiling for suing in small claims court is usually $1,000 to $1,500. In civil court it is usually around $10,000. You don't have to have a lawyer in either court and are actively discouraged from bringing one to small claims court. Basically, the judge or arbitrator will ask the questions of the defendant that your lawyer would ask. In California, Hawaii, Idaho, Kansas, Nebraska and Washington, lawyers aren't even allowed in small claims court. A useful book is *Everybody's Guide to Small Claims Court* by Ralph Warner (available from Addison-Wesley Publishing Co., Jacob Way, Reading, MA 01867). New York volunteer lawyers for the Arts puts out a useful booklet called *An Artist's Guide to Small Claims Court*.

HOW TO SUE IN SMALL CLAIMS COURT

Small claims courts are really the people's courts. Filing fees are low, cases can usually be scheduled in a fairly short time and the courts are set up so that they are accessible to those who need them. Any individual may sue in small claims court, but no corporation or partnership may. In addition, a corporation must be represented by a lawyer, which can easily run $500 for a little paperwork and the lawyer's court time. For this reason, a realistic threat to take a corporation that knows it owes you money to small claims court may result in faster action than you'd expected.

Before resorting to small claims court, write the deadbeat a last letter describing the situation and your version of the events leading up to it. State what you think would be a fair settlement and ask that it be paid to you on a certain date. Notify them that you will bring suit in small claims court if payment is not received. Keep a copy of this letter of course and send it certified mail so that you have evidence that it was received. This proof of receipt and the latter are valuable evidence in your case.

To sue a company you must go to small claims court within the jurisdiction where either you or your deadbeat live or do business. The court clerks are usually extremely helpful in showing you how to fill out the simple papers necessary to file suit. In most places, the filing fee is less than $5. Although this is no longer true in New York City, in some places you must have the legal name of the business you are suing. Generally this is more of a problem in nonprofessional suits, such as against the dry cleaners or the landlords. They may be doing business as "Mayflower Cleaners" but their legal name might be "Mayflower Two Hour Cleaners, Inc." Ask the clerk how to find out the defendant's legal business name if there is any question. Generally this is done by going to the County Clerk in the borough where the defendant does business. Another way is to call the State Department of Assessments and Taxation.

When you assess how much money to sue for, don't forget to add in any verifiable expenses that were incurred as a result of whatever it is that you are suing about. This includes telephone calls that you made daily while trying to collect, late charges on your credit card bill if you needed the money to make your credit card payments. Think along the same lines you would for deciding what are ordinary and necessary business expenses for tax purposes. Also try to get interest on what was owed you, even though you aren't necessarily entitled to this. Just be sure that you document all your claims. Remember that you can only sue for money in small claims court. The court doesn't have the power to decide more complex issues such as ownership of a work, libel or moral rights.

After you have filed, the defendant will receive a copy of the complaint and a summons for a given date. It is up to you to check in with the court clerk to see if a certification of summons has been received ensuring that the defendant has received the summons and can be expected in court.

This may be all it takes to prod a typical small business, which knows it owes you for a job, into paying. If it doesn't, you should be preparing your case by rounding up all the genuine documents, such as contracts, purchase orders and canceled checks. You may also present witnesses, and witnesses essential to your case can be subpoenaed. In fact, unless the witness is a friend, you should subpoena him to make sure he appears. You do this by paying a little more money and asking the clerk to help you. Generally, this won't apply in collection cases, but it might be essential in suits over car accidents or a painter's botched job.

If you can't get your witness to court, get an affidavit, which is just a signed statement that you can write up yourself and have the witness sign. You then have it notarized for a couple of dollars. Stationery stores often have notaries, identified by a Notary Public sticker on the window. Many accountants are also notaries.

At court check that your case is posted with the rest of the evening's cases. If it isn't, find a court officer and apprise him of this. Then wait for the defendant to show up. If she doesn't, you win by default unless she has had the case postponed. If she does show up, you will be asked whether you want to present your case before a judge or an arbitrator. Because there are fewer judges than arbitrators, you may find yourself waiting six hours for a judge. However, if a judge hears your case, you have the option to appeal whereas you cannot if it has been arbitrated. For simple cut-and-dried cases of nonpayment, an arbitrator will probably do. If your case is complex, bring a book and a picnic and wait for a judge.

You will be asked to tell your side of the story and trot out your exhibits and your witnesses. Then the defendant gets to do the same. Generally it takes about fifteen minutes. You will receive notification of the decision in the mail in a couple of weeks.

Now that you have a judgment against this deadbeat, your problem is exactly what it was when you started: how to collect the money? Collection is harder if you have won by default, because the defendant isn't even in court. It is up to you to tell the defendant of the judgment against him, which you do by sending a certified copy of the judgment and a letter asking him to pay up now without further delay. If he doesn't respond, call a few times; or drop in. "I have found that my physical presence in the office can often be slightly more effective in getting money from my publisher," says a writer. "When they owe me money I just go down to their office for the day and sit in the waiting room with my work. If you're like me and can work in that situation it's not so bad. It's pathetic that that is how low you have to stoop to get paid, but that's life. If you don't live in the same city, forget it. Some places never pay unless you can harass them daily by phone and in the flesh."

If you get no action, you can get a sheriff or a city marshal to help you. The county sheriff can be located in the Blue Page listings under "Government Offices." Marshals can be found in the Yellow Pages. Although you must pay either one up front, you can charge the cost of engaging a marshal to the defendant along with any additional costs you incur chasing her around. The marshal or sheriff needs to know either the name of the bank where the deadbeat does business or the name of the company which employs her. (The case docket card from small claims court will tell the defendant's name and address and business telephone.) Once you have managed to locate some assets that you can get your hooks into, the marshal or sheriff should be able to seize money or force the employer to pay part of the miscreant's salary to you until the claim is paid.

If you have to go this far, you may have trouble. If the business is truly broke or is a small, close-to-the-line operation, such as an independent publisher or a small theater group, they may be crafty enough to rent their office furniture and thus be judgment-proof: you can't collect because there is no money and nothing to sell. If you're lucky, you'll be able to have the company's bank account attached or the president's salary garnisheed. If you have any information as to the defendant's bank accounts or property that might be seized, do tell it to the marshal. You will have to pay a small additional fee up front for attachment or garnisheeing, but then this will be added to what the defendant owes you.

Thirty-five percent of all small claims court winners have difficulty in collecting.* The chances of difficulties increase if you win by default, because all that means is that the person is told he owes the money you both already knew you were owed plus whatever your inconvenience cost you. By defaulting, an insolvent company saves lawyer's fees and buys time. If they own nothing that the marshal can seize and sell, nothing much has changed for them, and you haven't gained either.

If you have gone ahead and sued a company that had no money, you may find that there is still no money, and you are now on the bottom of their payment list for being so ill-mannered as to take them to court. This is *not* to discourage you from filing suit against people who have ripped you off, it is simply a cautionary note: be realistic in your assessment of their financial straits. If you do decide to listen to their pleas of temporary cash flow problems, you might insist on a short meeting with the president of the company in

*Richard George, *The New Consumer Survival Kit* (Boston: Little, Brown, 1978), p. 331.

which you come to an agreement for a cut-off date on which you will either receive your money or sue. If the company's financial problems are temporary, this is a fair compromise, but you should make it clear that you really do expect that next bit of money that the company receives.

Some companies will offer to pay you in small bits, i.e., they will help you out with $100 handouts of the thousands that they owe you if you crawl to their door with your beggar's bowl. This sort of payment schedule is to be avoided as much as possible. Small amounts of money won't cover your important expenses. They will probably not go much farther than the corner bar or the restaurant where you go to console yourself. After a few of these payments, you will be short for your bills and will have nothing to show for what you did receive. Don't accept this unless you really are starving and need the money to buy food. They wouldn't think of paying their landlord or employees pocket money every week, so don't let them get away with it in your case just because you are a poor freelancer.

Your best defense against all this nonsense with insolvent companies is either to avoid them or to make them pay for the job up front or half on signing and half on delivery.

Collection can be difficult for writers and TV performers who expect royalties when the amount that is owed is not clear. Basically they owe you whatever they say they do on your royalty statement.

There have been so many complaints about royalty reporting, as it is done by even the largest publishers, that you must be on your toes here. In most publishing contracts you are given the right to hire an accountant and go in and audit the publisher. This is very expensive and not worth your while unless there is considerable money involved and a strong suspicion of fraud.

The Authors Guild has drafted a desirable royalty statement format. It is far from universally employed by publishers, but it has helped to make authors aware of what information their royalty statements should provide.

OTHER COLLECTION METHODS

Small claims court is definitely the best and cheapest way to collect if your case is eligible to be heard there. However, for larger amounts there are other ways. Here are the most widely used of them.

- If you have an accountant, have him do your billing as a matter of course. Psychologically, this may give you an advantage.
- See if your guild or professional organization has a collection service for members. The National Writers Club and the Graphic Artists Guild both do. Generally such organizations will have agreements with a national collection agency of some sort, and so the collection rates you pay will be close to those you would pay if you turned the account over to a collection service—usually about 25 percent of the first $2,000.
- Send a letter to the Better Business Bureau in the deadbeat's city. You may get a distressed or self-righteous reply from a deadbeat you have thus embarrassed, but you may also get your money.
- You can get an attorney to help you collect. Here the collection rate is

likely to be even higher—closer to 27 or 30 percent. In counties where bar collection rates prevail, this may be still higher. Naturally, before retaining an attorney for collection you would want to find out how much of your money would remain and whether you would be liable for any fees if your attorney also failed to collect.

• If you are a well-established freelancer who is doing business at a fairly consistent level, you may decide to factor your bills. Generally this is only practical for those who have a large outlay for each job (e.g., photographers). If your invoices look all right (i.e., your client's credit rating is good) a factor will basically buy your invoices, giving you usually about 80 percent of their face value minus the factor's fees (usually a flat rate of a few points above the bank's current lending rate per annum based on how long it takes them to collect from your client). Some accountants say that factoring is a good way to go broke. Some artists and small businessmen insist that, in practical terms, factoring your invoices provides you with operating money when you need it instead of when the client chooses to pay. Very busy freelancers say that factors leave their hands free to do their work instead of chasing people who owe them money. You have to decide what your situation warrants. Perhaps a short-term bank loan would be cheaper than the factor's quite steep interest rates. If you do decide to use a factor's services, you can locate one under factors in the Yellow Pages. However, a personal recommendation from a friend who has done business with one is safer, particularly as the percentage they charge you can vary widely.

• Support Services Alliance offers a credit reporting service to help you investigate a potential client before you get involved and a credit follow-up service which will also dun deadbeats. SSA will also assist you in finding a collection attorney if needed.

SPECIAL COLLECTION PROCEDURES
FOR PERFORMERS

Many performers are members of a union and/or a performing rights society, and their collection procedures are different from those described earlier in this chapter. Actually, you are less likely to have problems collecting with an organized body like one of these acting as an intermediary between you and a producer. If you do have problems collecting, this is a matter for you to take up with your agent or union.

If you are not a union member, but nonetheless expect to be remunerated for your services as a musician or entertainer, read the guidelines given earlier in this chapter for independent contractor writers and artists. The same sort of letter of agreement is appropriate, specifying all the particulars of what you will provide at an engagement and for what price. One can be drawn up between you and the private parties or club owners who engage you. If you are offered a contract to sign, never do so without a thorough reading—preferably by a lawyer.

Unfortunately, many performers who are not yet of the stratum where they have agents, unions or performing rights societies will have trouble getting either remuneration or a contract. The rationale for this is that the chance to showcase yourself is equivalent to pay—an unfortunate and brutal attitude, but one that is common throughout the entertainment industry. The best advice is to accept only those showcases that offer realistic exposure and try your best to work out a deal whereby your expenses are paid. A gig should be quite an opportunity before you should pay to play in this way. Some club owners are at least willing to pay you a percentage of the take if you can bring in a decent crowd. Try at least to discuss this possibilty.

Songwriters and composers, whether published or not, and even the estates of deceased composers, may find the services of the Songwriters Guild of America, formerly the American Guild of Authors and Composers, extremely useful. The Guild, a nonprofit song writers protective organization, reviews members' contracts (they also publish a model writer-publisher contract), offers medical and life insurance, sponsors workshops and song critique sessions and audits music publishers. The Guild will also take care of your copyright needs. For those having trouble collecting royalties from music publishers, the Guild will help you collect for a 5.75 percent fee. There's a fee ceiling of $1,750 at this writing. Once you have paid out this much (the fee on about $33,000 of royalties), the Guild will collect the rest free of charge.

You can get further information on contracts and collection problems from one of the following:

MUSIC

AMERICAN FEDERATION OF
MUSICIANS
1501 Broadway
New York, NY 10036
(212) 869-1330

AMERICAN FEDERATION OF TELEVI-
SION AND RADIO ARTISTS (AFTRA)
1350 Avenue of the Americas
New York, NY 10036
(212) 265-7700

AMERICAN GUILD OF MUSICAL
ARTISTS
1841 Broadway
New York, NY 10023
(212) 265-3687

AMERICAN SOCIETY OF COMPOS-
ERS, AUTHORS AND PUBLISHERS
(ASCAP)
1 Lincoln Plaza
New York, NY 10023
(212) 595-3050

AMERICAN SOCIETY OF COMPOS-
ERS, AUTHORS AND PUBLISHERS
(ASCAP)
2 Music Square West

Nashville, TN 37203
(615) 244-3936

AMERICAN SOCIETY OF COMPOS-
ERS, AUTHORS AND PUBLISHERS
(ASCAP)
6430 Sunset Blvd.
Hollywood, CA 90028
(213) 466-8410

BROADCAST MUSIC, INC. (BMI)
320 West 57th Street
New York, NY 10019
(212) 586-2000

SONGWRITERS GUILD OF AMERICA
276 Fifth Avenue
New York, NY 10001
(212) 686-6820

SONGWRITERS GUILD OF AMERICA
6430 Sunset Boulevard
Hollywood, CA 90028
(213) 462-1108

THEATER

ACTORS EQUITY
165 W. 46th
New York, NY 10036
(212) 869-8530

ACTORS EQUITY
6430 West Sunset Blvd.
Los Angeles, CA 90028
(213) 462-2334

AMERICAN FEDERATION OF TELEVISION AND RADIO ARTISTS (AFTRA)
1350 Avenue of the Americas
New York, NY 10019
(212) 265-7700

AMERICAN FEDERATION OF TELEVISION AND RADIO ARTISTS (AFTRA)
6922 Hollywood Boulevard
Hollywood, CA 90028
(213) 461-8111

SCREEN ACTORS GUILD (SAG)
1700 Broadway
New York, NY 10019
(212) 957-5370

SCREEN ACTORS GUILD (SAG)
7750 Sunset Blvd.
Hollywood, CA 90046
(213) 876-3030

SOCIETY OF STAGE DIRECTORS AND CHOREOGRAPHERS
1501 Broadway
New York, NY 10036
(212) 391-1070

CHAPTER NINETEEN
INSURANCE

Getting adequate insurance can be a problem for freelancers. Health insurance is sold far more cheaply to groups of employees; theft insurance for business premises and for equipment such as cameras, electric guitars and other easily resold items can be very expensive; and as for life insurance, you are often hassled into buying more than you really need, or into buying it when you really don't need any at all.

There are a few ways in which freelancers can save on insurance while still keeping themselves adequately covered in these three areas of health, theft and life insurance.

HEALTH INSURANCE

Health insurance is essential for everyone, yet it is one of the prime areas of discrimination against self-employed workers. Not only are your premiums higher, but you get less comprehensive coverage than does an employee at the same income level. This is because employers pay part of the bill and do some of the administrative work, and because insurance companies charge less on group policies.

Your health problems are not predictable, and with health-care costs what they are today, you and your business could easily be wiped out by medical expenses and the loss of income during the period of your illness. So you must have adequate coverage. But no more. Many people are put off by the idea of having to buy health insurance in the first place, and so they don't think through their needs. They wind up paying a lot for a policy that covers very little basic health care, or that makes only a small dent in expenses when a major medical mishap does befall them.

DIFFERENT TYPES OF HEALTH INSURANCE

The basic categories of health insurance are basic hospitalization, major medical and disability income.

Basic hospitalization coverage pays for most in-hospital costs: room, surgery, nurses and certain diagnostic tests done in the doctor's office. Usually this sort of coverage doesn't pay for routine office visits for checkups, minor illnesses, and local surgery and repair. But such plans should cover maternity care, abortion and emergency first aid for accidental injuries—even when received in a doctor's office—if the care is provided within twenty-four hours of the accident.

The basic hospitalization plan most likely to be familiar to you is Blue Cross/Blue Shield, a nonprofit voluntary hospital care system. Blue Cross pays for the hospital room, and Blue Shield pays for other reasonable and customary medical expenses connected with your hospital stay. Because it is nonprofit, Blue Cross/Blue Shield has a very high payout rate: they pay out in benefits about 90 percent of what they take in from subscribers.

One of the drawbacks to this sort of coverage is that it really doesn't pay for routine medical care, even though many subscribers seem to think it does. Another is that it pays a flat amount for each operation or service—usually quite a lot less than the going rate in large cities, where medical costs are almost double what they are in even medium-sized cities. Individuals buying Blue Cross/Blue Shield coverage for themselves and their families will find it expensive—on the order of $1,000 per year for individuals and $2,000 per year for families including children up to the age of nineteen.

Major medical coverage is designed to cover you in case of serious accidents or extended illnesses. While these disastrous situations are statistically unlikely, when they do occur they can totally deplete your coffers in one fell swoop. Since this sort of major medical expense is rare, the premiums are not outrageously high, as you might expect them to be. Your premium will depend partly on how high your deductible is, the deductible being the set sum you pay before the insurance company starts to pick up the tab. The higher the deductible, the lower the premium. Once bills rise above the deductible, major medical should cover at least 80 percent of the remaining expenses, both in the hospital and outside. These expenses include such things as medication, doctors' fees and nursing care. Some companies have an upper limit to what they will pay in a given year or over a lifetime. Other policies pay the 80 percent on the first $25,000 or so and 100 percent of any expenses beyond that. If your major medical policy states that it will cover "reasonable and customary" expenses, you are better protected than if it gives a dollar limit, since the cost of specialists' services involved in this sort of medical care can far exceed the fixed limits, leaving you holding the bag. You should also try to avoid a fixed dollar limit on the price of the hospital room.

Disability Income insurance. While employees are generally protected by workers' compensation laws under which their employers must have mandatory State Disability Protection, self-employed people have a harder time protecting themselves in case of disability. They must buy personal disability insurance, which is harder to get than the kind administered by employers. This is so for obvious reasons: it is harder to verify your disability when you work at home and are also sick at home. For all the insurance company knows you could be ripping them off and lying luxuriously in bed writing screenplays, or you could just quietly disappear to the beaches of Mozambique on the proceeds. Formerly, disability insurance paid 100 percent of lost income, but then the insurance companies got hip to the hustlers who were having long, paid sabbaticals on the basis of phony medical problems. Nowadays, disability payments are more limited in order to prevent lying and malingering on the part of able but unwilling workers. Generally there is a waiting period of between seven and thirty days before the company will start paying out, and payout is generally limited to between 40 and 75 percent of your normal monthly earnings.

The average freelancer who has not been in business long and may not yet have a very reliable income will find it next to impossible to get disability coverage. This is due to the supposed work disincentive of paying disability, especially where there is no third-party control over your honesty, coupled with the usual anti-artist bias. Apparently, the only way a freelancer can get a disability policy written is to show a high income over two to five years—so that there is some average income figure that can be used to compute your benefits.

If you have the good fortune to get someone to write a disability policy for you, be particularly aware of the wording of the policy's definition of "disability." Some define it as "the inability to perform duties pertaining to any occupation." This could mean that, although an artist might not be able to *draw*, he or she could be declared fit to work in an office and cut off from disability benefits on that ground. Look for wording more like "inability to perform duties pertaining to his or her work or a suitable occupation."

Make sure also that your policy is *guaranteed renewable*. This means (a) the company is obliged to renew your policy when it expires, and (b) it can't raise your rates alone (it can raise your rates only as part of a general rate increase which applies to all their customers).

Guaranteed renewable and noncancelable is even better, since the company then agrees not to raise your premium until you reach a certain age—usually sixty-five.

Avoid at all costs policies which say "renewable at the option of the company." This means that they can drop you (and they probably will) as soon as you make a claim.

CHOOSING EFFICIENT HEALTH COVERAGE

The traditional advice is to buy Blue Cross/Blue Shield plus major medical. However, Barbara Gilder Quint, a noted authority on money management, suggests a different strategy for freelancers who may not have the funds available to pay the high premiums for this sort of coverage every year. What you really need to be protected against is medical disaster, so she suggests a major medical policy with a fairly high deductible—$500 is good—because the premium won't be astronomical and the deductible won't be so high that you will have to be half-dead before you've run up enough costs for the insurance company to take over. She suggests that you try to set aside enough money for the other, more predictable medical expenses, such as checkups, plus a set amount to cover unexpected minor illnesses. This sort of budgeting should make it possible for you to avoid paying out yearly the fairly steep premiums for basic hospitalization. You do run a risk of having to pay fully for routine medical care, but since much of this is not covered by basic hospitalization anyway, you may save money. This sort of minimal health coverage is probably best suited to young, healthy, single freelancers. The older you are, the more likely you are to need routine care involving hospitalization; and if you have dependents, the financial aftereffects of an uncovered hospitalization are more serious.

Another approach involves a new concept in health insurance—the Health Maintenance Organization, or HMO. HMOs replace major medical and basic hospitalization with a prepaid plan which covers almost everything from hospitalization to eyeglasses. The costs are extremely reasonable. As of 1985, the average cost was $75 a month for individuals and $205 for families. While this may seem as expensive as Blue Cross/Blue Shield, you must remember that it covers most medical care while Blue Cross/Blue Shield really does not. The major difference between HMOs and traditional insurance is that you are limited to your HMO roster of participating doctors.

There are two types of HMO: group practice HMOs and Individual Practice Associations (IPA). The group practice HMO is generally housed in a health center where all your medical needs can be dealt with under one roof. Usually you have a choice of physicians and can make appointments. In other words, these are not clinics where you are herded around and given whichever doctor has nothing to do. If you need to go to the hospital, your physician has you admitted to a participating hospital. All your expenses are taken care of once you're there. IPAs are not all under the same roof. Rather, you will see the doctor in his office. Hospital care is taken care of in the same way.

Three great advantages that HMOs have over traditional insurance plans are coverage of dental care (some HMOs already provide checkups for children), increased mental health coverage, and the full or partial coverage of prescription drugs. Also, according to a 1977 report from Consumers' Union, a study involving 8 million federal employees revealed that the HMO's stress on prevention and consumer education results in 58 percent fewer hospitalizations than Blue Cross/Blue Shield. In HMO plans, the emphasis is on keeping you healthy and out of the hospital. HMO doctors are on salary and so have no incentive to do anything but keep you well—a comforting thought these days when consumers are increasingly suspicious of physicians.

The number of HMOs has increased dramatically. To obtain a list of HMOs in your area, contact the Group Health Association of America, 1717 Massachusetts Avenue, NW, Washington, DC 20036; (202) 778-3200.

If you want to have the option of going to world specialists in case of catastrophic medical emergency, you might want to join an HMO in addition to carrying a major medical policy with a high deductible.

If for some reason the idea of joining an HMO does not appeal to you, and you decide to buy more traditional coverage which you feel will give you greater latitude in picking your doctors, here are some possibilities for which you might qualify that could result in your getting that insurance as cheaply as possible.

You may be able to buy insurance at group rates if you are a member of a union, guild or some other professional organization. Check the organizations to which you belong, and if none offers insurance, join an organization which does.

Many, if not most, of the professional groups listed in this book offer group health insurance. However, if you are joining principally to take advantage of a group's insurance offerings, check first to make certain that you will be able to enroll in the insurance program without a long wait. Increasingly, these programs are oversubscribed, and you may have to wait longer than you feel safe doing or you might like to take out an interim policy with an insurance company.

Alternatively, you and as few as two other employees may form a group, if you all work together, and receive group rates on Blue Cross/Blue Shield and some major medical plans. If you happen to work with several other people, such as a dance company or a small studio group, you may be able to work out a plan to your advantage.

After reading the first edition of *Freelance Forever,* one freelance commercial artist wrote to me of another clever strategy for saving on health insurance costs:

"I was paying in excess of $900 a year for coverage. I discovered that the University of Missouri/Kansas City offers a policy that includes major medical expenses for only $126 per year. I needed to enroll just as a part-time student to become eligible for this protection. My tuition is tax-deductible as long as the classes I take are directly related to my field. Not only is it now costing me less for health insurance and tuition combined than it used to cost for just insurance, but soon I'll have a Master of Arts degree besides."

SPECIAL HEALTH CARE OFFERINGS FOR ARTISTS

The following is a listing, by no means comprehensive, of special medical programs offered free or at low cost to artists by individual medical care providers such as hospitals. Although some of these are tied in to research projects and are geared to one type of medical problem or one type of artist, it is worth checking out all such programs anyway if you are close by, because they may actually be willing to let other types of artists participate or they may be able to refer you to a similar setup that is more appropriate to you.

GENERAL ARTISTS

ARTISTS THERAPY SERVICE
60 Riverside Drive
New York, NY 10024
(212) 362-1096 or 982-5107
Psychotherapy for artists.

CALIFORNIA ARTISTS HUMAN SERVICES
1824 North Curson Street
Los Angeles, CA 90046
(213) 655-2247
Counseling for artists on a sliding fee scale. Workshops on stress, management, art business, career planning and legal matters are occasionally offered.

CLEVELAND CLINIC
9500 Euclid Avenue
Cleveland, OH 44106
(216) 444-2200

DOCTORS FOR ARTISTS
123 West 79th Street
New York, NY 10024
(212) 496-5172

INTERNATIONAL ARTS MEDICINE ASSOCIATION
19 South 22 Street
Philadelphia, PA 19103

OCCUPATIONAL HEALTH PROGRAM
Harvard School of Public Health/The Artists Foundation
10 Park Plaza
Boston, MA 02116
(617) 227-ARTS

PERFORMING ARTISTS

THE CLEVELAND CLINIC
9500 Euclid Avenue
Cleveland, Ohio 44106
(216) 444-2200

MASSACHUSETTS GENERAL HOSPITAL
55 Fruit Street
Boston, MA 02114
(617) 726-2000

MEDICAL PROGRAM FOR PERFORMING ARTISTS
Northwestern Memorial Hospital
250 East Superior
Chicago, IL 60611
(312) 908-2000
Director, Dr. Alice Brandfonbrenner
This program emphasizes maladies of musicians such as the hand problems of pianists and wind instrument players' lips.

THE KATHRYN AND GILBERT HEALTH CARE INSTITUTE FOR PERFORMING ARTISTS
St. Luke's Roosevelt Hospital Center
425 West 59th Street, 6th floor
New York, NY 10019
(212) 554-6314
This is a comprehensive health care program for people whose livelihoods depend upon their ability to perform. Treatment is by professionals who understand the special needs of performers. Although these services are not free, the Institute acts as your health care base, referring you to specialists and keeping your records in a central location close to Manhattan's theaters. Other offerings are a national health care referral service for performers on the road, a free cancer screening exam at the Institute's Duke Ellington Cancer Screening Center, a newsletter, conferences and workshops on the medical needs of performers, a voice laboratory and a performance evaluation unit.

GOVERNMENT HEALTH INSURANCE PLANS

Medicaid is a federally funded program which provides free or inexpensive medical and dental care for those of any age below a certain income. Although Medicaid is federally subsidized it is administered by the individual states, so eligibility requirements and benefits vary from state to state.

To apply for Medicaid, write or visit the medical assistance division of your local department of social services. If you meet local eligibility requirements, you will be sent a Medicaid card to present to doctors, dentists and pharmacists in lieu of payment. Not every doctor will accept Medicaid, but many do—even some outstanding ones with fees higher than the reimbursement they will receive from Medicaid. Be sure to determine in advance whether the doctor or dentist of your choice will accept Medicaid patients. You may also want to check with the department of social services to find out what procedures are covered. As you may already be painfully aware, many states will no longer pay for abortions with Medicaid funds.

Medicare is extremely important to older freelancers. Its insurance is available to Social Security beneficiaries from age sixty-five on and to disabled people. It is divided into two parts. You receive the Part A benefits free of charge, but you can pay a small additional premium (at this writing, in the neighborhood of $17.50 per month) for Part B, which will greatly extend your coverage. Part A will help pay hospital expenses and other costs connected with an acute illness. Part B allows for more extensive home health care (even if you haven't been hospitalized), as well as medical and dental care. As with private insurance, Medicare carries a deductible as of 1987. Part A carried a $520 deductible for the first sixty consecutive days in a hospital, but thereafter hospital expenses are covered; Part B carries a $75 deductible and then pays 80 percent of allowed charges thereafter.

In order to obtain Medicare coverage at age sixty-five, visit your local Social Security office at least three months before your sixty-fifth birthday and enroll. If you wait to enroll until later than three months after your birthday, you must wait until the first three months of the next year, and your premiums are 10 percent higher for every year you wait.

OTHER HEALTH INSURANCE FOR OLDER FREELANCERS

If you are between fifty and sixty-five and are still working, check the health insurance offered to you through the Action for Independent Maturity division of the American Association of Retired Persons.

If you are sixty-five or older, the American Association of Retired Persons offers an In-Hospital plan, an Extended In-Hospital plan, a Skilled Nursing Facility and Home Nursing plan, and an Out of Hospital Medical plan. To find out about these, contact the American Association of Retired Persons, 1909 K Street, NW, Washington, DC. 20049; (800) 523-5800.

THEFT INSURANCE

Anyone who hasn't lived through the infuriating and heartbreaking experience of coming home to find all his uninsured valuables gone may not be sufficiently aware of how necessary adequate theft insurance is. You cannot imagine how impotent you feel as your eyes sweep the room and you numbly note the absence of your TV, toaster, stereo, silver, cameras, typewriter and guitars. It's trying enough if you do carry some coverage, because you can be assured of spending the two next months on the phone to Hartford, Connecticut—the insurance capital of America—disputing bills of sale, depreciation and arithmetical errors until you are ready to throw in the towel. But nothing is worse than observing the same scene and knowing that there will be no more music or TV or typing in the foreseeable future, because you don't have any insurance or any money. You might as well sit down and have a drink or smoke (if your liquor and grass are still there), because you can't do much else until tax time when you may deduct some of your uninsured losses (see page 330).

GETTING THE RIGHT COVERAGE

In order to protect yourself against this sort of nightmare you need good theft insurance to protect your valuables in any premises that you rent or own. It is becoming more difficult and expensive to insure personal business premises. Understanding insurance agents suggest that if you are a writer or artist who works out of your home you insure the whole place simply as a residence.

Under most policies some business equipment (up to about $2,500 or $3,000) will automatically be covered under your homeowner's or renter's policy anyway.

Theft insurance generally covers the actual cash value of your belongings rather than their replacement cost. The difference can be rather startling. Say you bought a typewriter three years ago at a cost of $400, and it is stolen today. The insurance company may give you only about $50, which is what they figure the machine is worth after depreciation has been calculated. However, it may now cost you $600 to buy the same typewriter. Clearly then some other sort of insurance is needed. What many people don't realize is that you can also ask for replacement value insurance which will pay you much closer to what you actually need to replace a stolen object at today's prices. Adding this type of coverage will increase a homeowner's premium by about 10 percent, but renters and condo dwellers who are insuring only the contents of their homes will pay premiums about a third higher. Most companies will still limit the amount of depreciation they will absorb if you carry replacement value coverage.

Many companies also limit the amount they will reimburse for particular categories of objects or for particular types of losses. You can raise the coverage for these items by paying a higher premium called an endorsement. For instance, you may be able to increase the coverage on your silver by paying an endorsement of about $5 per $1,000 of extra coverage. You can also increase your insurance on particular items by taking out a separate policy called a floater which will insure the named item on an "all-risk" basis which means that the item is covered no matter how the loss occurred. A standard policy is written on a "named peril" basis which means that you will be reimbursed only if the type of loss is named in the policy. For instance, if you leave a camera on an airplane it might not be covered under a policy that lists only losses such as fire and theft. If you have a floater the camera would be covered.

Floaters are provided to cover specific items, and you generally have to have proof of the value of the item. If you don't have a sales receipt for the item, you may even need to have it professionally appraised. To locate an appraiser in your area who is experienced in appraising the type of property you want to cover, contact the Appraisers Association of America, 60 East 42nd Street, New York, NY 10017; (212) 967-9775.

The Federal Crime Insurance Program, run by the Federal Insurance Administration, which is part of Housing and Urban Development, offers quite cheap coverage on business and residential property if you live in one of the states where the program is in operation. The participating states are these:

Alabama	Illinois	Pennsylvania
California	Kansas	Rhode Island
Connecticut	Maryland	Tennessee
Delaware	New Jersey	District of Columbia
Florida	New York	Commonwealth of Puerto Rico
Georgia	Ohio	American Virgin Islands

One of the pluses of this program is that you can't be denied coverage no matter how many times you've been robbed. More important, they can't raise your premiums no matter how many robberies you've had, unless they raise everyone else's equally.

These policies cover burglary and robbery (burglary takes place in the home, robbery occurs away from one's premises), as well as damage to the home or business during a burglary or attempted robbery, burglary of a locked automobile trunk and theft from a night depository. The limit on household insurance is $10,000, and up to $15,000 on business property.

Federal crime insurance is available from some insurance brokers, although they often have to be urged to mention it. If you live in a state not covered by federal crime insurance, check with your state's insurance commission. As of the writing of this edition, states were being encouraged to offer this sort of insurance directly to their residents. For more information, write Federal Crime Insurance, P.O. Box 6301, Rockville, MD 20850; or call (800) 638-8780.

NOTE TO PHOTOGRAPHERS

One possibility for insuring photographic equipment is a policy called *Photopac* . . . .

Photopac is available nationwide through Burnham and Company, which also has other similar plans available to filmmakers. You can contact them at Box 1096, Englewood Cliffs, NJ 07632; (201) 568-9800.

IF YOU ARE ROBBED

- If you see that someone has broken in while you were out, never walk into the apartment or house. Instead, back off and call the police.
- Don't move things around before the police come. Occasionally they will dust the place for fingerprints, and the less you disturb things the better. If you have a camera, it never hurts to get a few snaps of the scene for the insurance company.
- Be sure to get the complaint number from the police. You need this for the insurance company. It is also a good idea to get the cops' names in case you need to contact them again.
- It will probably take you a day or two to realize exactly what is missing. This is why an inventory of your valuables is useful and something which you should draw up as soon as possible if you don't already have one. Don't forget to keep it current! You may want to put it in with your tax records so you'll be reminded at least once a year to bring it up to date. Give a copy of your list of stolen items to your insurance company and to the police.
- You will need receipts, sales slips or appraisals to substantiate your claim. If none of these exist, you may be asked to supply an appraisal from a dealer as to the value of what was lost. Often, for a ten spot, dealers will be helpful and stretch these appraisal prices to their highest limit. This is necessary if you are not to end up getting $100 on a brand-new $500 stereo after the deductible and depreciation. (Depreciation is brutal and commences—for insurance purposes anyway—as soon as the item crosses the store's threshold.)

• Notify the insurance company as soon as possible. Most have a twenty-four hour switchboard for logging thefts and accidents.

CRIME PREVENTION

All it takes to make you properly secure your house is one good robbery. But why not save yourself the suffering and prevent a robbery altogether by investing a little of your hard-earned money in a few simple security devices? It's getting to be more and more common to find that insurance companies won't insure against burglary unless certain specifications as to locks and window guards are followed. In order to be eligible for Federal Crime Insurance you have to comply with quite specific regulations: if the specified equipment is not installed, and you are robbed, you won't be able to collect on your claim. Here is what you need:

Locks. Police recommend *dead bolts* for real security. Second choice is a *drop bolt.* A dead bolt is preferable because it cannot be pried apart. What you should avoid is a spring lock, which can be opened with a credit card if the robber has any skill at all. You need a key to lock dead and drop bolts; a spring lock locks when the door shuts.

The other kind of lock to avoid is the kind which has a keyhole in the knob. These can be worked with a credit card, or the burglar can spread the door and doorjamb with a crowbar and disengage this sort of lock with a strong push.

In addition to the locking device which is on the inside of the door, you need a cylinder into which you put your key. The cylinder most often recommended by crime prevention experts is the pick-proof Medeco, in combination with a vertical dead bolt. This set should cost you from $75 to $125 installed. Medeco keys cannot be duplicated except by authorized, bonded locksmiths. You should also spend an extra $15 and buy a cylinder guard plate which prevents the cylinder from being removed.

It is essential that there be spare keys to which you have ready access. The superintendent should have a key, and so should one or two friends in case you are locked out when the superintendent is not at home. It is important to have spare keys in any case. Freelancers leading frenetic lives as performers or journalists often have to leave town virtually on a moment's notice. It is a comforting thought to remember that although you may have forgotten a few last-minute details, your friend Sally has a set of keys and you can reach her by telephone from your destination.

It's also a good idea to leave one more set in a place which you can always get to: your parents', if they live in the same area, or in your car, hidden in a small device known as a Hide-a-Key. If you live in the country, you can always hide the key under a particular rock or some other safe spot outdoors. But don't do this in suburbia where someone might notice where you go to get it.

If you move into a new space, you should change the cylinders, because you have no way of knowing just who has keys to it. If the door has a good lock, you may want to add another dead-bolt lock above it.

If you have a door with glass panels, you may want to install a double-cylinder lock: you need a key for one of these anytime you want to open the locked door from either the inside or the outside. This will prevent thieves from just smashing the glass and reaching in and undoing the bolt. Never use a double-cylinder lock in a house with small children, elderly people, or others who might not be able to open it quickly in an emergency. An alternative is a heavy metal grille over the glass which should be secured with carriage bolts.

If you have a weak door or a weak doorframe which could be easily pried apart, you may want to get a Fox Police lock, also called a buttress lock, which consists of a steel bar which fits into a floor fixture and braces the door.

One new type of locking system coming into use actually has several bolts at different places on the door—all of them locked with one cylinder.

Windows. Windows can be secured cheaply and fairly thoroughly by closing them so that wooden frames line up, then drilling holes through the inside window sash and three quarters of the way through the outside sash, and inserting quarter-inch cap screws, or eyebolts, through these holes. The holes should be drilled at a slight downward angle to keep the screws frimly in place when inserted. You will want to drill several sets of holes at varying heights, so that you have a choice of how far open you secure the window. You can also buy window locks with keys for about $10 apiece, but Consumer Reports does not recommend these, as all types are too easily pried open.

In moderate to high-crime areas you need window gates. The most secure kind is the fire department–approved ferrygate, which has a locking device which uses no key and can be opened easily from the inside. This way, in case of emergency, you can spring yourself in a minute instead of dying of asphyxiation as you fumble with a key and lock. These gates are made of case-hardened steel and cost upwards of $100. The cheaper kind is usually slightly flimsier and has a padlock. These run about $50 per window and are quite sufficient except in the heaviest crime areas. In most states it is illegal to secure all the windows with padlocked gates. At least one of them must be a fire department–approved ferrygate which permits emergency access from the inside.

Alarms. Burglar alarms are expensive. The most expensive type hooks up with the police or with the alarm company's central office. These cost upwards of $1,000, but if you can afford them they will buy peace of mind for all but certifiable paranoids. Less expensive alarms consist only of noise from an alarm bell, which is theoretically enough to scare away a burglar. According to the police, they don't generally do this, because the key to such an alarm is the alertness of one's neighbors, and unless you happen to live next door to a snoopy old woman (like the one who saved the day in the Hitchcock movie *Rear Window*), you will find that your neighbors habituate quickly to your false alarms and will probably fail to distinguish a real alarm if one ever sounds. If you want to install one of these alarms you might consider one of the models sold in electronics chains such as Radio Shack or Lafayette. You can also buy one which you assemble yourself from Heathkit.

A brilliant little device which you can buy for $300 can make one of these simple alarms quite efficient. It is a phone dialer which hooks up to your alarm system and your phone. It is programmed to dial up to four numbers and deliver a prerecorded message—to the police or anyone else you want. This is also handy when you are on holiday, since you can program it to call you where you are staying.

Before you buy an alarm, check with your Better Business Bureau as to whether the dealer is legit, because many shoddy operations have burgeoned in this field. You might ask the dealer for the names of some previous customers and find out how satisfied they are. Buy an alarm with a long warranty—some are as long as two or three years.

In the opinion of many, rather than buying a cheap alarm you do better simply by putting metallic or recording tape on your windows to look like an alarm. Be sure to observe carefully what the real thing looks like before you attempt it. Mail order houses often sell stickers with the logos of well-known alarm systems such as Holmes or Dictograph. However, according to the police, metropolitan thieves are getting more sophisticated and can often distinguish imitation stickers and tapes. Needless to say, you would not neglect to have window gates and locks if you were to decide to try to fake alarm protection. The physical barrier is what really keeps them out—alarms or fake alarms are only a further deterrent, and unless they somehow tie in to the police they are not to be counted on to protect a vulnerable home.

Operation Identification. Operation Identification is a major crime deterrent program run by police in each city. The rerobbery rate is extremely low among crime victims who have joined this program. To join, you get an electroengraver from the police which you use to mark all valuables that might tempt thieves. Generally you mark them with your driver's license number,* which is then filed with the police. You are also given door and window stickers which warn that all valuables on your premises have been marked for identification by the police. As long as you make sure to mark the items on parts which can't be removed, the stolen items cannot easily be fenced.

In some cities the police departments have Search and Recovery squads which go around to hock shops and recover marked stolen goods.

For further information on proper security, check with your police department. Each police precinct has a Crime Prevention Officer who will come around for free and go over your premises and tell you how best to secure them.

It is imperative that you keep a current list of all valuable items in your possession. This should include all work equipment such as photographic and darkroom equipment, musical instruments, hi-fi equipment and typewriters. Keep a detailed descriptive list of these and be sure to include any pertinent serial numbers or other identifying numbers.

Valuables unrelated to your work should be catalogued and photographed if they are unique. If you have valid appraisals for any objects such as jewelry, silver, artwork, antiques or fur coats, these should be filed along with the list.

Keep the list in some fireproof place such as a filing cabinet or, preferably, an inexpensive, document-size safe-deposit box at your bank (average cost: $10 to $15 per year). If your home security is not reliable, you might even consider putting some of your valuables (such as jewelry, or even silver) in a safe-deposit box instead of paying the high insurance premiums for coverage of these items.

---

*Don't use your Social Security number. The police do not have access to a central file of these.

LIABILITY INSURANCE

It used to be that people took some responsibility for their own mistakes. In an earlier world if you fell down because you had had too much to drink at lunch you blushed and walked away as best you could. Now you scream bloody murder and try to sue the property owner or some other "deep pocket." And the courts are backing up many of these litigants. There are several famous cases of thieves who hurt themselves while trying to rob someone's premises and actually won their cases! There is a movement afoot to limit some of the exorbitant awards made to these so-called victims, but it has hardly become a major trend.

Not every freelancer with a home work space will need extra liability insurance since your homeowner's or tenant's policy provides some personal liability coverage. The size of your operation and the frequency with which members of the public enter your premises to do business or whether you have employees will determine how you should handle liability coverage. If you are a writer or artist who uses your work space to produce work which is not sold on your premises and if you don't have many clients regularly visiting you "at work" you probably have no problem. Your homeowner's or tenant's policy will cover you if one of your friends gets hurt and meanly decides to go after you.

If you have a bit more contact with the public, but still don't run a business such as a gallery, you may be able to increase sufficiently your liability coverage by adding an incidental business operation endorsement to your homeowner's or renter's policy. This endorsement, which at present would cost you just under $50, would protect you when the occasional client came to work with you in your office or to audition your band or look at some artwork.

If you have a situation where you have a lot of contact with the public at your home workplace you should probably buy a business owner's policy in addition to your homeowner's policy. This would cover a small gallery that you have in a barn next to your house and similar situations where the public comes to your residence on a regular basis.

If you have an employee check to see whether your homeowner's or business policy covers him. If not, you can purchase a worker's compensation policy from your insurance company for $50 to $100 in most states.

LIFE INSURANCE

Not everyone *needs* life insurance, though after listening to life-insurance salesmen talk you begin to feel like a Bolshevik, or careless of your nearest and dearest, or in some vague way un-American, if you don't buy it anyway. These are the reasons you may need life insurance:

1. Creditor satisfaction—so that creditors can attack your policy rather than your estate if you die owing money.
2. Continuation of family income in case of your death.
3. Settlement of your estate taxes.
4. As collateral or supplemental retirement fund—the cash value of the policy can act

as a business reserve or as collateral for a loan, and the policy can be cashed in when you retire.

If you are single and don't have any significant estate, you don't need to buy any life insurance—or, at most, a minimal amount so that your heirs don't have to sell anything you left them in order to pay for your funeral. There is one reason, however, why it may make sense to buy life insurance anyway. You may be able to buy a policy when you are sound and young with a rider entitling you to buy more later on if you have a family, even if you have developed terminal maladies in the intervening years.

If you do have dependents, you have to think a little harder. While insurance need not make your survivors rich, it is supposed to fill in the gap in their budget after you have figured any Social Security benefits or personal assets which they will receive on your death. You'll want your family to have enough money to finish bringing up the children and an additional amount for their higher education.

Keep those goals in mind and hold fast when you come under assault by a pushy life insurance salesman. These strange people may call you out of the blue at inconvenient hours to try to sell you life insurance. The ones I have dealt with have been distinguished by their triumphant lack of sensitivity to the limits of patience.

TYPES OF LIFE INSURANCE

There are two basic kinds of life insurance: term insurance and whole life insurance.

Term insurance is purchased for a specified period or term. As you age, the probability of your dying increases, so that each time you renew, your premium goes up. Within term insurance there are two types: level term, in which the face value and the premium of the policy both remain static; and decreasing term, in which the value of the policy decreases at scheduled points during its term until your coverage ceases completely. The logic behind decreasing term is that your need for coverage also decreases as you get older and your children begin to assume their own expenses.

Whole Life insurance is also called ordinary or straight life. Both face value and premiums stay the same year after year. Whole life can be cashed in or borrowed against, because the company sets aside a percentage of each premium payment and lets these build up. If you suddenly have an emergency you can cash in your insurance policy for its accumulated cash value (a policy with a face value of $10,000 might be worth about $1,500 after ten years). However, after you have cashed it in, that's it: you lose the policy and the protection. Your alternative is to borrow money from the company at quite a reasonable rate, using your policy as collateral. This way your policy is still in effect, and your family would be covered if you died. However, when you do die, your family only receives the face value of the policy—the cash value disappears.

While whole life may sound better to you because of the accumulated cash value, and better to your agent because commissions are nine times higher for whole life policies, term life is cheaper: you can buy six or eight times as much term coverage for the same premium. Many people look on whole life as a substitute savings plan, but this is really not practical since you are paying to save money which vanishes at your death. A common mistake is to buy small amounts of whole life insurance (which would not be sufficient for your family if you were to die unexpectedly) because of the attractiveness of the cash value. Another mistake is to allow yourself to be bullied into buying a whole life policy that you can't afford and have to let lapse after a couple of years. If this happens, you will be dismayed to find that you have accumulated no cash value because most of the first few years' premiums pay the agent's commission. You would have been much better off buying term insurance.

LIFE INSURANCE BARGAINS

- Try to get your insurance through one of the unions or professional organizations you belong to.
- Look into a preferred risk policy. Some companies offer these to people who work in safe occupations or who don't smoke. Generally, however, this is only possible if you are buying whole life.
- If you live in New York, Connecticut or Massachusetts, you may buy savings bank life insurance which is sold by mutual savings banks in these states. There is a ceiling on the amount of coverage you can buy:

New York	$30,000
Massachusetts	$41,000
Connecticut	$5,000

HOW TO FIND AN INSURANCE AGENT

You will get the best policy by going to a reputable insurance agent, so don't be tempted to cut corners by buying insurance through magazines, television or door-to-door salesmen. Get a referral from a lawyer, an accountant or a canny business friend. If you don't number any of these types among your acquaintances, get a referral from your state insurance commission. A good agent should be helpful and willing to advise you in your own best interests.

No policy is any good unless it is attached to an insurance office which is quick at administering claims. You really shouldn't have to wait more than about a month for the settlement of a claim, although in practice it is usually longer and very tiresome because you must haggle about depreciation. Watch the claims department's arithmetic, too, in substantiation of your claim. I remember one valuable company employee who had a knack for repeatedly making downward arithmetical mistakes which I had to keep picking up and pointing out.

If you have a complaint against your insurance carrier, you do have some recourse. You can contact your state's insurance department. In some states, such as Connecticut, this may be subsumed under the Governor's Information Office.

SETTING UP A PENSION PLAN

If the words *pension plan* depress you, I don't blame you at all. They depress me too. None of us likes to think of the other end of life, but you can be sure it's going to come anyway and that you'll be a lot happier when it does if you have been wise enough during your working years to put something aside— enough to struggle on the way you are used to, rather than ending your life in some state-run almshouse, psychiatric hospital or worse. This occurs among aging artists more than you'd care to think. Employees are often forced to put money into pension plans or are given group life insurance, and they all have money deducted routinely for Social Security. The average freelancer's life is a constant battle for survival in the present. Most of them don't even consider the demands of the future twenty to thirty years in advance when they are struggling to pay the rent and the telephone bill twenty days overdue.

Self-employment tax on some freelance incomes can be quite little, because so many business expense deductions are taken that actual taxable income is reduced greatly. While this is essential to help you keep alive in the present, it also pretty much dooms you to low Social Security benefits. Likewise, any income you earn off the books doesn't work for you in the long run. It may look like a good deal while you are young and poor. When you're old and poor you may gnash your teeth and damn yourself for working off the books.

Many freelancers rightly decide against buying expensive whole life insurance, which is the only kind that has any redeemable cash value. Couple those imbalances with the sort of "gather ye rosebuds while ye may" attitude which has characterized the life-styles of many people in the arts, and you begin to understand why you hear so many sad stories.

The fact that so many people who have spent their lives enriching others with their art are then allowed to waste away points to yet another inequity in the economic life of freelancers. Until now, very little has been done to help freelancers even to know what benefits they are being deprived of, and most of them, accordingly, arrange for themselves. Except for big-name freelancers in various fields, who have agents or reps or managers to advise them, most freelancers neither get advice on financial planning nor know where to go to look for it. Consequently they don't even consider it until it may be too late.

The individual unincorporated freelancer has a couple of possibilities open, depending upon the reliability of her income and how much she can put aside, and how old she is when she starts. If you are making a good income, the tax-shelter advantages of certain pension plans will far outweigh the tax advantages of simply working off the books. If you are incorporated, either as a profit-making individual or as a not-for-profit corporation, you can save even more on taxes. This subject is far too complicated for a short discussion in this book to be of much help to you, and if you have made enough money to have formed an individual corporation you undoubtedly have advisers who can advise you far more shrewdly on these matters than I can. The average freelancer who is making enough to be able to squirrel some away has a less complicated set of options.

TYPES OF PENSION PLANS

An Individual Retirement Account or IRA is a retirement plan available to both self-employed people and employees. At this writing, you may put away $2,000 ($2,250 if you file a joint return with a nonworking mate; if you both work, you can each have an IRA) or 100 percent of your earned income, whichever is less. If you earn less than $2,000, you may not contribute any more than you earned. Your IRA contribution will be fully deductible as long as you are not covered by any other retirement plan, including a Keogh, or your adjusted gross income is below a certain ceiling (at this writing $40,000 before you figure your IRA contribution for joint filers and $25,000 for single taxpayers). If you make more than these ceilings but are below $50,000 for joint filers and $35,000 for individuals you will still be allowed to deduct some portion of your IRA contribution even if you are covered by another pension plan. If you are not covered by another pension plan, you may deduct the full IRA contribution regardless of how much you earn.

You may withdraw without penalty from your IRA when you reach age 59 ½ or if you become disabled prior to that time. By the time you are 70 ½ you must begin your withdrawals, and you aren't allowed to make any more contributions. Although you may deduct from your earned income the IRA contributions that you make each year, and the interest you earn is not taxed, the withdrawals that you make are taxed. If you withdraw funds from your IRA before 59 ½ you will be taxed and penalized.

You may set up your IRA with a bank, credit union, brokerage house or insurance company or with an individual who qualifies as a trustee. An IRA may be set up and funded as late as April 14 for deductions on the prior year's taxes.

Keogh Plans are retirement plans for self-employed people which, depending upon how they are set up, may allow you to put away as much as 25 percent of your net self-employed earnings (after the effect of the plan contribution). Keoghs can be set up as Defined Benefit plans in which you decide how much of a payout you want at retirement and your contributions are figured accordingly or as Defined Contribution plans. The latter comprises two types of sub-plans: a *profit-sharing plan* in which you may make a flexible annual contribution of up to 15 percent of your net earnings (under this plan, if you have a bad year you needn't contribute at all) or a *money purchase pension* in which you can deduct between 1 and 25 percent of your net earnings. However, the latter plan requires that you commit yourself to contributing a fixed percentage of your income each year. If you decide to change this you will have to amend your plan at considerable hassle. To maximize your deductions, you may elect to have both plans, although you may not deduct more than 25 percent of your net earnings.

Keogh Plans must be opened by December 31 of the tax year in which you wish to take the contribution deduction. You can open the account with a small amount of money if you wish and then pay it up by April 15 of the following year or up to the time you file your tax return, if you have a valid extension. You can start a Keogh Plan through many banks, mutual funds and insurance companies. As with an IRA, you may begin withdrawals from your Keogh at age 59½.

Because a Keogh does allow you to put more away each year, it is more advantageous to open a Keogh first. Then, if your income falls below the ceilings mentioned above under IRAs, you can contribute an additional amount to an IRA also.

CAN YOU REALLY AFFORD A PENSION PLAN?

Pension plans are obviously good investments for freelancers. However, a big mistake that people often make is to fix their eyes on the tax savings when they really can't afford to tie up so much of their money. You can open and fund an IRA right up till April 15 and don't even have to fund it in years when you are broke which allows you some flexibility. Certain types of Keogh Plans, however, require the investment of a set amount or percentage of your income each year. Before you decide to set up these types of Keoghs you must know how much money, on average, you are going to be making and how much of it you can live without. If you can't afford to maintain your Keogh after a few years, any tax benefits you might have had will be wiped out.

A whole life insurance policy can function as an IRA. You can buy a single premium whole life policy where the interest will compound free of income tax, just like an IRA. The beautiful part is that you can borrow against it, even before your retirement, at very low interest rates, and at the same time, you are getting life insurance protection.

SOCIAL SECURITY BENEFITS

In order to be eligible for Social Security benefits when you retire, you must build up work credits throughout your working life. If you are self-employed and net $400 or more in a given year, you are given credit for all four quarters. Depending upon how old you are when you die or become disabled, you will need anywhere from a year and a half to ten years' credit. For instance, if you were to die or become disabled at age twenty-eight or younger, you would need to have gotten credit for one and one half year's work in order to be fully insured. For this reason, it is important to pay some Social Security each year.

The *amount* of your benefits is determined by your average monthly earnings and the rate of Social Security tax you paid. In 1986 self-employment earnings were being taxed at 12.3 percent.

Many people miss out on benefits for which they are eligible because they don't realize that benefits do not automatically come to them upon retirement, widowhood, or in time of major disability. To activate your benefits, apply at your nearest Social Security office a few months before you retire. If you are seriously disabled at any age, check with the office to see whether you or your family are eligible for assistance.

CHAPTER TWENTY

LEGAL MATTERS

The purpose of this chapter is not to tell you how to be your own lawyer but rather to give you an idea of the range of legal difficulties to which freelancers commonly fall prey, some ways to prevent them, and to tell you how to find suitable counsel. It cannot be stressed too strongly that you will never win by trying to be your own lawyer except in small claims court, where it is set up so that you can be. You can get into such expensive trouble by being your own lawyer that you'll be paying for it for the rest of your career—if you're not wiped out altogether. As one freelancer said, "You need a lawyer every time you sneeze."

Collection of smallish amounts of money is really the only legal maneuver you should attempt yourself. More serious or complex matters definitely require counsel. If you are wise, you will try to have a lawyer friend who will help you with some of the minor technicalities of your life, such as looking over lcases. However, when something more specialized, such as a book contract or copyright infringement, is involved, be sure to go to a lawyer who is experienced in this particular area rather than to a family friend who, though a lawyer, may have absolutely no idea about that specialized area.

Aside from nonprosecutory situations, such as signing contracts or writing charters, you will be either a plaintiff or a defendant. In either case you will need a lawyer. As a plaintiff, you are suing somebody and need a lawyer to prepare your suit. As a defendant, somebody is suing you, and you need a lawyer to defend you.

SUING

Nobody likes to get involved in lawsuits. They consume time and money, and the experience of taking someone you formerly had dealings with to court can be fraught with anxiety. The time loss and the anxiety can become such a burden that your artistic work suffers—often to the point of not getting done. Still, sometimes you have to put aside your preference to look the other way and initiate a lawsuit. Chances are, if the damages involved are great enough to warrant a lawyer, rather than arbitration in small claims court, you are involved in a situation where you may have been seriously wronged and stand to recover significant quantities of money. And yes, it *is* possible that you, a lowly freelancer, will bring suit successfully and win redress of your grievances, but only if you arise from your apathy and do something about it.

You may be called upon to go after business contacts for a variety of reasons, but for freelancers the most common suits brought involve copyright infringement or breach of contract. In the next sections I will set forth some of the salient points to consider about each of these types of suit. Again, the scope of this book permits no more than a setting forth of the basic logic underlying each of these actions. Not only is each case unique, but there are fifty states with differing laws which need to be considered. Many of the landmark cases in arts-related law have been decided in New York State. Therefore the basis of much of the following discussion is New York law. Only a lawyer can determine if it applies to your case.

THE 1978 COPYRIGHT LAW

The copyright act of 1976, effective January 1, 1978, replaced one that had been in effect for sixty-nine years. The change has put the artist, rather than the user of the artist's material, in the driver's seat. The new system should simplify matters for every artist who produces copyrightable works (written, recorded, pictorial, graphic, audiovisual and sculptural works) by eliminating the former dual system. Basically, the change is that you have statutory copyright the moment you create your work. Formerly you did not have statutory protection of your work until it was either registered with the copyright office or published. What this means is that you have automatic and legally binding ownership of works you have created *whether or not they are registered or published*. Other people cannot use, publish, buy or sell any part of them without a written transfer of copyright from you.

Term. The term of the copyright is now the creator's lifetime plus fifty years. Formerly it was twenty-eight years with a renewal term of twenty-eight years. Another simplifying change is that the term will run through the last day, December 31st, of its year of expiration. However, works copyrighted prior to January 1, 1978 will remain under the jurisdiction of the old law unless the copyright was obtained between 1950 and 1977, in which case it can be renewed for a second term of forty-seven years. If a work has gone into the public domain under the old system it cannot be recognized under the new system. This is true even if the work would not have yet become public domain under the terms of the new law. However, work created prior to January 1, 1978, but neither published nor registered will receive automatic statutory protection under the new law.

Works produced anonymously or pseudonymously are granted a term of seventy-five years after the publication date or one hundred years after the creation of the work, whichever is sooner.

Your rights. Under the new copyright law, the holder of the copyright has the exclusive rights of reproduction, sale, public display and distribution of the work. Nobody can copy, publish or publicly display your work except with your written permission. New under this law is your right to retain the reproduction rights to a work that you have sold.

Another important new right you have is the right to terminate rights that you have previously signed away. Under the new law you may terminate such a transfer during a five-year period which begins thirty-five years after the transfer of the rights. If you transferred publishing rights, you may cancel them thirty-five years after the publication, or forty years after the initial transfer of rights, whichever is shorter.

In order to revoke these rights, you must give notice in writing to the holder two to ten years before you wish to terminate his rights, and you must contact the U.S. Copyright Office. You should send these notices certified mail so as to have proof of mailing, and you should keep copies.

Copyright notice. You must put a copyright notice on each copy of the work that leaves your work space. (It's a good idea to place the notice on the work as soon as you finish it.) This is to help protect you against innocent infringers who might not wish to crib your work but who do not know that it is copyrighted. This is the best way to give yourself immediate protection against accidental infringement.

A notice should comprise the following elements: the word "Copyright" or the abbreviation "Copr." or the symbol ©, your name and the year of first publication (under the new law, "publication" means public distribution, display or performance).

You should place the notice so that anyone can see it. This means on the front or back of the title page of a manuscript, on the front or back of a drawing, painting or photograph, or on any matting or frame in which it will be permanently displayed. Notice can appear on any visible portion of a three-dimensional work, or on the base. For films, the notice should appear with the title or credits, or near the end. The same is true of a series of slides as in an audiovisual show. A single slide should carry its notice on the mounting.

Registration. You do not have to wait until the publication of a work before you register it. Nor do you have to register the work in order to have copyright protection, as was true under the old law. *However,* you cannot recover statutory damages or attorney's fees if the work was not registered prior to the alleged infringement. This is not to say that you won't collect *actual* damages (i.e., any profits made by the infringer) even if the work was not registered—though you must register it before you can proceed with your suit. You have three months after publication in which to register the work and still qualify for statutory damages* and attorneys' fees arising from an infringement that took place prior to registration. In any case, you must register your work before you can sue for infringement.

In order to register a work you must complete the appropriate form (available from the U.S. Copyright Office, Library of Congress, Washington, DC 20559 [202] 287-8700 or 287-9100). Most works, published or unpublished, will be registered on one of the following forms:

---

*Statutory damages are damages that can be awarded in an amount ranging between $250 and $10,000 in cases where actual damages are hard to prove. If you can prove that the infringer acted knowingly, the amount can be raised to $50,000. If the infringer can prove that he acted unknowingly, the amount can be set as low as $100.

Form TX: Nondramatic Literary Works
Form PA: Performed Works (Musical, Dramatic, Cinematic or Choreographic)
Form VA: Visual Works (Graphic, Pictorial or Sculptural)
Form SR: Sound Recordings
Form RE: Renewal of Copyright of Works Copyrighted under the Old Law

Form CA: Corrections in Previously Registered Works
Form GR/CP: Used to register groups of works (in addition, you should file those which are appropriate of the first four forms listed above)

It will cost you $10 to register each separate work. You can save yourself a lot of money by registering groups of your works. To do this, you should arrange them into a single, orderly work and title it. You need get no more imaginative then "The Collected Poems of Felicity Freelancer."

You must send a copy of the best edition of your work to the Copyright Office along with your registration form and the fee.

In cases where it isn't possible for you to deposit actual copies of your work, you may submit certain alternative materials. You may choose to do this if:

1. Your work is an unpublished visual work.
2. Fewer then five copies of a graphic or pictorial work have been published.
3. It is a limited edition work, consisting of three hundred or fewer copies.
4. It is too valuable to deposit.

You have no choice but to send in an alternative deposit when your work is a three-dimensional one, or one that exceeds ninety-six inches in any dimension.

Acceptable alternative materials include:

1. Photographs, slides, drawings or photostats of graphic, pictorial, three-dimensional, oversized or valuable works.
2. A reproduction of the sound track of a motion picture, together with a description or a visual reproduction such as a frame enlargement from every ten minutes of running time.

This is a basic discussion of the nature of the rules pertaining to the deposit of works. If you are sending an alternative to an actual copy as deposit, an excellent guide is Tad Crawford's a *Legal Guide for the Visual Artist*, listed in the bibliography of this chapter.

Work for hire. There has been much ado concerning the "work made for hire" provision of the new copyright law. Some people maintain that it robs the freelancer of the copyright to work that is rightfully his. Others insist that it helps the freelancer because his rights to the work have to be *signed* away. It can certainly be said that when misused by unscrupulous consumers of freelance work, the "work for hire" provision can be dangerous to freelancers.

Under the new law, work is considered "made for hire" if it was produced by an employee within the scope of his employment or if the work was commissioned for inclusion in a collective work. In order for the creator to give up his usual rights in his own work, he must transfer them in writing. There is a defensible logic to the law which allows "work for hire," even though it came into being mainly thanks to pressure from publishers. It is that certain works composed of many small parts, e.g., magazines, anthologies, newspapers and other such works, are in effect the creations of the publishers who put them all together. In some cases you may be perfectly *willing* to allow this. Just don't allow yourself to be pressured.

The fact that you have actually to sign away your rights before your work can be considered "made for hire" may not help you as much as it should. Some crafty users of freelancers' works try to force artists either to sign "work for hire" or "all rights transferred" contracts or not to work at all. Some publishers now require this for all freelance work, making freelancers, in effect, their employees, with none of the fringe benefits of employment such as health or unemployment insurance. A few publishers have even tried to force freelancers to sign *lifetime* "work for hire" contracts! Almost all of the guilds and associations for visual artists and writers have promised to fight the "work for hire" contracts battle on grounds of restraint of trade and deprivation of the creators' rights. If someone does try to pressure you into signing a "work for hire" contract in a situation you think unfair, contact a professional organization in your field (e.g., the Authors Guild, ASMP, or Graphic Artists Guild). If you do elect to produce a work for hire, bear in mind that you are selling all future rights to your work: charge accordingly the one time you can.

Infringement of copyright. If somebody wishes to reproduce your copyrighted material he should have your written permission. If he hasn't bothered to obtain this and has made more than fair use (e.g., short portions quoted in a review or article about your work) of the work, this may be considered infringement of your copyright. If you open a book and see one of your photographs or a substantial number of your words reproduced therein, you have grounds for an infringement suit. Provided that you have registered the work prior to your discovery of the infringement or the infringement occurs within three months of the publication of your work, you will be eligible for actual damages, statutory damages and attorneys' fees should you decide to sue. If an unregistered work was pirated more than three months after its first publication, the creator is only able to recover any actual damages he can prove.

In order successfully to prove infringement, you must be able to show that you owned the copyright and that the work was actually cribbed by the person you are accusing. It is helpful to show that the accused individual had access to the work. The decision will also be based on whether an impartial person seeing both works would think that the one had been copied from the other.

PROTECTING YOUR IDEAS

One of my bitterest memories as a writer concerns a list of stories that I sent to an editor at a new glossy travel magazine that I had heard was looking for writers and article proposals. Among my ideas was an obscure one that I believed to be uniquely mine, arising out of my lifelong interest in horses. I suggested that a gorgeous illustrated article could be done on the royal Arabian stud farms. I told how I would slant the article and which stud farms would be most spectacular to photograph. Imagine my surprise when the first issue appeared on newsstands with the selfsame story emblazoned on its cover! Despondently I thumbed through pages that seemed a déjà vu. To this day I'll never know whether I was really a victim of idea theft or whether the situation arose out of the synchronicity that reigns among creative people the world over.

People are rightly nervous about the theft of ideas. Nothing is more powerful and valuable than an idea. At just about every freelancing seminar that I give, someone asks whether ideas can be registered for copyright. The answer is no. Ideas, names, titles and short phrases cannot be copyrighted. However, there are some steps that you can take to protect your ideas. First of all, write them down in as much detail as you can, for while ideas are not copyrightable, a two-page article or letter which sets them forth does have copyright protection.

Second, date any ideas that you write down and have the date notarized. You can also mail yourself or a trusted friend or lawyer a copy of the document that describes your idea. Leave the envelope unopened, and this will establish the date that you had the idea if you are ever called on to prove that it actually originated with you. Some professional societies for writers, such as The Writers Guild, will register your works or drafts of ideas to protect you against just this sort of dispute.

Beyond that, don't get drunk and blather your good ideas at parties, especially when there are others who could conceivably make use of them. Keep dated copies of all proposals that you send out (you should anyway) just in case you do see a too-familiar idea. However, do bear in mind that the outright cribbing of ideas is probably not as common as one might be tempted to believe. People who have never met do get the same idea and often at about the same time. Legitimate publishers or producers of works wouldn't stay in business long if they got the reputation of trafficking in stolen ideas. So don't get the reputation of being a paranoid troublemaker. On the other hand, if you are reasonably sure and particularly if the person or company you suspect did have a chance to review your idea, you may have a real problem. However, never go charging out into the breach until you have run the evidence by your agent or rep or a good lawyer familiar with your field. You don't want to be slapped with a countersuit for defamation.

CONTRACTS

Some sort of written agreement or confirmation is your best protection in the event of nonperformance or later disagreement (see chapter 18, Collecting What's Owed You). The failure to make contracts when appropriate is the mark of an inexperienced freelancer who is so anxious to please anyone who gives him work that he doesn't ensure his rights by asking that the agreement go on paper and be signed. Up to a point, this is understandable. You feel as though you are accusing the person of dishonesty before you even do any business with him. Rather than jeopardize the person's opinion of you, you just assume his goodwill and get to work. However, try looking at it this way: it makes you look unprofessional. Anyone doing any sort of business where goods, services or money are involved should ask for and receive a written contract signed by both parties. And anyone who feels threatened by your request for something on paper is probably a bad egg to begin with—someone looking for a gullible freelancer. A person more on the level might see your failure to insist on an agreement in writing and signed by both of you as a sign of your inexperience. Your insistence upon having a contract makes you look like a pro, and the type of people you want to be dealing with will recognize your wisdom in doing so and respect you for it.

Think of all the business dealings you have each day and some of the nonbusiness dealings, too, that involve agreements to perform services or deliver goods or make payments. Many of them involve written contracts, and probably many more should, the reason being that if someone breaks a promise agreed to on paper you have a better basis for a suit.

Examples of Transactions that Require Contracts

Consignment of artworks	Agreements for performances
Agreements with agents	Rentals and sales of work
Publishing agreements	Collaborations
Commissions	Loans

Certain types of contracts must be in writing to be binding. Most states require written contracts for purchases exceeding $500 and for services that won't be performed for more than a year. Other contracts can be verbal agreements or informal letters, but it is always safer to have them in writing and signed. Not everyone who burns you does so intentionally. Sometimes there is just a lapse of memory; sometimes the other's financial situation changes drastically, and it is very inconvenient for him to pay you (too bad—a contract is a contract!).

Sources for contracts for everyday transactions, such as commissions to produce work or sales of small pieces of work, are given in chapter 18, Collecting What's Owed You. You can photocopy a stack of these in advance so as to have them at hand when you need them. More complicated transactions, however, should be drawn up by a lawyer or an agent familiar with that sort of transaction. Contracts offered to you by other parties, even so-called standard contracts, should be gone over by a pro.

"Standard" contracts such as publishing contracts or management contracts are not rigid propositions that you must accept or reject without alteration. Nor are they really standard. This is why the advice of a pro in a particular area is essential. These people know the ins and outs of these contracts and will know which small but significant changes to insist upon so as to alter the "standard" more to your favor. Many unions and professional associations such as Artists Equity, The American Society of Journalists and Authors, and the Authors Guild have available suggested contracts and guides to the "standard" contracts frequently encountered by their members. These organizations are also excellent sources of lawyers or agents who can vet contracts for you.

Bringing suit for breach of contract. When you decide to sue someone for breaking their contract with you, you will first want to determine whether it is an action that can be handled in small claims court or not. This will be mainly determined by how much money is involved. Each state has a limit beyond which your case is not eligible for small claims. (For information on how to pursue a case in small claims court, see chapter 18.)

If a larger amount is involved, you should take your contract, and any evidence you have as to its not being performed to your satisfaction, and consult a lawyer.

BREAKING A CONTRACT

Another good reason for having a written contract is in case you have to break it. Your contract should have some provision for what happens if one or the other party has to break it. Whether any monies paid will be returned, who owns any finished parts of the work in progress and the procedure for notifying each other and terminating should all be noted.

If there is no contract or no termination clause, send a letter to the other party and tell why you cannot carry out your agreement. Be polite and try to mitigate the other person's inconvenience. The best way to do this is to offer to try to help her find a solution if your bowing out causes her problems. Perhaps you know another person who can do the job, or you can refer your client to a professional group which can refer others capable of doing it. Be polite and conciliatory and, as in all your dealings with clients, keep copies of all your correspondence. This way if the other party takes you to court you have proof that you did your best to help resolve the problem.

DEFENDING YOURSELF

If there's anything worse than suing a business acquaintance, it is being sued yourself. The threat of legal action against you immediately reawakens all your most childish fears of omnipotent others who can punish you for your every wrongdoing. The simplest way to protect yourself against this sort of terror is to prevent it by knowing a bit about some of the areas of law most pertinent to your situation. Copyright, defamation, obscenity, releases and relations with your publisher or gallery are some of the more common areas in which you can run into trouble if you aren't aware of how to prevent it.

COPYRIGHT INFRINGEMENT

As long as you are well intentioned and are aware of the correct procedure for obtaining permission to use someone's copyrighted material, you should never be called upon to defend yourself in a copyright infringement suit.

To get permission to use a portion of a copyrighted work, you should send a letter to the publisher or the artist involved. If you are not certain exactly who controls the copyright, you can have this checked out by the Copyright Office at $10 per hour (U.S. Copyright Office, Library of Congress, Washington, DC 20559). Once you have the name and address of the copyright holder, you should compose a letter which includes the following information:

1. How large a portion of the work you wish to use.
2. The context in which it would be used.
3. Whether or not people will pay to see it.
4. Explanation of how the artist will be credited.

You should then type up a separate agreement listing all of these points in separate paragraphs, date it, write "agreed to" at the bottom and leave a space for the person to sign. Have the copyright holder send you the signed letter, which you should then have copied. Send one copy to the copyright holder, one to the Copyright Office, and keep one for your records. If you want to be doubly certain, you can even send a follow-up letter asking that the copyright holder contact you before a given date if any change is to be made in your understanding. Obviously, you should hold on to all this correspondence, because it is your proof that you have received permission to use the work.

DEFAMATION AND RIGHT-OF-PRIVACY SUITS

Defamation and invasion of the right of privacy are two charges against which artists are commonly called to defend themselves. How far an artist may go in depicting the flaws of another person and what use an artist may make of his depiction are the basic issues. Both types of suit must be examined in the light of the First Amendment, which guarantees freedom of expression.

Defamation, basically, is injury to a person's reputation. It can take the form of *slander*, which is spoken, or *libel*, which is printed and published, or rendered in physical form. The individual being defamed need not be identified by name. It is enough that he is identifiable by a third party. If your work depicts a public person, you are less likely to run into trouble than if a private person is involved. Those who lead a public life give up some of their rights to protection of their reputations by so doing. In order for a public figure successfully to sue an artist for defamation he has to prove that the material was substantially untrue *and* that the artist maliciously and willfully propagated the untruth. A private person need only prove that you were negligent in determining the facts to have grounds for a suit.

There are several defenses against such suits. The most important is the truth. If you can prove the veracity of what you have written or depicted, the plaintiff will not be able to win his suit against you. No matter how damaging the truth may be to him, he cannot recover a penny in damages if what you have expressed is the truth and you can prove it to the court's satisfaction.

One way to prevent trouble in this area is to attempt in any of your dealings with editors, publishers, and others who may be putting your work into composite form, to limit your liability to only the work that you supplied. This means that if a publisher adds some flap copy or produces a cover illustration, or an editor changes your original work, and one of these alterations is the part of the work that is actionable, you won't be held responsible. There are ways of altering "standard" contracts to limit your liability in this important way. If you are a visual artist whose work carries a caption, always write your own caption and include it with the work. This way the user of your work will be held responsible if he doesn't use the caption you supplied and suit is brought against you.

You should also obtain a release form if you are a visual artist. This may help if later the subject of the work tries to sue for defamation, pleading that the work ridiculed him or made him the object of scorn.

The *right to privacy* is really a right to several types of privacy. You are protected against intrusion into your home, against unauthorized use of your name or likeness for advertising or trade purposes, against publicity that places you before the public in a false light and against the disclosure of private facts. As in the case of defamation, a public figure has considerably less right to privacy. Facts relating to a person's private life may be aired as newsworthy if they are related to his performance of his public role. Private persons whom you choose to dredge up from anonymity and incorporate into your work have more leverage in claiming that their privacy has been invaded.

The best way for visual artists to prevent charges of invasion of privacy is to get a release when taking the likeness of a person for use other than that intended by the subject. You should also get a release to use the likeness of someone's private property, but this is not necessary for public buildings unless admission is charged to enter them.

A *release* should state a subject's consent to your taking a visual likeness and to the artist's intended use of the finished work. Since you don't always know what use will finally be made of a work, it's wise to list all the possibilities and to try to get the subject to sign. The release should always be obtained on the spot. Both the release and the work, or the negatives, should be dated. This helps in two ways: you won't have to waste time trying to catch up with your subject later, and you establish a connection between the release and a particular work. This last is important in case the subject later insists that he signed a release that pertained to an entirely different work.

If you work in an area in which you will commonly be using releases, you should take a look at the various types of releases reproduced in *Photography: What's the Law?* (listed in the bibliography of this chapter). The same book suggests that, even if you don't have a release form for a particular work, you can protect yourself to some extent by stamping "This work cannot be used for advertising or trade" on the back.

DEFAMATION AND FICTION

The preceding discussion centered on realistic representation of people, usually in visual works. However, a frightening new trend is that, contrary to previous understanding, works of fiction can be shown to be libelous. A case that received much publicity has been the Bindrim case, in which Paul Bindrim, a nude encounter therapist from California, sued Doubleday and recovered $75,000 in damages plus attorney's fees amounting to $34,000. His charge was that Gwen Davis Mitchell, a Doubleday author, had violated a contract that she had signed in which she agreed not "to take photographs, write articles, or in any manner disclose who has attended the workshop or what has transpired." Davis ended up writing a novel called *Touching* and was promptly slapped with a libel suit. Doubleday later sued its author for recovery of what it had cost them in damages. Davis and Doubleday have recently come to what both sides consider a fair settlement.

There has been much controversy over this case. Many people in the publishing world have expressed fear that no book is safe any longer. Those parts of the book that were true were considered *identifying* and those that were made up were judged *libelous* because they were *false*. There is a danger here of a legal catch-22 being set up, with a chastening effect on the future of literature. Novelists generally do base characters on living people or on composites of living people. Will authors of fiction now have to indemnify publishers for any suits arising from ill-intentioned plaintiffs who insist that a particular character is created from them? Indeed, a novel with characters based on living people might almost by definition be judged libelous, since it is fiction, or untruth, and since both the author and publisher, knowing this, are guilty of malice!

These are chilling thoughts. One worries that the same sort of greed and ill will that made medical malpractice suits look like a good way to cash in on imagined slights may now move into the publishing world. In the future, will science fiction and historical fiction be the only fiction safe enough to write?

In order to defend yourself against insane libel or invasion-of-privacy suits it is, then, not enough to label your work fiction. It is recommended that you avoid writing untruths about identifiable characters' sex lives, criminal or unethical practices, or medical history. For if you make up fictional sex lives for your characters you risk libeling someone who comes forward and says you're describing him, and on the other hand, if you tell the truth and use an actual incident, you can then be hassled for invasion of privacy.

In *Law and the Writer* (see the bibliography of this chapter), it is suggested that you check in the phone book of the place you're writing about to see if any of your characters match names with people in that town. If they do, either change their names or get a release.

For those writing romans à clef (i.e., those who *want* some of their characters to be identifiable) this sort of advice is not helpful. If you fall within this category you may want to consider libel insurance (see below).

LIBEL INSURANCE

Because of cases like *Bindrim* v. *Doubleday* writers have begun to realize that they can be as vulnerable to libel suits as doctors are to malpractice suits. Writers of nonfiction always knew that they had to be accurate, but most novelists and screenplay writers felt safe behind their shield of created characters and situations.

Recently, some publishers have been offering to their authors insurance against libel, invasion of privacy and other related risks. If you are concerned about material that you are attempting to have published, then you may wish to investigate whether any of your prospective publishers either offer libel insurance or state in their contracts that they will undertake your defense (unless you have knowingly libeled someone). Short of either of these alternatives, many publishers will at least have one of their lawyers read your manuscript for potential legal problems.

HOW TO FIND A LAWYER
ARTS-RELATED CASES

If you are not making a great deal of money, you may be eligible for the services of Volunteer Lawyers for the Arts, a nonprofit organization founded in 1969 to give legal assistance to artists and arts organizations on arts-related matters.

In order to qualify for VLA assistance, individual artists must be below a certain income ceiling. Organizations with budgets of less than $100,000 may also qualify. There are regional offices of VLA throughout the country. A list of these appears below.*

You may also be able to get experienced legal counsel through a professional association or guild to which you belong. Almost all of these organizations have consulting lawyers or legal departments. Some offer legal assistance to individual members, but others reserve their legal departments to represent their membership as a class in such matters as copyright or artists' rights.

VOLUNTEER LAWYERS FOR THE ARTS ORGANIZATIONS BY STATE

NEW YORK CITY
Volunteer Lawyers for the Arts
1285 Avenue of the Americas
New York, NY 10019
(212) 977-9270
This branch serves primarily metropolitan New York but also other states and countries

California
LOS ANGELES
Volunteer Lawyers for the Arts—
Los Angeles
P.O. Box 57008
Los Angeles, CA 90057
(213) 489-4060

SAN DIEGO
San Diego Lawyers for the Arts
1205 Prospect Street
Suite 400
La Jolla, CA 92037
(619) 454-9696

SAN FRANCISCO
Bay Area Lawyers for the Arts
Fort Mason Center
Building C
San Francisco, CA 94123
(415-775-7200

Colorado
DENVER
Colorado Lawyers for the Arts
P.O. Box 300428
Denver, CO 80203
(303) 830-0379

Connecticut
HARTFORD
Connecticut Volunteer Lawyers
for the Arts
Connecticut Commission on the Arts
190 Trumbull Street
Hartford, CT 06103-2206
(203) 566-4770

District of Columbia
Lawyers Committee for the Arts/
Volunteer Lawyers for the Arts, D.C.
918 Sixteenth Street, NW, Suite 503
Washington, DC 20006
(202) 429-0229

Washington Area Lawyers for the Arts
2025 I Street, NW, Suite 608
Washington, DC 20006
(202) 861-0055

Florida
CLEARWATER
Volunteer Lawyers and Accountants for
the Arts Program
Pinellas County Arts Council

*For a complete listing of the programs and resources available from each of these VLA programs, look in the National VLA Directory available from the New York City VLA.

400 Pierce Boulevard
Clearwater, FL 33156
(813) 462-3327

FORT LAUDERDALE
Broward Arts Council
100 South Andrews Avenue
Fort Lauderdale, FL 33301
(305) 357-7457

MIAMI
Business Volunteers for the Arts/Miami
% Greater Miami Chamber of
Commerce
1601 Biscayne Boulevard
Miami, FL 33132
(305) 350-7700

Georgia

ATLANTA
Georgia Volunteer Lawyers for the Arts
P.O. Box 1131
Atlanta, GA 30301-1131
(404) 586-4945

Illinois

CHICAGO
Lawyers for the Creative Arts
623 South Wabash Avenue,
Suite 300-N
Chicago, IL 60605
(312) 427-1800

Iowa

CEDAR RAPIDS
Volunteer Lawyers for the Arts
Committee
Cedar Rapids/Marion Arts Council
424 First Avenue, N.E.
P.O. Drawer 4860
Cedar Rapids, IA 52407
(319) 398-5322

Kentucky

LOUISVILLE
Community Arts Council
609 West Main Street
Louisville, KY 40202
(502) 582-1821

Louisiana

NEW ORLEANS
Louisiana Volunteer Lawyers
for the Arts
% Arts Council of New Orleans

WTC Building, Suite 936
2 Canal Street
New Orleans, LA 70130
(504) 523-1465

Maine

AUGUSTA
Maine Commission on the Arts
55 Capitol Street
State House Station 25
Augusta, ME 04333
(207) 289-2724

Maryland

BALTIMORE
Maryland Lawyers for the Arts
% University of Baltimore School of
Law
1420 North Charles Street
Baltimore, MD 21201
(301) 685-0600

Massachusetts

AMHERST
The Arts Extension Service
Division of Continuing Education
University of Massachusetts
Amherst, MA 01003
(413) 545-2360

BOSTON
Lawyers and Accountants for the Arts
The Artists Foundation, Inc.
10 Park Plaza
Boston, MA 02116
(617) 227-ARTS

Minnesota

MINNEAPOLIS
Minnesota Volunteer Lawyers
for the Arts
% Fred Rosenblatt
100 South 5th Street, Suite 1500
Minneapolis, MN 55402
(612) 337-1500

Missouri

ST. LOUIS
St. Louis Volunteer Lawyers and Accountants for the Arts
% St. Louis Regional Arts Commission
329 North Euclid Avenue
St. Louis, MO 63108
(314) 361-7686

Montana

MISSOULA
Montana Volunteer Lawyers for the Arts
% Joan Jonkel, Esq., P.O. Box 8687
Missoula, MT 69807
(406) 721-1835

New Jersey

TRENTON
Volunteer Lawyers for the Arts
of New Jersey
A Special Project of Center for Non-
Profit Corporations
36 West Lafayette Street
Trenton, NJ 08608
(609) 695-6422

New York

ALBANY
Volunteer Lawyers for the Arts Program
Albany League of the Arts
19 Clinton Avenue
Albany, NY 12207
(518) 449-5380

BUFFALO
Arts Council in Buffalo and Erie County
700 Main Street
Buffalo, NY 14202
(716) 856-7520

POUGHKEEPSIE
Dutchess County Arts Council
39 Market Street
Poughkeepsie, NY 12601
(914) 454-3222

North Carolina

RALEIGH
North Carolina Volunteer Lawyers for
the Arts
P.O. Box 590
Raleigh, NC 27602
(919) 890-3195

Ohio

CINCINNATI
Cincinnati Area Lawyers and
Accountants for the Arts
ML003
University of Cincinnati
Cincinnati, OH 45221
(513) 475-4383

CLEVELAND
Volunteer Lawyers and Accountants for
the Arts

% Cleveland Bar Association
Mall Building
118 St. Clair Avenue
Cleveland, OH 44114
(216) 696-3525

TOLEDO
Arnold Gottleib
421 North Michigan Street
Suite D
Toledo, OH 43624
(419) 243-3125

Oklahoma

OKLAHOMA CITY
Betty Price
State Arts Council of Oklahoma
Room 640
Jim Thorpe Building
Oklahoma City, OK 73105-4987
(405) 521-2931

Pennsylvania

PHILADELPHIA
Philadelphia Lawyers for the Arts
251 South 18th Street
Philadelphia, PA 19103
(215) 545-3385

Rhode Island

NARRAGANSETT
Ocean State Lawyers for the Arts
96 Sachem Road
Narragansett, RI 02882
(401) 789-5686

South Carolina

GREENVILLE
South Carolina Lawyers for the Arts
P.O. Box 10023
Greenville, SC 29603
(803) 232-6970

Tennessee

NASHVILLE
Bennett Tarleton
Tennessee Arts Commission
320 Sixth Avenue North
Nashville, TN 37219
(615) 741-1701

Texas

AUSTIN
Austin Lawyers and Accountants
for the Arts

P.O. Box 2577
Austin, TX 78768
(512) 476-7573

HOUSTON
Texas Accountants and Lawyers
for the Arts
1540 Sul Ross
Houston, TX 77006
(713) 526-4876

Utah

SALT LAKE CITY
Utah Lawyers for the Arts
50 South Main, Suite 900
Salt Lake City, UT 84144
(801) 521-5800

Washington

SEATTLE
Washington Volunteer Lawyers
for the Arts
428 Joseph Vance Building
1402 Third Avenue
Seattle, WA 98101
(206) 223-0502

Canada

TORONTO
Canadian Artists' Representation Ontario
183 Bathurst Street
Toronto, Ontario M5T 2R7
Canada
(416) 360-0780

SPECIAL MATERIALS AVAILABLE FROM VLA ORGANIZATIONS

Many of the VLA branches publish or distribute special materials, books, tapes, newsletters and journals. Here are some materials of special interest. A fuller listing can be obtained either by contacting the individual offices or by looking in the *National VLA Directory*, available from VLA in New York City.

Available from Canadian Branch

Copyright for Canadian Visual Artists
Moral Rights in Copyright (Canadian Artists' Representation Ontario–OAAG
Artist–Public Gallery Exhibition Agreement)
Taxation Information For Canadian Visual Artists
Model Agreements for Visual Artists: A Guide to Contracts

Available from Chicago VLA

Resource Kits:
Dancers, Dance Companies and the Law
Legal Aspects of Photography
Legal Considerations for Filmmakers and Video Artists
Legal Issues for Independent Writers
Record Contracts for Musicians

Available from New York VLA

To Be or Not to Be: An Artist's Guide to Not-for-Profit Incorporation
The Artists' Housing Manual: A Guide to Living in New York City

Available from Philadelphia VLA

Legal Guide for Emerging Artists
*Bach Never Said It Would Be Easy: A Guide to Managing Your Classical
Music Career*

Available from Washington VLA

A Guide to Washington's Artist/Dealer Consignment Law
Graphic Crimes: Legal Issues in Graphic Design

OTHER CASES

For problems not related to your artwork, you have several alternative sources of inexpensive legal aid:

Legal Aid. Legal Aid, also known under the names Legal Aid Society, Community Law Office and Public Defender, is a government-funded legal organization which represents clients whose yearly income is below a certain ceiling. At the moment, Legal Aid lawyers can defend you in civil or criminal suits.

Bar association. Your local bar association probably has a referral service, though you won't necessarily be able to locate a lawyer by field since lawyers are not allowed to advertise by specialty. These referral services usually send you to a lawyer for a half-hour consultation costing $15 to $25. You then decide whether to retain the lawyer or not.

Legal clinics. Some "legal clinics" are just law firms which have adopted a more populist-sounding name. Although the name implies reduced prices, this is not always the case. However, there are some high-volume law firms calling themselves clinics and serving people whose incomes disqualify them from poverty law services. These clinics can be located through the local bar association or through the community legal department of a law school in your area.

Most lawyers will tell you that the best way to find a lawyer is through the grapevine. If you are a freelancer, talk to other freelancers who have dealt with similar problems in the past and find out if they were satisfied and who their lawyer was. Another good source is your union or guild.

Don't make the mistake of underestimating your need for legal advice. And don't rely on the advice of law students: this may be a tempting thing to do, but it is rarely helpful, except in the simplest matters, because they haven't yet had a chance to practice law and don't have practical experience. In any case, law students are prohibited from doing any sort of legal work for clients in every state except Oregon.

Prepaid Legal Plans. A fairly recent innovation in the legal world is the concept of prepaid legal service packages which function somewhat like a health maintenance organization. They are offered by such outfits as Amway, Montgomery Ward and Hyatt Legal Services. Although the deals vary, basically you pay somewhere between $8 and $20 per month and are entitled to certain basic legal services such as document reviews, telephone consultation with a lawyer or will probation for free, and you receive discounts on legal services in more complex matters.

Like HMOs, most of these packages only allow you to consult one of their approved lawyers. However, Prepaid Legal Services, Inc. of Ada, Oklahoma, the oldest and largest of these companies does allow you to use a lawyer of your own choosing.

Because these services haven't been around long enough for a thorough assessment of their real utility, some experts feel that you may be wasting your money if you need consultations in specialized areas of the law such as arts law or copyright. Unless you tend to have a lot of small, general legal problems on a regular basis these plans may not be useful to you.

ARTISTS' RIGHTS

Recently there has been a movement to give creators more control over their works and a fairer tax break in a couple of situations which are presently grossly inequitable toward the very people to whom the works of art involved owe their existence.

DROIT DE SUITE

In eleven countries of Europe, Africa and South America, artists or their estates have the right to share a percentage of the incremental gain when an artist's paintings take a jump in price. Suppose early in your career you sold a painting for $500 and ten years later it is resold for $5,000. In countries where *droit de suite* is the law you would be entitled to a percentage of the $4,500 price increase. So far, however, American artists have not benefited by this law even in countries where it is enforced.

Although we don't have a law of *droit de suite* in America, attempts are slowly being made to extend similar rights to artists here. California has enacted a 5 percent resale proceeds right for living artists, which provides that whenever a work is sold for more than $1,000 by a seller who is a resident of California, the artist must be paid 5 percent of the gross sale price within ninety days of the deal. This does not apply to the initial sale nor in sales where the price drops below what the seller paid for it. If the seller cannot locate the artist within the specified time, the money is to be deposited with the California Arts Council. If the artist still hasn't been unearthed after seven years, the money is used for the Council's programs. If the artist finds that the seller sold the work and did not pay, he has the right to sue for three years after the sale or one year after his discovery of the sale.

This law was challenged by a Los Angeles art dealer who contended that it violates the copyright law as well as property rights guaranteed by the Constitution. It was upheld by the U.S. Supreme Court in November, 1980. However, this does not mean that you should expect any change in the laws of most states in the near future.

Another innovation which would give artists *droit de suite* is "the Artist's Reserved Rights Transfer and Sale Agreement," written in 1971 by Bob Projansky, a New York lawyer, and Seth Siegelaub, a dealer. This contract asserts that the purchasers of the work agree that 15 percent of the appreciated sale value of the work will be paid to the artist or his estate. Under this agreement, the owner would notify the artist of any proposed exhibition and allow the artist to act as a consultant or to veto the exhibition altogether. The artist would also have all reproduction rights, half of any rental income, and the right to borrow the work for exhibition for two months every five years. If the work is lost in a fire, the artist receives 15 percent of the insurance settlement. So far, this type of contract is rare outside of California.

There is presently a heated debate between those who are for such measures as the Projansky contract or the California resale royalties law and those who oppose them (art dealers, for the most part). Many artists feel that such a measure would give them more financial security as well as more control over the fate of their work. They feel that a collector shouldn't begrudge a small royalty to the person who created the work that is sold for a windfall profit. Those on the other side of the fence argue that artwork "burdened" with a Projansky contract or a royalty requirement will be harder to sell: collectors will want to avoid all the extra bother and expense of selling one of these works. They say a wide acceptance of this type of arrangement will help a few of the better-known artists but inhibit the sales of younger artists' works. In a *New York Times* article on the subject, arts accountant Rubin Gorewitz says that it also works to the buyer's *advantage*, in that an artist who has more of a stake in the future of a work would be more likely to spend time doing restorative work. He also reminds collectors that the percentage paid to the artist could be deducted as a business expense. One disadvantage to both parties is that the true sale price would have to be noted and go on record.

DROIT MORAL

Any artist knows that certain pieces of his or her work are far more than mere products. In fact, they are more like children. While you may not feel this way about everything that you create, it would be nice to know that you have a legal right to assert this connection even after the work has been sold. In France, where such protection exists, it is called *droit moral*—moral right.

Droit moral comprises three separate rights: the right of integrity, the right of paternity and the right of divulgation. The right of integrity provides that works are part of an artist's personality and that changing or dismembering an artist's work may damage not only his professional standing but also his identity and personality.

The right of paternity gives the artist the unwaivable right to assert his or her association with the work. The right of divulgation gives the artist, rather than the person who commissions or buys the work, the sole right to decide whether and when the work is ready to be shown.

Although full droit moral protection doesn't exist in the United States, New York State has enacted an "Artists' Authorship Rights Act," effective January 1, 1984, for works of art by resident New York artists and sold to resident New York collectors when the work is shown in New York. This law extends some moral rights protection to artists. It prevents anyone other than the artist, or someone acting on her behalf, to display or publish an altered or mutilated version of a work under the artist's name. It also gives artists the right to claim or disclaim authorship of a work of art that has been altered without the artist's consent. Artists whose rights under this law have been violated may sue for actual damages and legal costs as well as punitive damages where appropriate.

Similar laws exist in California and Massachusetts and have been proposed in New Jersey and Pennsylvania. However, the laws and the exact protection they offer varies from state to state and usually protect state residents. Artists in other states may be able to secure some moral rights over their works, particularly the right of paternity, by making them part of their sales or consignment contract. The copyright law as well as the right to privacy and laws against defamation may also give some protection.

Senator Edward Kennedy has introduced a federal bill to amend the 1978 copyright law so as to provide moral rights and resale royalties as part of copyright protection. This bill also provides full copyright protection to all artworks even those without copyright notices accompanying them, thus guaranteeing full, no-strings copyright protection for artists. If passed, this broadened copyright protection for creators of artwork should discourage malicious infringers and increase compliance in obtaining permission to use copyrighted material.

CHARITABLE CONTRIBUTIONS
OF ARTWORKS

If an artist gives a work to a charity or a museum, he will only be able to take a charitable deduction for the cost of the raw materials that went into the work. But if anyone else, the artist's estate included, holds onto the work for six months, that person can donate it to a charitable institution and get a deduction for the full market value of the work provided the charity uses it in the course of carrying out its tax-exempt function. This is clearly inequitable towards artists, who deserve tax deductions from the contribution of their own works at least as much as collectors who donate them. The public is hurt by this law as well as the artist. Because of this law Stravinsky decided against bequeathing his papers to an institution in this country when he learned that his donation, valued at about $3.5 million, would bring his heirs no tax break in this country. He left them to Russia instead.

Many of the artists' rights groups across the country have been at work to get this law changed.

FURTHER READING

There are legal problems peculiar to each of the arts which are too specialized for discussion in a general reference book such as this one. I recommend that you purchase, or at least carefully read, one or more of the following:

Adams, Paul. *The Complete Legal Guide for Your Small Business.* John Wiley and Sons, 1982.

"Business Practices in Photography." Published by ASMP (The American Society of Magazine Photographers, 205 Lexington Avenue, New York, NY 10016).

Cavallo, Robert, and Kahan, Stuart. *The Business of Photography.* Outlet, 1981.

Cavallo, Robert, and Kahan, Stuart. *Photography: What's the Law?* Crown, 1976. Mr. Cavallo is the legal counsel for ASMP, now called the Society for Photographers in Communications, and has written a very thorough handbook containing what photographers should know about the law when creating and selling their work.

Crawford, Tad. *The Visual Artists Guide to the New Copyright Law.* Available through the Graphic Artists Guild, 30 East 20th Street, Room 405, New York, NY 10003.

Crawford, Tad. *The Writer's Legal Guide.* Dutton, 1978.

Crawford, Tad. *Legal Guide for the Visual Artist.* Madison Square, 1985. This book, and the others by Mr. Crawford, are full of information which is well explained and presented in such a way as to make sense to those who need it—not just to business school or law school graduates.

Crawford, Tad, and Mellon, Susan. *The Artist-Gallery Partnership: A Practical Guide to Consignment.* American Council on the Arts, 1981.

Davidson, Marion, and Blue, Martha. *Making It Legal: A Law Primer for the Craftmaker, Visual Artist, and Writer.* McGraw-Hill, 1977. This is an excellent guide to the legal problems encountered by people creating, distributing and selling their work.

Hale, William Storm, and Hurst, Walter E. *Music/Record Business and the Law.* Available from Seven Arts Press, Inc., 6605 Hollywood Blvd., Suite 215, Hollywood, CA 90028.

Hurst, Walter E. *The Music Industry Book: Protect Yourself Before You Lose Your Rights and Royalties!* Available from Seven Arts (see above).

Norwick, Kenneth P. Chasen, Simon, Jerry, and Kaufman, Henry R. *The Rights of Authors and Artists.* Bantam Books, 1984. Part of the excellent ACLU series on the rights of various groups such as gays, employees and others. Contains a particularly good section on copyright.

Polking, Kirk, and Meranus, Leonard. *Law and the Writer.* Writers Digest Books, 1985. An excellent compendium of articles by experts on legal problems facing authors. Among them: libel, First Amendment, copyright, subrights.

Shemel, Sidney, and Krasilovsky, M. William. *This Business of Music.* Billboard Books, 1977. This book is considered *the* reference guide to the music industry. I urge every musician to spend the money for his personal copy. Such topics as contracts, record deals, management, songwriter contracts, publishing, copyright, taxation and publicity are all covered in depth.

A *Writer's Guide to Copyright.* Available through Poets and Writers, Inc., 201 West 54th Street, New York, NY 10019.

CHAPTER TWENTY-ONE

PAYING YOUR TAXES

Everyone who earns or somehow amasses money has to file a tax return. There is no way legally to escape paying taxes, but you can avoid paying any more than you have to. If you keep track of exactly how much your business costs you each year, you will be able to recover most of those costs at tax time, as they are excluded from taxable income before you even start to figure your taxes. Nonbusiness expenses as well as employees' business expenses are deducted later on from the total income when figuring the adjusted gross on which you are taxed.

As a freelancer, you are totally responsible for assessing and paying your taxes. If you are an employee part of the time or, in some years, full-time in addition to your freelance work, you will have money withheld from your paycheck, and you will have to square away with the government at the end of the year.

THE WISE AND FOOLISH FREELANCERS

Laura B. and Cameron D., both freelance graphic designers, had the same income—$11,000 last year. Cameron paid $1,447 in federal taxes; Laura paid $996. Neither was incorrect. Laura did not cheat on her return. She simply took the trouble to keep accurate records of her business expenses all year while Cameron crumpled up his receipts with the wrapping paper and thus threw away all his valuable records. For the extra two minutes or so per day that he would have spent in record keeping, he paid $551.

The only point to record keeping is to be able to pay the lowest possible legal tax and have proof acceptable to the Internal Revenue Service showing how you arrived at the amount you pay. For the small expenditure of time and effort that this takes, it seems only masochistic not to give as little as possible of your hard-earned money to the government each year. The government is happy to accept what you pay them; the accountants at the IRS are not going to take a second out to give you a refund for deductions you didn't take. I'm certain that you can think of better ways to spend a couple of hundred dollars each year.

KEEPING RECORDS

WHY IT'S IMPORTANT TO KEEP RECORDS

You must keep detailed records of financial transactions such as money earned, money spent on your business, interest and dividend income, uninsured business losses and certain eligible personal spending such as medical bills and medicines. Your records should consist of such documents as purchase orders or bills, canceled checks, bank statements and receipts. In addition, you need a diary in which to annotate and explain each expenditure.

There are two reasons for this. (1) Keeping records helps you to get an accurate idea of how much money you spend. After a few months of careful record keeping, you may be surprised at how much you actually spend. Supplies and repairs and transportation add up alarmingly if you are scrupulous about recording them. You are very likely to find that your own estimates are substantially lower than the actual total amount of money you disbursed. This helps you, as the costs of your business are deductible from your gross income when calculating the amount of your earnings which is taxable. (2) You also need detailed records to back up your tax calculations if you should have your return examined by the IRS. Your personal testimony alone cannot substantiate a deduction for business-related expenses unless your claim is also supported by records and sometimes by witnesses. Even if you leave your tax preparation to someone else, he can't be of much help unless you have proper documentation.

WHAT ARE ACCEPTABLE RECORDS?

In order to back up your deductions you must keep all receipts for expenses over $25. You must have both an explanation in your diary and the receipt as proof. The diary or the receipt alone will not stand up. The burden is always on you to provide the proper documentation. If the receipts you do keep should show the nature and the amount of the expense, the date it was incurred, and the party to whom payment was made, you do not need the diary. If possible, the receipt should show a letterhead or similar identification. This is required in the case of hotel and restaurant receipts. A canceled check by itself won't stand up as proof of an expenditure. You may need written statements by witnesses in order to back up expenditures for which the only existing proofs are canceled checks. Credit-card receipts, however, are permissible. Write the nature of the expense, why it was incurred, and the date on them before you file them. Most credit-card receipts have spaces on the back of the customer's copy for this information.

It is simplest to keep a diary of your day-to-day expenditures along with as many receipts and canceled checks that correspond to those entries as you can collect. You must have both an entry and a receipt for expenses over $25. Although a canceled check is not, by itself, acceptable as proof of an expenditure, it is still useful evidence when substantiating a claim. It is recommended that you pay all your bills and business-related expenses by check or credit

card. The most convenient system, and one recommended by many accountants, requires an accordion file with one pocket for each type of expense—
e.g., rent, supplies, medical, etc. At the end of the year all you have to do is
tote up the contents of each pocket and enter that amount on the appropriate
line of your tax form.

I keep a separate diary of money received, but you may also note this on
one side of a ledger. Most convenient to use is a large accountants' ledger to
record monies received and disbursed in the same book. You use opposite
pages for each month's receipts and disbursements. Make automatic lines for
monthly expenses such as rent and utilities. You may also want to keep a small
pocket expense diary with you at all times, as it is very easy to forget small
expenditures that you've made in the course of a day. Some of the more flashy
stationery stores sell diaries made expressly for the purpose of recording tax-
deductible expenses. If these make you feel more businesslike, you can buy
them in versions ranging from Naugahyde to grain cowhide stamped in gold.

Whatever form of notebook you choose, the pertinent information you should
always note is amount paid, item purchased, what its purpose was, when and
where it was bought or when and by whom the service was performed. If you
entertain prospective customers, patrons or connections, record who, when,
where, how much and why you entertained them.

HOW LONG TO KEEP YOUR RECORDS

You should keep your diary for at least three years after the year of income to
which it pertains. By law, the IRS has this much time in which to assess
additional taxes. If for some reason you misstate your income by 25 percent
or more, you are liable to face a charge of fraud and the three-year limitation
will not apply. If you don't file any return there is no limit on how long the
government has to hunt you down. So don't leave yourself open to such
charges —you won't sleep well for years.

Records kept for years tend to accumulate into cumbersome piles that take
up a lot of your active space and invite vermin. You want to have them neatly
arranged in case there is ever any question from the IRS or from anyone with
whom you have had financial dealings, and you want them out of your way
and arranged into as little space as possible.

The way to accomplish both of these objectives is to separate your records
into active and inactive files. The present year and the two before it are active
and should be stored in your work area so that you can refer to them as you
may need to do—for instance, when you apply for a loan. The same accordion
file that you used to store your documents during the year they referred to can
be used to store them when they become inactive, or you may prefer to save
money (those files cost between $3 and $7, depending on size) by clipping the
contents of each pocket with a large paper clip and storing them all in a manila
envelope or a cardboard box. The point is that they must be organized so that
you can lay your hands on anything you need without having to take the whole
day to sort it all out. Keep your ledger with the receipts and other documents
for the year, and also keep handy photocopies of the filled-out IRS forms.

(Although loan departments can't force you to show your tax forms, if you have made enough money for the figures to establish you as a good credit risk, showing your tax forms can help you procure a loan.)

The inactive files should go back five more years. You will need these less frequently, so don't store them underfoot. A dry spot in the basement or attic, under your bed in a box, or in the back of the closet is fine. Fancy office supply stores offer a breathtaking array of organizers, but many people find that they do better in handling their business matters if they simply become a bit more obsessive-compulsive with their paperwork. (See in chapter 4 the section entitled Freelancers Tell Their Favorite Organizers.)

OTHER RECORDS

You should also keep records that prove your professional status in case there is ever a question from the IRS as to whether you're a professional or a hobbyist.*
These should include correspondence, reviews, published work and purchase orders or contracts.

WAYS OF SETTING UP YOUR BUSINESS

If you are self-employed, do not run any other profit-making enterprise and are not engaged in a licensed profession, such as medicine, you run what is called a *sole proprietorship*. This means that all your business profits are considered personal income by the IRS. This makes for vastly simplified accounting. If you don't qualify as a sole proprietor (the average reader of this book will) other options are a partnership or various types of corporation such as a professional corporation or a subchapter S corporation.

Incorporation is generally not worth your while unless you make considerable money, are in a licensed profession, run another profit-making business or need protection of your personal assets from liability suits arising from your work. If you think you fall into one of these categories you need the guidance of an accountant.

SETTING UP A SOLE PROPRIETORSHIP

You can run a sole proprietorship under your own name and use your personal bank accounts, or you can think up a company name. If you choose a business name, even if it is no more complicated than your name with the word "Enterprises" tacked on at the end, you need to get hold of Legal Form #201,

---

*It is hard to prove intent, and the IRS is becoming increasingly tough in distinguishing between a self-employed businessman and a hobbyist. Losses from a hobby are *not* deductible; they are considered personal losses. If you show a profit for three or more years out of five, you are considered to be *intending* to make a profit. If there is a question, but you anticipate showing a profit sometime in the next five years, you can delay the assessment of these items. In order to do this, you must complete Forms 5213 and 5214 within three years of the due date for the return of the year in which you began your business. This delay does not mean that your return can't be examined for mistakes in other parts during those years.

"Certificate of Doing Business Under an Assumed Name for Individual." You can generally get blank legal forms at large stationery stores. County clerks also have them. This form authorizes you to bank under your business name.

You must also contact your closest IRS office and get a federal identification number. If you're running your business under your own name, you use your personal social security number when you file.

CLASSIFYING YOUR INCOME

Most freelancers, be they writers, performers or visual artists, actually fall into three separate tax categories (though these categories are linked for fiscal purposes). Here is a description of each category and how to classify your different sorts of income:

1. *Self-employed professional or sole proprietor.* You make or intend to make a profit as a result of the practicing, teaching or selling of your work. Usually your clients will not withhold taxes from this type of earnings: it is your responsibility as a self-employed professional to determine your liability.
2. *Employee.* You receive a regular (or occasional) paycheck for your services from an employer. Your employer withholds money for federal, state and city taxes as well as FICA or Social Security.
3. *Private citizen.* We are all "private citizens" in this respect. As private citizens we have income and expenditures which are not work-related—such as medical expenses, dividends and alimony payments. It makes no difference whether you work freelance or as an employee when you are itemizing your nonbusiness deductions.

You may consider yourself all three if, for instance, you receive income from a studio where you are employed as a graphic designer, you run your own freelance book designing business from a spare room in your house and you receive interest or dividends as unearned income. The balance of these three categories may vary from year to year in your life. Perhaps you may decide to work only freelance in one year, but the next year you need some cash and work as an employee three days a week. In that case you would file as both a self-employed business person and as an employee. In addition, nearly everyone has some nonbusiness income such as bank interest or personal debts which are paid off.

The rules differ for taxation of the three categories. You or your tax preparer will be filling out different forms when accounting for the different types of income and expenses, so do be sure to classify accurately your expenses and income received as an employee, a sole proprietor or a private citizen. Here are the forms you will be filling out for each category:

Employee

Form 1040:	shows wages, tips and other employee compensation such as moving expenses or free lodging.

Form 2106:   shows your unreimbursed employee expenses.
Schedule A: see below.

Sole Proprietor

Form 1040:   see above.
Schedule E: shows passive royalty and residual income (writers, actors and musicians).
Schedule C: shows your business profits and expenses.
Schedule SE: is for the purpose of computing your self-employment tax. It takes the place of employee withholding for Social Security.
Schedule A: see below.

Private Citizen

Form 1040:   indicates unearned income such as dividends and interest if under $400.
Schedule B, —Part I: indicates interest and dividend income in excess of $400.
Schedule A: shows your itemized deductions, should it be worth your while to itemize.

As a freelancer, you actually have some tax advantages over those who work for others. The federal government gives you a better break for your pains than insurance or credit institutions. Unlike employees, who must either take the standard deduction or itemize work-related and personal expenses, you may itemize and deduct business expenses and still take the standard deduction instead of itemizing nonbusiness expenses. The standard deduction is excluded from your income. An employee does not have this privilege and thus must either take the standard deduction alone or itemize most work-related expenses and personal expenses together—which often means that he must pay more tax than he would have to do if he could take the standard deduction for personal expenses *and* itemize his business expenses as a freelancer may.

AM I AN EMPLOYEE OR AN INDEPENDENT CONTRACTOR?

It is important (because of employee withholding taxes) for you to know when you are considered an employee even though you may also work freelance. Generally, independent contractors don't have taxes withheld. Employees always do.

A *writer* is not an employee of a publisher, but a staff writer or editor on a magazine or paper is an employee. If you write a weekly column in a paper, you are not necessarily a staff writer.

Minor *actors* are usually employees of stage and film companies. A "star" like Dustin Hoffman is usually an independent contractor.

Musicians are treated as employees of a band leader if he pays them. If they split the fee amongst the band members, they are independent contractors. If single musicians are paid on a per job basis, they are independent contractors.

Artists or *photographers* are considered employees of the studios which supply their materials and supervise their work. Those who work on a per job basis are independent contractors.

BUSINESS DEDUCTIONS ALLOWED
SOLE PROPRIETORS

SCHEDULE C DEDUCTIONS

All of the amounts on the records and receipts that you keep pertaining to your business income are added up and recorded on Schedule C. You must file a separate Schedule C along with your 1040 if you are (1) the sole proprietor of a trade or business, or (2) a professional in your own practice or an independent contractor.

Most freelancers fall into one or both of these categories unless they have incorporated their business.

The deductions you list on Schedule C are subtracted from your business income when determining your taxable business income. They represent the "ordinary and necessary" expenses incurred in producing your income. Here is a partial list of allowable deductions for business expenses:*

Accompanist	Makeup
Accountant	Moving expenses for business premises
Agent fees	
Appearance clothes	Music scores
Auto	Newspapers
Auto rental	Periodicals
Ballet shoes	Piano tuning
Books	Parking and garage
Cabs and fares	Photos and photostats
Costumes	Postage
Dance coaching	Printing
Depreciation of equipment	Professional gifts
Drama coaching	Publicity
Professional dues	Records
Entertainment	Sanitation and maintenance of home office or studio
Film	
Hairdos	Salaries of assistants
Insurance premiums	Small equipment
Leotards	Stationery
Luggage	Subscriptions
Maintenance of clothing	Supplies

*At the time this book went to press, it was unclear whether the uniform capitalization rules of the 1986 Tax Reform Act were going to be extended to writers and others engaged in the production of "tangible personal property" such as films, videos and sound recordings. Most opinion held that artists would be exempted. If they are not, you will only be able to deduct expenses incurred in the creation of works in years when those works produced imcome. Expenses incurred in producing a work would not be deductible unless and until the project made money. Check with an accountant or tax preparer regarding this grossly unfair provision.

Telephone answering service	Travel
Tickets to lectures	Utilities
Tickets to concerts	Vocal coaching
Tolls	Voice lessons

Remember to obtain receipts for all such expenses over $25 and to make daily diary entries. Don't wait a few days and lump all the small ones together: eventually they will exceed $25 and you won't have a receipt.

YOUR OFFICE OR STUDIO

Many artists who work at home don't realize that the expenses of a home office are deductible. However, you must be able to prove (with photos if necessary) that you use your office exclusively as an office and on a regular basis. A corner of your living room will certainly *not* qualify. The rules change on this occasionally, as the IRS is becoming stricter about such deductions. The "Revenuers" do mean business, and it is best not to stretch these rules.

Although performers employed by a company or orchestra are considered employees and are thus not usually allowed to deduct home practice space costs, if you can prove, if questioned by the IRS, that it is a necessary business expense, you may be able to.

An appeals court overturned an IRS ruling that a musician employed by an orchestra couldn't deduct his home studio costs. The appeals court decided that since the orchestra didn't provide solo practice space to its musicians, this musician was entitled to deduct the cost of his home studio, since solo practice was, for him, a necessary business expense and not merely a personal convenience.

If you own your home you may write off mortgage interest, real estate taxes and depreciation. If you rent, you can deduct part of your rental payment. In either case, you can deduct for utilities and office cleaning. However, your deduction is limited to the percentage of the total space that represents your work area. For instance, if you live in a four-room apartment and use one room as an office, you may deduct only one-fourth of your rent, light, heat and any other related expenses. If you live in a loft, calculate the ratio of square feet of work space to your total area to find out what portion of the costs you can deduct.

Under the Tax Reform Act, your home office deductions can't exceed your gross income minus all your other business expenses. So, if you made $10,000 last year and had $2,000 worth of business expenses, such as materials and equipment, this figure is $8,000. Your home office deductions cannot exceed $8,000. This is so that you can not use home office deductions to produce a business loss. If somehow your office deductions do exceed the allowable limit, you may carry forward into other years any leftover home office deductions that you can't claim this year.

TELEPHONES

Get a separate business telephone if at all possible. This way you can deduct the entire cost at the end of the year. Otherwise, keep track of long distance calls that you make for business, and why, when and to whom they were made. You may also allocate whatever part of your monthly service charge and any other charges that represent business use.

COSTS OF MATERIALS

All materials (dance shoes, canvas, paints, paper, typewriter ribbons, musical instruments, film, etc.) necessary for you to perform or produce your work are deductible. You must apportion your deduction if you use the materials for both work and your own pleasure. For example, an actor would not be permitted to deduct the entire cost of his daily newspapers unless he read only the theater columns and didn't read the news or sports page. *Backstage* or *Variety* would of course be entirely deductible, because the actor can argue that he reads them only for professional purposes.

Clothes often cannot be deducted as ordinary and necessary business expenses. Deductions have been denied on the grounds that even though the clothing was used for business purposes (the sculptor's dress for lunching with potential patrons, the writer's single suit for a television appearance) it was later adaptable for general usage.

Uniforms, clothes, wigs and makeup which are worn only while at work or for the duration of a performance are all deductible, as are their cleaning and maintenance. Any items with useful lives of more than one year, such as cameras, typewriters, desks, etc., are "depreciated" over several years. Rather than deducting the full cost in the year you bought the item, you deduct a small part of it and spread the deduction over several years—the useful life of the item. Be sure to keep the bills for these items.

Resale License. If you are a painter, photographer, sculptor or craftsperson who uses raw materials in the creation of objects for sale, you can get a resale license so that you don't have to pay sales tax on the raw materials. You are required, however, to charge a sales tax to your customers. To get a resale license you usually apply to the State Sales Tax Bureau or the State Board of Equalization in some states for a Certificate of Authority. Your processed application will be returned to you with your resale number stamped on it.

MEALS AND ENTERTAINMENT

When you take clients or other work-related people out to a meal or a performance or some other form of entertainment, you may deduct 80 percent of the total amount you spent (tips and tax as well as food and drink or tickets). However, the deduction is only allowable if you incurred the expense directly because of your business. If the meal is billed to your client and reimbursed, it is 100 percent deductible. You must keep a good record of where you went, whom you took, how much you spent, the purpose of your meeting and what was discussed. Furthermore, you must discuss business directly before or after or during the meal or entertainment unless you happen to be on a work-related trip away from home. In this case, you don't have to talk about business with your companions, but you can deduct only the cost of your meal unless you do. In any case, you can deduct 100 percent of any transportation you take to these meetings.

TRAVEL EXPENSES

As long as you can prove that you had to travel in order to conduct business or work on a project, travel expenses can add up and be very significant deductions. You must follow the rules and keep good records. You can save yourself a lot of money if you just take the time to keep adequate records of where, when and why you went as well as saving canceled checks, credit card slips, meal and lodging receipts and tickets. In addition, you must keep a diary of these expenses.

When you must travel for your work, you may deduct the ordinary and necessary expenses on all working days. While you may deduct 100 percent of your transportation and lodging, your meals are still subject to the 80 percent maximum deduction that you can take at home. If, however, your meal costs are included, pension-style, with your lodging, then you may deduct the total.

If you are a musician in a band or a member of an acting or dance company, you are considered an employee of the group. (See page 322)

AUTO EXPENSES

You may either deduct the actual operating expenses of your car for business purposes (gas, oil, insurance, repairs, parking, tolls) or deduct a flat IRS allowance based on your annual business mileage. As of the writing of this edition, you are allowed 22.5¢ per mile for the first 15,000 miles of business travel each year* and 11¢ per mile after that.

If you use the IRS business allowance, remember that it includes depreciation, so don't deduct this twice. However, you may deduct tolls and parking in addition to the flat allowance. If your car is old or has poor gas mileage you might wish to deduct your actual operating costs, otherwise the IRS allowance is generous and far more convenient. If you deduct actual expenses you must also deduct for depreciation of the car which you should do with the help of a professional tax preparer.

You may deduct 12¢ per mile for any driving you do for charities and 9¢ for drives to medical appointments.

DEPRECIATION

Under the new tax law, the calculation of depreciation on different types of equipment and other assets is complicated to say the least. Yet depreciation deductions can actually be quite significant if you own expensive business equipment or vehicles. My advice is to hire a tax preparer if you have many depreciable assets, especially if you have just bought them. Despite the cost of preparing the return you'll probably still come out ahead. If, on the other hand, all you have is an auto, take the flat 22.5¢ per mile allowance which includes depreciation.

---

*If you use your car for both personal and business purposes, you must keep a very strict log showing what proportion of your total mileage is for business. Only this percentage of your total expenses may be claimed.

LOCAL TRANSPORTATION

As a self-employed professional, you may deduct costs necessary to your work: automobile and public transportation costs to and from meetings, rehearsals, lessons, errands pertaining to work. You may not deduct the cost of *commuting* from your home to your principal place of work (e.g., your studio downtown), but you may deduct the cost of going from your place of work to any other appointments during the day. If your principal place of work is in your home, you may deduct the cost of getting to your first business appointment of the day as well as all other business-related transportation costs during the day.

You may also deduct transportation costs that you incur while looking for work in your field, whether or not you are successful in your quest..

MOVING EXPENSES

A freelancer may deduct the cost of moving. The cost of moving business assets is 100 percent deductible in any case. To deduct the costs of moving personal assets in a work-related move, you must move at least thirty-five miles away and you must work at least seventy-eight weeks of the two years following the move. Deductible expenses include those for movers, gasoline, packing, meals eaten out while moving, and shipping. You may take the deductions even before you satisfy the seventy-eight-week rule, but if you move again before the seventy-eight weeks are up, you will have to square with the IRS the next year.

BUSINESS PROPERTY TAXES

These taxes are deductible by the self-employed person, even if he doesn't itemize.

PREMIUMS

Insurance premiums covering business property or activities are deductible.

LEGAL AND PROFESSIONAL FEES

These are deductible as long as they were incurred because of your business. The cost of an accountant to prepare your business tax returns is deductible. The preparation of your personal tax return can only be deducted if you itemize your nonbusiness deductions. Legal fees incurred for the protection of capital are deductible. The legal costs of slander, obscenity and paternity suits are not deductible unless they affect your ability to earn a living or arise from your work.

INTEREST CHARGES

Under the new tax law, you may still deduct all of the interest charges on your business loans and on first and second home mortgages with some limitations, but interest on consumer loans is being phased out. In 1988 you may deduct only 40 percent of your credit card, personal bank loan and store charge interest. In 1990 this drops to 10 percent and after that the deduction disappears altogether.

There is a special exception for homeowners which allows them to deduct the interest charges on qualified home mortgages equal to the purchase price of their house, plus the cost of any improvements they made, plus qualified medical and educational expenses.

TRAINING

You are usually allowed to deduct the cost of classes and clinics that are necessary for the maintenance and improvement of your skills. Dancers and other performers who must keep in shape may deduct gym fees and massages. Volunteer Lawyers for the Arts* says that the IRS may try to disallow this deduction on the ground that it is an educational expense instead of the maintenance of your skills at performance level. They urge you to fight that one.

RESEARCH EXPENSES

Research expenses are fully deductible as long as they are necessary for the production of work that you expect to earn money on. Examples of permissible expenses would be all travel and entertainment expenses connected with interviewing subjects or using special collections, photocopying in the library, and the cost of magazines and other research materials you might need.

COMMISSIONS AND AGENCY FEES

All commissions paid to reps and managers or galleries are fully tax-deductible.

SALARIES AND TIPS TO STAFF

These are all deductible for you as a freelancer. If you pay someone, such as an assistant or a typist, more than $600 a year, you must file a 1099 Form, but if you regularly pay salaries you must check with an accountant about setting yourself up as an employer and deducting necessary taxes from your payments to your employees. You must also cover them with workers compensation and state disability insurance.

HEALTH INSURANCE

The new tax law has provided one nice, although temporary, benefit to self-employed folk who aren't eligible under any employee medical plan including that of their spouse. Through the 1990 tax year, you can deduct directly from your gross income 25 percent of the cost of health insurance premiums you paid for yourself and your family. You can subtract the other 75 percent as a medical cost if you itemize rather than take the standard deduction.

This deduction can't be used to increase your business losses—it can only be deducted from your profit. For instance, if in 1989 you report a $2,000 loss from your graphics business and you spent $1,000 on health insurance premiums, you can't add $250 (25 percent of the cost of the premiums) to your $2,000 business loss for that year. If instead you showed a $19,000 profit, you can subtract the $250, and your tax liability will be calculated only on $18,750.

*For information about this group, see the section How to Find a Lawyer in chapter 20.

Also you must add the premium cost back to your net income when you calculate your self-employment tax.

THE SELF-EMPLOYMENT TAX

Schedule SE is used to compute your self-employment Social Security tax, since you do not have an employer to withhold this money from your salary.

If your net self-employment income is $400 or more after you have taken all your business deductions, you must file Schedule SE. Income that is not the result of actual labor in which you were directly involved (such as residuals or royalties, or other passive income) is not subject to the SE tax. For 1987 there was a ceiling of $43,800 above which self-employment income was not subject to the SE tax.

Since the SE tax does not apply to earnings below $400, if your income is this much or less from self-employment, you won't have to pay any Social Security tax, but you should file anyway as you can claim earned income credit.

If you earn both wages and self-employment income, only that part of your self-employment income which will bring your total from both sources up to the maximum subject to Social Security tax will be subject to self-employment tax.

EMPLOYEE BUSINESS EXPENSE DEDUCTIONS: A PERFORMER'S BREAK

Although unreimbursed employee expense deductions are sharply limited under tax reform, because they can generally only be taken if you itemize, one loophole has been created to aid performers. If you are a qualified performer who makes $16,000 or less per year, works for at least two companies or groups within the tax year and makes at least 10 percent of your income as a performer, you may deduct the costs of going to auditions, looking for work, agents' fees, professional dues and other business-related expenses even if you don't itemize.

NONBUSINESS DEDUCTIONS WHICH ARE ALLOWED ONLY IF YOU ITEMIZE

The following deductions can be taken only if you itemize. Except for qualifying deductions for medical costs, charitable contributions, interest and casualty losses, miscellaneous itemizable expenses are only deductible to the extent that they exceed 2 percent of your adjusted gross income and they have to exceed the standard deduction. If you don't have many itemizable deductions you are generally better off using the standard deduction.

MEDICAL AND DENTAL EXPENSES

You are allowed to deduct that portion of your medical and dental expenses which exceeds 7.5 percent of your adjusted gross income as entered by you on Form 1040. You may also deduct the cost of transportation to and from the doctor's office. If you drive, the current basis is 9¢ per mile.

HEALTH INSURANCE PREMIUMS

The 75 percent remaining after your 25 percent deduction (see page 328) is deductible to the extent that it exceeds 7.5 percent of your adjusted gross income.

HOME MORTGAGES

Interest on mortgages for your first and second homes is generally fully deductible.

INTERERST ON PERSONAL LOANS, CREDIT CARDS AND CHARGE ACCOUNTS

Interest on personal credit of all types ranging from credit cards to personal loans used to be fully deductible, encouraging people to buy lots on credit. This deduction is being phased out. In the tax year 1988, 40 percent of all your personal interest will be deductible, 20 percent in 1989, 10 percent in 1990 and none thereafter.

CHARITABLE CONTRIBUTIONS

You may deduct cash contributions to tax-exempt organizations. You may deduct your costs (taxis or supplies) as a volunteer, but not the estimated value of your time and services. You may also take a deduction of the fair market value of clothes and other personal property that you donate to a tax-exempt organization. If you donate a work of art which you have created, your deduction may not exceed the cost of producing the work and the recipient of the art has to use it as part of the organization's tax-exempt work. However, if anyone but the artist donates the work, he should check with an accountant to determine tax liability.

CASUALTY OR THEFT LOSSES

Itemizers may deduct personal losses that exceed insurance reimbursement. First subtract $100 from the amount of uninsured loss. Whatever part of this figure exeeds (for 1986) 10 percent of your adjusted gross income is deductible. If the stolen items were business property, the 10 percent limit doesn't apply.

PERSONAL ACCOUNTING AND
TAX PREPARATION FEES

The cost of hiring a tax preparer for your personal return is deductible if you itemize. The costs of preparing a will and investment advice for the protection of capital are deductible by itemizers.

HOW TO HANDLE UNEARNED INCOME

GRANTS, PRIZES AND FELLOWSHIPS

If you win a prize or award in recognition of past accomplishments, did not apply for it and do not have to perform any future services as a condition of receiving it, it is tax-free only if you transfer it *directly* to a governmental agency or tax-exempt organization. Scholarships and fellowships may be excluded from gross income only if you are a candidate for a degree at an educational institution. You can exclude from income only the amount you use for tuition and course-related costs. Scholarships or grants to nondegree candidates are tax-free up to $300 per month. You may claim this $300 exemption for thirty-six months during your lifetime. If you receive a grant or award, you should check with the grantor to determine the tax status of your money.

INTEREST

Interest is taxable unless it derives from state or municipal bonds (in which case it may still be subject to state income tax). Those who have paid you interest over the year will send you forms at the end of the year showing what you have earned.

ROYALTIES

Royalties from books, plays, etc., are taxable as self-employment income.

STATE AND LOCAL TAX REFUNDS

You may deduct state and local taxes from your federal taxes; but if you get a refund later, you must declare it as income the next year if you itemized in the prior year.

DEBT CANCELLATION

A cancellation of a debt is counted as income.

ALIMONY

Alimony received is taxable. Child support is not.

UNEMPLOYMENT

Unemployment income is taxable if your total income from unemployment, interest, dividends and wages comes to more than $20,000 for singles, or $25,000 for married couples filing jointly. If you are married and living with your spouse but file separately, all your unemployment may be taxed.

WHAT INCOME IS NOT TAXABLE?

Income from these sources is not taxable:

Life insurance proceeds
Interest from municipal bonds
Social Security payments, unless your income exceeds certain limits
Worker's compensation
Disability benefits, with some exceptions
Child support
Certain grants and prizes

Keep track of these nontaxable sources of income, because they may be added to your adjusted gross income on Form 1040 when computing your sales tax deduction from the tables on Schedule A.

OTHER TAX OBLIGATIONS

STATE AND LOCAL TAXES

Many people, once they have gotten over the hump of paying their federal taxes, feel that they can ignore the smaller sums involved in state and local taxes. This is a serious mistake. Willfully not paying state and local taxes can be almost as troublesome to you as ignoring your federal taxes.

Every state is different with regard to income taxes. Some states, (e.g. Connecticut) have no income tax at all though these states are exceptions. In some states, a person doing business must register with the Bureau of Revenue and file monthly reports on earnings.

TAX CREDITS

Tax credits are available under special circumstances for those with low incomes or dependent children. You can be self-employed or an employee and still qualify for the following tax credits. The amounts are to be subtracted directly from your taxes.

EARNED INCOME CREDITS

You are eligible for earned income credit if:

1. You paid more than half the cost of a home where you lived with your child who is either under nineteen, disabled, or a full-time student. As with all tax matters, keep good records in order to establish your child's status.
2. Your adjusted gross income is below a certain level.

HOUSEHOLD AND DEPENDENT CARE

Freelancers and employees may claim work-related dependent and household-care credits if they paid more than half the cost of a home in which they cared for a dependent under fifteen or a disabled person. In calculating the percentage of the cost you paid, you may include all food and other expenses of your dependent, as well as ordinary domestic services in the home which allow you to leave for work, plus day-care, nursery-school or day-camp costs and baby-sitters' fees.

You must have *earned* income in order to be eligible for this credit; and if you are married both spouses must work at least part-time unless one is a full-time student.

HOW TO PROCEED AT TAX TIME

If your tax situation is complicated by capital gains, large figures or money earned abroad, I suggest that you use all of the information in this chapter as a guideline, but that you consult an accountant. Whoever prepares your final return can do a much better job for you, whatever your income level, if you do a good job of bookkeeping throughout the year. As I have stressed repeatedly, you must keep receipts and make entries in some form of ledger. If you don't, you are simply wasting your hard-earned money.

FINDING AN ACCOUNTANT

There are many accountants who specialize in different branches of the arts. Naturally, if you can find one of these, it will be to your benefit, since he may know of various tricks not familiar to you or even to most accountants who do not specialize as he does. To find these accountants, look in the trade papers or magazines relating to your field. A call to your local arts council or the closest Volunteer Lawyers for the Arts (see page 308 might also help, as might a call to any professional guilds or associations to which you belong.

For straightforward tax returns with no major arts-related calculations you don't need an arts accountant. Most other accountants will charge you between $50 and $500, and their help is usually well worth the price. Around tax time many tax preparers hang out shingles. Not all of them are equally good. Stick to large, reputable firms such as H & R Block. Also, some banks provide tax preparation for a nominal charge.

DOING YOUR OWN TAXES

For small or straightforward income with no capital gains or tax shelter plans, you shouldn't feel that doing your own taxes is an insurmountable difficulty.

All you have to do is start with Schedule C, read the instructions carefully and then provide the information you are asked. Some people are needlessly put off by all those blank lines. Don't be. But don't, on the other hand, feel that you're a fool because you only make $7,000 per year and can't even calculate your own tax liability on that. Even if you get an accountant, you should have kept all your receipts and diaries meticulously all year. Otherwise, no one will be able to help you sort it all out.

WHAT IF YOU CAN'T AFFORD TO PAY YOUR TAXES BY APRIL 15?

Cash flow is often a problem for even freelancers with a good income and plenty of work. So what do you do if you can't afford to pay your taxes on April 15? There are actually a couple of options:

1. You can work out a payment plan with the IRS. To do this, file your 1040 form anyway. (If you don't, you will be assessed a large penalty for filing late.) The IRS will bill you for your unpaid tax, the delayed payment penalty (½ percent of the unpaid balance per month that it's overdue) plus, currently, 9 percent interest. Despite these charges, it's cheaper, in effect, to borrow the money from the IRS than from a bank at commercial interest rates. However, do bear in mind that the IRS doesn't care for this and may pay more attention to your future returns.

   Once you have received your bill, you should *immediately* contact the IRS, preferably by letter with a photocopy of the IRS notice enclosed, to negotiate a monthly payment plan that you can meet.

2. Leave the country. Lots of people aren't aware that you can get an automatic two-month extension to file and pay your taxes, although you will have to pay interest as of April 15. If you are a married couple, the law states that only one of you need be out of the country to qualify for the extension. By the way, if you're looking for a nearby foreign country, skip Puerto Rico. The IRS doesn't consider it outside the United States.

   When you get back from your vacation and file your return, attach a statement on your return explaining that you were away, where you went, and be prepared to prove it.

3. File your return on time even if you can't pay what you owe and file Form 1127 for an extension of the time to pay up. You will have to show that you don't have any money beyond what you need to exist and can't sell anything or get a loan with which to pay the IRS. If you have a house or some other important asset that you could sell, you have to show that you would be selling it at a sacrifice. You must also send a complete list of your assets and liabilities as well as records of all your monthly income and disbursements for the three months before your taxes were due.

   If the IRS decides to give you an extension, it will usually be for six months. Even so, you are still assessed interest during the period of the extension.

4. Borrow the money from a bank or private sources.

HOW YOUR RETURN IS EXAMINED

When your return is received it is first checked out for the accuracy of your computations. If you have made a mistake in your arithmetic you will receive either a bill or a refund.

Some returns are screened more thoroughly to determine such things as:

1. Whether you have claimed more than the IRS allows as a mileage rate for auto expenses.
2. Whether you have claimed medical expenses without attending to the 7.5 percent adjusted gross income limit on deductions.
3. Whether you have claimed questionable home office or travel or entertainment expenses.

You are notified by letter if you are going to be audited. In some cases only part of your return, e.g., your medical expenses, is considered in the audit. The IRS has three years in which to assess additional taxes. If you filed no return there is no limit on when they may get you.

If your return isn't complicated and does not involve a lot of tax, you may want to handle an audit yourself. An audit is merely an examination—not a bust. The examination of your documents may take place at an IRS office or at your home or office if you have a great deal of supporting records.

If, after the examination, you agree to the agent's assessment of additional taxes, you sign Form 870. If you disagree, you may appeal your case, but it is wise in this case to get an experienced accountant.

Artists are notorious among IRS auditors for being badly organized and unable to support their deductions. This is the absolute key: you will be fine as long as all your deductions are supported with the proper receipts and daily records. Now that you know what a difference records can mean, do yourself a favor (which could amount to a couple of thousand dollars' worth) and keep clear, detailed records.

Sometimes rules about what you may deduct, and the supporting records necessary, as well as cash allowances (e.g., for auto use) change. It's never a bad idea to check this sort of thing out in an up-to-date edition of one of the books listed on page 336.

If you really don't feel up to doing your return yourself, try at least to be organized and sort your records into those pertaining to freelance income, to other earned income and to unearned income. This step will make your tax preparer's job a little easier.

ESTIMATED TAX DECLARATIONS

Although we think of April 15 as the day we pay taxes, in fact taxes are paid on an as-you-go basis. This is done for employees through withholding taxes from wages, and for the self-employed through estimated tax returns on form 1040-ES.

You must file a 1040-ES if you expect to owe more than $500 in tax.

You do not have to file the 1040-ES if your tax liability is less then $500.

Form 1040-ES has four declaration vouchers attached. These are due on April 15, June 15, September 15 and January 15. If you are self-employed, don't forget to include the self-employment tax in your declaration.

You may figure your estimated taxes by basing your calculations on last year's total taxes. Even if this figure doesn't turn out to be near your tax liability for the present year, you will not be subject to penalty. Normally, if you have not paid 90 percent of the previous year's taxes by January 15, you are subject to a penalty.

If you pay 100 percent of the previous year's tax liability, you won't be penalized no matter how much tax you owe.

Even though you file estimated taxes quarterly for a given year, you must still file a Form 1040 on or before April 15. At that time you compute the difference between what you have already paid and your total tax liability. If you overpaid, you will be mailed a refund; or you may have the overpayment credited to next year's taxes.

AMENDMENTS

If after figuring your taxes and mailing the check you find that you have deductions that you didn't take, you can file an amendment for up to three years. For instance, if in 1989 you find that you didn't include all your business deductions, you can file an amended Schedule C for any year back to 1986. This is done by filing Form 1040X plus an amended Schedule C. This can also be done with itemized, nonbusiness deductions on Schedule A.

FURTHER READING

Here are several publications which you may find useful if you wish to read about tax rules in more detail:

Holzman, Robert S. *Take It Off!* Harper & Row, 1982.

IRS publications:
  "Preparing Your Individual Tax Return"
  "Tax Guide For Small Businesses"

Frankel, Sandor and Fink, Robert S. *How to Defend Yourself Against the IRS*. Fireside/Simon & Schuster, 1987. This book is useful and highly entertaining. It tells, via well-written anecdotes, how you can and cannot slip past the IRS and gives detailed information on how your return is examined and on audits.

Kamaroff, Bernard. *Small Time Operator: How to Start Your Own Small Business, Keep Your Books, Pay Your Taxes and Stay Out of Trouble.* This handbook is written by a CPA and includes ledgers and worksheets. It is available from Bell Springs Publishing, P.O. Box 640, Laytonville, CA 95454.

Lasser, J. K. *Your Income Tax.* Prentice-Hall (annual).

Volunteer Lawyers for the Arts. *Fear of Filing* available from Volunteer Lawyers for the Arts, 1285 Avenue of the America, New York, NY 10019.

APPENDIX

ALL ARTISTS

ALLIANCE OF INFORMATION AND REFERRAL SERVICES
1100 W. 42nd St.
Indianapolis, IN 46208
A national office for state and local information referral services.

AMERICAN COUNCIL FOR THE ARTS (ACA)
1285 Avenue of the Americas
New York, NY 10019
(212) 245–4510
ACA is an advocacy group for the arts which provides information on legislation pertaining to the arts and advises art administrators, patrons, educators, elected officials and the general public. ACA also provides information on legal and tax matters to individual artists. ACA's library in New York has a large collection of books, periodicals and other materials relating to arts research, policy and advocacy. In addition, ACA publishes numerous useful books of interest to individual artists, fund-raisers and arts educators. Call them for their most recent catalogue.

AMERICAN HOME BUSINESS ASSOCIATION
60 Arch Street
Greenwich, CT 06830
(800) 441–2929
This group offers services and benefits to individuals who operate home businesses. These include tax information, discounts on office equipment, car rentals and travel, as well as low-cost health insurance and a newsletter and special reports.

THE ASSOCIATION OF FREELANCE PROFESSIONALS
P.O. Box 42809
Houston, TX 77242

THE ARTISTS FOUNDATION
10 Park Plaza
Boston, MA 02116
(617) 227–ARTS

CENTER FOR ARTS INFORMATION (CAI)
1285 Avenue of the Americas
New York, NY 10019
(212) 977-2544
CAI is a national information clearinghouse and library that provides information on individual professional development, arts organizational management and economic and other trends in the arts. CAI has a research and reference library which comprises over 6,500 reference books, directories and pamphlets as well as extensive files on arts service organizations and funding agencies nationwide. Of particular use to the individual artist are the subject files on topics of interest to artists such as accounting, taxes and housing. Use of the library is by appointment only. CAI also publishes books, pamphlets and newsletters of interest to artists.

CONSUMER INFORMATION CENTER
Department TD
Pueblo, CO 81009
The U.S. government puts out a lot of useful consumer information on topics ranging from financial and career planning to diet, housing and child care. I

find it useful to have their Consumer Information Catalog *close at hand.*

FOUNDATION FOR THE COMMUNITY OF ARTISTS (FCA)
280 Broadway
New York, NY 10017
(212) 227–3770
FCA is an advocacy and research group. It offers the largest nonunion health plan in the country along with disability insurance and a buying service. FCA also offers counseling and job placement through Artwork, a federally funded employment agency. Artists Hotline is a twenty-four hour information number: (212) 285–2121. FCA has assumed a major role in artists' rights and artists' housing. The Artists Housing Hotline number is (212) 285–2133. FCA also publishes information on art hazards as well as one of the most informative newsletters, Art and Artists.

MATERIALS FOR THE ARTS
Department of Cultural Affairs
2 Columbus Circle
New York, NY 10019
(212) 974–1150
Materials for the Arts is a clearinghouse for resources available to artists. Donors ranging from businesses with a surplus of office furniture to individuals wishing to get rid of a typewriter or a camera can hook up with needy individuals and groups. Since its inception, the service has generated more than $250,000 in donations. As of late 1981, the only such program was in New York City, but other cities have expressed interest in starting similar programs. Check with your local Department of Cultural Affairs.

THE MEDIA DISTRIBUTION CO-OP
1745 Louisiana Street
Lawrence, KS 66044
(913) 842–3176
This outfit's services are available to artists, filmmakers, journalists, writers, musicians and photographers. They have a research department, publicity services, and put out various publications of interest.

OPPORTUNITY RESOURCES FOR THE ARTS
1457 Broadway
New York, NY 10036
(212) 575–1688

Opportunity Resources is a placement center for individuals looking for jobs in their artistic field. OR also refers personnel to nonprofit professional arts organizations for administrative jobs. OR provides advice on career development and résumé writing.

THE PRINT CENTER
Box 1050
Brooklyn, NY 11202
(212) TR5–4482
The Print Center offers printing services well below the cost of typical commercial operations to nonprofit arts organizations in the eastern U.S.

PUBLISHING CENTER FOR CULTURAL RESOURCES
625 Broadway
New York, NY 10012
(212) 260–2010
The Publishing Center provides editing and production assistance to nonprofit educational and cultural groups. Book distribution and short-term loans for publishing projects are also provided.

SCORE
(Service Corps of Retired Executives)
26 Federal Plaza
New York, NY 10278
(212) 264–4507
SCORE is a federal project which matches up retired executives with small business operators who need free advice. There are over 400 SCORE chapters throughout the country.

SUPPORT SERVICES ALLIANCE INC.
251 Main Street, P.O. Box 130
Schoharie, NY 12157
(518) 295–7966
(800) 322–3920 (in NY State);
(800) 892–8925 (outside NY)

Mid-West Office
612 Fondulac Drive
E. Peoria, IL 61611
(309) 699–2453
A service organization founded with help from the Rockefeller Foundation to provide group contracts and services to self-employed people. This group offers excellent deals on insurance and travel, low-cost loans through its credit union, a buying service, a credit reporting and collection service and workshops and other services of real interest.

READING FOR ALL ARTISTS

See also books listed at the end of each chapter as well as books and other materials offered by various branches of Volunteer Lawyers for the Arts, page 305–311.

Directory of Artists' Organizations. National Association of Artists' Organizations, Suite 607, 930 7th Street, NW, Washington, DC 20004. A comprehensive listing of nonprofits that sponsor and present artworks or provide services to artists in all disciplines.

Puer Aeternus, A Psychological Study of the Adult Struggle with the Paradise of Childhood. Marie-Louise Von Franz. Sigo Press, Santa Monica, CA, 1981. I think all artists should read this psychoanalytic exploration of the struggle to grow up fully by a student of Jung.

VISUAL ARTISTS

THE ART INFORMATION CENTER
280 Broadway
New York, NY 10007
(212) 227–0282
The Art Information Center acts as a reference point for visual artists looking for dealers, buyers looking for artworks and dealers looking for new artists. The Center maintains an "Unaffiliated Artists File" which contains slides and résumés of young artists seeking galleries and the "Affiliated Artists File" to help you locate the work of living artists. Anyone may request information from the center by sending a stamped, self-addressed envelope. The Center will also look at an artist's slides and refer them to appropriate galleries.

ARTISTS EQUITY ASSOCIATION
116 F Street NW
Washington, DC 20004
(202) 628–9633
AEA is a national advocacy and educational group for artists. There are many local chapters throughout the country. The national office, listed above, can supply you with their addresses.

AEA disseminates information on legislation of interest to visual artists, legal problems and art business. Some chapters offer medical insurance, access to a buying service and a credit union. AEA also has a welfare fund which provides interest-free loans to members and nonmembers who have suffered financial hardships. AEA has developed a "Declaration of Artists' Rights" to serve as a guide to fair practices and artists' rights for individuals and art associations.

ARTS RESOURCE AND INFORMATION CENTER
Minneapolis Institute of the Arts
2400 Third Avenue South
Minneapolis, MN 55404
(612) 870–3131
The Center is an excellent source of information on all aspects of the visual arts.

ASSOCIATION OF ARTIST-RUN GALLERIES (AARG)
164 Mercer Street
New York, NY 10012
(212) 226–3107
AARG is the coordination point for cooperative galleries throughout the U.S. and Canada. AARG offers information and guidance in setting up and running co-op galleries. AARG sponsors an exhibition exchange program among galleries here and in Canada and also a slide registry.

BOSTON VISUAL ARTISTS UNION
700 Beacon Street
Boston, MA 02114
(617) 266–1101
BVAU was founded to bring together artists and the public and to foster connections between artists. BVAU maintains a slide registry, studio-space files and a job file. There is a program of discounts for supplies and a cooperative buying plan. BVAU is active in artists' rights and has developed contracts, minimum compensation schedules and minimum exhibition standards.

CHICAGO ARTISTS' COALITION
5 West Grand Street
Chicago, IL 60610
(312) 670–2060
The coalition serves visual artists in the area. They offer workshops, insurance, a slide registry, a job file, lectures and art business information.

JOINT ETHICS COMMITTEE
P. O. Box 179
Grand Central Station
New York, NY 10017
Sponsored by a consortium of visual artist professional organizations, this committee mediates disputes between graphic artists and clients.

SOCIETY OF PHOTOGRAPHER AND ARTIST REPRESENTATIVES (SPAR)
1123 Broadway
New York, NY 10010
(212) 924–6023
SPAR is the reps' professional society. Through them you can get a directory of reps listed by specialty. Artists seeking representation may list themselves for free in SPAR's newsletter.

SOCIETY OF PUBLICATION DESIGNERS
25 West 43rd Street
New York, NY 10036
(212) 354–8585

SOHO CENTER FOR VISUAL ARTS
114 Prince Street
New York, NY 10012
(212) 226–1995
The Center houses a reference library and information service for visual artists. Artists from anywhere may call with queries about grants, housing and other concerns.

VISUAL ARTISTS AND GALLERIES ASSOCIATION
141 Fifth Avenue
New York, NY 10001
(212) 505–2280

READING FOR ALL VISUAL ARTISTS

The Artist-Gallery Partnership: A Practical Guide to Consignment. Available through the American Council on the Arts, 1285 Avenue of the Americas, New York, NY 10019. A useful book that also includes sample contracts.

The Artists' Guide to Getting and Having a Successful Exhibition. Available from: The Photographic Arts Center, 127 East 59th Street, New York, NY 10022. This useful book describes how to contact galleries and other exhibition spaces, publicity, agreements and self-promotion.

Chamberlin, Betty. *The Artist's Guide to His Market.* Watson-Guptill, 1975. A very useful and informative guide written by the director of the Art Information Center.

Cummings, Paul. *Fine Arts Market Place.* R.R. Bowker, 1977. A compendium of publishers, dealers and exhibitions plus a useful resource section.

Directory of Artists' Slide Registeries. American Council on the Arts, 1285 Avenue of the Americas, New York, NY 10019.

McCann, Michael. *Artist, Beware.* Watson-Guptill, 1979. The best source available on art hazards.

New York Fine Artists' Source Book. compiled by the New York City Department of Cultural Affairs. Published by Addison-Wesley, Jacob's Way, Reading, MA.

Way to Go! Crating Artwork for Travel. Available from: Gallery Association of New York State, Box 345, Hamilton, New York 13346. All about crating, wrapping and shipping two- and three-dimensional works of art.

MAGAZINES AND NEWSLETTERS

AMERICAN ARTIST BUSINESS LETTER FOR PRACTICING ARTISTS
2160 Patterson Street
Cincinnati, OH 45214

NATIONAL PERCENT FOR ART NEWSLETTER
Technoart
311 East 17th Street
Spokane, WA 99203
$24/year
This newsletter tells of towns and developers who are looking to commission artworks for their building projects.

TODAY'S ART AND GRAPHICS
6 East 43rd Street
New York, NY 10017
(212) 949–0800

A magazine of business and artistic information for commercial and fine artists.

THE SQUEAKY WHEEL
P.O. Box 14584
Richmond, VA 23221
(804) 359–2540
If you happen to live in Virginia or Washington, this is an excellent newsletter for professionals in the communications industry with local news of interest to freelance folk and employment ads. In addition, the newsletter's founders also maintain a file of local freelancers which prospective users of their work can access for a reasonable charge.

GRAPHIC ARTISTS

AMERICAN INSTITUTE OF GRAPHIC ARTS
1059 Third Avenue
New York, NY 10021
(212) 752–0813
AIGA's purpose is to promote the graphic arts, disseminate information and provide continuing education. There are chapters in major cities nationwide. AIGA holds several large juried shows annually in its gallery. There is also a small gallery open to submissions by members and nonmembers. Seminars and workshops are held throughout the year. Group health insurance is available to members.

An AIGA affiliate called "The Guild of Book Workers" is dedicated to promoting excellence in the book arts.

GRAPHIC ARTISTS GUILD
11 West 20th Street
New York, NY 10011
(212) 463–7730
GAG has taken a particularly strong arts advocacy stance. It is especially helpful to graphic artists and illustrators in need of legal advice or those who desire information on business practices. GAG publishes the very useful Pricing and Ethical Guidelines.

READING FOR GRAPHIC ARTISTS

Crawford, Tad, and Kopelman, Ari. *Selling Your Graphic Design and Illustration.* St. Martin's Press, 1981.

Goodchild, Jon, and Henkin, Bill. *By Design: A Graphics Sourcebook of Materials, Equipment and Services.* Quick Fox, 1981.

Los Angeles Workbook. Available through AIGA, 8753 Chalmers Drive, Los Angeles, CA 90035. A directory to LA graphic arts and artists.

PHOTOGRAPHERS

ASMP: AMERICAN SOCIETY OF MAGAZINE PHOTOGRAPHERS
205 Lexington Avenue
New York, NY 10016
(212) 889–9144.
ASMP was founded to safeguard and promote the interests of photographers. ASMP has various insurance plans open to professional photographers as well as legal counseling and other business help. Other benefits include an ASMP press card.

INTERNATIONAL MUSEUM OF PHOTOGRAPHY
900 East Avenue
Rochester, NY 14607
(716) 271–3361
The museum is one of the largest photographic archives in the world. It also includes a collection of related materials and files. Members and nonmembers may attend symposia on topics of interest to photographers.

NIKON PROFESSIONAL SERVICES
Nikon, Inc.
Garden City, NY 11530
(516) 222–0200

This service is available to Nikon owners who need emergency repairs, equipment or just information.

PHOTOSOURCE
Osceola, WI 54020
This outfit, a husband and wife farmer team, puts out three newsletters of interest to professional photographers looking to sell stock shots. The newsletters consist of listings from book and magazine publishers looking for specific shots. Photoletter is a monthly listing for the beginning stock photographer and costs $75 per year. Photomarket and Photobulletin cost more and can be accessed weekly by computer via MCI Mail. Freelancers who don't own computers can get printed copies.

PROFESSIONAL PHOTOGRAPHERS OF AMERICA, INC.
1090 Executive Way
Des Plaines, IL 60018
(312) 299–8161.
An organization that offers insurance and a bank card for members as well as various programs of interest to photographers.

READING FOR PHOTOGRAPHERS

The Art Director's Index to Photographers, Available from John S. Butsch Assoc., 415 West Superior, Chicago, IL 60610; (312) 337–1901. A directory of photographers with samples of their work. Bought by art directors, editors and buyers of photography.

Hedgecoe, John. *The Photographer's Handbook*. Knopf, 1977.

Index to Kodak Information. Free from Kodak, Dept. 454, Rochester, NY 14650. Kodak publishes much useful technical information, and this is a guide to it.

Lewis, Steven, McQuaid, James, and Tait, David. *Photography: Source and Resource*. Turnip Press, 1973. Available from: Turnip Press, 144 Clinton Avenue, State College, PA 16801.

Nathan, Simon. *In Focus: A Rated Guide to the Best in Photographic Equipment*. Harper & Row, 1980. Very worth buying if you are contemplating buying new equipment.

Owens, Bill. *Documentary Photography*. Addison House, 1978. Available from Addison House, Morgan's Run, Danbury, NH 83230. A useful book for the freelancer. Includes good information on getting published and grants.

The Photography Market. Fred McDarrah, ed. R.R. Bowker, 1977. A guide to buying and selling photographic works, edited by an old pro.

Professional Business Practices in Photography.
Stock Photography Handbook.
Both are available from ASMP (see above).

ALL PERFORMERS

AFFILIATE ARTISTS INC.
37 West 65th Street
New York, NY 10023
(212) 580–2000
Affiliate Artists runs a residency program which is funded by corporations, foundations and individuals to help bring performers into U.S. communities by arranging residencies. Artists chosen for this program receive a fee plus travel expenses.

THE DRAMA BOOK SHOP
723 Seventh Avenue
New York, NY 10019
(212) 444–0595
This shop is an excellent source of printed material on the performing arts.

HOSPITAL AUDIENCES
1540 Broadway
New York, NY 10036
(212) 575–7676
Hospital Audiences was organized to bring performers into such institutions as prisons, hospitals and nursing homes and to send institutionalized individuals to performances. HA sends groups of performers to tour several institutions in a day for a very fair fee. In New York State, there are affiliates in Rochester and Syracuse. Your performing group can also donate tickets to HA so that people can attend your events too.

TECHNICAL ASSISTANCE PROJECT
570 Seventh Avenue
New York, NY 10018
(212) 302–6709
TAP provides consultations, referrals and other assistance to performing artists and groups. Their placement service refers technicians and other production assistants to companies. An equipment service aids groups and individuals who wish to rent or purchase sound, lighting or other stage equipment.

READING FOR PERFORMERS

Papolos, Janice. *The Performing Artist's Handbook*. Writer's Digest Books, 1984. A good practical sourcebook on all sorts of issues in a performing arts career.

Performing Arts Directory. Annual. Published by *Dance* Magazine. This exhaustive reference book to the music and dance worlds includes addresses and information on individual artists, companies and orchestras, unions, sponsors, service organizations, spaces, competitions and resources.

Shagan, Rena. *The Road Show: A Handbook for Successful Booking and Touring in the Performing Arts*. Available from: American Council for the Arts, 1285 Avenue of the Americas, New York, NY 10019 ($14.95).

MUSICIANS

AMERICAN COMPOSERS ALLIANCE
170 West 74th Street
New York, NY 10023
(212) 362–8900
Represents composers of concert music and gives information on practical matters of concern such as copyright, contracts and management.

AMERICAN MUSIC CENTER
250 West 54th Street
New York, NY 10019
(212) 247–3121
AMC was formed to promote the composition, performance and publication of contemporary music. AMC maintains an extensive library and information center with scores of tapes, records, reviews and files.

CONCERT ARTISTS GUILD
850 Seventh Avenue
New York, NY 10019
(212) 333–5200
The Concert Artists Guild was founded to assist and promote gifted young classical musicians. The Guild offers advice on such management topics as booking, publicity and funding. In addition, it sponsors concerts in the greater New York area to provide performing experience to young musicians. An annual audition is held to discover exceptionally gifted, performance-ready musicians who are then presented in debuts at Carnegie Hall.

NATIONAL INSTITUTE FOR MUSIC THEATRE
John F. Kennedy Center
Washington, DC 20566
(205) 965–2800
A national advocacy group for opera artists which offers grants, workshops and internships among other services.

SONGWRITERS GUILD OF AMERICA
276 Fifth Avenue
New York, NY 10001
(212) 686–6820

6430 Sunset Boulevard
Hollywood, CA 90028
(213) 462–1108
The Songwriters Guild is a voluntary songwriter's protective association which acts as an advocate for authors and composers in their dealings with music publishers. They will help you get the best contract, collect your royalties, administer your catalogue and aid you in numerous other ways. They also offer insurance and hold workshops. (see also page 277.)

YOUNG CONCERT ARTISTS
250 West 57th Street
New York, NY 10019
(212) 307–6655
Young Concert Artists is dedicated to launching the careers of exceptional young classical musicians. Those who are chosen receive the benefits of management and publicity advice and booking assistance. Artists who are chosen remain affiliated until they are signed by a manager or for up to nine years.

READING FOR MUSICIANS

Dearing, James W. *Making Money in Music No Matter Where You Live.* Writer's Digest Books, 1982.

Erickson, J. Gunnar, *The Musician's Guide to Copyright.* Available from: Bay Area Lawyers for the Arts, Fort Mason Center, Building C, San Francisco, CA 94123.

Harris, Herby, and Farrar, Lucien. *How to Make Money in Music.* Arco Books, 1980.

Rapaport, Diane. *How to Make and Sell Your Own Record.* Headlands Press, 1979.

Shemel, Sidney, and Krasilovsky, M. William. *This Business of Music*, Billboard Books, 1979. The major reference for those who work in any sector of the music world.

DANCERS

AMERICAN DANCE GUILD
570 Seventh Avenue
New York, NY 10018
(212) 944-0557
ADG was founded to provide a forum for the exchange of ideas and methods. ADG serves dancers, teachers and choreographers. It acts as a clearinghouse for professional material and information. ADG offers insurance, a book club and a job information service.

CAREER TRANSITION FOR DANCERS
The Actors' Fund
1501 Broadway
New York, NY 10036
(212) 221-7300

203 North Wabash
Chicago, IL 60601
(312) 372-0989

444 North Larchmont Blvd.
Los Angeles, CA 90004
(213) 464-4171
This program helps dancers expand their employment opportunities, particularly aging or injured ones who must plan for new careers.

CHOREOGRAPHERS THEATRE
225 Lafayette Street
New York, NY 10012
(212) 925-3721
Worldwide employment information on dance teaching. Information on housing, medical services, spaces and more.

THE KITCHEN CENTER FOR MUSIC, VIDEO AND DANCE
512 West 19th Street
New York, NY 10011
(212) 255-5793
This performance space sponsors work in all the above media plus film.

PENTACLE
104 Franklin Street
New York, NY 10013
(212) 226-2000
Provides administrative services, grant preparation, résumés, tour management, publicity and more to performing artists and companies.

READING FOR DANCERS

Jacob, Ellen. *Dancing.* Addison-Wesley, 1981. An encyclopedia on every aspect of dance from finding the right teachers to treating injuries and launching a career.

Kupersmith, Judith R.F., and Horosko, Marion. *The Dancer's Survival Manual.* Harper & Row, 1987.

Mueller, John. *Dance Film Directory.* Princeton Book Company, 1979. An annotated guide to dance films.

Vincent, L. M. *The Dancer's Book of Health.* Sheed, Andrews and McMeel, 1978. A truly useful book on the dancer's special body, written by a doctor who has had experience as a dancer and as a medical consultant to dancers. Dr. Vincent covers injuries, massage, anatomy, diet and rehabilitation.

White, David R., ed. *Poor Dancer's Almanac: A Survival Manual for Choreographers, Managers and Dancers.* Available from Dance Theatre Workshop, 219 West 19th Street, New York, NY 10011. A must-have reference book with the spirit of this one.

Two excellent sources of dance books are:

DANCE ETC.
5897 College Avenue
Oakland, CA 94618

THE DRAMA BOOK STORE
723 Seventh Avenue
New York, NY 10019

THEATRE ARTISTS

EUGENE O'NEILL MEMORIAL THEATRE CENTER
230 West 49th Street
New York, NY 10019
(212) 246–0220
The O'Neill Center sponsors many programs of interest to theater professionals, including the National Playwright's Conference, a prestigious competition for playwrights. Winners receive a living stipend and have their play produced. The Monte Cristo Cottage Museum and Library houses a collection of books and theater memorabilia. The Center publishes The National Playwright's Directory, a showcase for new plays that also contains biographies of several hundred American playwrights.

THEATRE COMMUNICATIONS GROUP
355 Lexington Avenue
New York, NY 10017
(212) 697–5230
TCG provides information and assistance to all professional theater personnel. They maintain referral files of actors, directors, technicians, stage managers, etc., and a biannual roster of new scripts called New Plays. TCG holds annual national auditions in Chicago for college and conserv-

atory students. In addition, TCG provides information on fund-raising and maintains a research library. The organization has done a lot of advocacy work and also researches legislation germane to the theater.

THEATRE DEVELOPMENT FUND
1501 Broadway
New York, NY 10036
(212) 221–0013
TDF is an organization dedicated to expanding audiences for music, theater and dance by subsidizing tickets. There is a voucher system for members and TDF runs two half-price ticket booths near Broadway. TDF maintains a collection of 50,000 costumes which can be rented by nonprofit groups nationwide.

THEATRE HAZARDS PROJECT
Center for Occupational Hazards
5 Beekman Street
New York, NY 10038
(212) 227–6220
This group researches and provides information on health hazards of materials encountered by performers in theaters.

A list of theater unions appears at the end of chapter 18, "Collecting What's Owed You."

READING FOR THEATER ARTISTS

Boleslavsky, Richard. Acting: The First Six Lessons. Theatre Arts Books, 1970. Available from Theatre Arts Books, 153 Waverly Place, New York, NY 10014. Although not brand new, many of the actors I talked with felt that this book was not to be missed. A book of dialogues between the "teacher" and the "creature."

Hagen, Uta. Respect for Acting. Macmillan, 1973. A meticulous book on acting.

Matson, Katinka. The Working Actor. Penguin, 1978. A guide to the acting profession which covers training, finding work, the markets, auditions, unions, agents and more in a lively style interspersed with interviews.

Players Magazine (University Theatre, Northern Illinois University, DeKalb, IL 60115). A bimonthly magazine with information on playwriting and performing, contests, auditions and awards.

Simon's Directory of Theatrical Materials. Available from Package Publicity Service, 27 West 24th Street, New York, NY 10010. Information for the U.S. and Canada on unions, awards, professional associations and more.

Other useful publications:

Backstage, 330 West 42nd Street, New York, NY 10039.

Show Business News, 1501 Broadway, New York, NY 10036.

Variety, 154 West 46th Street, New York, NY 10036.

These three are weekly trades which publish casting information, reviews and columns of interest to those in the theater.

WRITERS AND EDITORIAL FREELANCERS

AMERICAN SOCIETY OF JOURNALISTS AND AUTHORS, INC.
1501 Broadway
New York, NY 10036
(212) 997–0947
ASJA is a service organization for professional writers. Its offering include DialA-Writer, which matches journalists with potential clients, group insurance, buying services and a committee on writer-editor relations which mediates disagreements.

THE AUTHORS GUILD AND THE AUTHORS LEAGUE OF AMERICA
234 West 44th Street
New York, NY 10036
(212) 391–9198
The Authors League involves itself in matters of concern to authors as a group, such as legislation concerning writers, contracts and freedom of expression. The Authors League is the parent of both the Authors Guild and the Dramatists Guild. This is one of the largest and most influential of the writers' organizations listed here. Members receive a bulletin, and periodic workshops on such topics as agents, children's books and contracts are held in New York.

THE BUCKLEY-LITTLE BOOK CATALOGUE CO. INC.
Kraus Building, Route 100
Millwood, NY 10546
William F. Buckley and Stuart Little of the Authors Guild devised this catalogue in which writers can advertise books that publishers have let go out of print. Warehousing, reprint, distribution and marketing services are now offered, basically allowing authors to resurrect books that publishers have let die. The catalogue is distributed widely throughout the book trade world.

THE DRAMATISTS GUILD
234 West 44th Street
New York, NY 10036
(212) 398 9366
The Dramatists Guild is a professional organization of playwrights, composers and lyricists which functions similarly to the Authors Guild.

EDITORIAL FREELANCERS ASSOCIATION
30 East 20th Street
New York, NY 10003
(212) 677–3357
This organization is very useful not only to writers but to all sorts of editorial people. It offers monthly meetings, health insurance, a newsletter, a directory listing writers geographically and by profession, and the job phone, a recording listing writing and editorial jobs available.

NATIONAL WRITERS CLUB INC.
1450 South Havana
Aurora, CO 80012
(303) 751–7844
NWC was founded to aid and protect freelance writers. They offer a press pass to members, a collection bureau, a very good newsletter, and workshops and seminars.

P.E.N. (POETS, ESSAYISTS, EDITORS AND NOVELISTS)
568 Broadway
New York, NY 10012
(212) 334–1660
P.E.N. is a distinguished international writers' organization, with many foreign chapters worldwide. P.E.N. has become a major voice for freedom of expression throughout the world. Its programs include an emergency money fund for needy writers. The Prisoner Writer helps put aspiring writer inmates into contact with P.E.N. members who are willing to read their work and also with publishers. P.E.N. offers a number of important literary prizes. Lectures, workshops and social events are held at the various centers. P.E.N. has devised a set of standards to guide editors and writers of magazine and newspaper assignments and also publishes an excellent listing of grants, Grants and Awards Available to Writers. Membership in P.E.N. is by invitation.

POETRY SOCIETY OF AMERICA
15 Gramercy Park South
New York, NY 10003
(212) 254–9628
The oldest poetry group in America. PSA sponsors readings and workshops and awards annual prizes.

POETS AND WRITERS INC.
201 West 54th Street
New York, NY 10019
(212) 757–1766
A service organization for American poets and fiction writers. The Information Center will answer general literary questions or help locate a contemporary writer. Members receive Coda, an excellent newsletter packed with information. P&W also publishes A Directory of American Poets and Fiction Writers.

WASHINGTON INDEPENDENT WRITERS
National Press Building
Washington, DC 20045
(202) 347–4973
A clearinghouse for independent nonfiction writers, WIW holds monthly workshops and social events for members. Members have access to a job bank, group medical insurance and legal aid.

THE WRITER'S CENTER
7815 Old Georgetown Road
Bethesda, MD 20814
(301) 654–8664
Geared more to writers of fiction, poetry and plays then WIW, the Writer's Center offers workshops and has word processors, phototypesetters and graphics equipment for rent.

WRITERS GUILD OF AMERICA
555 West 57th Street
New York, NY 10019
(212) 245–6180
or
8955 Beverly Blvd.
Los Angeles, CA 90048
(213) 550–1000
The Writers Guild acts as a collective bargaining body for screen, television and radio writers.

READING FOR WRITERS

Balkin, Richard. A Writer's Guide to Book Publishing. Hawthorne Books, 1980. A well-written book that takes you step by step through the publishing process and helps answer many of the questions that people feel silly asking.

Burnett, Hallie and Whit. Fiction Writer's Handbook. Barnes and Noble, 1975. Practical advice on writing long or short fiction from the former co-editors of Story magazine.

Evans, Nancy, and Appelbaum, Judith. *How to Get Happily Published.* Harper & Row, 1978. A deservedly popular book with excellent information on the professional writing world.

Goldman, William. *Adventures in the Screen Trade.* Warner Books, 1984. Perhaps the best and most realistic guide to the movie world. Certainly the most readable by the writer of *Butch Cassidy and the Sundance Kid, Marathon Man* and other favorites.

Henderson, Bill. *The Publish-It-Yourself Handbook.* Harper & Row, 1980. A guide written by the founder of The Pushcart Press, a self-publisher who knows what he's talking about.

Jerome, Judson. *Poet's Market.* Writer's Digest Books.

Kleinman, Maggie. *Writer's Guide to Southern California.* Available from: L.A. Writer, 4102 E. Seventh Street, Long Beach, CA 90804. This sourcebook lists professional and service organizations, workshops, contests and funding sources, book shops and publications among many other items of interest to writers in the area. Included also are features written by working writers about different aspects of survival.

Literary Marketplace. R.R. Bowker. This is probably the most important reference book in the publishing business. Contains information on agents, conferences, publishers, magazines, television and film companies, associations and events.

The Chicago Manual of Style. University of Chicago Press, 1969. The major rule book on standard American English for writers and editors.

Polking, Kirk. *A Beginner's Guide to Getting Published.* Writer's Digest Books.

Scriptwriters News. Available from Writers Publishing Co., 250 West 57th Street, New York, NY 10019; (212) 582-1371.

Strunk, W., and White, E.B. *The Elements of Style.* Macmillan, 1979. No writer should be allowed to pick up a pencil without having first read this classic primer of good English. It is delightful and informative and deserves frequent rereading. Your work will show it.

Tomajczyk, S.F. *The Children's Writer's Marketplace.* Running Press, 1987.

Writers at Work: The Paris Review Interviews. George Plimpton, ed. Viking Press. This series is my favorite reading on writing. It is similar to the Hersey book, but it is presented in interview format.

The Writer's Craft. John Hersey, ed. Random House, 1974. An anthology of writers on writing.

Writer's Market. Writer's Digest Books. A necessary shelf item for any free-lancer. Your fingers can do the walking through the market whether you be selling articles, greeting card fillers or books.

FILM AND VIDEO ARTISTS

AMERICAN FILM INSTITUTE
John F. Kennedy Center
Washington, DC 20566
(202) 833–9300
or
501 Doheny Drive
Beverly Hills, CA 90210
(213) 278–8777
AFI is an affiliate of the National Endowment for the Arts. It offers a variety of programs for film and video artists. These include a grant program which is a very important source of funds for individual filmmakers. AFI regularly holds all-day seminars at different locations throughout the country on such topics as scriptwriting, scoring and grant-getting. Both branches maintain extensive libraries. AFI operates the Center for Advanced Film Studies, a graduate school in Beverly Hills.

ASSOCIATION OF INDEPENDENT VIDEO AND FILMMAKERS (AIVF)
625 Broadway
New York, NY 10012
(212) 473–3400
AIVF was founded to aid film and video artists, and to encourage public exhibition of their work. AIVF maintains a referral file for job opportunities in the New York area. In addition, workshops and screenings are held regularly. AIVF does a lot of advocacy work and publishes an excellent newsletter.

COLLECTIVE FOR LIVING CINEMA
41 White Street
New York, NY 10013
(212) 925–3926
The Collective is a nonprofit film art center. It offers a showcase to emerging filmmakers who have previously had a chance to show their work. The Collective also offers intensive workshops, publishes the journal Motion Picture *and offers internships.*

INDEPENDENT FEATURE PROJECT (IFP)
21 West 86th Street
New York, NY 10024
(212) 496–0909
or
309 Santa Monica Boulevard
Santa Monica, CA 90401
(213) 451–8075
IFP is a service and advocacy group for independent producers and directors of feature films. IFP, along with the Film Society of Lincoln Center, sponsors the American Independents Festival, a major showcase for independent features.

SCRIPT CITY
1765 North Highland Avenue
Suite 170-WE
Hollywood, CA 90028
(213) 871–0707
This outfit has the script of every movie you've ever heard of plus posters and other memorabilia. Send $1 for their catalogue.

WOMEN IN FILM AND VIDEO, INC.
Friendship Station
P.O. Box 39049
Washington, DC 20016
(202) 463–6372
WIFV is a nonprofit organization that provides professional and educational support to women in all areas of the film and video industry, including actresses. Branches exist in Atlanta, Boston, Dallas, Los Angeles, New York, San Francisco, Chicago and Toronto. WIFV sponsors workshops on all aspects of working in the industry, conducts special study groups, publishes a newsletter which features job leads and a resource directory of its membership and has special screenings. Its international film festival, Women Make Movies, *held at the Kennedy Center, is the oldest and largest held in this country.*

YOUNG FILMMAKERS FOUNDATION
817 Broadway
New York, NY 10012
(212) 673–9361
This group has available editing-room facilities for film and video as well as equipment rental. They also offer classes and workshops on topics of interest to film and video artists.

READING FOR FILM AND VIDEO ARTISTS

Backstage's TV, Film and Tape Syndication Directory. Jaguar Productions. A highly useful directory of film and video business, with the names and addresses of editors, animators, props, insurance companies and many others across the country.

Bensinger, Charles. *The Video Guide and The Home Video Handbook*. Available from Video Information Publishers, P.O. Box 1507, Santa Barbara, CA 93102.

Brenner, Alfred. *The T.V. Scriptwriter's Handbook*. Writer's Digest Books, 1980.

Films for Film Study. Available from: Audiovisual Services, Kent State University, Kent, OH 44242. A listing of films on all aspects of film art.

Gregory, Molly. *Making Films Your Business*. Schocken Books, 1979. This useful book discusses proposals, grants, distribution, budgets, copyright, contracts and other matters of importance to filmmakers.

Jackson, Bruce. *Get the Money and Shoot*. $15 postpaid from: Documentary Research Inc., 96 Rumsey Road, Buffalo, NY 14209. A great funding book for filmmakers with the true spirit of *Freelance Forever*.

Lipton, Lenny. *Independent Filmmaking*. Simon & Schuster, 1972. This book's valuable advice is the next best thing to experience.

Matrazzo, Donna. *The Corporate Scriptwriting Book*. Available from: Communication Publishing Co., 548 NE 43rd Avenue, Portland, OR 97213.

Monaco, James. *Who's Who in American Film Now*. Available from New York Zoetrope, 80 East 11th Street, New York, NY 10003. New York Zoetrope is an excellent source of books on film.

Motion Picture, TV and Theatre Directory. Available from Motion Picture Enterprises, Inc., P.O. Box 276, Tarrytown, NY 10591. A semiannual directory with information similar to that in the Backstage directory but in vest-pocket size.

Reickert, Julia, et al. *Doing It Yourself: A Handbook on Independent Film Distribution*. A well-written book, full of information for the independent on such topics as promotion, credit, caring for prints, shipping and European distribution.

Sayles, John. *Thinking in Pictures*. Houghton-Mifflin, 1987. A great book on movie writing by a great contemporary writer-director.

Shanks, Bob. *The Cool Fire: How to Make It in Television*. Vintage Books, 1976. This book is a guided tour through the television with enjoyable and informative anecdotes.

Wiese, Michael. *Film and Video Budgets* and *Home Video: Producing for the Home Market*. Available from: Michael Wiese, Box 406, Westport, CT 06881; (203) 226–6979.

SOFTWARE FOR SCRIPTWRITERS

Scriptor. This program will put your screenplay into standard industry form and will run on IBM, MacIntosh and CP/MS. Available from Screenplay Systems, 150 East Olive Avenue, Burbank, CA 91502.

INDEX

ABOUT THE AUTHOR

Marietta Whittlesey has been a freelance writer for twelve years. She has published two books in addition to *The New Freelancer's Handbook* and has contributed articles to the *New York Times Magazine, Self,* and numerous other publications. She is currently working on a novel.